Making Good the Claim

Making Good the Claim

Holiness and Visible Unity
in the Church of God Reformation Movement

RUFUS BURROW, JR.

Foreword by Barry L. Callen
Afterword by Gary B. Agee

☙PICKWICK *Publications* • Eugene, Oregon

MAKING GOOD THE CLAIM
Holiness and Visible Unity in the Church of God Reformation Movement

Copyright © 2016 Rufus Burrow, Jr. All rights reserved. Except for brief quotations in critical publications or reviews, no part of this book may be reproduced in any manner without prior written permission from the publisher. Write: Permissions, Wipf and Stock Publishers, 199 W. 8th Ave., Suite 3, Eugene, OR 97401.

Pickwick Publications
An Imprint of Wipf and Stock Publishers
199 W. 8th Ave., Suite 3
Eugene, OR 97401

www.wipfandstock.com

PAPERBACK ISBN: 978-1-4982-3765-9
HARDCOVER ISBN: 978-1-4982-3767-3

Cataloguing-in-Publication data:

Burrow, Rufus (1951–)

Making good the claim : holiness and visible unity in the Church of God reformation movement / Rufus Burrow, Jr. ; foreword by Barry L. Callan ; afterword by Gary B. Agee.

xvi + 284 pp. ; 23 cm. Includes bibliographical references.

ISBN: 978-1-4982-3765-9 (paperback) | ISBN: 978-1-4982-3767-3 (hardback)

1. Church of God (Anderson, Ind.). 2. Church of God (Anderson, Ind.)—Doctrines. 3. Holiness churches—Doctrines. I. Callan, Barry L. II. Agee, Gary B. III. Title.

BT75.2 B87 2016

Manufactured in the U.S.A.   02/15/2016

For James Earl Massey of Greensboro, Alabama, and the late Theodore Baker, Sr. of Anderson, Indiana. Two Movement giants along the way who endeavored to make good the claim about holiness and visible interracial unity in the Church of God Reformation Movement.

Contents

Foreword by Barry L. Callen | ix
Introduction | xiii

1 The Church of God in Sociological Transformation | 1
2 John Winebrenner and the Churches of God (General Eldership) | 33
3 Daniel Sidney Warner: Charismatic Personality | 62
4 The Next Generation: Seeking to Clarify Ideas and Practices | 106
5 Continued Expansion and Diversification | 153
6 Making Good the Claim: What Whites and Blacks Must Do | 166
7 Conditions for Making Good the Claim about Holiness and Visible Unity | 198

Afterword by Gary B. Agee | 241
Appendix A: Letter from James Earl Massey | 251
Appendix B: Validity of Oral and Written History | 255
Acknowledgments | 263
Bibliography | 269
Index | 277

Foreword

Humans seem inclined to discrimination based on selfish definitions of insiders and outsiders. We create exclusive clubs, encourage nationalisms, nurture family and tribal loyalties, and pour great amounts of money into political party preferences. Often the price is high for indulging in such popular discrimination.

We typically tend to exempt ourselves from the mass guilt—"maybe everyone else, but not me. I am free of prejudice." Despite considerable rhetoric to the contrary, Americans who speak highly of "all created equal" emerged from the British colonies in North America that were hardly societies practicing equality. Native American people and lands came to be conquered without mercy or payment, and imported Africans were forced into dehumanizing slavery. Some people obviously were considered more equal than others, whatever the national slogans.

One would expect—or at least hope—that it has been very different in the churches that seek to have "the mind of Christ." Jesus announced that, once having found new life in Him, there no longer is to be discrimination based on race, gender, or national origin (Galatians 3:28). Sadly, however, Christian churches routinely have followed social patterns of their host cultures and divided into "denominations" that have checkered histories of competition and even combat among themselves.

Christians, like people in general, have gathered memberships of like-minded and often like-colored people who share cultural preferences as well as Christ commitments. They have tended to exclude those who think, act, or look differently. Usually this is done in the name of strict adherence to what is understood to be Bible teaching or orthodox theology. In fact, too often it is little more a shallow rationalization illustrating the tendency to mirror surrounding social patterns that are unlike Christ, patterns sometimes directly contrary to the teachings and modeling of the Master.

Our author points straight at this deep irony. Dr. Burrow feels strongly about Christian holiness and unity, the founding principles of non-discrimination of the Church of God movement (Anderson). He also is disturbed about the limited degree of the actual realization to date of the "visible" part of these high-sounding ideals. He observes that the new converts to the Church of God in the 1880–1900 period—a few whites and many blacks—experienced a high level of exuberance for this reform movement's message about visible unity and its ethical implications among Christians. In their excitement "they simply did not pay much attention to civil law and the custom of racial separation." It appears, however, that this excitement waned over time and racial separation slowly crept back into the church's life.

Despite the unusual unifying instincts of the Church of God movement, including between races, Burrow records a typical sociological process that soon took over, one far from the rich rhetoric of the movement's prophetic pioneers. As the early unity zeal began to diminish among the white members after a generation or two, "the process of routinization began picking up steam." Pragmatic matters became prominent, including "developing organizational structures that would effectively institutionalize the collective life, norms, and values of the group, as well as meet its emerging needs."

Consciously or not, this reform movement was influenced negatively, being reformed itself by prevailing societal customs and practices that tend to keep racial groups apart. Even in the midst of high idealism about being one in Christ, we Christians are citizens of heaven and, let's admit it, are still in the world and inclined to act too much like the world.

Consequently, a driving question behind this book is: "Why have Afrikan Americans remained in the Church of God, and continue to join it, in light of their unequal treatment and second-class standing in the group? Why did they not do what blacks did in the Methodist Episcopal and Baptist churches in the nineteenth century? That is, why did they not leave the Movement?"

Rufus Burrow Jr. wades right into this crucial and complex scene with his love and concern on full display. His analysis is instructive for all bodies of Christian people, even though his emphasis is primarily a case study of a particular Christian community, the Church of God movement (Anderson). This is a reform movement that has tried very intentionally, in light of biblical teaching about equality and unity, to separate itself from the common cultural accommodations of the many racially insensitive and divided churches.

This reform body has stressed holiness, reflecting the very nature of God, and unity, practicing the equality and oneness called for by Christ. It has dropped all lines of discrimination based on race and gender—at least in intent, principle, and rhetoric. It has reached loving arms of acceptance "to all blood-washed ones" and proclaimed that God's church is to be gifted and led by whomever God calls—regardless of race, gender, or ethnic origin. And it has been relatively successful compared to most Christian bodies.

So what's the problem that our author finds himself facing? Just this. Noble idealism is not always accompanied by proper practice. The one who steps out of the crowd and commits to a higher standard must withstand the inevitable spotlight of critical analysis. The Church of God movement passes—and fails—such close scrutiny, particularly on the issue of race relations in church life. Our author insists that there are lessons to be learned by us all, and much more ground yet to be gained.

Burrow reaches back for baselines to the sociological studies by Aubrey Forrest in 1948 and Valorous Clear in 1953 and to the historical reporting and book-length analysis by James Earl Massey titled *African Americans in the Church of God* (Anderson University Press, 2005). This present book is dedicated to Massey and his colleague Theodore Baker, Sr., key African-American leaders of the Church of God who greatly impacted Burrow's life and thought.

But why another book if the Massey volume on the present subject is rather recent and well done, in fact "seminal" according to Burrow? There are at least two reasons. One is new research by Burrow on this exceptional fellowship of Christians, the Church of God movement (Anderson) that at least has rightly envisioned the God-intended inclusiveness of all members of the Body of Christ. The other reason is to issue an urgent call to all followers of Jesus. This call is to become *more intentional* and make *more visible* the noble words about holiness and unity that flow admirably and easily from the mouth.

Insists our author, it's time to move from theory to practice, from right theology to a practical church life that is more congruent with stated ideals. Thus, this book's title, *Making Good the Claim*. The right call already has been sounded by Massey and others, but now Burrow seeks to sharpen the keen insights of yesterday and magnify the trumpet sound directing disciples of the Master to actually *be* what God desires and to make really *visible* what God is prepared to enable in the world of race relations.

In order to highlight the problems and point the way forward, Burrow traces the changing attitudes and practices of the Church of God movement (Anderson) over its generations from the 1880s to date. This study spotlights the socio-ethical visions, experiments, and limited even if substantial results. We see laid bare the hopes and dreams and also the shortcomings that create an ongoing agenda for this and coming generations, an agenda facing this reform movement and the Christian community in general.

If the world today is to know that God really was in Christ on its behalf, the church must provide more than quality buildings, ornate ideas, and sophisticated programs. The church must *visibly be* what the world needs and cannot provide for itself—real love, real community, real resolution to the ugly divides of tribe, gender, and race. The world will never believe in what it cannot *see in practice*. So the church must continue announcing the good news, of course. And it also must become a living and very public model of the good news that all believers, regardless of racial, gender, or ethnic heritage, are indeed *one in Jesus Christ*!

Dr. Barry L. Callen
Editor of Aldersgate Press and Anderson University Press
Corporate Secretary of Horizon International
and the Wesleyan/Holiness Consortium, and theologian
and historian of the Church of God movement (Anderson)

Introduction

ALTHOUGH I GREW UP in the Church of God Reformation Movement (hereafter the Movement) but am no longer formally affiliated with it, I still have a passion for its two founding principles—holiness and visible unity. Indeed, having grown up in the Movement, I have known for many years that however long I live I will carry strains of it in me that will influence my behavior in the world. So strongly do I feel about these founding principles that I chose to devote the time and energy to researching and writing this book. In addition, writing this book was truly a labor of love, prompted by my utmost respect and admiration for two Movement giants: Dean Emeritus James Earl Massey and the Rev. Theodore Baker Sr.

Holiness and visible unity are the founding core principles of the Church of God Reformation Movement. Standard works on the Movement, e.g., *When the Trumpet Sounded* (1951), *The Quest for Holiness and Unity* (1980), *I Saw the Church* (2002), and *African Americans and the Church of God* (2005), suggest that from the beginning Movement pioneers interpreted the visible unity principle broadly to include not only spiritual and church unity, but interracial unity as well. Such interpretation could easily lead one to believe that the founder and pioneers were advocates of progressive ideas on race relations at a time when overt racial discrimination and white supremacy were as American as cherry pie, but we will see that there is reason to question this.

Reading the standard works on Church of God history, one gets the sense that more than any other religious group during the first two decades of the Movement's existence all people, regardless of race, were welcome to join and were received on the basis of equality with all others. Presumably, Movement pioneers' exuberance for the holiness-visible unity ideal readily and easily translated to a determination to draw in all races of people, regardless of social custom and civil law, and that only after approximately two decades did questions begin to emerge among white members about worshipping with blacks without racial barriers, e.g., a dividing rope, in the church. The problem is that when I began reading the standard Movement histories, and issues of its weekly magazine, *The Gospel Trumpet*, during its first fifteen years of existence, I was not able to verify these claims to my satisfaction. The more I read, the more questions I had about the level of commitment that Movement pioneers had to interracial unity that was linked to the principle of equality. I had no doubt that they were advocates of visible unity, and that a few even connected this to unity along racial lines, even if they did not add the all-important principle of equality. However, it did not seem to me that the pioneers were as devoted to and passionate about interracial unity and equality as the blacks who were so eager to join the group because of its teaching on holiness and visible unity.

Important doctoral dissertations by Aubrey Leland Forrest (1948)[1] and Valorus B. Clear (1953)[2] provide instructive sociological studies on the Church of God Reformation Movement. The studies by Forrest and Clear were influenced by the sect-church typology of the German historical theologian and social philosopher Ernst Troeltsch,[3] but as mediated through the work of the Americans Liston Pope and H. Richard Niebuhr, respectively. Forrest and Clear studied changes in the Movement from its inception in 1880 as a sect (an unstable protest group) to a denomination (an established and stable group). Their studies sought to show how attitudes, ideas, ethos, and practice changed as the Movement progressed along the basic sect-church continuum; how, in the language of H. Richard Niebuhr, it moved from the sect posture of "Christ against culture" to the denomination

---

1. See Aubrey Leland Forrest, "A Study of the Development of the Basic Doctrines and Institutional Patterns in the Church of God (Anderson, Indiana)."

2. See Valorus B. Clear, "The Church of God: A Study in Social Adaptation," later published as *Where the Saints Have Trod*. I am most proud and honored to say that Val Clear was my academic advisor, from whom I took several courses in sociology and criminal justice. He introduced me to the writings of literary artist James Baldwin who became one of my three favorite writers. During my student days at Anderson University, Dr. Clear was truly one of the good guys who took seriously the idea about making good the claim about holiness and visible unity. He distinguished clearly between the Church of God Reformation Movement and the Church of God, and argued that the former's job is to work itself out of existence. "Our task is to build the Church of God," he proclaimed, "not the Church of God Reformation Movement, and to the extent that we lose sight of that fact we likewise lose sight of the original call to D. S. Warner," which was to unite holiness and visible unity; see Clear, "Uniting Holiness and Oneness," in *A Time to Remember: Projections*, 50.

3. Troeltsch actually included a third type of Christian thought that he referred to as *mysticism* (roughly what is known today as "cult," or "New Religious Movement," the preferred nomenclature of present day sociologists of religion; but scholars have frequently only named church and sect when referring to his work. See Troeltsch, *The Social Teaching of the Christian Churches*, 2:993–99.

posture of "Christ of culture."⁴ Essentially, Forrest and Clear tracked the life cycle or sociological transformation of the Movement from its sect beginnings to its mature denomination phase.

My book differs significantly from the work of Forrest and Clear. Although like theirs, this book is interested in and discusses aspects of the sociological transformation of the Church of God, it more assertively addresses the socio-ethical implications of various changes in the ideas and practices of the Movement as it transformed itself along the sect-church continuum to where it is today. This book is particularly interested in showing how attitudes and practices have changed in light of the two basic founding core beliefs: holiness and visible unity, and more especially, their relation to interracial unity in the group. This latter was of basic concern to blacks entering the group during the Post-Reconstruction period, and continues to be today. What did these core principles mean, and what was their relationship to interracial unity during early Movement days? In light of these foundational beliefs, how have attitudes and practices changed regarding interracial unity over the course of the Movement's life cycle? What is the moral responsibility of Movement people to make good the founder's claim about holiness and a visible unity that all may see and believe? What can be done to make good this claim nearly 130 years after the founder's declaration?

Because of the failure of pioneers and subsequent members of the Church of God to adequately and consistently link the teaching on holiness and visible unity to unity along racial lines—a connection that pioneer Movement blacks and their successors made almost instinctively—I will attend to this particular subject in several chapters. I do so because of my sense that most white Movement people generally interpret(ed) these teachings to mean spiritual and-or church unity among the many religious groups. This is the way they seem to interpret the founder's numerous references to *visible unity* in the church. However, this is quite different from how early and subsequent blacks who heard the preaching on holiness and visible unity interpreted these principles. From the beginning, blacks' interpretation was inclusive of interracial unity on the basis of equality with all others in the group.

Whatever else blacks may have heard when the core principles were preached by white Movement pioneers, they most assuredly linked them to the ideal of interracial unity. Historically, a significant strand of black Christians adhered to the liberation and justice interpretation of the Bible. Furthermore, by the time the first blacks heard Movement pioneers preach on

---

4. See Niebuhr's discussion of his five-fold typology in *Christ and Culture*.

holiness and visible unity they had been "emancipated" from enslavement for approximately twenty years, and had lived through the Reconstruction period (roughly 1865–1877). It should not be difficult to understand why such preaching and teaching would be so appealing to people only recently freed from physical bondage. So when Jane Williams and other blacks heard Movement pioneers preach on holiness and visible unity in the mid-1880s, it was easy for them to interpret this to include interracial unity or blacks and whites—*all* people—worshipping together in the house of the Lord with no barriers between them, regardless of custom and civil law. In any event, it is important to note at the outset that the relationship between holiness and visible unity to race, especially among early Movement people, will be addressed a number of times in the chapters that follow.

As a theological social ethicist who was trained by one of the founding Christian social ethicists in this country, third generation Personalist Walter G. Muelder (1907–2004) of Boston University, I am not—like Forrest and Clear—a pure sociologist. Nor am I a trained historian. As a social ethicist trained in the Muelderian tradition, I understand the discipline of theological social ethics to take seriously the methodologies and findings not only of history, sociology, other social sciences, and philosophy, but those of the behavioral and natural sciences as well. These methodologies and findings, coupled with my own experiences and the relevant experiences of others, provide a reasonably clear sense of the existence and status of racism in church and society, for example. Consequently, they help to clarify the answer to the question: What is the actual state of affairs relative to the issue of racism in church and society? This is the question that the social scientist asks. But even when the answer to that question has been provided, the work of the theological social ethicist is not complete, for such a one must not only know the actual state of the alleged social problem in church and world. She must then focus on the normative question: What ought to be in light of the gospel, and especially a gospel of liberation concerned not only about the well being of the individual, but of individuals in relation to social, political, religious, and economic structures? Therefore, by definition the theological social ethicist is at once concerned about the empirical question (*what is*) as well as the normative question (*what ought to be*). It should come as no surprise, then, that the theological social ethicist inevitably challenges the way things are, in light of her understanding of what ought to be according to the gospel mandate of agape and the best in the Jewish and Christian traditions.

Consequently, to merely address the sociological transformation of the Church of God and to report on shifts in attitude, thinking, and practice is not sufficient for the theological social ethicist. Such a one is compelled to determine not only whether social problems like racism exist in the group, but what must be done about them in accordance with the highest religious ideals of his faith. More specifically, having reported on the actual state of affairs regarding the Movement's founding core principles, one must then proceed to suggest what ought to be done in light of those principles in particular, and other relevant teachings and principles of Jesus Christ, in general. This book focuses on both *what is*, and *what ought to be.*

What is essentially provided here is a socio-ethical examination of the Church of God Reformation Movement. Holiness is the group's chief cornerstone and is that which (presumably) makes it possible to live a life free of sin. Holiness is also important because of its relationship to the principle of visible unity. One cannot live in complete accord with holiness if she fails to do all she can to honor and live in accordance with the principle of visible unity. My reading of early Movement literature, particularly the writings of its founder, Daniel S. Warner, convinces me that visible unity has not merely to do with spiritual and-or denominational unity, but with *visible* unity among people—a unity that all can actually see, and thus believe in its possibility. I want to be clear, that among other things, unity of this type has also to do with the face of the church and its institutions in terms of racial-ethnic makeup. And yet, it will be seen that unity of this type was not the express concern of most white Movement pioneers, and if the founder had such concern, little hard evidence was left to confirm it. This is not to say that Warner was not concerned about interracial unity, but only that little hard evidence exists to verify it. Nevertheless, in this book, the reference to *visible unity* has primarily to do with unity along racial lines, whatever else Warner and Movement whites took (and take) it to mean. Visible unity is indeed about spiritual and church unity, but it is also about concrete flesh and blood human beings of all races physically uniting as one in Christ and worshipping together on the basis of equality, regardless of color line rules and practices in the wider society. The church's guide in matters of ethical behavior is the teachings and basic principles of Jesus, not the customs of society. In matters of ethics the church at its best is the headlight, not the taillight. This means that the church is to provide moral leadership for the world; it does not (or should not!) uncritically follow the customs and practices of the world.

As I grew up in the Movement I was, even as a child, fascinated by the core principles of holiness and visible unity. I was always curious to know how the unity principle was related to the issue of race. My pastor, Rev. Matthew Moses Scott, preached on unity periodically, and I often heard other Movement preachers, white and black, preach on it. I never heard one of them preach explicitly on the relevance of visible unity to the matter of race. Not only did I not hear sermons and lessons on this in local Movement churches, I did not hear them at state and national camp meetings and the International Youth Convention. However, because we regularly fellowshipped and worshipped with white Church of God congregations in the state of Michigan, I think the black members assumed that the holiness-visible unity principle was inclusive of unity along racial lines. We were not explicitly taught different from this. Even the *assumption* of such a connection by pioneer blacks speaks volumes about their level of faith and their understanding of the biblical message about visible unity.

By the time my mother, Mrs. Fannie B. Burrow, the charter member of the Eastside Church of God in Pontiac, Michigan, introduced her eight children to the Movement I was a twelve year old. Although I had to that point grown up in mostly black low-income housing projects and attended predominantly black secondary schools, I was quite familiar with racism and the devastating problems it caused us. Consequently, it did not take much to get me wondering about race and the Movement either when the pastor preached about unity, or when we sang so often, "The Church of God one body is . . ." In any event, I have always wondered whether D. S. Warner and other Movement pioneers were primarily or only concerned about spiritual and denominational unity, or whether they were also concerned about visible unity along racial lines. For many years my experience in the Movement confirmed that they were at least aware of the implications of their teaching for interracial unity, even though they seldom preached and taught about it explicitly.

When I read James Earl Massey's book, *African Americans and the Church of God* (2005) not long after its publication, it became clear to me that although D. S. Warner was most assuredly concerned about spiritual and church unity, he was also aware of and concerned about the significance of visible unity in a much broader sense. The world could not believe that such unity existed in the church if it did not *see* it. Warner saw that Jesus was not praying about an abstract, unseen, up-in-the-sky unity. His reference—to spiritual and church unity—was also to the more inclusive visible unity, an important implication of which was his desire for persons of all racial-ethnic groups to be joined together as one in the church. It was the desire of Jesus that the world *see* evidence of this unity in the church.

At any rate, I credit Massey's book with having prompted me to begin reading (for the very first time) works by and about D. S. Warner and other Movement pioneers, but also publications by and about John Winebrenner. Warner was for ten years a member of the Churches of God (General

Eldership) founded by Winebrenner around 1825.[5] As I read and pondered Massey's seminal book, I became convinced that although the Movement had been founded on the principles of holiness and visible unity, most early and subsequent leaders—primarily whites—basically focused on spiritual unity or denominational unity, while giving scant attention to the importance of the more broadly inclusive visible unity along racial lines so clearly implicit in Warner's teaching and preaching. Unfortunately, Warner himself said little about this in his writings and sermons. Nevertheless, my reading of the literature revealed that efforts were afoot even during the early years of the Movement to water down the true meaning of the powerful principles of holiness and visible unity, giving them a more abstract character such that the focus was not to be on a visible unity with racial and related connotations, but on spiritual and-or church unity.

In addition, I could see that the transition from the emphasis on visible unity, to spiritual or denominational unity, seemed to fit quite well into the general schema of the sociological transformation of religious organizations that focuses on the natural history of religious groups.[6] That is, I could see how the Movement was founded by a charismatic leader who was primarily interested in teaching his newly found doctrines to others, and was not concerned about societal expectations and pressures, but within a few years there were signs of an erosion of the true meaning and implications of the founding principles. Not long afterward the founder died, and leaders began interpreting his ideas, often in ways that accommodated the spirit and practices of the broader society, especially racial practices in the South, but in the rest of the country as well. In fact, we will see that even before Warner died some Movement leaders and members were already moving in the direction of accommodating the expectations of the surrounding society. Also consistent with the sociological transformation of the group were signs of structures or institutions of various kinds being developed in the Movement that would insure the group's continuation. Because the sociology of church group transformation is not an exact science, we will see that some of these signs (which generally occur in the second and third stages) actu-

---

5. The name of the group that Winebrenner founded was changed from "Church of God" to "Churches of God" at the meeting of the General Eldership in Muncie, Indiana, in 1896, approximately thirty-six years after Winebrenner's death. See Forney, *History of the Churches of God*, 788.

6. The concept of the sociological transformation of religious groups has been around at least since the time of Ernst Troeltsch (1866–1923), who was much influenced by his German colleague and teacher, sociologist Max Weber (1864–1920). This has been enhanced by H. Richard Niebuhr, J. Milton Yinger, David Moberg, Elizabeth Nottingham, Bryan Wilson, Barbara Hargrove, Keith Roberts, and a host of other sociologists of religion.

ally occurred within the first year of the Movement's existence. All of this seems to me to follow a basic sociological transformative path, so much so that it even appears that at this writing, the Church of God has come full circle in the sense that some Movement people are seriously wondering why the group has not yet actualized all that is implied in the two founding core beliefs, especially since the group has made tremendous progress; has taken in so many members; and has become so prosperous. In other words, some in the group are surely wondering why the Movement has not yet made good the claim of holiness and visible unity, particularly as these pertain to race.

The sociological transformation of religious groups involves at least three basic stages of the group's life cycle. The first stage is generally dominated by a strong charismatic leader whose aim is to preach and teach her message oblivious to what is occurring in the broader society. The illness or death of the founder generally ends stage one. Typically, during this stage there is no attempt to develop an organization or institution, since the primary emphasis is on getting the message out. But we will see that this was not quite the case for the Church of God. Its path deviated from the general sociological tendency in that second stage signs actually began to appear during the first phase.

In the second stage of the cycle the successors of the founder find themselves needing to respond to societal pressures and to interpret the meaning and application of the founder's basic ideas and teachings for the growing group. Members and new converts want to know what the founder's basic teachings meant and what is required of them in light of those teachings. This is also the stage in which efforts are begun to insure the sustainability of the group. Ideas and teachings of the founder and early leaders begin to take on the appearance of being routinized or institutionalized, especially as structures and agencies are put into place, such as publication facilities, to accomplish the goals of the group and to insure that the founding principles are continuously put forward on a wide scale. In addition, the adding of various departments or agencies, such as a publishing house and schools, also helps to establish and further stabilize the group, thus providing a stronger foundation for its continuation. This second stage, then, is generally the beginning of organizational and institutional development, even though the pioneers typically fight hard to avoid such occurrence.

In the third phase of the group's life cycle, there tends to be further organization, diversification, expansion, and stabilization of the group, often done through the adding of more schools, service agencies, etc. The period might also be characterized by phenomenal membership growth, increase in wealth, and deepening institutionalization. By this time, the group is truly established, but frequently the members appear dissatisfied still. They may be frustrated by the recognition that having gained significantly in membership, financial stability, and achieved all they have in terms of building construction, the group has not yet actualized the basic principles of the founder; has not made good the claim.

All of this implies a drive toward a fourth stage. At this point, the group might be energized by rediscovering its roots and basic teachings, and may be compelled to put its energy and resources into the matter of actually taking steps that will lead to their living up to the best in their heritage. I think there is strong evidence that the Church of God is in the fourth stage of its natural history. All that remains is for members to decide where to go from here, how best to get there, and to *vow* to adhere to the Movement's foundational core principles: holiness and visible unity.

I discuss the sociological stages of the Movement's life cycle more fully in the chapters that follow. For now, suffice it to say that my sense is that a socio-ethical discussion on the Movement, its two founding core beliefs and their relation to racial-ethnic unity, as well as the stated desire of many in the group for reconciliation, could in fact help to fill a longstanding void not only for Afrikan American members, but for all members of the Church of God.

Important as church or spiritual unity has been throughout the Movement's history, the time is long past due for members at all levels, and in all agencies and institutions of the group, to make good the implicit claim of the visible unity emphasis regarding concrete interracial unity in the church. For years, members have talked, preached, taught, written, and sung about being one body in Christ. Acknowledging the importance of Warner's work as reformer, Andrew L. Byers declared in 1921 the need for a subsequent constructive stage. Of this stage he wrote: "*The responsibility is to make good the claim*, and this means much."[7] The Church of God is still in this constructive stage. It is time to make good on the claim about holiness and visible unity as they pertain to interracial unity.

In the most concrete sense, what would the Church of God look like in a racial-ethnic sense in every area of its operation if it took this claim seriously? We can be sure that at the bare minimum, it would mean that the mere token presence of a person of color here and there would no longer be seen as acceptable or even viewed as "progress." Rather, every conceivable effort would be made to insure the presence of a *critical mass* of Afrikan Americans and other people of color in every Movement agency and school. Local churches would be much more intentional about joining together for

---

7. Byers, *Birth of a Reformation*, 32 (my emphasis).

regular interracial worship services throughout the year and not just annual special occasions such as Christian "brotherhood" Sunday; engaging in other interracial activities intended to foster understanding, racial-ethnic-cultural appreciation, and interracial unity; and cooperating with each other to do serious, meaningful social ministries as a contribution to establishing a more just society and the community of love.

The term "generation" is used loosely in this book. That is, I will not in all instances be referring to a 20–25 year period of time before a subsequent stage of the Movement's life cycle begins. When discussing the sociological transformation of religious organizations one usually discusses a number of phases that are generally separated by a generation (more or less). But this is only an approximation, since sometimes there will be less, and sometimes more, years involved in a given stage of development. In this regard, it will be important to remember Val Clear's helpful observation when discussing the life cycle of religious groups, namely that it is virtually impossible to pinpoint definite dates for passage from one stage to the next.[8] Furthermore, it will be seen that there are often various degrees of overlapping of the stages. For example, while in the first stage of the life cycle some characteristics of the second stage may present themselves, just as traits of the third phase may begin to emerge during the second period. Or, it might be the case that because of the way the group develops, some aspects of a given stage might not appear at all. Val Clear illustrated this point when he argued that the Movement essentially skipped what sociologists call the established sect stage of its life cycle.[9] It may also be that characteristics of the second stage may appear even before the founder is no longer on the scene. Indeed, we will see that this was precisely the case with the Movement, and that during the very first year of the Church of God's existence signs of institutionalization (a second stage trait) began to appear. In addition, only a few years—not a generation—separates the first from the second stage of the Movement's life cycle. The Movement began around 1880, and Warner died fifteen years later. Technically this was less than a generation. However, we will see that there were clear signs that, by sociological definition, the second stage of development was beginning even before Warner died.

While there is evidence that some pioneer leaders in the Church of God intentionally sought to actualize concrete visible unity along racial lines, there is also considerable evidence that not only did many whites succumb early to the race ethic of the wider society, but the hard evidence is lacking that white pioneers themselves made interracial unity a priority,

8. Clear, *Where the Saints Have Trod*, 52.
9. Ibid., 122.

or that the stance of most was qualitatively different from the racism that characterized and affected so many whites throughout the country. There is little solid evidence that they actually interpreted the visible unity motif as broadly as the blacks who heard the message and instinctively joined the Movement. Blacks joined because they believed the visible unity message was consistent with their understanding of the Bible's teaching on the unity of all people under the one God of the universe. Indeed, one looks in vain for evidence that white Movement pioneers, as a rule, intentionally and systematically evangelized among blacks (a practice that was not unusual in itself, or unique to the Church of God during that period). Large scale proselytizing among blacks was done primarily by blacks themselves. And yet, this would seem to contradict the standard Movement histories that teach that white pioneers had a "zeal" for interracial unity that presumably was lacking in other religious groups. The possession of such zeal should have compelled white Movement pioneers to evangelize among blacks as readily as they did among whites, but this was not the case.

Researching and writing this book has convinced me that the vision of interracial unity based on the principle of equality was the primary basis on which Afrikan American members—from the early days of the Movement to the present—joined and remained even when they received only minor support from their white counterparts; even when whites have worked decisively against the ideal of visible racial unity in the church, its agencies, and educational institutions. Blacks joined the Movement because of what they took the teaching on holiness and visible unity to mean, namely that all of God's people—regardless—are one and equal under God and should be treated accordingly.

Chapter 1 provides an overview of the sociological transformation of the Church of God Reformation Movement. The focus is on the stages that are generally involved in the life cycle of a new religious group, from inception to maturity. One will see how the Movement began as a sect-like group (in the sociological sense) that had been affiliated with a larger, established group, the Churches of God (General Eldership). It will be seen how the small group, with its leader, left the parent group because specific practices and issues, doctrinal or otherwise, were not satisfactorily resolved. Sociologically, the protesting group tends to break away from the parent group, generally under the leadership and inspiration of a charismatic leader. This chapter applies these and related sociological dynamics to the Church of God Reformation Movement and shows why and how it began, and how, before long, and without even desiring or planning to do so, it began to take on institutional and other characteristics similar to those of the larger, established group from which it separated. These changes typically occur over a period of two or more generations. The basic emphasis in the chapter is on how the Movement was established on the principles of holiness and visible unity, but failed early on, and subsequently, to make good this claim in the fullest sense, especially along the line of interracial unity. The chapter introduces the reader to the broad outline of the sociological transformation of new religious movements generally, and the Church of God more particularly.

In chapter 2, the reader is introduced to John Winebrenner, the founder of the Churches of God (General Eldership), the group from which Warner was ultimately excised when he refused to stop preaching and teaching what he learned to be the truth, namely holiness or entire sanctification as a second work of grace. This is a particularly important chapter because even though Warner never met Winebrenner, it is probable that he was much influenced by his strong abolition and anti-enslavement stance, and also his later, more moderate position. The latter may suggest why Warner said so little publicly and in his writings about interracial unity, although he believed in it. Warner was also likely influenced by Winebrenner's thinking on the doctrine of holiness and visible unity. In addition, the chapter reveals that Warner differed from Winebrenner and others in the General Eldership primarily because of his insistence that conversion and entire sanctification did not occur simultaneously. Rather, according to Warner's interpretation of the Scriptures, holiness was a second blessing. The initial conversion experience was not all there was, but a necessary step leading to entire sanctification. Inasmuch as Warner spent about a decade in the General Eldership, it seems reasonable to examine Winebrenner's thought to determine the nature of the influence he and-or his teachings might have had on Warner.

The discussion in chapter 3 focuses primarily on the first phase of the life cycle of the Church of God, the stage that is generally dominated by the strong personality of a charismatic leader. The emphasis, then, is on Daniel Sidney Warner, founder and leader of the Church of God Reformation Movement. This chapter tries to determine whether, and to what extent, Warner possessed charismatic traits in the sociological sense, and what this meant in the early stage of the newly found group. In addition, the chapter sheds light on the extent to which Warner might have been influenced by the time he spent at Oberlin College; by Winebrenner's early abolition and anti-enslavement activities, and how this may have affected Warner's treatment of blacks and how genuinely he accepted them into the Church of God. To what extent was Warner committed to interracial unity in the church, since he stressed the need for visible unity? To what degree did early Movement whites and blacks buy into the visible unity concept, particularly as it pertained to interracial unity? What were circumstances that created conditions for interracial division in the group? This chapter examines these and related issues.

Chapter 4 covers a lot of ground, even continuing and deepening some of the discussion in the previous chapter. The longest chapter in the book, it examines aspects of the second stage of the group's life cycle, i.e., its movement from the charismatic leader (or sect) stage to the established sect or denomination phase. The second and subsequent stages of the group's natural history typically occur after the founder has left the scene, often through illness or death. It is generally during this stage that successors try to clarify and interpret key ideas, principles, and practices of the founder. For example, second generation leaders seek to define the basic ideas or core principles of the founder; what these mean—or should mean—for members, and how members should behave toward each other and people in the wider society. Sociologically, these interpretations are generally not quite in line with what the founder had in mind. For example, in the case of Warner's successors, the general inclination was for white Movement leaders and pastors to focus more on spiritual or denominational unity than on visible interracial unity. And yet, we will see in this chapter that there is some muddiness of this issue, since there is not much extant solid evidence that Warner and other pioneers intentionally and persistently emphasized interracial unity in their sermons, teachings, and public practice. Warner stressed the importance of visible unity in the church as well as spiritual and church unity. For reasons that elude us, and about which we can only speculate, however, Warner himself was generally silent on the issue of interracial unity in the church. However, James Earl Massey recalls having read letters written by two Mississippi blacks who said that Warner preached justice for black people during the Mississippi tour in 1890 (see Appendix A). Nevertheless, had Warner been more vocal about interracial unity in the church, there would be a more natural, identifiable sociological progression whereby the founder's core teachings give way to or get altered by second and subsequent generations of leaders when they begin interpreting them. In truth, we will see that the seeds of one of the things Warner dreaded most, namely, division along racial lines in the church, were present even during his time. The proof of this was clearly manifested two years before Warner died when white members began publicly questioning the viability of blacks and whites worshipping together on the basis of equality. The more precise sociological tendency would have been for such change to have occurred as the leader was losing influence or was otherwise passing from the scene, which was not the case of D. S. Warner.

Chapter 4 also discusses the early concern about race, and the sacrificing of the visible unity principle while Warner was still alive, i.e., during the first stage. There is also consideration of racial separation in Movement churches in the northern cities after Warner's death. The chapter revisits the infamous confrontation of 1912 (introduced in chapter 1), and also examines the significance of oral history for Movement blacks especially, and all Movement members more generally. It is argued that written literature need not be privileged over the oral tradition in every situation; that the oral tradition is just as legitimate, particularly when written and other sources are either questionable, have been lost, or are otherwise non-existent. Oral tradition and written literature may be mutually supportive. The importance of this tradition is addressed more extensively in Appendix B. It will be seen that precisely because there is not much hard evidence to support the standard Church of God party line that Warner and some white pioneers possessed great enthusiasm for interracial unity—a fervor, we are told, that only began to dissipate as the group moved into the second stage of its development, it is necessary to look to the supportive oral tradition passed down by blacks, and whites as well.

In chapter 5 we turn to a consideration of the third stage and the beginning of a fourth stage of development, the point at which, among other things, the group begins to re-examine its core principles and what members need to do to live them out. During this period, the group may very nearly approximate an established sect or a denomination. It will have taken more and more of the world—its beliefs, schemes, and practices—into itself, and begins accommodating to the ethic of society, rather than clinging to the rigorous requirements of the ethic of the gospel, or the ethic promulgated by the founder. There is also further elaboration in the chapter on the period of expansion and the implications this might have for the group. It will be seen that during the late third stage and the beginnings of the fourth, the group is thought to be more established as an organization, and when—in the case of the Church of God Movement—members begin to wonder whether or not enough has been done to make good the claim about holiness and visible unity.

It is during the third phase, i.e., what David Moberg refers to as the institutional stage, that the group may begin to experience tremendous growth in membership, wealth, building construction, and more diversification of all kinds. The group's vitality begins to be drained by the demands of institutionalization or bureaucratic demands, and before long it is "more concerned with perpetuating its own interests than with maintaining the distinctives that helped bring the group into existence."[10] However, as a group that is now more established, members *may* begin to wonder whether they have done enough to live in accordance with their founding principles. In the case of the Church of God, members might well begin to wonder whether enough has been done to make good the claim about holiness and visible unity. This opens the way for the possibility of a fourth stage of development in the group. This chapter therefore further elaborates on the period of expansion and implications for the group.

Chapter 6 turns to a consideration of things that Movement people will need to do if they are truly serious about making good the claim about holiness and visible unity. The focus is on what Afrikan Americans and whites should do, and cease doing, if this is to be a real possibility. There is also reflection on the theological and socio-ethical meaning of the holiness principle and its significance in the work toward visible interracial unity.

Chapter 7 is the final chapter in this book. It offers and discusses seven conditions that I believe will position Movement people to make good the claim. These seven conditions, influenced both by Massey's book on Afrikan Americans in the Church of God, and numerous conversations I had with the late Theodore Baker, Sr., are essentially challenges to Movement leaders and members at every level and in each of its agencies and academic institutions. My hope is that this book will serve as a catalyst, along with Massey's important book (*African Americans and the Church of God*), to challenge Movement people in their churches, schools, and agencies to get on with the business of making good the claim about uniting holiness and visible unity, particularly as it relates to unity along racial-ethnic lines.

Rufus Burrow Jr.
Distinguished Visiting Professor of Theological Social Ethics
and Black Church Leadership
United Theological Seminary of the Twin Cities
December 2015

---

10. Moberg, *The Church as a Social Institution*, 121.

1

The Church of God in Sociological Transformation

RELIGIOUS GROUPS GENERALLY PASS through at least three distinct stages before ultimately reaching a more settled phase and becoming stabilized in relation to other religious groups and the broader society. Indeed, by the time stabilization occurs, some religious groups will have entered a fourth stage. This is the stage in which church members might begin to intentionally look back to their roots, for by this time they are at least three generations removed from the time the group was founded. By now, members may have a strong desire to rediscover the teachings of the founder(s); to re-examine and ponder the founding core beliefs of the group—what they meant to the founder and pioneers and what they should mean today, both in theory and most especially, in practice. My sense is that the Church of God Reformation Movement has entered just such a stage in its lifecycle. This might well be the time when Movement members will consciously and determinedly consider committing themselves "to make good the claim" of their founder—Daniel Sydney Warner—the claim about uniting holiness and visible unity in the church.

The sociology of religion teaches us that when members of religious groups are on the social, economic, political, or religious fringes of society there is a strong likelihood that they will form a sect (i.e., a protest group) that comprises members of their group or community. The group bonds in protest against real or imagined injustices against them; or they bond in protest against various ideas and practices of the parent group. The emergence of the new group is a result of complex multiple causes. These include, but are not limited to: migration and transplantation of members, social disorganization, social change, conflict over doctrinal issues, socioeconomic differentiation, and charismatic leadership.[1] Once the group emerges as a sect the sociological tendency is for it to be transformed multiple times before reaching the level of stabilization. These transformations are affected by occurrences both within and outside the group. The implication is that if a new religious group survives it will go through a series of stages over the course of several generations. A new religious group can go through its entire natural history in one generation or, what is more commonly the case, over the course of several generations. What does this process *generally* entail?

THE BASICS: SECT AND CHURCH

Following H. Richard Niebuhr's discussion in his classic text, *The Social Sources of Denominationalism* (1929), sociologist of religion David O. Moberg provides an instructive portrait of the life cycle of new religious bodies.

> According to [the process of a religious group's life cycle], children born into the families of first generation sect members begin to change the sect into a church even before they reach adulthood. With their coming the sect must become an educational and disciplinary institution in order to make the new generation conform to its ideas and customs. The second generation holds its convictions less fervently than pioneers of the sect, whose convictions were formed in the heat of conflict and sometimes at the threat of martyrdom. With each succeeding generation isolation from the world becomes more difficult. Wealth may also increase, giving sect members vested interests in the economic order. Compromise is an inevitable result; the ethics of the sect, increasingly become like those of church-type bodies.[2]
>
> In time the sect's administration also tends to become church-like. An official clergy replaces lay leadership; easily taught creeds replace the unwritten, enthusiastically held doctrines of the emergent sect. Infant baptism or dedication becomes a means of grace as children's salvation is sought . . . Sectarian organization theoretically can endure in pure form for only one generation.

1. See Moberg, *The Church as a Social Institution*, 108–17.
2. Ibid., 100.

> Even the sect or cult that originates as a protest against ritualism, ceremonialism, and formalism is soon likely to have its own ritual. Regular religious services make emergence of repetitive patterns inevitable. Although the group may insist that it has no liturgy or ritual, any deviation from the customary pattern may produce insecurity or a feeling that something important is left out.[3]

Without question, members become alarmed if and when someone ignores or forgets the functions of the rituals or does not perform them as they have always been performed. However, the formalizing and establishment of ritualism and other practices only contributes to the group's movement from sect toward church; from less to more stability; from charismatic to bureaucratic leadership. These are all ideas to be developed in this book.

At any rate, my contention is that once a group reaches the third stage (i.e., the denominational stage) and becomes stabilized, it is from this point that other religious movements *may* arise, or, it might be that other significant dynamics may occur instead. I emphasize "may" because it is not necessarily the case that another group will arise from the more stabilized one. Sociologists of religion such as Max Weber, Elizabeth Nottingham, Barbara Hargrove, J. Milton Yinger, C. Eric Lincoln, Ronald Johnstone, Meredith McGuire, Keith Roberts, and Grace Davie have advocated that from this stabilized position new religious movements may emerge. That is, internal dissension may arise that could lead to division or schism and possibly the development of a new religious group. My contention, however, is that what *could* happen, instead, is that the stabilized group may enter a fourth stage in which it begins to focus in serious and creative ways on internal renewal and regeneration, which may also entail a looking back, remembering, and re-examining the meaning and implications of the founding principles. I believe that the Church of God Reformation Movement has entered or is on the verge of entering such a stage, or is at least poised to do so if enough of the members have the will, courage, and moral resolve to press ahead in this regard. How the members and leaders respond and behave at this point in their history will likely have important implications for their success or failure to actualize the meaning and requirements of their founding core beliefs.

Sociologists of religion have long held that sectarian elements (which are potentially explosive, creative, and even divisive) are always present in the church, although in varying degrees. This is a different way of saying that generally we find both church and sect type tendencies (which may be

---

3. Ibid., 100–101.

viewed as end points on a continuum) in religious groups. In an early work, sociologist J. Milton Yinger described these two basic types of tendencies or religious groups (sect and church). According to Yinger the sect type organizations tend to,

> refuse to compromise their ideal in any thoroughgoing fashion and are forced by this decision to withdraw from normal participation in the dominant structure. They prefer to maintain their ideal, to the extent of human ability, in a small, intimate community, rather than have it sharply reduced in the competition with secular powers that it would face to a much larger degree if they tried to control the whole society. Being outside, in a sense, the dominant social structure, the sects . . . are in a position to make a radical challenge, either directly (as in the case of sixteenth-century Anabaptists) or implicitly (as in the case of medieval monastics), to those aspects of society which contradict their ideal.[4]

The tendency of the sect to refuse to compromise its ideals and view of what is the true gospel and church implies an attitude of rigidity and exclusivism. This frequently points to not wanting to fellowship with other denominations, or to acknowledge that they are legitimate churches. We will see that this was precisely the case of the early Church of God Reformation Movement.

Unlike the sect, the church type organization tends to compromise its ideal, become more accepting of the outside world, and accommodate to the ethic of society. The church tends to do this primarily because it is an "all-embracing" institution that makes universal claims, and as such must be able to live in the world; must be able to get along with the world; and must be able to receive the world into itself. That is, it receives members of virtually every socio-economic grouping into its membership, giving preference to the financially able. Moreover, Ernst Troeltsch taught that the church, unlike the sect, is able to receive the masses, and to adjust itself to the world.[5] The church therefore has "the power to stir the masses" in significant ways. It views the sect type response to society and the world as too narrow and limited; or as too rigid, and realizes that such a response is not conducive to gaining a place of power in society; not conducive to receiving the world and its masses into itself. Both the sect and the church know this, for the former has no interest in gaining a place of power and acceptance in society, while the latter does. The church type organization "gains more

---

4. Yinger, *Religion in the Struggle for Power*, 220.
5. Troeltsch, *The Social Teaching of the Christian Churches*, 2:993.

formal influence than the sect because it compromises its ideal, accepts the basic pattern of the *status quo* in society despite its failure to come up to the religious ideal, and thereby establishes itself alongside the ruling powers. By this means the church maintains a good deal of influence."[6] It wins a place of power and influence within religious and societal circles, which means there is a degree of mutual acceptance between church and world such that the church tends to water down or compromise its highest ideals in order to accommodate the world.

The literature on the sociology of religion reminds us, however, that notwithstanding this, sect-like traits generally exist even in church type groups. What this means is that sect-like tendencies, e.g., the spirit of protest, can act as a leaven to either transform the church from within—what could happen to the Movement as it enters and moves through the fourth stage—or prompt it to take more militant positions on matters of faith. And if all else fails, that faction within the church that possesses sect-like characteristics may break away completely from the church and form its own organization. Yinger had this in mind when he said: "The compromise of the churches . . . is seldom complete, for there is a sectarian element in religion which defies institutionalization. Not all of this is located in the sects. It seems apparent, in fact, that religion maximizes its power as an agent in social change when the church and sect tendencies are combined by some kind of organizational principle."[7] Indeed, it may be said that Christianity always retains within itself an "explosive element," i.e., sect type tendencies, which is evidenced by the periodic appearance of charismatic and-or prophetic type personalities in history.

It appears that the degree or amount of the sectarian elements in a church is not as important as the fact that this element exists at all. The point is that it is an important factor in the matrix of those elements that may ultimately lead to a re-examination of the fundamental core beliefs of a group and their socio-ethical and other implications. But this explosive element, i.e., the sect-like elements in the church, can also lead to schism, and possibly even to the development of a new religious organization of some kind. Presently, we will see that sociologically, something like this happened with Daniel S. Warner and the small bands of believers affiliated with churches in the Northern Indiana and Northern Michigan Elderships of the Churches of God at Beaver Dam, Indiana and Carson City, Michigan, respectively, in 1880. Unable to convince the entire membership of those congregations of the viability and significance of holiness or pure sanctification as a second

---

6. Yinger, *Religion in the Struggle for Power*, 220.
7. Ibid., 221.

work of grace, Warner and a small group of devoted ones left each of those congregations and became the first two churches of the Church of God Reformation Movement.

For our purpose "explosive element" and "sect-like tendency" is equated with the "prophetic" or "ethical prophetic tendency" in the church. Consequently, my inclination is to use these terms interchangeably. Although I later discuss the Movement's understanding and rejection of "sect" and "sectarian," the primary usage of the terms in this book is consistent with that of the sociology of religion and theological social ethics. It is in light of this understanding that I equate sect-like tendencies with prophetic tendencies, although I am not claiming that every sect-like tendency is synonymous with an ethical prophetic tendency such as we find in the Hebrew prophets of the eighth century BCE. The tendency of a segment of a religious group to engage in divisive practices merely for the sake of its own selfish interests, for example, is not considered to be an ethical prophetic tendency. Such a tendency will only be equated with those actions of a group—even if they are potentially divisive—that fights for the larger group's strict adherence to God's expectation that justice be done in righteous ways, for example. In this book, then, prophetic tendencies always have significant ethical connotations that are consistent with the best in the Jewish and Christian traditions.

ABOUT THE CHURCH OF GOD

It might well be that the Church of God's conservatism, its strictness about adhering to teachings relative to matters of personal morality such as drinking, tobacco usage, gambling, and dancing,[8] may be contributing factors to

---

8. It is of interest to note here that the Movement, or more specifically Anderson University, has relaxed the restriction on dancing by permitting some forms of religiously motivated dancing on the campus—dancing, by the way, that looks every bit like dancing in non-religious settings. I witnessed the very spirited, rhythmic, performance of an interracial group of talented Anderson University students (comprised mostly of white students) at the first annual Afrikan American Alumni Luncheon at the 2006 North American Convention of the Church of God in Anderson, Indiana. Such was not permitted during my student days at the University in the early 1970s. This change, which may seem insignificant to most, is really quite important from a sociological standpoint, since it is further evidence of how religious groups that intend to sustain themselves are so affected by what is occurring in the broader society that they invariably make subtle (and not so subtle) adjustments here and there to their earlier beliefs and practices. I could see during my student days at Anderson that at some point the University would have to make some adjustments around the issue of dancing and partying. For although these were not at the time allowed on the campus, vast numbers of white and black students found ways to engage in these off campus. I knew then that

its continual growth at a time when many of the mainstream white denominations, e.g., Presbyterian USA, Disciples of Christ, and United Methodist, are experiencing decline in membership.[9] From a low of 74,497 members in 1940, to a high of 250,905 in 2007–2008, the Church of God Reformation Movement has, unlike many groups, experienced continuous growth for all but eight years from 1933 to 2009.[10] For all but fifteen years during the same time period it experienced growth in the number of local churches, from a low of 1,201 in 1933, to a high of 4,095 [sic][11] in 1971. There were 2,192 congregations in 2009.[12]

Sociologists of religion believe that although the growth in membership of conservative churches may be attributed to many factors, two of these include recruits from other conservative groups, and high fertility rates in the more conservative groups generally.[13] Typically these groups are able to retain members because of their "commitment mechanisms," which contribute greatly to the retention of members. One does not generally find much focus on commitment mechanisms in the more liberal and moderate churches. Citing several sociological studies of religious groups, Keith A. Roberts reports that: "The conservative churches in the United States employ more commitment mechanisms, have higher fertility rates, and have more religious training in the home, accounting for better overall membership trends."[14]

It is also known that Afrikan American congregations in white denominations often exhibit membership growth even as the overall membership of the denomination declines. This is a provocative and instructive phenomenon, one that Lawrence Mamiya and the late C. Eric Lincoln address in their outstanding study, *The Black Church in the African American Experience* (1990). The authors show not only that black church growth generally remains healthy. They also show that of the mainline white churches only

---

over time various internal and external pressures—which might also have implications for recruitment and retention—would prompt the University to relax this restriction. Young people today are much more free-spirited than in my college days, and we too were free-spirited! I was therefore not at all surprised to witness the performance of those student dancers, right there on the campus.

9. Hartman has listed a number of reasons he believes the Church of God has experienced such steady membership growth. See Hartman, "Reasons for our Growth," in *A Time to Remember: Evaluations* ed. Callen, 79–83.

10. The ARDA (Association of Religious Data Archives), http://www.thearda.com/Denoms/D_1349.asp, accessed 4/3/2015, 1–2.

11. The Church of God Yearbook of 1971 places the number at 2,326.

12. The ARDA, 1–2.

13. See Roberts, *Religion in Sociological Perspective*, 131.

14. Ibid.

the Roman Catholic Church has experienced a surge in black membership since 1985, and that most middle class Afrikan Americans tend to join the larger, more prestigious mainline black churches.[15]

As noted above, the Church of God has experienced a steady growth in membership at least since 1940. Indeed, James Earl Massey contends that since the late 1970s Afrikan Americans have been the Movement's fastest growing racial-ethnic group.[16] This is a very interesting phenomenon considering the essentially second-class status that Afrikan Americans have held in the group since the 1890s. A driving question in this book is: Why have Afrikan Americans remained in the Church of God, and continue to join it, in light of their unequal treatment and second-class standing in the group? Why did they not do what blacks did in the Methodist Episcopal and Baptist churches in the nineteenth century? That is, why did they not leave the Movement in mass and form their own completely separate denomination?

Doctrinally the Church of God is orthodox Trinitarian. One does not miss this emphasis in Cecil Carver's book, *Church of God Doctrines* (1948), where he writes about the Godhead: "I believe there is in the Word enough light for us to understand this matter . . . , if we are willing to be open-minded about it. The simple truth is that they are one in spirit, will, desire, aim, duration, etc., and are three in individuality, mind, and body; that is, in the sense that spirits have bodies."[17] Throughout the entire book Carver essentially bases Church of God doctrines on what he considers the appropriate biblical texts. Like many in this group he does not question words and ideas in the biblical text. He merely takes them at face value. The Bible is thought to be the undisputed, infallible word of God, pure and simple. Nevertheless, in addition to being orthodox Trinitarian doctrinally, Church of God polity is congregational. The worship style varies according to locality and group. When I was growing up in the Movement it was not unusual to find very spirited worship services—both during the singing and the preaching—in both white and black congregations.

---

15. Lincoln and Mamiya, *The Black Church in the African American Experience*, 159.

16. Massey, *African Americans and the Church of God*, 7. Of course, with the explosion of the Latina/o population throughout the nation and its status as the largest "minority" group in the country it is quite possible that the Movement's membership rolls may benefit mightily if concerted efforts are made to reach out to that group.

17. Carver, *Church of God Doctrines*, 8.

CHURCH OF GOD: A DENOMINATION?

Historically, members of the Church of God thought of themselves as a "movement" within the church rather than a sect or denomination. Carl Williams has written of this distinctive feature.

> [A]s long as we are a reform group within the church universal, working as leaven to better the existing order of the universal church, we are a *movement*. When and if we should formulate ourselves into an organization (formally or informally) to the exclusion of other Christians, we would then become a sect or denomination . . .
>
> Again, the Holy Spirit is the governing power in the universal church. If we as a group set up other governing powers, we cease being a movement and become a denomination . . .
>
> . . . *we as a group of people are not the church but a movement within the church to bring about Christian unity*. To bring about Christian unity simply means to establish the church (properly, and biblically speaking).[18]

Williams argues that when and if the group fails to preach and teach the doctrine of unity, it will become a denomination, which Movement people believed to be based on separateness or sectarianism.

Thinking of itself as a Movement, the Church of God wishes to give the impression that it is a group that is "on the move," or that "is going somewhere." While it disagrees with the way things are, the Movement has chosen to remain within the mainstream of Christianity and to work to reform it from the inside rather than to form a separate group.[19] However, we will see that it is a real problem, at least from the perspective of sociology of religion, as to whether the mere teaching and preaching of visible unity is sufficient for the group to avoid being viewed as a denomination. From 1893, efforts were already afoot by white Movement pioneers to instigate racial separateness. If, as early Movement people believed, separateness is a criterion for being viewed as a denomination, then the Church of God has been a denomination for a very long time, despite the continued preaching and teaching to the contrary. The Movement has unquestionably displayed racial separateness at some level at least since the 1890s.

Although Movement people do not consider themselves to be a sect or denomination in the sociological sense, they nevertheless come very close to being a classic example of an established sect or a denomination. In the

---

18. Williams, "Are We a Sect?," 23.
19. See Callen, ed., *A Time to Remember: Evaluations*, 35.

sociological sense, the Church of God falls somewhere between the established sect and the denomination. Perhaps it will be helpful to list some of the basic characteristics of these two types.

The Established Sect

Sociologist Ronald Johnstone contends that the established sect manages to retain elements of its radical protest and a strong commitment to ideology, while avoiding the accommodation and modification that would turn it into a denomination. Some denominational characteristics, however, usually become incorporated into the group, which becomes bureaucratized; its norms and procedures become formalized; some of its members gain higher social status. Yet, it does not become a denomination, even though it is no longer a pure sect. An institutionalized or established sect is halfway between the denomination and the sect on the sect-church continuum.[20] The established sect seems to be stuck between the sect and the denomination, and thus is essentially in "a state of arrested development . . ."[21]

Characteristics of the established sect include:

- Tends to be an outgrowth of a sect or cult (New Religious Movement or NRM).
- Tends to be more stable than a sect.
- Is likely to be occasioned by a sect whose initial emphasis was upon societal evils. This was the case of the Anabaptists, and to a lesser degree, the Quakers.
- Tends to be more inclusive and less alienated from society.
- Tends to be more organized, structured, and institutionalized, and thus closer to the denomination.[22]

We will see later that it is quite possible that the Church of God skipped the established sect stage.

The Denomination

The sect that is likely to become a denomination is that which is comprised of large numbers of individuals who are burdened with problems of anxiety

---

20. Johnstone, *Religion in Society*, 75.
21. Ibid.,
22. See Yinger, *The Scientific Study of Religion*, 266–73.

and sin. The focus of such groups is on "individual regeneration." The difficulties of middle class sects tend not to be of the financial or social injustice types. Rather, the basic issues tend to be "a feeling of inadequacy, confusion of standards in a highly mobile world, guilt, and physical pain."[23] Consequently, the sect that appeals to such people "has no real need to make a sharp challenge to the society and the established churches."[24] Because the protests of such a sect, e.g., Christian Science, are easily "absorbed into the dominant religious stream" without seriously challenging societal injustices and structural problems "and without the necessity for a reorganization of the religious pattern," the group easily becomes much more accommodating of society, and thus a denomination.[25]

Characteristics of the denomination include:

- Achieves less universality than the church.
- Unlike the sectarian tendency to withdraw from society and criticize it, the denomination tends to compromise its ideal with society.
- It tends to be limited by class, racial, and at times, regional boundaries.
- Because it is in close relationship with the power structure of the society, it may still be classified as a church type group.
- It is an intermediate or mid-point on the sect-church continuum.
- The key activity in the movement from sect to denomination is the development or focus on education. One no longer just gets religion through a conversion experience; it can now be taught![26]

It is important to remember that in the case of both the established sect and the denomination these traits are general tendencies. This means that some of them may or may not appear, depending on the group and the context. It is also helpful to remember that some denominations are characterized by more sect-like tendencies than others, e.g., the United Churches of Christ. Others, e.g., the Lutheran Church, tend to have fewer sect-like tendencies and therefore tend to be more accommodating of society and more prone to compromise their ethical ideal.[27]

---

23. Yinger, *Religion, Society and the Individual*, 152.
24. Ibid.
25. Ibid.
26. Yinger, *The Scientific Study of Religion*, 264–66.
27. Yinger, *Religion, Society and the Individual*, 150.

DANIEL SYDNEY WARNER AND SECTARIANISM

Daniel Sidney Warner (1842–1895) became a member of the General Eldership of the Churches of God in North America around 1867. He was licensed by the West Ohio Eldership at its eleventh annual meeting in Findlay, Ohio on October 16th of that year.[28] By this time, John Winebrenner (1797–1860), founder of the Churches of God (General Eldership), had been dead approximately seven years.

In 1874 Warner was at the center of a controversy in the West Ohio Eldership that came about as a result of his involvement with a holiness group in Sandusky, Ohio.[29] This group taught the doctrine of entire sanctification or the idea of a "second blessing" after conversion. In 1914, Churches of God historian Christian Henry Forney summarized the minutes of the 1874 annual meeting of the West Ohio Eldership in which the incident was addressed: "The beginning of trouble between D. S. Warner and the Eldership is foreshadowed in an action on the adoption of his Report, which stated that he had 'organized a church in Upper Sandusky contrary to the Rules of Co-operation,' and regarding this as 'a schismatic movement,' 'highly disapproved of his cause in organizing said church.'"[30] Warner was later brought up on charges in 1877 by W. H. Oliver, who expressed annoyance over his constant teaching and preaching on holiness and entire sanctification.

On September 16, 1877, Oliver preached against holiness as a distinct work of God, and instigated the charges against Warner.[31] In that same year, the Eldership reported that the Warner case had been "acted on charitably." This included a renewal of his license, but "with certain restrictions—that he cease to spring this so-called 'Holiness Alliance Band,' or any other outside party he may stand connected with, upon the Churches of God."[32] The Eldership tried to convey that any theology based on sanctification as a second act of grace was unacceptable and would not be tolerated. But Warner was so taken by the doctrine that he simply could not hold his tongue or his pen. Consequently, on January 30, 1878, charges were brought against him by G. A. Wilson for violating the conditions of the Eldership's earlier decision. This time Warner's license was withheld.[33]

---

28. Forney, *History of the Churches of God*, 561.
29. See Byers, *Birth of a Reformation*, 115–16.
30. Forney, *History of the Churches of God*, 565.
31. Warner, *D. S. Warner's Journal 1872–1880*, 292.
32. Forney, *History of the Churches of God*, 567.
33. Warner, *D. S. Warner's Journal*, 294.

However, this was not the end of the matter. The minutes of the 22nd West Ohio Eldership in 1878 reveal that more attention was given the Warner case, albeit "indirectly." The Committee on Resolutions declared, without citing Warner's name: "That any minister of this body that may presume to preach the dogma of a second work for sanctification shall be deemed unsound in the theology of the Church of God, and should not hold an ecclesiastical relation as a minister in this Eldership."[34] Whoever else the Eldership had in mind, Warner was certainly one of them. Warner was censored for his involvement with the Holiness Alliance, and also for his affinity with the belief in sanctification as a second work of grace, the view that after the initial conversion experience and justification by faith one must still undergo the experience, through faith, of sanctification. That is, one must achieve a state of holiness, purity or perfection. Presumably justification by faith gives the convert peace with God and frees her from all committed sins, while sanctification by faith is "a second definite instantaneous work of grace, which frees us from the inherited, or adamic, sin (1 John 1:7; Titus 3:5; John 15:2)."[35] Warner was convinced of the truth of this second work of grace, and thus refused to cease believing in and teaching it. Despite the actions taken by the General Eldership, Warner's belief in the truth of entire sanctification deepened daily and he could not give it up or stop preaching and teaching it. Forney reports that the Eldership "had finally to resort to the old remedy of excision in order to prevent the spread of the disease and restore the body to good health."[36]

A Second Work of Grace

Adherence to the idea of a second work of grace—different from the dreaded *Zinzendorfism*, the theory that justification and complete sanctification occur simultaneously, and a potentially schismatic issue for the Movement in 1899—is what places the Church of God in the category of *perfectionist sect*. This type of sect believes "that moral perfection, spiritual holiness, and total eradication of sinful desires should be the goal of all Christians."[37] The purpose of this second work of grace is twofold: "(1) restoration of the soul from innate depravity and uncleanness, the destruction of that carnal element which antagonizes the godly purpose of the soul, and (2) the infilling and indwelling of the Holy Spirit. In short, it is the doctrine of Christian

---

34. Forney, *History of the Churches of God*, 567.
35. Rowe, "What We Believe," 71.
36. Forney, *History of the Churches of God*, 185.
37. Moberg, *The Church as a Social Institution*, 91.

perfection, the state of loving God supremely and of living victorious over every form of sin."[38] This implies a total, absolute purging of the "saved" person such that sin and corruption will not be a problem in their daily living. The claim is that one is completely separated from sin and completely given to God.[39]

Warner himself claimed to have experienced "entire sanctification" and "embraced the cause of holiness" in 1877, having previously been hostile toward that doctrine.[40] Indeed, Warner had some contact with the doctrine when he attended Oberlin College (known for its teaching on perfectionism[41]), but he was not much influenced by it then. In the November 11, 1872 entry in his journal, Warner criticized adherents of sanctification, saying: "Nearly all blew loudly the horn of sanctification but manifested little of its fruits . . ."[42] Actually, this was less a criticism of sanctification as such, but more a recognition that proponents of it did not live accordingly. Warner began to be sympathetic toward the doctrine of entire sanctification when he started associating with the National Association for the Promotion of Holiness. He was influenced in this direction by his wife, Sarah Keller, and her parents who had all been converted to the doctrine and were affiliated with a holiness group in Upper Sandusky, Ohio. It was the Baptist minister, C. R. Dunbar, who most influenced Warner in the direction of entire sanctification.[43]

Holiness, Warner maintained, is a unifying principle. "It makes Christians one, in accordance with our Savior's prayer: 'That they may all be one: as thou, Father, art in me, and I in thee, that they may also be one in us; that the world may believe that thou hast sent me' (John 17:21). True holiness is destructive of divisional elements."[44] This latter point, we will see, had serious socio-ethical implications for the Church of God in the matter of race. Holiness was viewed as "a distinct experience," "the fullness of God in man," said Warner.[45]

Inasmuch as there was no meeting of the minds on the matter of sanctification or holiness as a second work of grace, Warner ultimately separated from the parent group, the Churches of God, and founded the Church of

---

38. Byers, *Birth of a Reformation*, 125.
39. Ibid., 194. See also 392.
40. Ibid., 115. See also 119–123.
41. Brown, *When the Trumpet Sounded*, 53.
42. Warner, *D. S. Warner's Journal*, 1.
43. Byers, *Birth of a Reformation*, 115.
44. Ibid., 131.
45. Ibid., 194.

God Reformation Movement around 1880. Although clearly based on protest, Warner's separation from the Winebrennerians (a characterization that John Winebrenner detested[46]) was not a schism as such, since he was seeking not to leave the church, but to reform it from within. Restoration, not separation, was his aim. Moreover, sociologist Val Clear observed that those who followed Warner represented "at least eighteen different denominations," so that it could not be said that as a new group they shared a common religious background or heritage.[47] Generally, the schismatic group shares a common religious tradition, but this was not the case of those first Movement pioneers. Warner and his followers thought of themselves as having withdrawn from denominationalism, or "all organized Christianity and return to the purity of the one church which Christ found."[48]

As observed before, in a little church near Beaver Dam, Indiana (Northern Indiana Eldership), Warner and five other persons declared their freedom from so-called sectarian Christianity. During this same period, some members of a congregation in Carson City, Michigan (Northern Michigan Eldership) walked away from what they considered to be sectarianism, and joined Warner. Andrew Byers, early Warner biographer, maintains that these two churches were the first to join Warner and the Church of God.[49] Warner declared that the Church of God "denotes the called out of God or separated unto God."[50]

Rejection of Sectarianism

Without question, the Church of God has never considered itself to be either a sect-type organization or a denomination in the sociological sense. In fact, D. S. Warner had much to say about the need to renounce and avoid all forms of division and sects of all types. Warner was interested in the biblical

---

46. One might be tempted to refer to the followers of John Winebrenner as "the Windbrennarians," but this is a characterization that was rejected by Winebrenner and others in the Churches of God (General Eldership). Forney reports: "With one voice, including Winebrenner's, and with some degree of ungentle and trenchant diction, they resented the charge that they were Winebrennerians. 'They reject the name Winebrennerian and utterly abhor that or any other human appellation.' 'It is entirely discarded by all the members of this body of Christians.' 'The Church discards every human invention.' 'The name Winebrennerian is entirely disowned by the Church, not one member being willing to wear it'" (Forney, *History of the Churches of God*, 66).

47. Clear, "The Church of God," 130.
48. Ibid., 131.
49. Byers, *Birth of a Reformation*, 289.
50. Ibid., 194.

sense of the term sect. It is of interest to note that the Church of God has at times been referred to as a sect in the pejorative, non-sociological sense.[51]

Warner held that in the biblical meaning one who causes divisions is a heretic. Accordingly, he asserted that the Greek term *hairesis* (heresy) is found ten times in the Second Testament. In five instances the word is rendered "sect," which refers to divisiveness or a faction. After looking into the meaning of the other five meanings of the term Warner concluded: "So then it is clearly seen that a heresy is a 'sect,' 'faction,' 'party,' or 'division'; while a heretic is a man who causes divisions, foments sects; or he may be simply a 'party man'" or 'a sectarian man.'"[52] Warner considered sectarianism or what he called "sectism" to be among the worst of sins, claiming that "there is no sin more utterly abominated by the Word of God than that of sectism," and that "there is in the Inspired Volume no sin mentioned that is more hateful in the sight of God."[53] The Bible, he held, teaches against all forms of sectarianism, and views the practice as being among the most despicable of all sins.

Warner did not know anything about sect in the sociological sense, although the term would be popularized by two of his younger contemporaries (whose names he may not have known), the German sociologist Max Weber (1864–1920) and his student and colleague, historical theologian Ernst Troeltsch (1865–1923). These men popularized the term sect in their sect-church typology (to which Troeltsch added mysticism as a third type). In any event, the sociological meaning of sect is important for our discussion, as well as the biblical meaning of the term that was popular with Warner and other Movement pioneers. Warner was convinced that Satan's most effective weapon is the dividing of the church into sects, for which proponents must answer to God.[54] "If you are a true, intelligent Bible Christian, a holy, God-fearing man," he writes, "you must cast off every human yoke, withdraw fellowship from, and renounce every schismatic and humanly constituted party in the professed body of Christ. Instead of belonging to 'some branch,' you will simply belong to Christ, and be a branch yourself in him, the 'true vine.'"[55]

Whatever one does, according to Warner, she must avoid sect membership and join the fellowship "with, the one and indivisible church that

---

51. See Norwood, *The Story of American Methodism*, 300.

52. Warner and Riggle, *The Cleansing of the Sanctuary*, 249. At Warner's death this manuscript was not complete. Riggle tells the reader that he "added about one-half more to the book than what was originally written" (Preface). Unless noted otherwise, citations will be to Warner's contribution.

53. Ibid., 250.

54. Warner, *Bible Proofs of the Second Work of Grace*, 302.

55. Ibid., 300.

God has on earth and which is made up of all who are born of the Spirit." Jesus, Warner held, requires not only a union of hearts, but "*a visible organic union*" as well.⁵⁶ The requirement in the Church of God is not merely the achievement of a spiritual unity, but a visible unity as well. This latter, we will see, is where the breakdown early occurred among white Movement people. They were eager for and sold on the idea of spiritual and church unity, but the idea of visible unity—particularly with its implications for unity along racial lines—was apparently too much for them. In this regard, many quickly came to prefer the divisive racial ethic of the larger society.

According to Cecil Carver, sectarianism or "sectism" is absolutely wrong, and is rejected and hated by God. Not unlike Warner, he cites a number of scriptures that he believes support his point.⁵⁷ Sectism, Carver writes, "is abhorrent to the very heart of God. We know with what displeasure God looks upon adultery. Well, He likens being joined to any of the man-made organizations, calling themselves churches, as being in adultery."⁵⁸ To further clarify what he means, Carver writes: "We are to be joined unto one husband, and that husband is Christ. When we are converted, or born again, we are born into Christ's church, or wife. Then if we go and join an organization of men, we have placed ourselves in such a position that Christ would have to be a bigamist to recognize us as His. He is not married to the many divisions of sectism. His bride is One."⁵⁹ The beauty of the church, Carver maintains, is cited in the twelfth chapter of Revelation, while the "awfulness of sectism" is depicted in the seventeenth chapter. Warner himself said that sectism is the result of carnality, and carnality is most effectively destroyed by perfect holiness, which "removes both sectism and its cause."⁶⁰ The reference to perfect holiness, of course, is what Warner regarded as the second work of grace.

However, despite all of the young Movement's preaching and teaching against sectarianism, the group was, in the strict sociological sense, a sect. Indeed, Church of God scholar Barry L. Callen is not wrong when he declares that Warner "was even a 'sectarian' in the modern, sociological sense."⁶¹ Warner and others who left their respective groups and banded together did so because they believed their groups had strayed from biblical teachings, whether on the nature of the church and church organization

---

56. Ibid., 301 (my emphasis).
57. Carver, *Church of God Doctrines*, 100.
58. Ibid.
59. Ibid.
60. Warner, "The Experience of Oneness," 17.
61. Callen, *It's God's Church*, 161.

matters; too much emphasis on institutional structures; failure to adhere to the biblical requirement of a second work of grace, etc. Warner and his followers wanted to return to what they considered the true church—the New Testament Church; a church that took seriously the doctrine of entire sanctification as a second work of grace.

Leaving their respective groups for the above reasons may, in the sociological sense, be equated with a protest. Sociologically, the sect is a protest group; typically tends to be small in terms of members; and aggressively separates itself from other groups and the larger society. Almost immediately an air of exclusiveness and of *being against* sets in. The stance of the group is what H. Richard Niebuhr characterized as "Christ against culture."[62] There is no question that Movement pioneers fought long and hard to distance themselves from other denominational groups. They were, after all, part of what they believed to be the last reformation at the end of Christian history. They were the "Evening Light" church; the church that was the beginning of "the restoration of the true New Testament church in all of her original holiness and unity."[63] In their view, all true Christians, regardless of religious affiliation, were to be members of the Church of God (the only name given to the church in the New Testament[64]). There was no place for sects and denominations, which for Warner were little more than pretenders of what it meant to be church. They were not thought to be legitimate churches at all. Consequently, those in the Church of God must isolate or separate themselves from other groups. There was thus a

---

62. See Niebuhr, *Christ and Culture*, Chapter 2.

63. Strege, *I Saw the Church*, 96–97. See also Warner and Riggle, *The Cleansing of the Sanctuary*, 266; also Wickersham, *A History of the Church*, 287–88.

64. In his small book, *The Church of God* (n.d.), Warner lists a dozen instances in scripture where the name, "Church of God," appears (20). He argued that there is but one church, and that its name came from the mouth of the Lord. (See also Warner and Riggle, *The Cleansing of the Sanctuary*, 255–56). Warner totally rejected what he referred to as "party names" or denominational names of churches. In *Bible Proofs of the Second Work of Grace* he asked: "Can it be said of professors of holiness that they have 'one heart' and 'one mind,' while some have a mind to be Presbyterian, others Baptists, others United Brethren, and others have a mind to adhere to the several different sects of Methodism" (299)? Warner might well have been influenced by the writings of John Winebrenner in some of this. Winebrenner wrote: "We nowhere read of the 'Christian Church,' or of the 'Disciples of Christ,' nor of the 'Brethren's Church,' etc." He went on to say that it was dishonorable and unscriptural "to lay aside all Bible names, even the divinely appointed name, Church of God, and assume a human name: such as Roman Catholic, Episcopalian, Lutheran, Presbyterian, German Reformed [from which he broke away], Baptist, Methodist, Menonist, Unitarian, Universalist, or something else, equally inappropriate, unscriptural, and unmeaning"; see his chapter, "History of the Church of God" in *History of All the Religious Denominations in the United States*, 171.

rigid exclusivism that characterized the Movement in its first thirty or forty years—a sect trait in the sociological sense.

Early Movement people considered themselves to be the sole true church, which essentially meant that they did not acknowledge the legitimacy of other groups and did not actively seek to fellowship with them, a practice that would change only very slowly. Church of God national historian Merle D. Strege aptly characterizes a thirty-year period that may have been the Movement's "most sectarian period," and here the reference is to the sociological meaning of sect. According to Strege:

> The saints of the Evening Light claimed to be the restored church of the New Testament, an exclusive church that admitted no sin, certainly not the sin of dividing the body of Christ. During these three decades [from the 1880s to the mid-1920s] the majority of saints refused to recognize the legitimacy of other Christian bodies and therefore refused cooperation as well. Church of God ministers were loath to join interdenominational ministerial fellowships. They warned the saints to keep their children away from Sunday schools operated by the "sects" and discouraged attendance at non-Church of God revivals . . . Non-cooperation, grounded in apocalyptic exclusivism, was the watchword of this era.[65]

This early sense of exclusivism and refusal to acknowledge other sects and denominations as legitimate churches was without question a sect-like trait in the sociological meaning. Warner totally rejected the view of those denominational ministers who held that they could accept his teaching on the biblical idea of the church, if only he would accept that their denominations were also God's churches. Instead, Warner insisted on strict exclusivism, declaring: "There is but one household of faith. Christ does not have a plurality of wives. He has but one bride, and she has no sisters."[66] He acknowledged that there were many denominations calling themselves churches, "but the Lamb's wife owns no kin to them. They are of an entirely different family."[67]

Although Warner founded the Church of God Reformation Movement on the basic core principles of holiness and visible unity, even before he died in 1895 there was evidence of white Movement people resisting unity along racial lines in the church. Before going further it seems reasonable to discuss this in more detail.

---

65. Strege, *I Saw the Church*, 104.
66. Warner and Riggle, *The Cleansing of the Sanctuary*, 266.
67. Ibid.

HOLINESS, VISIBLE UNITY, AND RACE IN THE CHURCH OF GOD

Is there a connection between the Movement's teaching on holiness and visible unity and the existing racism among many of those who became members? Did the pioneers intend that the principle of visible unity include unity along racial lines? In a word, was unity along racial lines part of, or inclusive of, the pioneers' claim about visible unity?

In the case of the Church of God Reformation Movement there was—among a few pioneers at least—such enthusiasm generated over the emphasis on holiness and visible unity during the first decade (1880s), that there were a few significant instances of blacks and whites actually worshipping and praying together in southern white churches without the legally required ropes or partitions to separate them. Although required by civil law, to my knowledge, blacks were not initially required by Movement pioneers to sit in the balcony in southern churches, nor were they the last to be served during communion, as was the case in most southern white churches.[68] Although there was no manifest attempt to systematically violate the prevailing custom of racial segregation in the wider society and in most existing churches, the new converts to the Church of God—a few whites and many blacks—experienced such a high level of exuberance for Warner's message about visible unity and its ethical implications that they simply did not pay much attention to civil law and the custom of racial separation. This tendency was consistent with what we find in the process of the sociological transformation of religious groups. In the first stage the group generally exhibits little or no concern for societal practices and prohibitions. Rather, the group tends to focus solely on its own teachings and the sense of revivalism that is occurring. Its eyes are generally on nothing else, but evangelizing or proselytizing. Essentially the aim is to grow the membership of the group. Therefore, it is understandable that initially some new converts to the Movement, regardless of race, paid little or no attention to the prevailing social custom and practice of racial segregation. But sadly, these few among whites were the exceptions.

Without question, there were instances in which a few early white pastors and leaders of the Movement actually preached against the custom of the separation of the races in the South. It is not clear that they did so *because* of their interpretation of the holiness and visible unity doctrines,

---

68. The great orator, statesman, and abolitionist Frederick Douglass wrote of witnessing just such practices, i.e., black worshippers having to wait until all whites were served communion. See his selection, "The Church and Prejudice," in *Narrative of the Life of Frederick Douglass*, 143–45.

or for some other reason, or a combination thereof. At any rate, at the Alabama Camp Meeting near Hartselle in 1897, two years after Warner's death, Lena Shoffner (later Lena Shoffner Matthesen), a white woman, preached against the separation of the races. (Six years before the 1897 camp meeting, Warner and his five member evangelistic team held a meeting near there in February, 1891.) The Shoffner meeting was an interracial one, separated only by the *legal* requirement of a rope that was strung down the middle aisle of the tent where worship services were held. Church of God historical theologian Charles E. Brown reports that Shoffner preached a sermon about tearing down the wall or partition that separated God's children. On this one occasion, at least, she seems to have made the connection between the principle of visible unity and interracial unity in the church. According to Brown, Shoffner was apparently so passionate and forthright about the matter that, while she was preaching, "Someone took the rope down and whites and blacks knelt at the same altar together."[69] For those brief moments the worshippers seemed to forget about civil law and custom and behaved only in accordance with divine law. In those moments, nothing mattered but what they believed God expected of them. They were caught up in the Spirit, and gave no thought to the requirements of custom and civil law. However, as might be expected for that period in American history, the group was immediately attacked by a mob of white racists. Brown tells what reportedly happened next.

> They threw dynamite under the boardinghouse and the camp houses and ferreted out the preachers like hounds hunting rabbits. The preachers fled. One man stood in a creek all night. Another preacher put on a woman's clothes and escaped. Next night the mob followed them to the homes where they had fled, in some cases fifteen miles away from the campground. Otto Bolds fled to a home five miles away, walking in a creek to avoid his pursuers and arriving at this friend's house at two o'clock in the morning. The next morning five more of the preachers arrived at this friend's home. On the following day an unsaved friend guarded them with a shotgun till they had crossed the river on the road to Huntsville.[70]

Brown also writes of two black Church of God ministers who were at the Alabama camp meeting and also heard Shoffner's sermon against the partition between blacks and whites in the church that day. Brown does not tell us how he knows of the two black ministers' presence at the camp

69. Brown, *When the Trumpet Sounded*, 266.
70. Ibid.

meeting. However, reportedly one of these was Henry Robinson, who also fled for his life.[71] The other was Daniel F. Oden who became pastor of the Bessemer, Alabama congregation established in 1895 by Beatrice Sapp, a black woman. Oden later moved to Detroit, Michigan where he became pastor of a new black congregation, "a group newly separated from whites following controversy over the color line."[72] The core of the blacks who remained organized themselves into the Church of God of Detroit. Oden succeeded Christiana Janes, a black woman, who was forced to resign what had been a racially mixed congregation.[73] The black members were forced out and Oden was called to be their pastor. Oden also served as vice-president of the National Association of the Church of God (comprised primarily of blacks) and worked closely with the white Detroit pastor, Charles E. Brown, who later became editor-in-chief of the Gospel Trumpet and a professor at the Anderson School of Theology.

It is of interest to observe that in a talk given at the North American Convention of the Church of God in June 2008, Douglas Welch reportedly said that an examination of Lena Shoffner's diary and other sources reveals that on the day she allegedly preached the sermon against the partition she was not actually present.[74] When I discussed this with James Earl Massey a few days later, he helpfully replied: "That her diary and other sources record nothing about the sermon she reportedly preached on the day to which witnesses refer does not mean she did not preach that sermon, although it might well mean that she did not preach it on the particular day to which witnesses report. The story about Shoffner's sermon and the events that followed circulated quickly and widely throughout the Hartselle area and other parts of the state. Many blacks quickly picked up on the story and it became part of the oral history. No less was this the case with whites." Massey is confident that the oral history around that incident is accurate, even if the reported date and a detail or two of the incident is not. (Because of the historical importance of orality among Afrikans on the continent and in diaspora, I discuss it further in chapter 4, but more thoroughly in Appendix-B. Much of what we know about early blacks' membership in the Church of God was conveyed by word of mouth, since blacks had a tendency to "speak" their

---

71. Ibid.

72. Massey, *African Americans and the Church of God*, 163.

73. Ibid.

74. This was reported to me by one of my Master of Theological Studies (MTS) students, Matthew Upchurch, who heard Welch's lecture. Upchurch himself is a Movement man who engaged in painstaking research in the Church of God archives at the Anderson University School of Theology as he worked toward completion of his thesis, "No Holiness without Unity, No Unity without Holiness."

history, rather than write it down. This had much to do with the fact that historically blacks were an oral people, and in addition, it was against the law for them to learn to read and write during slavery. Oral tradition, then, is most important among blacks.) Moreover, as previously observed, Charles E. Brown reports that when the worshippers and ministers were attacked by white racists after Shoffner's sermon, a number of the ministers fled for their lives, including Henry Robinson. Afterward, Robinson reported that he had been to Hartselle, implying that he had heard Shoffner's sermon.[75] Although he did not explicitly say this was the case, it is quite possible that Brown obtained this information about Robinson and Oden from one or more of the "hundreds of letters" he received (at his request) from around the world as he researched and wrote his history of the Movement, *When the Trumpet Sounded* (1951).

Nevertheless, it is of no small moment that Lena Shoffner's reported sermon against the dividing rope has remained in the collective memory of Movement people—regardless of race—as long as it has, and has also been so important for so many. Even if Shoffner did not preach that sermon, it is significant that many in the Movement *wanted* to believe that she did; *wanted* to believe that at least *some* white ministers among the pioneers explicitly preached against racial division in God's church. This most assuredly would have been appealing to blacks and would have been a powerful drawing card for them to join the Church of God. In addition, it would also supply part of the reason that blacks remained in the Movement even when whites in the group began calling for separation of the races and the need to abide by custom and civil law in matters of race, even in church. Furthermore, the oral history around the sermon preached by Shoffner may have much more significance than Movement people have acknowledged. In addition, we will see later that dating from 1893 there is clear evidence of a number of other white Movement pastors, e.g., Joseph F. Lundy, A. J. Kilpatrick, and Thomas Carter who expressly addressed the race question and sought to clarify that racism was a divisive belief and practice and thus a contradiction of the Movement's holiness and visible unity principles. They therefore invited people of *all* races to their church services.[76] We do not see strong written evidence of this practice in Warner the founder, although it is generally believed that his services were always open to any who would come.

Clearly, in light of what reportedly occurred during Lena Shoffner's sermon in 1897 there was excitement and enthusiasm among many black,

---

75. See Smith, *When the Trumpet Sounded*, 266.
76. See Massey, *African Americans and the Church of God*, 29, 30–31.

and some white, Movement people regarding the *visible* unity that Warner preached and taught about. (It is not clear that by visible unity Warner meant to include unity along racial lines, for we know of no instance in which he explicitly said so.) Here and there, small groups of white Movement people had gotten it right on the race question; had made the connection between visible unity and unity along racial lines. However, as typically happens when the charismatic leader leaves the scene, much of the initial zeal for the founder's message and practices diminishes, and before long, less emphasis is placed on the original vision and ideals. This was precisely the case in the Movement.

D. S. Warner died in 1895. Two years later, Lena Shoffner preached against division along racial lines in the church, making it clear that such division contradicted the Movement's teaching on holiness and visible unity. However, during this same period, early Church of God leaders were sending out contradictory and confusing messages regarding the matter of race. For example, during the same year that Shoffner preached against partitions between the races, Enoch E. Byrum, Warner's successor as editor of the *Gospel Trumpet*, wrote an article that gave the following advice regarding race relations in the group.

> There are no certain rules that can be laid down nor lines drawn that will govern every community, except those set forth in the word of God, as customs in various places widely differ, and oftentimes it is wisdom and to the glory of God to follow customs of the country, though they differ from those of our native place.
>
> However, when the customs of the people conflict with the word of God, then Peter's advice should be followed—obey God rather than man; forsake the customs of the people rather than forsake God. *We do not believe in white and colored people mixing in marriage, or in any other way that is unnecessary. We believe it would be better, if it were convenient to have it so, that they meet in separate meetings*; but there are places where it is almost necessary for them to meet together, and they do in many places harmoniously and to the glory of God.
>
> *But when all prejudices between the race is removed, that does not give them liberty to intermarry*, but if custom is not too strong against them, they can meet together in harmony.
>
> All we desire is to see the word of God fulfilled. We do not require the white brethren to greet the colored brethren with the Holy kiss. If they feel it is a duty according to the word of God, let them fulfill the word, and God will get the glory.[77]

---

77. Quoted in Smith, *Quest for Holiness and Unity*, 166–67 (my emphasis).

If only Byrum had ended his statement after "forsake the customs of the people rather than forsake God!" Nevertheless, let us be clear. Already, by 1897 (and possibly earlier), two years after Warner's death, Movement leaders were talking about the convenience of blacks and whites worshipping in separate meetings. Furthermore, lest we think that Byrum's article carried little weight and influence we should be clear about the role and influence of the editor of the *Gospel Trumpet*. Warner had essentially chosen Byrum to succeed him as editor. Indeed, after Warner's death Byrum and his brother Noah became the sole owners of the Gospel Trumpet Publishing Company when they bought out Mrs. Warner's interest.[78] When Byrum succeeded Warner as editor "he was unanimously acknowledged everywhere as the leader of the movement everywhere," writes Charles E. Brown. He was not the forceful, eloquent speaker like Warner, but his "character and upright life" were such "that he commanded the confidence of the churches and ministers everywhere." Brown writes further that: "Not only so, but in any dispute as to whether a minister was accepted or not, the editor of the *Gospel Trumpet* always had the last word. He would listen to the trial, if he could. If not, he would receive the evidence. Always he decided whether the person accused should be renounced or whether to set aside the judgment of the ministerial court and continue to publish the man's reports. *From his decision there was no appeal.*"[79] It was known that Byrum's was a much more authoritarian leadership style than Warner's and some other pioneer leaders who "at least nodded in the direction of democratic participation."[80]

This is all to say that Byrum had a tremendous amount of authority, power, and influence. For Byrum to have given the confusing advice he gave in his 1897 article, "The Color Line," that clearly opened wider the door to racial division, therefore, was certainly taken seriously, especially by many white Movement people who already had inclinations in this direction but needed official counsel and support for their stance. They found this in the advice given by the editor of the *Gospel Trumpet*. One can only wonder about what might have been the practice of Movement whites had Byrum chosen to write and speak explicitly and forcefully against division along racial lines in the Church of God. Strege has written of Byrum's willingness to risk the possibility of huge defection from Movement ranks when in 1899 he "imposed a strict doctrinal discipline" on those who subscribed to

---

78. Strege, *I Saw the Church*, 50.

79. Brown, *When the Trumpet Sounded*, 366 (my emphasis).

80. Strege, *I Saw the Church*, 57. Warner did in fact exhibit "heavy-handed authoritatianism" in his use of the *Trumpet* "to portray Sarah Keller Warner [his then estranged wife] as both theologically and ethically outside group norms" (52). See also Byers, *Birth of a Reformation*, 321–24.

Zinzendorfism, the view that justification and sanctification occurs simultaneously.[81] This view was contrary to Movement teaching. Nevertheless, the Movement was able to weather this crisis. Byrum's risk in this controversy was no small matter. But in the case of race he was not willing to take such a risk, i.e., to risk the possible defection of large numbers of white racists. Why?

My point here is not that Enoch Byrum's decisions and advice—whether about matters of race or something else—could not be challenged by pastors and the laity. We know that there were both whites and blacks who questioned his "rulings" and advice on the separation of the races.[82] Nevertheless, Massey has shown that when, several years later, successive articles appeared in the *Gospel Trumpet* in 1909 in response to Byrum's advice to southern blacks regarding Christian unity, all of the articles sought "to reinforce the editor's logic,"[83] even some of those pioneers who were most supportive of interracial unity, although not on the basis of equality.

Frankly, Byrum's advice had nothing to do with logic as such, but everything to do with his own racism. Therefore, the articles to which Massey refers actually reinforced Byrum's racism, even as they exposed the racism of the writers. In any event, we must not pretend that whites generally were not influenced by all of this in their racial thinking and behavior, or that blacks were not supremely offended and disappointed by Byrum's concession to racism. In some instances blacks chose to no longer make the effort to worship and fellowship with whites as a result. Some must have left the Movement. Most chose to remain—which I find incredible—while many simply opted to worship only among their own race. It should be borne in mind, however, that this turn of events was a result of blacks' *reaction* to white racism. It was not a choice that blacks would have made had whites not consistently invited into the church the societal practice of racial segregation. It is important to make this distinction because there are always those who are quick to claim that both blacks and whites desired racial separation in the church, as if to imply that both groups were equally culpable in the division that occurred. This simply is not true. Whites instigated separation along racial lines, and blacks reacted to it. Blacks and whites were not equally complicit in this divisive practice.

The advice that Byrum gave regarding race relations was absolutely devastating to the teaching on holiness and visible unity. It therefore seems to me that Massey is much too soft in his assessment of Byrum when he

---

81. Ibid., 41–43.
82. See Massey, *African Americans and the Church of God*, 59–64.
83. Ibid., 60–61.

writes of, "Byrum's concern for a 'sound economy and efficiency' as editor (and thus leader of the new movement)—that doubtless influenced his approach to shaping a social code for the movement's young but ever-widening work."[84] Byrum's was clearly nothing more than a rationale—and not at all a good one—for accommodating the Movement's ethic of holiness and visible unity to the racist ethic of society. Massey, however, offers a different interpretation of Byrum's article. To get the full flavor of his line of reasoning I quote the relevant passage from his book.

> Byrum viewed all happenings in light of what seemed at stake at the time. The publishing work was burgeoning in 1897, experiencing a growth that had taken the Gospel Trumpet Company far beyond being a 'tiny, almost one-man operation' under Warner. It was becoming 'a reasonably well-established business whose impact was even then reaching far around the world' through its periodical, tracts, and books. New building plans were under way at the Gospel Trumpet office, new publications were appearing, and new management was showing itself admirably, with Byrum the chief moving figure behind the new growth and progress. Having assisted Warner as 'Office Editor,' managing the publishing work as an ailing Warner withdrew more and more from the business details, Byrum was mindful of protective measures which could serve the business interests along with the spiritual interests of the publishing work. His 1897 article about 'The Color Line' was published as a policy statement about race relations *with an interest to protect the church.*[85]

According to this line of thought, then, Byrum, notwithstanding his troubling advice on race, essentially sought only to protect the growth of the church. But the church is supposed to be one body under God. How does one protect the church by opening the door to racial division, for *any* reason? I do not question that Byrum sought to "protect" the church. What is at issue is that he sought to do so at the expense of racial unity—at the expense of the Movement's ethic of holiness and visible unity. That, to me, is a problem of monumental importance. It seems to me that the only way to make any real sense of Byrum's stance is to be forthright in naming his racism and his willingness to advise the church to accommodate to the ethic of a racist society. The truth is that Byrum compromised the Movement's teaching on holiness and visible unity, instead of holding firm to the ideal of the church

---

84. Ibid., 17.
85. Ibid., (my emphasis).

as a counter-cultural community that advocates a far superior ethic to that of society and refuses to compromise it. Byrum might well have had the best interests of the Church of God Reformation Movement in mind, but this does not exonerate him for having opened the door to division along racial lines. Furthermore, can it be said that he had the best interests of the *Church of God* (as distinguished from the Church of God Reformation Movement) in mind? The *Church of God* is absolutely against racial division in the body.

Massey also offers a rationale for why Byrum advised blacks at the 1912 Anderson camp meeting to find their own place to worship. Discussing the "clouded . . . racist mood" of the state of Indiana and Church of God practices such as the "holy kiss," Massey writes: "Perhaps Byrum and others considered an open and prolonged fellowship between the races, however honorable by Scripture standards, to be inappropriate because of the social risks involved."[86] However, it is important to remember that the Christian ethic is a "radical imperative," a countercultural ethic, and thus is one that is always poised to challenge the status quo, rather than give in to it. As such, any person or group that lives this ethic knows—or must be made to know—that there will be both "social risks involved" as well as reprisals for choosing not to accommodate. Byrum's actions were more in line with the broader society's ethic of racial separation than the Christian ethic of racial inclusivity. Remember, in 1897 he had written about the feasibility of blacks and whites worshipping in separate meetings, so the advice he gave to that small group of blacks in 1912 was merely a continuation of this line of reasoning. So important was the confrontation in 1912 that I take it up in more detail in chapter 4.

In light of the process involved in the sociological transformation of religious groups, it makes sense that Byrum and other Movement people of his generation—the second generation of the group's life cycle—wished by this period to survive as a group and to continue to perpetrate some semblance of the ideals of the founder, which necessarily meant that they needed to routinize or institutionalize their collective life, ideals, rules, and norms. This process of routinization or institutionalization would also necessarily entail the need to further develop and maintain existing organization structures, e.g., the Gospel Trumpet Company, as well as to introduce other sustainable organizations and agencies to help carry out the group's work. In this sense, Byrum was quite on the mark from a sociological standpoint. His aforementioned egregious error was a moral, not a sociological one. Byrum went too far in that he contributed heavily to the slaughter of interracial unity on the altar of church survival and socio-political convenience.

86. Ibid., 90.

To his credit, Massey acknowledged that Byrum's teaching on racial division in the church served to "dull the prophetic edge of the reform to which D. S. Warner had been openly committed."[87] It is not at all clear, however, that Warner was "openly committed" to racial unity, a point to which we return in chapters 3 and 4. Nevertheless, Massey could see clearly that Byrum and other Movement pioneers were off the mark regarding interracial unity.

Byrum frequently obliterated the Christian or prophetic aspects of his instructions on race relations by inserting comments that revealed his disdain for racial amalgamation. Indeed, he often seemed less concerned about Warner's emphasis on holiness and visible unity. In the same article in which he said, "when the customs of the people conflict with the word of God, then Peter's advice should be followed—obey God—rather than man; forsake the customs of the people rather than forsake God," he also felt compelled to say, "we do not believe in white and colored people mixing in marriage." He wanted to assure otherwise good, but racist Movement people that under no circumstances did the group endorse marital intermingling of the races. Byrum was more interested in political, rather than moral, correctness. It was more important to appease various white factions in the group and the wider society than to actualize the earlier vision of D. S. Warner regarding visible unity.

Byrum seemed to have no problem with unity among the races as long as it was not based on equality, and there was no intermarrying. It seems that many churchgoers of the period, including much of white America, were preoccupied with the idea of interracial marriage or amalgamation. Indeed, in the late nineteenth and early twentieth centuries "social equality" was for many whites a euphemism for interracial relations that could lead to the dreaded interracial sex and miscegenation. With all the socio-political corruption and massive injustice occurring during the period, it is peculiar indeed that nineteenth- and early twentieth-century "church fathers" were more concerned about mature adults who might desire to intermarry than they were about establishing justice and the community of love, or about retaining interracial worship services, and eradicating racism in all its manifestations. Indeed, what Bertrand Russell, the British philosopher and Nobel Laureate, said about Medieval church fathers such as Ambrose, Jerome, and Augustine applies as much to early white Church of God pioneers. Said Russell:

> It is strange that the last men of intellectual eminence before the dark ages were concerned not with saving civilization or expelling

---

87. Ibid., 18.

the barbarians or reforming the abuses of the administration but with preaching the merit of virginity and the damnation of unbaptized infants. Seeing that these were the preoccupations that the Church handed on to the converted barbarians, it is no wonder that the succeeding age surpassed almost all other full historical periods in cruelty and superstition.[88]

It is indeed strange that this type of mentality seems always present in the church of every age, even as poor and oppressed peoples are being treated unjustly, brutalized and even annihilated all around. This was also the case of Byrum and other pioneers of the Movement. With so many serious, indeed devastating problems in the aftermath of the Emancipation Proclamation and the Reconstruction era, Byrum and many other whites throughout the country focused their energy and resources on trying to discourage and offset racial amalgamation.

At any rate, E. E. Byrum not only raised the specter in 1897 of whether it might be better for the two races to meet in separate places of worship, but also in 1909. Interestingly, the issue of separate places of worship was also raised by Lena Shoffner-Matheson in 1909 at the Oklahoma Assembly. She wrote about a controversy in the meeting, and said it was concluded that an investigation be done "to find out whether or not it would be better to have separate meetings there. This must be mutually agreed on by both colored and whites of the congregation,"[89] she wrote. It is not clear whether Shoffner-Matheson agreed with the conclusion of the investigation, or whether she was merely reporting on the incident. What is clear is that at the 1897 Alabama camp meeting twelve years earlier she was convinced that racial dividing lines in the church was wrong. By 1909 however, she seemed not to be quite as certain. This was yet another indication of the lack of consistency among even well intentioned Movement whites about unity along racial lines.

We learn from the sociology of religion that during the first stage of the founding of a new religious group the question of discipline and rules is generally not a major concern for leaders, for the energy and emphasis goes into proselytizing and evangelizing. Nowhere is this more evident than in D. S. Warner's journal. That Warner traveled as frequently as he did to spread the truth about entire sanctification leaves one wondering how it was humanly possible for him to do all the other things he did, e.g., read, write, and study on a regular basis, and also manage the Gospel Trumpet Company and its affairs. In any case, during the first stage of a group's natural history,

---

88. Russell, *A History of Western Philosophy*, 366.
89. Mathesen, "Miscellaneous," (column 1), 10.

few well thought-out answers are given to questions about either the nature of the founder, his ideals, or the authority for his mission. Little attention tends to be given the ranking of persons in the new religious movement or to the development of an organization as such. Indeed, it is known that from the beginning Warner and some other pioneers shunned organization, preferring only to be ruled and led by the Holy Spirit.[90] Charles Brown rightly observed that Warner's fault in this regard was his failure to differentiate between organizing the church and organizing the work of the church in order to accomplish its tasks as efficiently as possible.[91]

Essentially, the first generation of Movement people and many in the second generation advocated for what C. E. Brown called the "leader principle," as opposed to "spiritual democracy" as the best means of church governance. The former was based on the idea that the church was to be governed by the Holy Spirit, who gifted selected men (primarily) and women for leadership. Consequently, it was believed that only the most minimal organization or institutionalization was needed during this early stage of the Movement.

We will see that as the Movement progressed through its life cycle—indeed by the middle of the second stage of development—the leader principle would give way to "spiritual democracy." This transition would not happen either quickly or without causing deep resistance and pain among those who wanted to retain what they considered a most important practice of early leaders. Although Brown—the fourth editor of the *Gospel Trumpet*—and others came to believe that the older model of church governance that required the absence of all organization was one of the early Movement's most egregious errors,[92] it is a sociological fact that charismatic leadership, with its de-emphasis on organization, tends to be a trait of virtually all new religious groups during the first stage of development. What is not clear in the case of the Church of God is how unusual it was that Movement people fought so hard and long to retain the "leader principle" while simultaneously decrying institutionalization as they sought to respond pragmatically to more and more problems of a growing organization and concerns raised by the membership.

Although some attention has been given the teaching on holiness and visible unity and how or whether these are related to the matter of race, I return to the subject subsequently. In the meantime, before taking up the sociological stages of the Church of God Reformation Movement, it is

---

90. Smith, *The Quest for Holiness and Unity*, 92.
91. Brown, *When the Trumpet Sounded*, 94, 101.
92. Strege, *I Saw the Church*, 217, 288.

important to examine the contributions of John Winebrenner, founder of the Churches of God (General Eldership). D. S. Warner was initially a member of this group. In what way(s) was Warner influenced by Winebrennerian ideas and practices before he founded the Church of God Reformation Movement? What beliefs and practices of the parent group did Warner and his followers retain? To what extent, if any, was Warner influenced by Winebrenner's or the West Ohio Eldership's stance on race? These and related matters are examined in the next chapter.

2

John Winebrenner and the Churches of God (General Eldership)

Two years after President Abraham Lincoln signed the Emancipation Proclamation Daniel Sidney Warner was converted to the Christian faith and enrolled in Oberlin College.[1] He preached his first sermon in a Methodist Episcopal Church on Easter night in 1867 and became a member of the Churches of God (General Eldership) that year. Warner was much influenced by the fact that this group had no written creed, and considered the Bible to be its primary article of faith. I discuss Warner more extensively in the next chapter. For now, it is important to take a closer look at John Winebrenner, founder of the Churches of God in North America, since a number of Warner's theological and socio-ethical stances may be linked to Winebrennerian ideas and practices. In addition, this discussion on Winebrenner may contribute to our understanding of Warner's position on race.

Many members of the Church of God Reformation Movement know little or nothing about John Winebrenner and what may be important similarities and differences between his group and theirs. James Earl Massey has written that D. S. Warner was likely influenced by Winebrenner's abolitionism and his anti-enslavement stance. This claim needs to be examined more closely. For example, we need to know what type of abolitionist Winebrenner was, and what he required of the church regarding the issue of enslavement. Did he adopt the view of Alexander Campbell (of the Disciples of Christ) and other revivalists of the period, namely that the slavery issue was one chiefly for politicians, not for the church and its ministers

---

1. Byers, *Birth of a Reformation*, 46, 49.

and members? Did he believe it to be a political, rather than a moral or theological issue? Was he the type of abolitionist who believed blacks to be the equals of whites? Did he believe that enslavers should be allowed to join the Church of God? In addition, what might Warner have taken from the West Ohio Eldership of the Churches of God (to which he belonged from 1867–1878) regarding the race question? Winebrenner helped to establish the West Ohio Eldership that quickly became an anti-enslavement eldership like most of the others.

We have seen that Warner would ultimately grow beyond the West Ohio Eldership and would be expelled because of his persistent espousal of the idea of entire sanctification as a second act of grace. Warner also came to believe that the group had become too dependent on "man-rule" and had become a sect. Nevertheless, there were still a number of beliefs and practices that Warner continued to share with his former group, not least the emphasis on church unity, and the centrality of the Bible.

The party line among Church of God Movement people has been that Warner also exhibited sensitivity toward blacks and their plight and welcomed them into the Movement on the basis of equality with whites. Although this book takes issue with that line of thought, we will see that depending on what Warner actually knew of Winebrenner (who died seven years before Warner joined the Churches of God), he might have learned much about his consistent abolitionism and anti-slavery stances, which could have contributed to Warner's own view of blacks and their place in the church.

In the discussion that follows, I most especially highlight Winebrenner's early abolitionist stance and his emphatic writings against the enslavement of blacks. I also list and discuss reasons that led him to moderate his stance. In addition, I discuss his influence on the General Eldership in 1845 to pass two strong resolutions against involuntary enslavement. One of these advised that any member involved in the sinful practice should be excommunicated. Although soon thereafter Winebrenner capitulated and significantly softened this stance, we will see that D. S. Warner knew about his abolitionist and anti-enslavement positions, and that he quite likely learned some things from this that helped to shape his own point of view and practice regarding blacks during his leadership of the new Church of God. We need to keep in mind, however, that Warner only *knew about* Winebrenner, for when the latter died Warner was not yet of college age. By the time he began studies at Oberlin College in 1865 Winebrenner had already been dead five years. Nevertheless, the question remains: Were Warner's racial views influenced by Winebrenner's abolitionist and anti-slavery stances? Did his position supplant or go beyond that of Winebrenner? Was he able to avoid the mistakes made by Winebrenner regarding the matter of race, or did he essentially remain silent, despite his strong emphasis on holiness and visible unity? These and related matters are addressed below, and in the next chapter. Before proceeding, it will be instructive to briefly discuss Winebrenner biographically.

JOHN WINEBRENNER

John Winebrenner was born the third son of Philip and Eve C. (Barrick) Winebrenner on March 25, 1797 in Frederick County, Maryland, an enslavement state. The parents were of German descent, and German was spoken in the home. They were members of the German Reformed Church. Winebrenner's father had limited formal education, but was a successful farmer. His mother was "a gentle, pious woman, of remarkably good mind, and more of Scotch than of German origin."[2]

John Winebrenner wanted to be a minister from the time he was a boy. Although his mother was supportive of this from the beginning, his father's support came only belatedly. The more his father opposed, the stronger was the boy's desire to be a preacher of the gospel. Winebrenner later wrote that, "nothing, I believe, in all the world would give me permanent satisfaction and contentment but preaching the gospel."[3] He clearly understood this to be his calling or vocation. He was known to be an impressive preacher from the start. His personality and preaching were such that he possessed qualities of charisma, thus easily drawing people to himself and his beliefs. "His sermons had great power in convincing men of sin . . . ," and "his force of character itself contributed intensely to rivet conviction upon the people."[4] His preaching had such power that "crowds flocked to hear him."[5] We have already seen that generally charisma is a key characteristic of leaders of new religious groups. John Winebrenner was not lacking in this regard.

Winebrenner was ordained on September 24, 1820. He preached his first sermon as pastor of the Salem Reformed Church in Harrisburg, Pennsylvania. He remained a resident of that city until his death on September 12, 1860.

Churches of God historian, Christian Henry Forney tells us that Winebrenner, like all human beings, had his faults and his limitations. He often exhibited a sense of not quite knowing how best to accomplish stated

---

2. Ross, "Biography of Elder John Winebrenner" (1880), 2.
3. Quoted in ibid., 3.
4. Ibid., 11.
5. Ibid., 12.

goals, and was at times overly optimistic about the possible outcomes. In this regard Forney writes:

> He had a constitutional weakness which led him to see future things in too large proportions. He was often too sanguine as to the efficiency of means to reach results. He was not so much a chimerical theorist, or lacked in practicalness and want of prevision; but his executive powers were disproportioned to his faith in results. Hence, some of his enterprises may seem utopian. In the light of experience this seems true of the constant hope he held out of the money-making power of *The Gospel Publisher*, through which relatively so much was lost. Also in the Texas mission project he so earnestly advocated, and which in the end created such bitter antagonism.[6]

And yet, to the extent that Winebrenner possessed charisma, these were not necessarily destructive limitations, for one who possesses charisma can generally get away with a great deal that others cannot. Organizational skills, for example, need not be such a one's forte, and it was not Winebrenner's. However, the evidence suggests that on his best day Winebrenner had the ability to draw others to him and into his message, an important attribute of the charismatic leader.

Notwithstanding his limitations Winebrenner, by all accounts, was known to be a man of honor and integrity. "He was accustomed to perform, and to insist on others performing, every part of social justice. Fidelity to every trust and contract; tenacious of every promise; disdaining to dissemble or prevaricate, and regarding every act of injustice as a meanness to which he would scorn to stoop—these were ingredients in his character. Integrity was to him only entireness of one's moral being in unison with moral law."[7] Not unlike the stance of Socrates in *Gorgias*, Winebrenner was known to prefer to suffer wrongdoing rather than to inflict it on others.[8] In addition, rather than return injustice for injustice, he preferred to simply dismiss the injury that was inflicted on him.

Winebrenner gave his first views on the Church of God in a sermon in 1836 in a Mennonite meetinghouse.[9] About a year previous he started *The Gospel Publisher* in which he strongly advocated against dividing the church into denominations because he believed it promoted sectarianism. He argued emphatically, as Warner would later do, that the Church of God

---

6. Forney, *History of the Churches of God*, 132–33.
7. Ibid., 134.
8. See Plato, *Gorgias*, 53.
9. Forney, *History of the Churches of God*, 52.

John Winebrenner and the Churches of God (General Eldership)   37

was the only name of God's church, and that it was neither a sect nor a denomination.[10] It was also said that he "met with wonderful success: in his efforts to obliterate sectarianism."[11] In addition, Winebrenner also argued for the unity of the church, i.e., "the oneness, or unity of all true believers in one holy Church of God . . . ,"[12] although he was not the only one to do so during that period. Leaders in other churches did the same. For example, "On May 9, 1839, 'a meeting was called at New York of several gentlemen of various denominations for the purpose of devising and adopting a plan to unite Christians of different denominations in a more intimate and friendly alliance.'"[13] Winebrenner believed that denominationalism does nothing but promote sectarianism, also an idea that Warner would take as his own.

Inasmuch as he was primarily trying to restore the church to early or "primitive" Christianity, Winebrenner was part of the restoration movement. He therefore argued that the basis on which all questions were to be answered was the Bible, the Church of God's "only creed, discipline, church standard, or test-book . . ."[14] For example, since the church was essentially a Bible institution, the naming of it must be a Bible name. The Bible, therefore, was the place to turn in order to find the appropriate name for the church. "There they found, again and again, the title, 'church of God,' and no other church name, and that settled the first and one of the most important questions."[15] Winebrenner (as Warner would do later) attested that one nowhere finds in the Bible "Christian Church," "Disciples Church," "Brethren' Church," "Roman Catholic," "Episcopalian," "German Reformed," etc. One finds only "Church of God."[16] He was as passionate and vigilant about seeking a Bible name for the church as he was about preaching against sectarianism, or about the need for regeneration.

Winebrenner and his early followers (not unlike D. S. Warner and his) were most passionate about "soul winning" for salvation. And yet he clearly had other strong passions.

> He was the harbinger of that charming symphony of union of the twentieth century. But his own utterances on 'Church of God' as the only proper name for the church, being 'more ancient,' 'more descriptive,' 'more scriptural' and 'more appropriate,' and his

10. Ibid., 66.
11. Ross, "Biography of Elder John Winebrenner," 11.
12. Winebrenner, "History of the Church of God," 175.
13. Forney, *History of the Churches of God*, 53.
14. Winebrenner, "History of the Church of God," 176.
15. Yahn, *History of the Churches of God in North America*, 35.
16. Winebrenner, "History of the Church of God," 171.

opposition to 'baptism as the door into the church' were distinct and without a shadow of compromise. The voice of the Church of God those years gave no uncertain sound on the question, 'Who should be members of the church?' Regeneration the door, and credible profession of godliness the only terms of admission into the fold. Otherwise there is no salvation.[17]

Baptism was important, to be sure. However, one had to undergo the salvific experience that alone could change one's life, giving her the new look. Therefore, in order to be member of the Church of God, Winebrenner argued, one had to experience regeneration or conversion. Salvation was the criterion for membership in the church, but there was no talk of the need for a second work of grace. So strongly did Winebrenner feel that many of the people in the church had not been converted, that one of his favorite texts in the early years of his ministry was, "Ye must be born again."[18]

WINEBRENNER, THE CHURCHES OF GOD, AND THE SLAVERY QUESTION

Prejudice against others, whether class, cultural, or racial seemed to have no place in John Winebrenner's life. We are told that he simply would not tolerate it. According to Christian Forney, "There were no barriers between him and the poor or the rich, the cultured or the illiterate, the white or the black, the children of toil or the elite."[19] He appeared in these ways to be a genuinely good person who sought to do the right thing and expected others to do the same. And yet, there is no clarity as to whether he, or later, D. S. Warner, believed Afrikan Americans to be the equals of whites. We will see that this has frequently been a problem with otherwise well meaning white people throughout United States history, namely to be virtually free of racial prejudice while simultaneously contending against the equality of whites and blacks. Interestingly, this phenomenon has been as prevalent among believers as non-believers. Indeed, in my own experience I have known many whites—in and out of religious institutions—who appear to be free of racial prejudice, while at the same time struggling with the idea of blacks being on equal terms with whites and being granted the same opportunities and life-chances in education, housing, employment, healthcare, etc.

---

17. Forney, *History of the Churches of God*, 52. See also 99–100.
18. Yahn, *History of the Churches of God in North America*, 29.
19. Forney, *History of the Churches of God*, 134.

Born and reared in the slave state of Maryland, Winebrenner was no stranger to being around enslaved Afrikans. His family was even involved in the sordid practice. He spent a good portion of his life in the company of abolitionists, however. He joined the anti-slavery society that formed in Harrisburg in the mid-1830s and during this period he used his magazine, *The Gospel Publisher*, to advocate for the abolition and emancipation of the enslaved Afrikans.[20] Winebrenner's articles and editorials about this subject began appearing in 1835 but abruptly stopped after the August 1838 issue of the *Publisher*.[21] The publication of these articles and editorials was an experience that influenced Winebrenner's way of thinking about ministry as well as his sensitivity to the enslavement of Afrikans and his sense that the practice was something much deeper than a political problem, or one to be left solely to politicians. It was not merely a secular issue to be left to the non-religious. According to historian Richard Kern the slavery issue was, for Winebrenner, "no more a secular matter beyond the reach of the church, than was any other form of sin . . ."[22] Winebrenner early saw (in the 1830s) that the enslavement of the Afrikans was a moral and theological problem. Nevertheless, we will see that he later began to adopt the much more conservative but popular position that it was primarily a political problem, and therefore was chiefly the concern of political and civic leaders, but not of Christians and the church.

Although Winebrenner did not believe that the Bible classified slavery as such to be a sin, he held tenaciously to the belief—especially in the 1850s—that certain forms of the *practice* of it were sinful. For example, Winebrenner's family had enslaved Afrikans and he had known "of instances where diseased or aged slaves who had outlived their usefulness were freed so that their masters would not have to provide for them. This, according to Winebrenner, was nothing short of sin. Although Winebrenner did not declare slavery itself a sin,[23] there were in fact times when he did characterize it as a "great crying sin." This appears to have been a point on which he vacillated. Nevertheless, Winebrenner seems to have believed that

20. Ibid., 54.
21. Kern, *John Winebrenner*, 104.
22. Ibid., 107.
23. Kern, ed., *A History of the Ohio Conference of the Churches of God*, 19. James Earl Massey claims that Winebrenner saw enslavement as "a moral issue, a form of sin . . ."; see his *African Americans and the Church of God*, 12. However, if one looks closer she will see that Winebrenner ultimately came to see slavery as sinful, but tolerable. Over time his stance softened. He even held that certain sins, e.g., sectarianism and war, are greater evils than slavery. See Kern's excellent and instructive discussion on Winebrenner and anti-slavery in *John Winebrenner*, chap. 6, especially 107–17.

the general drift of the biblical message was against the enslavement and inhumane treatment of the Afrikans.

In 1830 Winebrenner helped to form four Elderships: East Pennsylvania, West Ohio, West Pennsylvania, and Indiana. These met annually for the purpose of "cooperation, and not legislation."[24] In 1845 he was successful in forming the General Eldership which met triennially. This group passed resolutions intended to influence the behavior of church members. Interestingly, the introduction of the General Eldership ultimately caused critics to say that it contributed to the group taking on a sect-like look.[25] In any event, in 1845 Winebrenner himself was successful in urging the General Eldership to pass two strong resolutions against the enslavement of Afrikans.

In his chapter, "History of the Church of God," Winebrenner includes resolutions adopted by the Committee on Resolutions in the first meeting on May 26, 1845. The two that are pertinent to our discussion follow:

> *Resolved*, That it is the unequivocal and decided opinion of this General Eldership of the Church of God, that the system of involuntary Slavery . . . is a flagrant violation of the natural, unalienable and most precious rights of man, and utterly inconsistent with the spirit, laws and profession of the Christian religion. *Resolved*, That we feel ourselves authorized by the highest authority, and called upon by the strongest ties and obligations, to caution our brethren in the Church of God, against supporting and countenancing, either directly or indirectly, the said iniquitous institution of involuntary slavery; and should any of our ministers or members ever become guilty of *this great crying sin*, we do most *earnestly and religiously recommend and advise* that all such be excommunicated or cast out of the church, and denied the right of Christian fellowship among us.[26]

An important point to observe is the reference to *slavery as sin* in the second resolution, for this is evidence of Winebrenner's acknowledgement of the theological character of the practice. It was a violation of the biblical stance that, out of one blood God created all people as equals under God. Kern tells us that the above resolutions were "drawn up and offered by Winebrenner himself."[27] This adds weight to the claim that during an earlier period, especially the abolitionist period from approximately 1835–38,

---

24. Winebrenner, "History of the Church of God," 182.
25. See Byers, *Birth of a Reformation*, 55–56.
26. Winebrenner, "History of the Church of God," 185 (my emphasis).
27. Kern, *John Winebrenner*, 109.

John Winebrenner did in fact consider involuntary enslavement to be a sin and a theological problem, although by the time he published his "Letter on Slavery" in 1858 his emphasis was no longer on slavery as sin. Rather, by this time he held that "the sinfulness was in its abuse."[28] This point is implied above in the reference to Winebrenner's view that the abuse of elderly or sick enslaved persons was sin. What is clear, however, is that by the 1850s Winebrenner was more concerned about sustaining the church, which, sociologically, is an established sect or denomination trait. He was more willing to moderate or compromise his earlier anti-slavery ethic, thus accommodating to the broader society.

Not surprisingly in a society in which racism was endemic to all social structures, including religious institutions, not all in the Churches of God supported and lived in accordance with the resolutions pertaining to slavery. Indeed, it is even questionable as to whether Winebrenner himself adhered to a literal interpretation of the resolutions. For example, it is possible that he never intended that enslavers literally be excommunicated from the church. Whatever was the case with an aging Winebrenner, the General Eldership soon began receiving negative feedback regarding the resolutions, as indicated in the minutes of subsequent meetings in 1851, 1854, 1857, and 1860, the year of Winebrenner's death (four months after the last meeting).

The 1851 meeting was that of the East Pennsylvania Eldership. To its credit, that Eldership held its ground against elders and laity who argued "that the bare relation of master to slave not debar from Christian fellowship in all cases." Not surprising by this period, Winebrenner voted in favor of the proposition (albeit in a close losing cause, 19 to 17).[29] The small majority of the members were not only being courageous. More importantly, they were being faithful to what they believed God required of them and of all believers. It will be helpful to quote at length the relevant statements regarding the matter of the 1845 resolutions.

> At the meeting of the 23rd East Pennsylvania Eldership in November 1851: The peculiar position in which the Eldership was placed by its action on the slavery question, and on [George U.] Harn's report in 1850, led to the adoption without debate of a resolution declaring it to be 'the opinion of this Eldership, that the relation of master and slave, as authorized by the laws that make and sustain American slavery, is a sufficient bar to

---

28. Ibid., 138.
29. Corbin, "Slavery and the Civil War as Viewed by the Churches of God," 7.

membership in this body, and ought to be a bar to membership in all the churches where this institution exists.'[30]

The 4th General Eldership on May 29, 1854: The resolutions on slavery that were adopted in 1845 were reaffirmed, with the statement that *'they were understood to teach our uncompromising hostility to slavery at the time of their adoption, and that they still express our unwavering resistance to this institution in any form of its representation.'* And that 'any person sustaining the relation of master and slave is disqualified for membership in the Church of God.'[31]

At the 5th General Eldership on June 1, 1857: The slavery question was irrepressible. Ober's letter was referred to the Committee on Slavery. This Committee, however, reported that 'we deem it unnecessary to take any further action at this time.' But this could not repress discussion, and the subject monopolized nearly two sittings before the report was adopted and the Committee discharged.'[32]

At the 6th General Eldership of May 1860: Yet again there was discussion of the slavery issue. 'A notably long and trenchant debate was precipitated by the Report of the Committee on Slavery, of which Harn, the fiery, ultra abolitionist, was Chairman. It characterized slave-holding to be 'man-stealing;' 'turns human flesh, blood, bones, sinews, nerves and muscles into articles of common merchandize; sets a price on souls, morals, religion and the image of God,' and that 'all who perpetrate said sin are classified by Paul along with the lawless, disobedient, ungodly, unholy and profane sinners, such as murderers of fathers and mothers, manslayers and whoremongers, liars and perjurers.' The mildest of its eight resolutions related to the Texas missionaries, simply deeply 'deploring the course' of these missionaries on the subject. [The Texas missionaries, with the backing of a changed Winebrenner, had allowed enslavers to join the church.] George Thomas offered a substitute, reaffirming the resolutions of 1845, with some additional sentiments better suited to existing exigencies. On this the yeas and nays were called, the vote on substituting the Thomas resolutions for

---

30. Forney, *History of the Churches of God*, 327–28.
31. Ibid., 762 (my emphasis).
32. Ibid., 764.

the Report of the Committee standing 21 to 14, and they were adopted."[33]

It is commendable, and virtually unprecedented for a white religious group of this period of U. S. history to have passed such resolutions and then for leaders, for several years, to consistently affirm them even in the face of deteriorating support by some of the members, including the leader, Winebrenner. This fact alone suggests that there was tension in the group regarding the Resolutions of 1845, with almost as many being against as in favor. Of course, an important question is: Did the General Eldership address the race question after 1860? For, after Emancipation (1863) the race problem did not simply go away. This is a topic that warrants further investigation, but is beyond the scope of this book.

It is important to point out that blacks were members of the Winebrennerian churches. Moreover, a group of blacks in Arkansas established an Eldership in the 1890s and was officially admitted in 1896.[34] Forney observes that, "In no Eldership did the pastors labor with such insufficient support."[35] Moreover, we know that this group was unwilling to permit a woman to be a pastor, although it was acceptable for women to be evangelists and to hold revivals. When Mrs. Eliza B. Dupree sought to be appointed pastor at the church at Zeaney's Chapel in 1901 the Standing Committee of the Arkansas Eldership ("colored") ruled that because she was a woman she could not be the pastor, and that "'she shall not be pastor of any of the churches on the same ground.'"[36] Significantly, both before and after leaving the Churches of God, D. S. Warner would have nothing to do with the practice of banning women from the pastorate. Indeed, while still a member of the West Ohio Eldership, Warner preached a sermon on March 11, 1873, in which he advocated for the right of women to speak and pray in the church.[37] Interestingly, although the third meeting of the Arkansas Eldership ("colored") in 1898 passed a resolution disallowing any minister among them to hold a license or certificate of ordination who consumes alcoholic beverages,[38] there is no mention of the race question in the minutes of any of the meetings cited. It is not known by this author whether Forney simply failed to include such references in his history of the Churches of God, or whether such was simply not included in the minutes of that Eldership. This

33. Ibid., 765.
34. Ibid., 789.
35. Ibid., 747.
36. Ibid.
37. See Warner, *Journal of D. S. Warner*, 22.
38. Forney, *History of the Churches of God*, 746.

too is a matter that warrants further investigation, since it is just as important to know what blacks in the Churches of God said about race in church and society.

It is known that long before the establishment of the Arkansas Eldership, blacks attended Winebrenner's revivals and preaching services, since he seemed to possess an openness toward all races and classes of people. Bishop Sybert of the Evangelical Association reported that Winebrenner "is no respecter of persons or station. He preaches to the wicked and the good, among the high and the low, the rich and the poor, white or black."[39] Furthermore, the East Pennsylvania Eldership licensed the first and second black pastors, P. Stanton and Henry Goings, in 1844 and 1848, respectively.[40] As further evidence that blacks were early attracted to the Churches of God, it is known that a white pastor in Uniontown, Maryland reported having baptized nearly a dozen persons of color.[41]

MODERATION OF WINEBRENNER'S STANCE ON SLAVERY

It is commendable that the General Eldership and some of the state Elderships, e.g., East Pennsylvania, Michigan, and West Ohio consistently reaffirmed the resolutions of 1845, even though there was considerable disagreement and tension among some pastors and lay people, especially regarding the resolution to excommunicate enslavers and the refusal to fellowship with them. The General Eldership saw involuntary enslavement as the gravest of social questions, and was therefore adamant about keeping the issue and the position of the Eldership before the people. "The preachers denounced slavery from the pulpits. The congregations sang their anti-slavery sentiments from the old hymn book. The question was discussed through the church paper by the editor and contributors."[42] (Unfortunately, we will see nothing of this sort in Warner and the Movement.) Indeed, expressing his disdain for slavery in *The Gospel Publisher*, Winebrenner expressed his dismay over the murders of abolotionists Elijah Lovejoy (1802–1837) in 1837, and Anthony Bewley (1804–1860) in 1860. Both men were Christian

---

39. Quoted in Gossard, "John Winebrenner," in *Pennsylvania Religious Leaders* ed. John M. Coleman et al., 93.

40. See Forney, *History of the Churches of God*, 324, 325. Also, on 357 it is reported that Stanton was licensed in 1835. This is an obvious discrepancy since it is said on 324 that he was licensed in 1844.

41. Gossard, "John Winebrenner," 93.

42. Yahn, *History of the Churches of God in North America*, 115.

ministers. "These men," he wrote, "fell martyrs to the holy cause of Abolition by the hands of cruel, blood-thirsty bands of ruffians and murderers . . ."[43] Moreover, he wrote that "the anti-slavery meetings encountered violent opposition, hissing, mobs, pelting and personal abuse, and was followed by social ostracism of the reformers."[44] And yet, as observed before, Winebrenner himself came to soften his stance and to render a more conservative interpretation of the profound enslavement resolutions of 1845. What possible reason(s) can be given for this significant change?

One possible explanation may be the storm of dissent that ensued as a result of Winebrenner's writings on abolitionism from 1835–38 and the resolutions of 1845. As might be expected, not everybody in the Winebrennerian churches had abolitionist sentiments, although by 1836 Winebrenner himself was unquestionably in the abolitionist camp.[45] This is not to say that his abolitionist and anti-slavery views were those of the more militant William Lloyd Garrison and Sarah and Angelina Grimké, or that he adhered to and advocated the more militant views of the Constitution and "Declaration of Sentiments" of the American Anti-Slavery Society. They were not, and he did not.[46]

While a member of the Harrisburg Anti-Slavery Society, Winebrenner actually adhered to a more cautious, watered down version of abolitionism than that which was advocated by the likes of Garrison and the Grimké sisters. Winebrenner signed the Constitution and "Declaration" of the Harrisburg Antislavery Society, "which documents were based upon the Constitution and 'Declaration of Sentiments' of the American Anti-Slavery Society," which were partially written by Garrison. *However*, Kern reports that upon closer inspection one discovers that "the Constitution and 'Declaration' of the Harrisburg Anti-Slavery Society, as printed in the *Gospel Publisher* [edited by Winebrenner], omitted several statements found in their prototypes,"[47] including:

- That every American citizen who retains a human being in involuntary bondage as his property, is [according to Scripture] a MAN-STEALER.
- We further believe . . . that all persons of color who possess the qualifications which are demanded of others, ought to be admitted forthwith to the enjoyment of the same privileges . . . as others; and that the

---

43. Quoted in Forney, *History of the Churches of God*, 54.
44. Quoted in ibid., 54.
45. Kern, *John Winebrenner*, 104.
46. Ibid., 103, 104.
47. Ibid., 102.

paths of preferment, of wealth, and of intelligence, should be opened as widely to them as to persons of a white complexion.

- We shall aim at a purification of the churches from all participation in the guilt of slavery.[48]

Each of these significant statements were excluded from the document of the Harrisburg Anti-Slavery Society, thus weakening it considerably in relation to the Constitution and "Declaration of Sentiments" of the American Anti-Slavery Society.

Winebrenner received letters to the editor from friends in the Churches of God, as well as subscribers to the *Gospel Publisher* regarding his views on abolitionism. Needless to say, these were not always letters of support. At least one of those who complained was an abolitionist. Some believed that Winebrenner was focused too much on what they considered more secular than spiritual matters. During this period he rejected the popular view that social evils like enslavement were the business only of politicians, not ministers and churches; that they were political, not theological problems. "Slavery was no more a secular matter, beyond the reach of the church, than was any other form of sin—only 'time-servers,' those who obsequiously complied with the spirit of the times, would hold the contrary."[49]

There is a second reason that may have contributed to the moderation of Winebrenner's stance on slavery. After August 1838 he might well have been concerned about saving the *Gospel Publisher*, which was already experiencing low subscription purchases and low readership. The continued existence of the *Gospel Publisher* was at stake.[50] This might have contributed to his decision to abruptly stop publishing abolitionist and anti-enslavement articles and editorials. "For over a year next to nothing appeared in the paper which even faintly had an abolitionist ring to it."[51] Some might argue that this was quite understandable. But this would let him off the moral hook too easily, for Winebrenner had the option of exhibiting another, more prophetic type of witness and response. His editorials and articles in the *Gospel Publisher* from 1835–38 spoke a truth that church members—however many or few—might not otherwise have been exposed to. Winebrenner was surely not the only editor of a religious magazine who received criticisms and threats to stop subscribing because of his editori-

---

48. Ibid., 103.

49. Ibid. 107.

50. Beset by financial problems in 1845, publication of the *Gospel Publisher* was suspended, but reappeared as the *Church Advocate* on the first day of May, 1846, with Winebrenner as editor.

51. Kern, *John Winebrenner*, 104.

als in favor of abolition and anti-enslavement. The same thing happened to Daniel Wise in the 1840s, editor of the *Sunday School Advocate*, a publication of the Methodist Episcopal Church.

Wise was severely criticized before Annual Conferences and there were threats of boycotting the *Advocate*. Possessing agency and autonomy, Wise surely could have opted to tone down his editorials or, like Winebrenner, stop including them altogether, in the hope of insuring the survivability of the publication, as well as his own livelihood. But Wise chose to take the more difficult moral high road. He replied to critics saying: "The *Advocate* is expected to teach our children the doctrines and ethics of our Church; that slave-holding is a violation of Christian and Methodist ethics; and consequently it is my duty to teach the children to think of it as a sin; so long as I am Editor of the paper I shall firmly but judiciously so instruct them. If the General Conference shall condemn my course, it can of course, replace me with another Editor."[52] Clearly this was not the stance of Winebrenner after the 1830s.

A similar illustration of prophetic courage involves a white Quaker woman named Prudence Crandall. In 1833 she admitted a "free" black female, Sarah Harris, to her school in Canterbury, Connecticut. Harris was the only Afrikan American student. It just did not seem to matter what states blacks lived in, or whether they were enslaved or nominally free like Harris. The ugly face of racism was omnipresent in the nation. The white parents in the non-slavery state of Connecticut went into a real uproar over the young black girl's presence in the school, criticized Crandall for encouraging social equality between whites and blacks, and claimed that this could only lead to intermarriage between the races. They demanded that Crandall dismiss Harris from the school or they would withdraw their daughters.[53] Crandall refused to dismiss the girl, declaring instead: "The school may sink, but I will not give up Sarah Harris."[54] Of course, the white parents withdrew their daughters as threatened. The school was closed, but Crandall then reopened it for Afrikan American girls only. The white community was outraged and did all kinds of ghastly things to force closure of the school. They filled Crandall's well with manure; "a minister was not allowed to preach in the Canterbury Church because he had visited the school; a physician summoned to attend a sick [black] girl warned Miss Crandall not to send for him again; a druggist refused to sell her medicines; fires were started in the building, windows repeatedly broken, and one temporary teacher was

---

52. Quoted in Singleton, *The Romance of African Methodism*, 53.
53. Hine and Thompson, *A Shining Thread of Hope*, 122.
54. Quoted in Sherwin, *Prophet of Liberty*, 50.

pelted with addled eggs."[55] The building was finally severely vandalized, and Crandall took the advice of friends to close the school.

The witness of Daniel Wise and Prudence Crandall are the truest examples of prophetic witness and courage as exhibited by the Hebrew prophets of the eighth century BCE. If a group has a firm abolitionist and anti-enslavement stance as part of the requirement for membership (as the Churches of God did), the leaders should be committed to it to the point of not granting the right hand of fellowship or membership to those who disagree with it. Such persons can join another religious group or begin their own with persons who share the like-minded, albeit foul belief that it is neither wrong nor sinful to degrade and dehumanize human beings solely because of their race. But such beliefs and practices should not be permissible in the Church of God.

It should never be the case that the humanity and dignity of any group of human beings are compromised or sacrificed on the altar of denominational or spiritual unity, as was the case of blacks in the Churches of God, and later in the Church of God Reformation Movement. Christianity that is worth something costs those who are converted. If it is permissible for the converted person to continue engaging in practices that clearly cannot be pleasing to God, such as forcibly enslaving and dehumanizing others of God's children, then what is the point of claiming conversion to the Christian faith? Indeed, what does it say about a religious group that requires no change of beliefs and practice of members, and requires no discipline and restraint? The behavior of one who has converted to Christianity ought to progressively become radically different from one who does not subscribe to Christian principles. If Christianity deems involuntary enslavement to be both unacceptable and a sin, then one who professes Christianity simply does not participate in or support such a practice.

Even when letters were not sent to the editor, Winebrenner nonetheless heard about the incredible dissension that was developing in the Churches of God around the enslavement question, and the matter of granting or not granting membership to enslavers, or continuing to fellowship with them. Concern about this dissension and the possibility that conflict and divisiveness might develop in the church and could lead to schism was a third contributing factor that might have led Winebrenner to soften his views on slavery. Barely three years after the passage of the resolutions of 1845 he editorialized on the issue of church membership for enslavers, but did so in the context of comments on war and slavery. Writing in the *Church Advocate* on July 1, 1848 he said: "We are opposed to War and Slavery. Yet

---

55. Ibid., 52–53.

we believe there are Christian soldiers and Christian slave holders. Though, therefore, we go with all our might for the abolition of War and Slavery, yet we cannot feel free to unchristianize and condemn everybody who is a warrior or a slave holder."[56] Winebrenner was essentially rejecting "ultraism" (the more radical strand of abolitionism) in favor of moderation, but there is no question that his present stance was milder than what appeared in the 1845 resolutions. Kern observes that although no one immediately connected Winebrenner's statement to the second resolution of 1845 where the churches were "advised" to excommunicate enslavers, it was clear that there was no consensus among the churches on this issue "and that Winebrenner himself was trying to moderate what he considered an extremist antislavery position."[57]

It was 1850 before Winebrenner's moderating stance was challenged. Rev. A. D. Williams of the Free Will Baptist church inquired of Winebrenner as to the East Pennsylvania Eldership's true position on the enslavement question. Winebrenner responded in "Position of the Eldership on . . . Slavery" in the December 2, 1850 issue of the *Church Advocate*. He reiterated the stance of the resolutions of 1845, but then proceeded to say that there was no unanimity in the Eldership regarding fellowship with enslavers; that some accept the resolutions' advice to bar fellowship, and others reject it. He said further:

> Those who take the negative side of this question, [including Winebrenner] think that the decision of it ought always to be made to turn on the circumstance of the case—that there are *mitigating circumstances* connected with many cases, which require the exercise of Christian toleration and forbearance, and hence the bare relation of master to slave does not, always under all circumstances, furnish a sufficient bar to Christian fellowship.[58]

Although in 1849 Winebrenner referred to enslavement as "a great moral wrong," he went on to declare that, "there are mitigating circumstances which forbid a wholesale unchristianizing of all who are guilty of the wrong."[59] This illustrated a clear softening of his earlier stance in the 1830s. Winebrenner also sought to assure Williams that there had not yet been the strife and division around this issue in the Churches of God as experienced by other religious groups. By all indications Winebrenner hoped

---

56. Quoted in Kern, *John Winebrenner*, 110.
57. Kern, *John Winebrenner*, 111.
58. Quoted in ibid., 112 (Kern's italics).
59. Quoted in Forney, *History of the Churches of God*, 81.

to avoid this occurrence in the Churches of God. We will see subsequently that a similar concern may have been part of the reason that D. S. Warner was virtually silent on the color line in church and society, even though the evidence suggests that he himself favored visible unity and equality along racial lines.

Reminiscent of a principle elaborated in the Book of Matthew, Winebrenner then observed that when a church member is in error such a one should be corrected, warned, and instructed according to the Bible. However, one does not get the sense that this idea of mutual correction and responsibility was for him one of the basic marks of the Churches of God, as it is for the Believers' Church, for example. The latter group seems to have in mind the *principle of mutual correction and responsibility* between members and the church, with each understanding the importance and necessity of this discipline and of restoring members to the fold. One of the central marks of the Believers' Church is that "they accept the necessity of being 'reproved, corrected, cast out, or excommunicated,' according to the principle of Matthew 18:15-20. True Christian love [Believers' Church members] contend, consists not in an easy tolerance, but in faithful admonition and edification. Being a disciple means being under a discipline, which is not legalism at its best, but rather like the loving chastisement of concerned family members."[60] One does not get the sense that the Winebrenner of this period (1850 and beyond) expected that the already churched enslaver, for example, should understand and accept the need to be reproved, corrected, or even excommunicated should he refuse to give up the practice of enslavement after a specified period of time. There seemed to be no requirement for the Winebrenner of this period such as exists within the Believers' Church, that mutual correction is what one should expect, and is what one expects to provide where others are concerned.

At least at this stage in Winebrenner's development regarding the enslavement issue, one does not get the sense that much at all was required of members other than to make the verbal claim of having experienced regeneration or conversion. This, he insisted by 1850, is the only criterion for membership that one finds in the Bible. Nothing beyond a commitment to personal morality, e.g., the avoidance of alcohol consumption, dancing, or swearing seems to be required beyond that point. That is, the enslaver who joins the church is disallowed the consumption of alcohol, for example, but the Winebrenner of this period gave little advice as to what such a one is to do about her practice of enslavement. After all, having told A. D. Williams in 1850 that one who errs should first be reproved or corrected, Winebrenner

---

60. Durnbaugh, *The Believers' Church*, 32.

goes on to say that notwithstanding this "there is no warrant to expel them from the church, or declare them unworthy of Christian fellowship, so long as they, in the judgment of Charity, may be deemed in favor with God."[61] Of course, I am certain that the enslaved person who was a Christian would have had a very difficult time seeing such a one as being "in favor with God." By this stage in his life Winebrenner's Christianity was considerably cheaper than it was in the years leading up to the 1845 anti-enslavement resolutions. Winebrennerian Christianity of this period cost the enslaver of Afrikan humanity virtually nothing. Such a one could go right on being an enslaver while looking forward to being received into Christian fellowship, and expecting no criticism of his enslavement of Afrikans. According to Winebrenner's line of thought such a one did not have to worry about church members hounding him all the day long about his practice of enslaving his black sisters and brothers.

During the mid-1850s and beyond, Winebrenner held that the refusal to admit enslavers to church membership, or to excommunicate members who were already enslavers and refused to relent was wrong. Logically, this would seem to make sense for one who taught that the only criterion for church membership is an experience of regeneration or conversion. J. Harvey Gossard makes an instructive comment in this regard. He contends that since "the born-again experience, nothing more and nothing less," is the sole test for church membership, Winebrenner could easily have concluded that "there was more chance of changing the slave holder's mind if he was an active member of the church, than if he were estranged from it."[62] This seems a reasonable claim about Winebrenner. However, what I miss is a more explicit emphasis on the need for the church and its members to be vigilant in working with the member enslaver to change his thinking and practice regarding enslavement. I also miss the sense that the enslaver who wishes to join the church will be explicitly and continually informed that the continued recognition of his membership with the group hinges on his willingness to give up enslavement by an agreed upon specified period of time.

From around 1850 onward John Winebrenner was without question seeking to moderate the position of the resolutions of 1845. He gave no clues as to what he had in mind when he referred to "mitigating circumstances" that might permit fellowship with an enslaver, although Kern is probably right in his contention that it is not assuming too much to say that Winebrenner's background of involvement with family and friends who were enslavers and with churches that fellowshipped with enslavers

61. Quoted in Kern, *John Winebrenner*, 112.
62. Gossard, "John Winnbrenner," 10.

might well provide for the "mitigating circumstances" argument.[63] A. D. Williams, however, was not persuaded by Winebrenner's response, and said that he simply could not reconcile the two resolutions, "'according to their obvious meaning,' to the 'mitigating circumstances' which would allow a slaveholder to be received into the church."[64] Winebrenner later responded, but this was no more convincing than his previous response. He tried to convince Williams that enslavement was not the greatest social evil in the world, or at least that it was not the only great social evil. Moreover, some sins, according to Winebrenner of this period, including but not limited to sectarianism and war, "are greater evils than slavery."[65] Consequently, even if Winebrenner continued to believe enslavement to be sinful, this belief was overshadowed by the simultaneous belief that it was also bearable. He apparently felt that he was better positioned to make this judgment than those who were enslaved. If Winebrenner had been a hero on the enslavement question up to the 1845 resolutions, he had completely lost hero status from 1850 onward. By this time others, such as A. D. Williams, were the staunch champions against enslavement and fellowshipping with those who refused to get out of the enslavement business.

In trying to determine why Winebrenner's stance on enslavement degenerated from his earlier abolitionist and anti-slavery position, we are wise to remember that even during the earlier period he was not an adherent of the most militant principles of the "Declaration of Sentiments" of the American Anti-Slavery Society. For example, the statement about "the 'purification of the Churches from all participation in the guilt of slavery'" was omitted from the "Declaration" of the Harrisburg Anti-Slavery Society to which Winebrenner belonged. In addition, we are invited to consider the possibility that Winebrenner's response to church membership for enslavers in the July 1, 1848 issue of the *Church Advocate* that people ought not be barred from the church or condemned because they are enslavers might very well have been his real position during the abolitionist period as well as when he drew up the resolutions of 1845. Kern found no evidence that suggests that this could not have been the case. However, he writes: "If we assume this to have been his position consistently, then we must also assume that even when drawing up the 1845 'Resolutions on Slavery,' he meant them as a general expression of the Church of God rather than as a categorical denial of church membership to slaveholders at all times and at all places. The fact that the Resolutions only 'religiously commend and

---

63. Kern, *John Winebrenner*, 117.
64. Ibid., 113.
65. Ibid., 114.

advise' that slaveholders be excommunicated would allow for individual interpretation and evaluation on the part of the local elderships."[66]

The Resolutions of 1845 therefore would have been the equivalent of general advisement, and not at all a requirement for continued membership in the church. Each of the local elderships could then decide whether or how best to apply such general advice. This would mean that each had the freedom to interpret and apply the Resolutions on Slavery as it deemed appropriate. In addition, it would mean that many members of the Churches of God could believe—as Winebrenner came to believe—that the intention of the Resolutions was not that enslavers should be barred from membership in the church. Therefore, one could, simultaneously, continue one's membership in the church while enslaving human beings at the same time.

It would have been wise for Winebrenner and church leaders to hold firm to the stance that the practice of enslaving people is both morally wrong and a sin, and thus is not permitted in the Church of God. Any member found guilty of this practice and was yet desirous of remaining in the church would have to submit to sustained correction and instruction for an agreed upon period of time. At the end of that time, such a one would have to be finished with the practice of enslavement if he wished to remain in fellowship with the Churches of God. By failing to institute something like this the leaders of the Churches of God themselves opened wide the door to church memberships that would be largely comprised of people who believed it was acceptable to be in Christian communion while simultaneously abiding by the prevailing social custom of enslavement and racism. Among such people it would be acceptable to be a Christian while not having to worry about one's racism being challenged by the church. What a convenience! What a dishonoring of the Christian ethic! What a tremendous contradiction—to be Christian and racist at the same time!

Winebrenner, like Warner would subsequently, feared and hated divisiveness that might lead to schism. We have seen that this too was reason for the softening of his stance on slavery. He had seen schisms in other religious groups, such as the Methodist Episcopal Church in the 1840s, as a result of the different positions held on the enslavement issue and the membership of enslavers. He surely did not want this to happen in his beloved Churches of God, since one of his primary aims in founding it was to insure unity—church unity.[67] Remember, Winebrenner had said to A. D. Williams that sectarianism is an even greater evil than involuntary enslavement. Apparently he was for church unity, no matter the cost; church unity even if it

66. Ibid., 115.
67. Ibid. 177.

meant being in complicity with the enslavers of Afrikans; church unity even at the expense of the enslaved Afrikans. Surely one must wonder, as I do: At what cost this unity? Is church or denominational unity really worth it, and for whom? That is, who benefits from a church unity that does not include unity along racial-ethnic lines?

The unity that was of central importance to John Winebrenner, and later to D. S. Warner, was church unity or spiritual unity, not unity along racial lines. And yet, interracial unity was implicit in each man's message on visible unity. Furthermore, interracial unity was an immediate concern and emphasis of blacks who early gravitated toward the Churches of God, and later the Movement. Blacks thought—wrongly or rightly—that the unity principle of Winebrenner, and subsequently of Warner, was broader than mere church unity and spiritual unity, and therefore was inclusive of unity along racial lines. Blacks immediately, indeed instinctively, saw the ethical implications of the unity principle relative to race in the church. They thought—indeed wanted to believe—that Winebrenner and Warner were staunch advocates of, and champions of, interracial unity; of blacks and whites worshipping together on the basis of equality. Although there are places in the writings of these men (more especially Winebrenner) that unmistakably imply such a connection, one searches in vain for evidence that either of them explicitly linked the core principle of visible unity with interracial unity in the church. Had Winebrenner explicitly joined his earlier stance against enslavement to a sound theological principle or foundation he would likely have had a more difficult time backing away from, or greatly moderating that stance. This raises the question, therefore, as to the source of the abolitionist leanings of Winebrenner, and the alleged openness and friendliness that Warner exhibited toward blacks. We have seen some of the difficulty of sorting this out regarding Winebrenner, especially since he was from a family of enslavers, and also had close friends who enslaved blacks.

EFFECT OF FAMILY MEMBERS AND FRIENDS

In a sense, John Winebrenner was really caught between a rock and a hard place. Not only did he grow up in a family that enslaved blacks, but he had close friends who did as well. Some of these family members and friends were people he remained in close relationship with even after he left the state of Maryland. Therefore, it must also be the case that Winebrenner found it difficult, if not impossible, to sever all ties with them, or even to be too outspoken against their practice of enslaving the Afrikans. But as difficult as this might have been for him, we need to remember that Winebrenner alone made the choice that led to his continued relationship with the enslavers of Afrikans.

There is also the matter of the Churches of God in Maryland—churches that were in association with and fellowshipped with enslavers. "Elder G. U. Harn had reported that upwards of thirty of the 'oldest and ablest' East Pennsylvania ministers had fellowshipped at the Lord's Table and washed the feet of slaveholders at ordinance meetings. Without question, Winebrenner would have been included in the thirty. His ties with several of the Maryland churches were extremely close."[68] Winebrenner apparently fraternized and worshipped with enslavers in his hometown as well as in the East Pennsylvania Eldership. The argument here is not that he should have cut off all association with family members and friends who continued in the enslavement business. Rather, the stance put forth here is that he should have been for them a constant, courageous, and emphatic Christian witness against the immorality of slavery. However, I have found no evidence that this occurred.

Thomas Fudge writes that, "Winebrenner's position on slavery was that the institution and practice was indeed sinful but not necessarily intolerable. His position curiously shifted in the late 1830s from 'the sin of slavery' to the 'sinfulness of its abuse.'"[69] Fudge writes further: "Winebrenner considered the Church of God a peace church. When forced to choose between war and slavery, though being opposed to both, Winebrenner asserted that war was a greater evil than slavery."[70] It seems to me that this is not a call that whites—Winebrenner or otherwise—can make when it is not their own, but another group that is forcibly enslaved and oppressed. Enslaved Afrikans likely felt that there was *nothing* more dreadful and evil—including war—than the system of enslavement to which they were subjected in

---

68. Ibid., 117.

69. Fudge, *Daniel Warner and the Paradox of Religious Democracy*, 172.

70. Ibid. Winebrenner clearly opposed the Mexican-American War on both theological and pragmatic grounds. By the beginning of the Civil War, however, he was dead. It is known that many in the Churches of God, ministers and laymen, enlisted to fight against slavery, but mostly, to save the Union. S. G. Yahn writes that, "the General Eldership of 1863 (the only session of that body held during the Civil War) adopted clear and unmistakable resolutions in support of the Union cause, its armies and those who were engaged therein. Such has been the attitude of our people with reference to all the wars waged during our history, up to and including the World War. They have never taken the position of 'non-resistants' or 'conscientious objectors.' They have always done their part in a spirit of heroism. This does not mean that they have warlike tendencies. On the contrary, like all right-thinking people they favor peace and abhor war"; see Yahn, *History of the Churches of God in North America*, 116.

the United States. Oppressors are never in the best moral position to make the call that Winebrenner made.

By 1853 Winebrenner's stance on enslavement had clearly shifted to a more moderate position. He still found enslavement to be repugnant, but nevertheless tolerable. In addition, Winebrenner seemed no longer to believe with the resolutions of 1845 that under no circumstance should enslavers be permitted to be members of the church. Forney writes that by the 1850s Winebrenner "called slavery 'a great moral wrong, but there are mitigating circumstances which forbid a wholesale, unchristianizing of all who are guilty of the wrong.'" Two years earlier, in 1851, he published an editorial, 'Our Position on Slavery Re-defined,' in which similar views are expressed, and declares that the resolutions on slavery adopted by the General Eldership in 1845 'do not bear the construction that they are intended to disallow any one, under any circumstances, who bore the relation of master to slave to be received or retained in the Church, or to be at all entitled to the exercise of Christian forbearance and toleration.'"[71] At best, Winebrenner exhibited a conciliatory stance by this period.

In West Virginia and in Green County, Pennsylvania, trouble erupted in the Churches of God regarding the resolutions of 1845. The church in West Virginia "had 'excluded pro-slavery persons from Christian and church fellowship.' This Winebrenner seemed to disapprove and 'censure.' But he explained by saying: 'I do not censure churches for excommunicating slaveholders when the action of the church is regularly had, but I condemn all irregular and proscriptive proceedings.' 'The church alluded to did not exclude slaveholders from their communion, but those members who cast their votes in favor of slave-holding candidates for civil office. Now, the exercise of such proscriptive power was evidently not intended to be sanctioned by the General Eldership."[72] Just months before he died, Winebrenner came to a position of "non-interference" with already existing enslavement in a locality, and "non-extension" of enslavement where it did not already exist.[73] This was a position held by moderates and conservatives of all kinds.

GENERAL ELDERSHIP AND PRO-SLAVERY STATES

Forney maintains that the reason that the Churches of God did not experience schisms as a result of the slavery issue like many other groups did was because it had no churches and elderships in pro-slavery states prior to the

71. See Forney, *History of the Churches of God*, 81.
72. Ibid., 59.
73. Kern, *John Winebrenner*, 136.

Civil War. The one instance in which Churches of God missionaries were sent into the enslavement state of Texas in 1856 nearly proved disastrous. This was a mission that Winebrenner strongly supported, although he likely would not have done so had this event transpired in the 1830s. When confronted by Texans about their reason for being in Texas, the two missionaries who were sent declared that they were "not abolitionists in the sense of that term as understood; nor yet members of an abolition Church.' Violence was threatened them, and it became necessary to use the press as well as the pulpit to defend themselves and explain their position."[74] But this offended the northern churches, causing the editor of *The Church Advocate*—who by this time was James Colder, son-in-law of Winebrenner—to re-publish the anti-slavery resolutions of 1845 as well as those of a number of elderships in the North, all of which had the effect of strengthening the charges of the pro-enslavement Texans against the two missionaries.

The missionaries argued that they had the support of Winebrenner through word of mouth as well as printed publication, i.e., through the columns of *The Church Advocate*. This led to Winebrenner being barred from publishing in the *Advocate* for some length of time. After all, he was no longer the editor. In addition, a serious stir was raised when the Texas missionaries organized a church, though without the support of the General Eldership, and allowed enslavers to join. The two missionaries, Benjamin Ober and E. Marple, then decided to form a Texas Eldership, although it was not immediately acknowledged by the General Eldership. At the July 31, 1857 meeting of that Eldership a resolution was passed saying that since "slavery is a religious and political question, and greatly agitated at the present time by both religious and political men North and South, we think it not expedient for the Church of God to interfere with it."[75] In effect, the missionaries were arguing that churches could only be organized in Texas if enslavers were permitted to join.

The response of Editor James Colder was that if churches could not be established without allowing enslavers to join, no churches should be organized in Texas. Allowing enslavers to join the church was in clear violation of the resolutions of 1845 passed by the General Eldership. One can see that this venture into the pro-slavery state of Texas could have had disastrous consequences for the Churches of God. Although a number of resolutions were issued by various elderships against what happened in Texas, reports from that state indicated that the two churches established there were

---

74. Forney, *History of the Churches of God*, 102.
75. Ibid., 103.

prospering. The Texas Eldership was not officially received in the General Eldership until 1875, fifteen years after Winebrenner's death.

There is no question that Winebrenner was tolerant of the Texas situation and as much as said so in his "Letter on Slavery" in 1858. Responding to the (unofficial) Texas Eldership's allowance for the admission of enslavers in the church, Winebrenner wrote: "I have charity enough to believe that there are many Christian slaveholders, as well as Christian soldiers, Christian masons, Christian Odd fellows, Christian Pedo-Baptists, and Christian Catholics."[76] By now, Winebrenner's behavior was more denomination or church-like ("Christ of culture") than prophetic or sect-like ("Christ against culture"). He was willing to accommodate the church's ethic to the enslavement practices of society, rather than requiring that enslavers abide by the tough, demanding ethics of the gospel and the anti-enslavement resolutions of 1845. He moved from advocating a prophetic stance and a desire to radically reform church and world during the mid to late 1830s, to advocating an accommodationist ethics in the 1850s that was calculated to keep the peace by any means, including allowing church members to believe that they could be Christians and enslavers of Afrikans at the same time. In effect, they could be guilty of the sin of presuming to own a sister or brother, and remain a member of the Church of God. This meant that whites must not be dis-fellowshipped merely because they were in the enslavement business *and* refused to get out of it. Nor must they be refused admittance to the Winebrennerian churches. This is the stance to which Winebrenner, the drafter of the anti-enslavement resolutions, came.

We have seen that Winebrenner's stance on the enslavement of blacks changed significantly. From the beginning he was in the abolitionist camp, albeit of the more moderate type. Nevertheless, his position softened drastically. "In his abolitionist days, Winebrenner was concerned about the sin of slavery; by the time of his *Letter on Slavery*, in 1858, the sinfulness was in its *abuse*. The procolonizationist of 1835 and the 1850s bore little resemblance to the staunch anticolonizer of the later thirties. Most obvious to one who follows his statements on slavery between 1836 and 1858, is the gradual diminution of antislavery zeal."[77]

Sociologically, John Winebrenner's moderated stance was an important ingredient in the recipe for numerical church growth. His changed position allowed the church to be open to taking the world and all of its foul ideas and practices into itself without requiring that such ideas and behaviors be relinquished for the more perfect way based on the teachings

---

76. Quoted in Gossard, "John Winebrenner," 95–96.
77. Kern, *John Winebrenner*, 138.

of the Hebrew prophets and Jesus Christ. It seems that by this period of his life Winebrenner was more interested in the numerical growth of the membership of the Churches of God and thus its long-term survival. The advice of the resolutions of 1845 would—if taken seriously—lead to the formation of a strong visible unity here and there, but these would most likely be churches with smaller memberships than might be the case if they followed Winebrenner's tactic and simply reinterpreted the meaning of those resolutions. Few whites would likely have joined—or been allowed to join—those local churches that stood their ground and abided by the resolutions of 1845. But unlike the larger churches, these smaller ones would have been in conformity with the gospel ethic.

At the end of the day, we can only speculate as to the reasons that John Winebrenner changed his position on the slavery question, and most especially the issue about barring enslavers from church membership. In addition to strictly adhering to the resolutions of 1845, I think that what we can say in Winebrenner's case (as well as Warner's), is that he needed to: 1) provide a solid theological foundation for his abolitionist and anti-enslavement stance; 2) explicitly link his core idea of unity to the principle of interracial unity in the church; and 3) add the principle of equality among the races. Unfortunately, Winebrenner failed on all counts. Consequently, it should not be surprising that his views on enslavement and the question of whether to grant fellowship to enslavers fluctuated and ultimately moderated with the winds of change, such that how societal views and practices went, so went his views on enslavement and the church membership of enslavers. In addition, I wonder whether Winebrenner was made out to be more of an abolitionist and advocate for anti-enslavement than he really was. I also wonder whether his theology around the issue of enslavement was sound. For reasons to be delineated subsequently, I wonder similarly about D. S. Warner, although to a large extent Warner's difficulty may have been solved had he explicitly connected the theological principle of holiness or entire sanctification to visible unity along racial lines and the principle of equality.

One has to wonder whether and to what extent the West Ohio Eldership (formed in 1857) that granted Warner a license at its eleventh annual meeting in Findlay in October, 1867, addressed issues pertaining to race, either before or during Warner's membership. Winebrenner helped to organize the Ohio Eldership in 1836 and was selected as its first speaker.[78] We have seen that in the eldership meetings from 1860 through 1865 there were either condemnations of the sin of slavery or praise for Emancipation.[79]

---

78. Kern, ed., *A History of the Ohio Conference of the Churches of God*, 15.
79. Forney, *History of the Churches of God*, 557–61.

By all accounts the West Ohio Eldership was an anti-slavery eldership. In the minutes of the Fourth Eldership meeting in 1860, for example, we find: "'The sin of slavery' was declared to be 'increasing most alarmingly' and 'making fearful inroads upon the interests of humanity,' and the Eldership resolved to 'do everything within the province of Christians, and especially ministers of the gospel, to arrest the progress of this evil, and ultimately to erase it from our land.'"[80] In the minutes of the meeting of the 6th West Ohio Eldership on October 20, 1862 we find: "The President's Proclamation of Emancipation was 'hailed with joy' by the Eldership, 'as the harbinger of a new era in the affairs of our country,' and the hope expressed 'that the time will speedily arrive when universal emancipation shall be proclaimed throughout the land.'"[81]

Interestingly, however, in Forney's record of the minutes, there was silence about race related matters in 1866, the year before Warner joined the West Ohio Eldership. It was the same throughout his tenure in the eldership. This is an oddity considering that many problems arose relative to race matters after Emancipation; problems that were experienced all over the country. Nothing is said in the minutes about race and the Reconstruction era (roughly 1867–1877). How were the recently liberated blacks to fit in to American society? What were the responsibilities of white members of the Churches of God regarding the ongoing problems of race? Would the principle of the equality of the races apply in the Churches of God? And yet, the West Ohio Eldership (as others) was less vocal on the issue of race throughout Warner's membership from 1867 to 1878 when he was excised from the group because of his teaching on holiness as a second act of grace.[82] Warner was considered to be one of the Eldership's best and brightest pastors, and unquestionably exhibited charismatic qualities.

We are now in a good position to begin examining more explicitly the stages in the lifecycle of the Church of God Reformation Movement. What are these? What are the roots of the Movement, and how was it transformed into the nearly church-like organization we know it as today? Sociologically, is it a *sect, established sect, denomination,* or *church* type group? To get at these questions it will be helpful to look briefly at Church of God history, and then to consider biographical, sociological, and other aspects of its evolution. Where one or more charismatic leaders is involved in the founding of a religious group it is necessary to look, at least briefly, at the biography of that person. One of the things that need to be determined is whether the

80. Ibid., 558.
81. Ibid., 559.
82. Ibid., 185.

founder of the group possessed *charisma*. As noted earlier, this book examines four stages of the transformation of the Church of God Reformation Movement. The fourth stage is generally that of a stabilized religious group. The biographical and historical information about the Movement will be discussed in the context of the sociological stages of transformation. The next chapter, therefore, begins with the first stage, which tends to be dominated by a strong charismatic leader and a de-emphasis on organization and organizational structure.

3

Daniel Sidney Warner

Charismatic Personality

IT IS IMPORTANT TO remember that D. S. Warner was nearly a generation behind John Winebrenner. The two men never met. When Winebrenner died in 1860 Warner was about eighteen years old and was not yet converted. It is of interest to note, however, that on June 29, 1873 Warner, in route to Nebraska, preached at the Church of God (General Eldership) in Chicago where he met Winebrenner's wife, two sons, and daughter, all who were members of that church.[1]

Warner possessed a deep love, admiration, and respect for his mother.[2] He had at best a strained relationship with his father, who was an alcoholic, and who would sometimes abuse him, thereby robbing him of "much of the brightness and joy of childhood."[3] In his unpublished journal (1872–1880), Warner records having felt the need to visit his father in Williams County in Ohio in June 1878. He found his father to be dying, and by June 16th to be "declining very fast." What troubled Warner most was that his father was "yet unsaved." He recalled that two years previous when his mother was dying she held his father's hand "and exhorted him until he trembled," but he

---

1. See Byers, *Birth of a Reformation*, 79.
2. Ibid., 39, 111–12.
3. Byers, "Warner: Life in Brief," 9.

gave no indication of desiring to live a different life.[4] Warner's father did not convert to the Christian faith, even on his deathbed, although he did express a desire to be made well (physically).

D. S. Warner converted to the Christian faith in 1865. Two years prior he served a brief stint in the Union army, having offered to serve in the place of his brother, Joseph, who was a family man.[5] Warner was discharged early as a result of a lung disorder he contracted, possibly during a forced march through inclement weather in Virginia.[6] His biographer tells us that after his conversion he was known through the remainder of his life for his "earnestness." Moreover, "He was sincere and intense in his devotion and his Christian work . . . When he yielded to God, he meant it as the decision of his very soul, and his conversion was for him an actual change for time and eternity."[7] It was for Warner a life-changing event that would color all else he would do for the rest of his life.

A few months after his conversion in 1865 Warner matriculated at Oberlin College. Initially he stayed for two months, left to teach school through the winter in Corunna, Indiana, returned to Oberlin in the spring, and after the summer break, returned there in September. However, he soon began experiencing the sense of being called to ministry. Sensing the need to get at the work of ministry sooner rather than later, he opted not to remain at Oberlin, but instead left in order to devote fulltime to the study of the Bible, to prayer, and related matters pertinent to ministerial preparation. Indeed, in his journal we find entry after entry where he was found studying the Bible, history (including church history), moral philosophy, theology, psychology, physiology, phrenology, etc. In 1877 Warner took courses at Vermillion College in Hayesville, Ohio but did not earn a degree. Although eager to learn, and "a believer in education . . . his personal choice of primary preparation for ministry was not found in schools."[8] Although he would later defend his informal preparation for ministry, Warner was never critical of education as such. "What he opposed," according to Church of God scholar Barry L. Callen, "was a lack of reliance on the governance and gifting of God and the denominational use of colleges to further divide the church by insistence on their human distinctives."[9] But this stance did not preclude his belief in the importance of education.

4. See Byers, *Birth of a Reformation*, 179–181.
5. Ibid., 42.
6. Callen, *It's God's Church*, 38.
7. Byers, *Birth of a Reformation*, 46.
8. Callen, *It's God's Church*, 42.
9. Ibid., 43.

Although Warner did not complete degree requirements at Oberlin, it is quite possible that he was influenced to some extent by the school's national reputation as the leading abolitionist school, and that he at least became aware of the doctrine of entire sanctification in the teaching and preaching of Charles G. Finney, president of the school. There is no extant physical evidence that Warner was affected by this perfectionism at the time, but it is reasonable to surmise that he heard talk of it—whether or not it was of interest to him—while at Oberlin. Because of our concern to identify factors that led to Warner's stance on race, it may be instructive to explore further his experience at Oberlin and what that might have contributed.

OBERLIN COLLEGE

It is significant that Asa Mahan (1799–1889), former professor at Lane Seminary in Cincinnati, Ohio, vigorous defender and advocate of anti-slavery and abolition, was appointed president of Oberlin in 1835; significant because Mahan was adamant that he would only accept the offer of president if blacks were allowed to enroll on equal terms with whites.[10] Mahan's successor, Charles Grandison Finney (1792–1875), also said that he would not accept an appointment as a college president unless blacks were allowed admission on the basis of equality with whites.[11] Oberlin had already determined that it would be a coeducational institution. The school granted a theological degree to Antoinette Brown in 1850, although obtaining ordination proved to be more than a notion, and was prolonged because of her gender.[12]

Mahan's demand aroused strong protest among some trustees. Indeed, Louis Filler claims that even Finney was initially "a conservative on the subject. Painful arguments preceded the final announcements: that Mahan was to head Oberlin, that Finney had been made professor of theology, and that $10,000 had been received for buildings."[13] Historian Benjamin Quarles tells us that although the trustees voted in favor of Mahan's demand, they did so "by the narrowest of margins . . ."[14] In any event, Oberlin was the first coeducational college in the nation and the first to admit blacks on equal terms with whites. It was not long before Oberlin became a sanctuary for enslaved runaways. Indeed, Charles E. Brown writes about Finney's house

---

10. Macy, *The Anti-Slavery Crusade*, 51.
11. Dorchester, *Christianity in the United States*, 460.
12. Ahlstrom, *A Religious History of the American People*, 643.
13. Filler, *The Crusade against Slavery 1830–1860*, 69–70.
14. Quarles, *Black Abolitionists*, 113.

being a station on the underground railroad, and tells how "in 1858 the United States marshal arrested a runaway slave in Oberlin and started south with his prisoner."[15] Refusing to be outdone, more than two dozen Oberlin professors (and other supporters) overtook the marshal and freed his prisoner. For that, they were all arrested and jailed.

Charles Finney was appointed professor of theology at Oberlin in 1835. He later served as president from 1851–1866, "and his dynamic presence made Oberlin a center of influence for revival theology, the 'new measures,' and a growing emphasis on perfectionism—all combined with an urgent sense of Christian activism."[16] The latter was so important to Finney that, "From the first he demanded that some kind of relevant social action follow the sinner's conversion . . ."[17] What is important for our purpose is that Warner's student days at Oberlin coincided with Finney's presidency. Previously we saw that Warner first enrolled in 1865 (the year he was converted) and remained for just a couple of months before leaving to teach at Corunna, Indiana. He returned to Oberlin in the spring, and again in September, 1866.[18] It is not clear as to exactly how long Warner remained at Oberlin, but it is known that he was there long enough to have been affected by his abolitionist professors and the president (if he indeed was).

The incident about the professors rescuing the enslaved runaway occurred seven years before Warner arrived on campus, but he must have heard about such events, and he most assuredly must have known that Oberlin had been a powerhouse abolition institution that was also co-educational. "[Oberlin] had a corps of very able professors who were, without exception, active Anti-Slavery workers."[19] Moreover, Warner must have been aware of the institution's stance on sanctification and the need for relevant social action after one is converted to the Christian faith. One cannot help but think that the time that Warner spent at Oberlin must have impacted his stance on racial equality and the importance of social action to address social evil. And yet, there is no evidence that Warner wrote about any of this in the journal he kept from 1872–1880. Nor is there extant evidence that he wrote, preached, or taught about such matters. Although we do not get an obvious sense of the extent to which Warner may have been influenced by the stance on race and slavery held by his Oberlin teachers, we are surely on solid ground when we conclude that the influence was not negligible. And

15. Brown, *When the Trumpet Sounded*, 53.
16. Ahlstrom, *A Religious History of the American People*, 461.
17. Ibid., 460.
18. Byers, *Birth of a Reformation*, 49.
19. Hume, *The Abolitionists*, 207.

yet, we are faced with the enduring question of why Warner seldom spoke and wrote about race, both during his time in the West Ohio Eldership, and during the fifteen years he led the Church of God Reformation Movement; why, at no period, did he openly, forthrightly, and consistently advocate for the rights of blacks and their acceptance in the group on terms of equality with whites. Oberlin was the first college in the country to be both coeducational and inclusive of blacks as the equals of whites. Warner resided in that community for a period of time, and attended classes, most likely with some of his black peers. Surely his views on women and race were influenced to some extent by his experience there.

Notwithstanding this we do not find Warner being the champion of blacks' rights that some Movement scholars would have us believe. I return to this important point later. For now, suffice it to say that Warner preached his first sermon in the Cogswell schoolhouse in Williams County, Ohio on Easter Sunday night in 1867.[20] He must have been a reasonably good preacher from the start, since it is known that even as a boy he exhibited excellent public speaking skills. Sociologically, such skills can come in handy for one who introduces and leads a new religious group, particularly if he also possesses charisma. Did Warner possess the characteristics of charismatic leader?

CHARISMATIC LEADERSHIP

D. S. Warner had an out-going personality, was known to be a passionate and fiery speaker, and was able to draw people to himself. He was a powerful speaker "and wrote convincingly, presenting in an incendiary manner an attack on the religious system of his period."[21] Warner inspired "undying loyalty in all who knew him and loved him."[22] Barry Callen assures us that without question, Warner "had personal magnetism and unusual persuasive ability."[23] These, we will see, are characteristics of the charismatic personality.

In his chapter, "As Others Knew Him,"[24] Andrew Byers included the memories of some individuals who knew Warner. A number of these described his preaching as well as his demeanor when preaching. One person remembered that Warner "preached with such power" that one preacher

---

20. Byers, *Birth of a Reformation*, 73.
21. Clear, "The Church of God," 131.
22. Brown, *When the Trumpet Sounded*, 133.
23. Callen, *It's God's Church*, 152.
24. See Byers, *Birth of a Reformation*, chap. 20.

in attendance said that it was too much for him and had to leave. Another reported: "When he was preaching on Sunday morning, the power of God came down on him and on the people. All wept and shouted. He leaped up a foot or more, turned completely around, and came down facing the audience." And yet another: "He had great power with God and men." And another: "When he sat down, we were surprised to find that he had preached just three hours, which seemed such a short time to all of us."[25] Robert L. Berry, a Movement preacher, and Mother Sarah Smith, a member of Warner's five member evangelistic team that began in 1884, made corroborating comments about Warner's tendency to preach long sermons and his ability to hold the attention of an audience. According to Berry, "People would be held spellbound while he preached for one, two, and sometimes three hours."[26] Similarly, Sarah Smith wrote that despite Warner's frail body, "he often would preach from two to three hours."[27] In addition, J. W. Byers said that in 1892 Warner preached three sermons each for three hours at a church service in Los Angeles. "Those who ever heard D. S. Warner preach," said Byers, "know why those hours passed quickly."[28] By all accounts, Warner was a powerful and persuasive preacher and had the ability to attract others to himself and his message. When Warner was a boy he was not only known to be entertaining as a speaker, but could hold a crowd and make his points convincingly enough to frequently win over listeners to his point of view. This trait was obviously advantageous in that it would later aid significantly in the growth of the Church of God Reformation Movement.

From what is known about D. S. Warner, he possessed the characteristics of Max Weber's concept of the *charismatic leader*. Weber was the first literary sociologist to exhibit fascination with the concept of charisma and charismatic leadership. In his sociological studies he found a number of patterns in the founding of new religious groups. One of these depicted a particular type of individual toward which others seemed to gravitate. Such persons tended to have dynamic personalities and what appeared to be an ability to almost mesmerize people, thereby attracting them to their vision. These individuals, e.g., Aimee Semple McPherson, founder of the International Church of the Foursquare Gospel, frequently appear to be beyond ordinary and somehow *set apart* from others.[29]

25. See ibid., 457, 458, 459, 462.

26. Berry, ed., *Golden Jubilee Book*, 11.

27. Quoted in her brief autobiographical sketch, in *A History of the Church* by Wickersham, 313.

28. Quoted in Berry, *Golden Jubilee Book*, 35.

29. See Epstein, *Sister Aimee*.

Max Weber did much to clarify the meaning of charisma and charismatic authority, saying: "The term 'charisma' will be applied to a certain quality of an individual personality by virtue of which he is set apart from ordinary men and treated as endowed with supernatural, superhuman, or at least specifically exceptional powers or qualities. These are such as are not accessible to the ordinary person, but are regarded as of divine origin or as exemplary, and on the basis of them the individual concerned is treated as a leader."[30] Indeed, such a one need not *actually* possess such "exceptional powers and qualities." The key is that followers and potential followers perceive or believe such a one to possess those qualities. Nevertheless, in ways that most persons cannot, the charismatic personality is able to use her power of persuasion to mobilize persons to join whatever venture she might be involved in. Indeed, her charisma is such that she is able to arouse in the people a sense of mission. When this happens, of course, persons often become committed followers, frequently to the point of being virtually uncritical of the one being followed. It is as if such a person has complete control over the faculties of her followers, many who appear to be completely devoid of the ability to think or to be rational regarding the beliefs and practices of the leader.

According to Weber the charismatic leader is more often anti-establishment and is frequently a catalyst to revolutionary changes in society. For example, the Hebrew prophets of the eighth-century BCE were charismatic leaders of this type. Although there have been instances when a charismatic personality was the stimulus to revolutionary movements and change, there is no way to predict that every charismatic leader will be such a force, nor whether such a one will be anti-establishment. And yet, generally this tends to be the case. Sociologically, it is known that typically the charismatic leader has little use for rules, organization, and institutions.

In the early years of the Church of God Movement, D. S. Warner was without question the dominant personality. Although critical of the failure of the Churches of God (General Eldership) leadership to acknowledge and accept the truth of sanctification as a second act of grace, Warner still remained indebted to the group. He retained some of its key teachings and practices, e.g., the teaching on unity, the primacy of biblical authority, foot washing, condemnation of drinking, smoking, dancing, etc. The sociological principle involved here is that new religious groups that begin as a result of a parting of the ways by members of an already established group do not generally begin from scratch; do not commonly relinquish every teaching, doctrine, or practice of the parent organization. The Church of God

---

30. Weber, *The Theory of Social and Economic Organization*, 358–59.

Reformation Movement is no different. Sociologist Elizabeth Nottingham is instructive in this regard when she writes: "Although founders of religious movements are often critical of existing religious organization, their own religious and ethical message, however new in certain respects, *inevitably owes much to the religious tradition in which the particular founder has been nurtured*. Thus the teachings of Jesus are both critical of organized Judaism and yet grounded in it."[31] Unquestionably, the same can be said of Warner and the Church of God, in the sense that they were both critical of various beliefs and practices of the General Eldership of the Churches of God, and yet retained some of its best teachings, and to this extent remained grounded in it. Indeed, although this writer grew up in the Church of God but left after more than twenty-five years, I continue to be committed to various of its teachings, e.g., holiness and visible unity, although I am intentional and adamant about expanding these principles to include visible unity along racial lines, since I believe the doctrine of holiness requires it. I examine this idea later in this chapter, and more fully in chapter 6. Suffice it to say that although I left the group I remain grounded in and committed to its two founding core principles.

Ordinarily, the one who breaks away from a parent religious group does not reject all of its beliefs and practices. This was the case of the early Church of God Movement. Early membership was fed by members of various other denominations, especially Methodist and Methodist related groups, Mennonite, United Brethren, and the Churches of God (General Eldership). The point being made here is that in a number of cases, those who left their denomination for the Movement took with them various religious beliefs and practices. Some of those ideas and practices survived in the Movement, others did not. Foot washing, for example, was inherited from the Churches of God, and became an enduring practice among many Movement people. Those from Mennonite and United Brethren backgrounds, e.g., E. E. Byrum and his brother Noah, brought with them a staunch commitment to pacifism, but there was great difficulty in sustaining this as a widespread practice in the Movement. There was, in the writings of E. E. Byrum, for example, ambivalence on the pacifist stance when the United States entered World War One.[32] The Movement leadership did not outright reject pacifism, but only "a small but determined minority kept this practice alive."[33]

---

31. Nottingham, *Religion*, 225 (my emphasis).

32. See Strege's instructive discussion on the pacifist question during the Movement's first decades in *I Saw the Church*, 117–21.

33. Ibid., 130.

A schismatic group may separate from the parent organization because of specific practices, doctrinal and-or other disputes, but seldom (if ever) does it reject all of the parent group's teachings, ideals, and practices. The new religious leader attempts to go beyond the teachings and practices of the parent group, but usually ends up retaining some of these in what he deems to be the higher or truer view. This is reminiscent of the idea (presented in chapter 1) that there tends to be an ongoing dialectic between church and sect elements, i.e., that church and sect qualities exist side by side in virtually every church organization and impinge upon each other in some form or fashion. Therefore, the church never completely compromises with the world, for it must always contend with the sect-like qualities (which might also be prophetic elements) within the group for stricter adherence to the ideals of the gospel and those of the founder. Sociologically, this means that every church group has in it the seeds or potential for prophetic outcry and socio-ethical and spiritual regeneration. In a way, this is captured in Yinger's reflection that, "the church cannot live with the sect in a mobile society, but cannot live without it either."[34]

But this also means that the group is always faced with a potential quandary. Yinger writes of this dilemma as referring "to the struggle between a religious interest and loyalty . . . and other powerful interests of men which often contradict the religious teachings."[35] Churches generally make one of two responses to this quandary. "Religious groups face the dilemma either of asking more than they can get from often recalcitrant constituents (motivated in large measure by other than religious interests) or of so modifying their demands that the concrete realization of their ideal in history is largely given up. In the former case, the group can hold the allegiance of only a small number; in the latter case, it can hold, in the concrete, to only a small part of its ideal."[36] But the flip side of the church only being able to retain a small part of its ideal is that it is easier to expand its membership. That is, it is easier to obtain and sustain membership because the requirements of membership are not as rigorous as what we find in the sect. Those members who refuse to compromise their highest religious ideals generally find that if they remain in the group they have to "withdraw from normal participation in the dominant social structure. They prefer to maintain their ideal," rather than have it become so diluted (to accommodate others) as to have no real meaning.[37] This is the sect or prophetic type of response to the dilemma.

---

34. Yinger, *Religion, Society and the Individual*, 147.
35. Yinger, *Religion in the Struggle for Power*, 219–20.
36. Ibid., 220.
37. Ibid.

The church type response, on the other hand, tends to be accommodating, thereby taking steps to draw in as many people as possible, and "to win a place of power." By softening or compromising its ideal, as Winebrenner came to do regarding the enslavement issue, the church tends to have more influence in the broader society. But it obtains this influence at the high cost of watering down its own ideal. In addition, the church generally inclines towards the acceptance of the status quo, while also tending to turn deaf ears and blind eyes to the plight of the poor and the oppressed. Since it does not require that society and the powers measure up to its ideal, the church comfortably "establishes itself alongside the ruling powers."[38]

CHARISMA AND THE TRANSFORMATION OF RELIGIOUS GROUPS

Although the concept of the charismatic leader has already been introduced, it will be helpful to say more about it in light of its significance in the process of the sociological transformation of religious organizations. As an *ideal type*[39] there are other characteristics of the *charismatic leader* of which we should be aware. Weber actually borrowed the concept of "charisma" from the Strassburg church historian and jurist Rudolf Sohm. For Sohm, based on its Greek origin, the term literally meant "*gift of grace.*"[40] As a sociological term charisma means a particular quality that a person possesses which appeals to the non-rational factors or motives in others.[41]

As we saw above, the person who possesses charisma has some "*extraordinary quality,*" and it *does not matter whether this quality is actual, alleged or imagined.*[42] The person who possesses charismatic authority may be viewed as having, "a rule over men . . . to which the governed submit

---

38. Ibid.

39. "Ideal" refers not to value or that which is normative, but to "pure" or "abstract." For example, in sociology *charismatic leader* is an ideal type of leader. One tries to determine whether there is evidence of such leaders in the everyday world. Because it is a pure or ideal type we may not expect to always find all of the traits in the actual world. In any case, many of the defining traits of the ideal type are generally observable in day-to-day experience. There may be ideal types of leadership, bureaucracy, democracy, capitalism, religious organizations, etc. Weber said that the ideal type is essentially "an instrument for classification," which made it possible for social scientists to make generalizations about religious and other behaviors.

40. Gerth and Mills, ed., *From Max Weber*, 52, 246.

41. See Weber, *The Protestant Ethic and the Spirit of Capitalism*, 281n105.

42. Gerth and Mills, ed., *From Max Weber*, 295.

because of their *belief* in the extraordinary quality of the specific person."[43] What is important here has less to do with the actual qualities of the charismatic leader than with what is in the mind of the follower. That is, what matters is whether a person(s) *believes* that Katie Doe possesses some extraordinary quality that compels him to be committed to her and to her vision, and to be committed to the point of not being able—or perhaps willing—to question anything that she says or does. Furthermore, as noted before, the "extraordinary quality" need not—and often does not—exist in fact. What is important is that the followers *believe* that the quality is present in the leader. As long as the followers believe that the charismatic leader is meeting their needs and is moving toward the stated vision, they ordinarily tend to believe in and follow him to the ends of the earth, as over 900 people of various races, ages, and socio-economic groups did under the influence of "cult" leader Jim Jones in November 1978. Jones's group had its beginnings in Indianapolis, Indiana prior to moving to California and becoming the Peoples Temple. The group then moved to Guyana, South America where the murder-suicide rites occurred. Most of the members were simply mesmerized by Jones and *believed* that he was truly leading them to a better place and life. So they followed him uncritically—and for all intents and purposes blindly—because they *believed*. The few who ceased believing stopped following him. One of these, Hyacinth Thrash of Indianapolis, was in the camp when Jones and his followers consumed the poison beverage. No longer believing in his leadership, Thrash hid in the camp and was rescued. She told her story to Marian K. Towne in *The Onliest One Alive*.[44]

When it becomes apparent that the charismatic leader is no longer able to deliver the goods, e.g., miraculous works or victory in social movements, the belief that her followers had in her usually diminishes and soon disappears. If it is no longer evident (or believed) that she has those magical or extraordinary qualities, she is finished as far as her followers are concerned. According to Weber, failure to perform heroic, magical, or seemingly miraculous feats inevitably leads to her ruin.

The charismatic leader is ordinarily self-appointed and his followers tend to be the disinherited and alienated. They follow him because they *believe* him to have extraordinary qualities. Founders of world religions and prophets, military and political personalities, may be charismatic leaders, e.g., the Hebrew prophets, Jesus, Adolph Hitler, Mohandas K. Gandhi, Aimee Semple McPherson, Malcolm X, Fannie Lou Hamer, Martin Luther King, Jr., and Oscar Romero. We will see that time and again, D. S. Warner

---

43. Ibid.
44. See Thrash, *The Onliest One Alive*.

proved that he could deliver the goods regarding entire sanctification, and because of it, his following grew.

Charismatic leaders are of utmost importance in times of social upheaval and crisis. But they are also important in times when groups feel a sense of alienation in a parent organization to which they belong, or to society at large. The times will generally be defined by much emotionalism, excitement, tension, and conflict. Although there may be other social forces at work, the charismatic leader can, and often does, make the difference between the failure and success of a movement. Moreover, the charismatic personality is frequently a revolutionary force in history. This was no less true of D. S. Warner, particularly in the context of the Church of God Reformation Movement.

PERSONAL CHARISMA AND D. S. WARNER

As the dominant personality during the first stage of the Church of God Movement, D. S. Warner unquestionably possessed charisma in the Weberian sense. Herein lay the source of Warner's appeal, authority, and responsibility—personal charisma or "the gift of leadership." Warner was the leader because he could lead and there were people who desired to follow him. No one asks or appoints such a one to lead. Instead, he leads "because he finds people following him. The personal charisma," Val Clear writes, "is self-validating."[45] Personal charisma is different from public or "official charisma." One who possesses the latter has authority by virtue of having been appointed to her position, or having assumed it at the death or ousting of her predecessor. She may or may not be qualified for the position. The point of validation for such a one is not from within, but from without. "With official charisma the charisma is in the office, not in the occupant."[46] Indicators are that this was the case of Warner's successor, E. E. Byrum. However, without question, Warner's charisma was of the personal or self-validating type. This is commonly the case of the protest leader. According to Val Clear, Warner "led his people with firmness in love, effectively exorcizing contrary persons in the interest of unanimity, which is a prerequisite to an effective protest group."[47]

The first phase of a religious movement, then, is typically characterized by two important factors. The first is the *personality of the leader*, which tends to be a dominant force. There might even be multiple leaders, each of

---

45. Clear, *Where the Saints Have Trod*, 67.
46. Ibid., 68.
47. Ibid.

which may possess charisma. But it is frequently the case that at least one of the leaders possesses this trait, and this was most certainly the case of D. S. Warner. The second factor is that of *"extraordinary enthusiasm"* on the part of the leader and her followers, and with little or no attention given to existing social customs, e.g., separation of the races or classes. We see overwhelming evidence in Warner's journal of his enthusiasm for ministry and for the doctrine of entire sanctification. There was frequently unspeakable excitement on his part whenever he had the opportunity to preach and teach holiness as a second act of grace. Moreover, there is no solid evidence that Warner was concerned about the custom and law regarding the separation of the races. The message he preached was for all to hear and receive.

During this first stage, the emphasis of the leader and followers is on commonness, not differences. It should be noted, however, that not unlike the religious organization itself, the *charismatic leader is also affected by the society and culture* of which she is a member. Just as the appearance of the charismatic leader may have a revolutionary impact upon existing institutions of society and culture, she cannot escape at least some influence of these upon her life. Nor can she avoid influencing them to some degree. Those who are familiar with the eighth century prophets know that as critical as they were of their culture, each was also much influenced by the society in which he lived and developed, even as such ones influenced their culture and surroundings. Yinger has written about this phenomenon. "Even the religious innovator—the prophet or 'charismatic leader,' the ascetic, the mystic—although he is often thought to be a spontaneous new force in history, does not escape the imprint of his society and culture. When social patterns change or when a religion is transplanted into a new society, the changes it undergoes further indicate the close interconnection of religion and society."[48] Every person is always a part of some culture or society, and thus is both influenced by, and influences it. Each makes and is made by her culture. The charismatic leader comes into prominence both because of personal or individual characteristics, and because of situational or societal factors. She does not develop in a vacuum. D. S. Warner was no exception.

It is also important to point out that during the first stage of the natural history of a religious group little to no attention is given organization. The emphasis, after all, is on the charismatic leader and her ability to get her message to as many people as possible. It is known that Warner was initially "opposed to any kind of organization." He also failed, in the beginning, to distinguish between "organizing the church and organizing the work of the

---

48. Yinger, *Religion, Society and the Individual*, 126.

church" in order to get the work of the ministry done.[49] Experience taught Warner that this was a mistake; that there truly is a significant difference between organizing the church, and organizing in order to carry out the tasks of the church.

THE PRIMACY OF HOLINESS OR ENTIRE SANCTIFICATION

D. S. Warner was ecstatic that the Winebrennerian churches had but one creed, namely the Word of God as espoused in the Bible. The other articles of faith of the group also appealed to him. "They hold the doctrine of the Trinity, believe in human depravity, the atonement of Christ, justification by faith, the resurrection, future punishment, and are, in general, orthodox. Through these articles of their faith, and the fact that they took the Scriptural name, Church of God, the followers of Winebrenner made their appeal to D. S. Warner."[50] But as noted earlier, Warner had kept company with workers in the holiness movement and was very much influenced by the doctrine of sanctification as a second act of grace, whereas the Winebrennarian elderships rejected it, causing Warner to believe that they were "outside the Holy Spirit control of believers."[51]

Initially, Warner was closer to the view that one receives full salvation at the point of conversion or justification; that they occurred in one and the same act. We get this sense from his journal, where he writes on July 5, 1877, that he presented himself at the altar for "entire sanctification," a blessing he said he enjoyed ten years previous. "But I had all this time repudiated the second work . . ." in part because of disgust "with the fanaticism I saw mixed with the professors of the second work, which had steeped me with prejudice through and through."[52] At that time, Warner believed that to adhere to the principle of sanctification as a second work of grace was to imply that God works by "piece meal" rather than making "a full and complete finish of it at once." Still looking back, he wrote:

> I attributed their second experience to the fact that after conversion we are weak infants and not able to carry into action the pure nature, that God had given us until we grew to that degree of strength, that we could successfully cope with outer

---

49. Brown, *When the Trumpet Sounded*, 94, 101.
50. Byers, *Birth of a Reformation*, 55.
51. Ibid., 56.
52. Warner, *Journal of D. S. Warner*, 207.

temptation and that holy nature given to us in regeneration would have reached a degree of development in strength, that it would no more be under subjection to sin in the world around us.[53]

By his own admission, Warner struggled long and hard, and was often at the altar before arriving at the "double cure" stance, or the belief in complete sanctification. His earlier stance was little different from what was known as Zinzendorfism, the view that entire sanctification occurs at the point of conversion or justification.[54]

It is of interest to note that Warner was aware of and had occasion to reflect on John Winebrenner's stance on sanctification. Winebrenner stressed "the necessity of a virtuous and holy life,"[55] citing Hebrews 12:14, 5:9, 16 to support his claim. It seemed to Warner that Winebrenner believed that regeneration or justification by faith to be insufficient by itself. He quoted Winebrenner's definition of sanctification as "a perfect conformity of heart and life to the will of God."[56] The biblical text that Winebrenner cited as an illustration of this was 1 Thessalonians 4:3, where we are told of God's will for our sanctification. This message is to those who are already Christians, and thus have already undergone justification or conversion. Warner interpreted this as implying the need for a work of grace beyond conversion or regeneration which implies that justification alone is not enough. Winebrenner's error, Warner charged, was a failure to make the pursuit of holiness or perfect purity an explicit part of the salvation process. Otherwise, Winebrenner seems to have been on a good track. "According to Eld. W[inebrenner's] theology," said Warner, "to be born again is not to be made perfectly holy. In describing the grace yet needed, he quotes 2 Cor. 7:1; and here the Apostle identifies 'perfecting holiness,' with 'cleansing from all filthiness of the flesh and spirit.' Hence, Paul and Bro. W[inebrenner] both concur in teaching a work of purification after regeneration."[57] What Winebrenner only implied, namely the need to seek perfect holiness or purity *after* justification, D. S. Warner made explicit and central in his theology.

Arguing for the "double cure,"[58] i.e., for justification *and* entire sanctification as two separate but related works of grace, Warner came to

---

53. Ibid., 207–208.

54. In the November 20, 1877 entry in his journal Warner acknowledged the presence of "Zinzendorfs" in their meeting. See *Journal of D. S. Warner*, 264.

55. Winebrenner, "History of the Church of God," 180.

56. Quoted in Warner, *Bible Proofs of the Second Work of Grace*, 231; also 21.

57. Warner, *Bible Proofs of the Second Work of Grace*, 230.

58. This is but one of three historical views of sanctification that have dominated

reject the view that these are identical and that full sanctification occurs at the point of justification or regeneration. They are not simultaneous,[59] as the Zinzendorfs believed. Thought to have originated with Count Graf Nicholas von Zinzendorf (1700–1760), the doctrine of Zinzendorfism was viewed by Warner as heretical. In 1898 a group of Movement pastors and Gospel Trumpet Company members began teaching the doctrine and were dis-fellowshipped by E. E. Byrum, editor. However, after a brief period of discontent and separation most of the dis-fellowshipped returned to the Movement.[60]

In any case, D. S. Warner was certain that regeneration and sanctification do not occur simultaneously, and thus are two separate but related acts of God's grace. Sanctification is that which happens to the sinner who has already been justified, and thus is already a Christian. "We never read [in the Bible] of sinners commanded to repent and be sanctified," wrote Warner. "This grace [entire sanctification] is always enjoined upon such as has already been justified, hence it is distinct from, and subsequent to justification."[61]

WARNER'S UNDERSTANDING OF HOLINESS

Holiness was in no way a principle founded by Warner. In some ways it was based on the Wesleyan principle of perfection. Holiness, in my judgment, is *the* revolutionary theological principle in the thought and practice of D. S. Warner; possibly *the* "principal foundation-stone." After all, had Warner not said on the last day of January 1878 that God had given him "a new commission to join holiness and all truth together and build up the apostolic Church of the living God?"[62] According to Warner, not even truth is mightier than holiness. "Truth," he said, "is mighty; but holiness, being the fullness of God in man, is almighty."[63] Holiness was a powerful term

---

Christian thought. The others include: 1) The Roman Catholic view which contends that sanctification is infused in the soul at baptism, and 2) The stance of most Protestants that because of the constancy of sin there can be no perfect holiness until that eschatological moment when all things are brought to perfection. Until then the most we can hope for is a gradual increase in purity or holiness. Although sanctification begins with regeneration, it remains incomplete until the eschaton. In this sense it is simultaneously gift and goal.

59. Warner, *Bible Proofs of the Second Work of Grace*, 228.
60. See Strege's excellent discussion in, *I Saw the Church*, 41–43; 61n17.
61. Warner, *Bible Proofs of the Second Work of Grace*, 221.
62. Byers, *Birth of a Reformation*, 173.
63. Ibid., 194.

that was intended to inform all else, including one's actions; including one's thinking and practice regarding visible unity. Indeed, one might wonder just how much more powerful and significant the term holiness becomes when visible unity is added to it.

It is also my sense that holiness, as a fundamental core belief, has been misunderstood by most people in the Movement, from its beginning to the present. By his own admission Warner certainly misunderstood holiness when he was initially introduced to it.[64] And yet, vast numbers of Movement people have exhibited a shallow understanding of the principle that virtually saturated Warner's life when once he understood and accepted it. Many in the early Church of God Movement understood holiness no better than many in the various holiness alliances. Warner's biographer made the point about holiness groups and their relation to sects:

> They seemed to believe sects were a necessary evil and they opposed the idea of coming out of sects. This is as far as the majority in the holiness movement would go. They deplored sects, but seemed to think that to be outside of all sects would be to have no church relation at all. Had they walked in the light they would have comprehended the true body of Christ and been led out of sectarian entanglements; but failing to follow the true leading of God, they receded, and their holiness degenerated into what was mere sect holiness. To this day they have their holiness associations and their conventions, but fellowshipping as they do the sects and factions of almost every description, they are left to grope in their own darkness and confusion, *still making an effort but accomplishing nothing toward Christian unity.*[65]

Warner saw that many in the holiness movement of his day did not fully understand, and most certainly did not apply, and live by, their own doctrine. Many in the Church of God, during and since Warner's time, have similarly blundered, especially regarding the issue of race in the church. Warner may have seen more clearly that the life of holiness implies human conduct that far transcends that which does not seek to be in harmony with God's expectations. True holiness, he came to believe, *affects one's entire life and conduct*. It must therefore affect how one thinks about race, gender, class, etc. One cannot claim to understand and adhere to the true meaning of holiness and be a racist, for example.

---

64. Ibid., 115, 119, 134.
65. Ibid., 132 (my emphasis).

Warner agreed with George Campbell of Scotland. Holiness or sanctification is but "an apt metaphor for moral purity . . ."[66] It is the perfectly sinless life and depicts the life that has undergone radical moral transformation. It affects in the most positive way one's moral conduct in every facet of her interpersonal *and* group relations. Warner thus concluded that, "if this purging from all inbred turpitude, this perfecting of love and wonderful increase of spiritual power and wisdom, does not constitute a great moral change; then it is difficult to conceive what would."[67] In light of such a view, it was not uncommon for Church of God ministers to declare, as J. D. Smoot (a black minister) did at the 1913 Anderson camp meeting that, ". . . God's word and God's salvation will clean a man or woman from the rubbish of sin and take away isms and everything else that is unlike God."[68] We will see that such a view, if taken literally, is problematic regarding the removal of the sin of racism, for it implies that all that is needed is the experience of justification or conversion. The problem is that the facts of experience and human history do not bear this out.

A logical conclusion to be drawn from Warner's stance (one which he, unfortunately, did not draw in his writings), is that many had not seen clearly that one cannot live the holy life, or a life of holiness, if one supports or is in ongoing complicity with the sin of division along racial-ethnic lines. Holiness requires that one be holy in every facet of his conduct, individually and collectively. One who thoroughly applies the holiness principle must know that race prejudice is an emphatic denial of the unity that believers have in Jesus Christ, for in Him there is neither Jew, or Greek, slave or free, male or female. All are one in Christ Jesus (Galatians 3:28). Part of God's holy purpose, at least, is that we humans be visibly united. To live the life of holiness, then, means that there has been a radical and permanent break with all of the sordidness of one's past life. If one was previously racist, he now understands that to aspire to be what the Holy One expects of him he must work relentlessly and tirelessly to liberate himself from his racism. He must, in the words of 1 Peter, become holy in *all* aspects of his life and conduct; "for it is written, 'You shall be holy, for I am holy'" (1:15, 16). This necessarily means that one must be holy in her relations with human beings, regardless of race or other God-given difference. At the bare minimum, to be holy toward others is to treat them as equals to self and one's group and to acknowledge their absolute dignity. One does this because God is holy, and expects human beings to be holy in our treatment of others.

66. Warner, *Bible Proofs of the Second Work of Grace*, 21; also 26.
67. Ibid., 37.
68. Smoot, "Our Mission in the World," 263.

There was already massive division along racial lines throughout the United States when D. S. Warner became the leader of the Church of God Reformation Movement. White members could not repair or avert the impending division along racial lines within the group—then or now—because they had a shallow understanding of the holiness principle and what it required of them. But for a few exceptions, whites did not understand holiness as a *purifying and unifying principle* as Warner did. In addition, Movement whites did not acknowledge their own racism and lack of support for the idea that blacks should be treated according to the principle of equality.

Warner maintained that holiness "is the one all-important, and absolutely essential attribute of the divine church."[69] Based on Ephesians 1:4, he determined that from the foundation of the world God determined that human beings should be holy and without blemish. This, he held, is why human beings were imbued with the divine image. Although through sin humans presumably lost this image, Warner argued that it is restored through sanctification.[70] Moreover, he believed that holiness is the means to visible unity.

As Warner came to understand it, holiness or sanctification comes *after* pardon, and thoroughly cleanses one's soul of sin and other depravities. In addition, it is a unifying principle that makes Christians one, as Jesus prayed in his prayer in John 17:21. Holiness is therefore destructive of all forms of division and sectarianism. Although not addressed forcefully and consistently by Warner and Movement pioneers, it should be said that true holiness is also destructive of divisiveness along racial lines, no matter the custom and-or civil law. After all, the church at its best is a countercultural community sworn to obedience to God's will and expectations. The church is that community that critiques all worldly ideas and practices in light of God's requirement that justice and righteousness be done; critiques practices in and out of the churches that are contrary to the gospel principles of Jesus Christ. To his credit, Warner was able to "face squarely the issue of holiness" and to embrace it fully in 1877 because of his company with the workers in the holiness movement.[71]

Holiness, Warner believed, was not purity in an abstract sense, for one is actually purified and *set apart* for God's use.[72] Persons are cleansed of sin for the purpose of being set apart for God, to do God's work in the world. This is the sense that Warner gathered from Titus 2:14. God requires that

---

69. Warner and Riggle, *The Cleansing of the Sanctuary*, 268.
70. Ibid.
71. Byers, *Birth of a Reformation*, 115, 134.
72. Warner, *Bible Proofs of the Second Work of Grace*, 24.

Daniel Sidney Warner

human beings be made holy for God's self and the work of transforming the world in ways that are consistent with God's expectations. Human beings, then, are sanctified and set apart for God's work in church and world. To be holy, then, is to be purified and "set apart from a common to a sacred use . . ."[73]

We have seen that members of the West Ohio Eldership were critical of Warner's acceptance of the idea of a second work of grace. Having been brought up on charges before the Eldership, Warner expressed his own sense of shame for having lost his composure during the proceedings; for having failed to "keep that perfect calmness and sweetness in the midst of the storm of unexpected accusation."[74] And yet, he believed that the fact that he was not angry with his accusers and had not the least harsh feelings toward them was attributable to God's complete and thorough sanctification of him.[75] Since he held that complete sanctification purifies the soul and cleanses it of all sin, Warner was all the more convinced of the truth of holiness, notwithstanding the fact that he was expelled from the West Ohio Eldership on January 30, 1878.

The idea of a second work of grace is the view that one must "achieve" a state of holiness, purity or purification. One does not literally achieve such a state as if by one's own actions, however, for holiness is a gift of God. *Justification by faith* gives the convert peace with God and frees her from all committed sins, while *sanctification by faith* is "a second definite instantaneous work of grace, which frees us from the inherited, or adamic, sin (1 John 1:7; Titus 3:5; John 15:2)."[76] Warner himself expressed concern about the man who thought "it impossible to get rid of the Adamic nature while we live."[77] Against those who argued that a state of sinlessness is unattainable in this life, implying that entire sanctification is possible only after death, Warner came to believe that God has sufficient power "to save from all sin in this life," such that once one experienced entire sanctification sin would no longer be a problem for him.[78] However, Warner was not so naïve as to believe that members of the church would never be tempted to commit sins of various kinds. He was quite aware that human beings are susceptible to weakness and therefore members of the church must be ever vigilant about their faith and practice. Not only may such a one be tempted to sin, but

---

73. Quoted in ibid., 19.
74. Byers, *Birth of a Reformation*, 151.
75. Ibid.
76. Rowe, "What We Believe," 71.
77. Quoted in Byers, *Birth of a Reformation*, 145.
78. Byers, *Birth of a Reformation*, 142.

may actually succumb, and if not checked, may go on pretending to be a member of the Church of God. "Such characters [sinners] may, and do assemble with the church," said Warner, "and may seek to pass for members of the body, and where the church is deficient in discerning, such may actually pass undetected, and yet they are not in the church."[79] The Christian realist in the tradition of Reinhold Niebuhr can at least agree with this much of Warner's theology. Niebuhr, of course, argued emphatically and relentlessly that the judgment of God is upon every human achievement in history,[80] and that the truth of the myth of the fall is that we humans *cannot* escape sin in history.[81]

Although Warner did not believe that to merely succumb to sin was itself sufficient reason to consider one to be unworthy of continued membership in the church, he did believe strongly that if such a one made no efforts to repent and seek forgiveness for whatever sin is committed, he is "unfit for membership in the body of Christ . . ."[82] Warner further maintained that no person who ceases to be holy, and makes no honest efforts to rectify the situation can remain in the church.[83] Why, moreover, would a serious Movement person be unwilling to heed the counsel of another serious Movement person and especially the counsel of the church? "Under ideal conditions," writes Charles E. Brown, "the man who will not do this is no brother, and it is time to close the books on such a case."[84] This point has significant implications for past and (most especially) present day racists in the Church of God, for is it not the case that such persons, by virtue of their continued racism, forfeit their holiness, and thus their membership in the church? Past and present Movement people have either not known this—whether because they were not taught or were inaccurately taught—or they chose not to abide by it. In either case, there is a serious credibility problem that needs to be addressed, which has implications for teaching, understanding, and applying the core principles of holiness and visible unity.

Nevertheless, we must not lose sight of the fact that Warner's teaching implies the need for ongoing vigilance and efforts to retain one's holiness. In one's humanity she might well succumb to sin, but she need not merely accept this and uncritically live that sin. She must choose to overcome the sin or wrongdoing. Warner writes that "whoever committeth sin and does

---

79. Warner and Riggle, *The Cleansing of the Sanctuary*, 271–72.
80. Niebuhr, *The Nature and Destiny of Man*, 2:286.
81. Niebuhr, *An Interpretation of Christian Ethics*, 71, 74–75, 86.
82. Warner and Riggle, *The Cleansing of the Sanctuary*, 270.
83. Ibid.
84. Brown, *The Church Beyond Division*, 137.

not continue to overcome, his name is blotted out of the book of life. 'And the Lord said unto Moses, Whosoever hath sinneth against me, him will I blot out of my book' (Ex. 32:33). But, 'He that overcometh, the same shall be clothed in white raiment; and I will not blot out his name out of the book of life (Rev. 3:5).'"[85] The point is not to destroy such a person(s) through discipline, but to restore her more fully to the community. This is what Paul gets at in Galatians. Such effort is to be made with humility, lest we forget our own susceptibility to fall out of harmony with the community: "My friends, if anyone is detected in a transgression, you who have received the Spirit should restore such a one in a spirit of gentleness. Take care that you yourselves are not tempted" (Galatians 6:1). Based on the practice of racists, sexists, and heterosexists in the Church of God it would seem that they have not known about this aspect of Warner's teaching. Not only does this teaching imply that one who is guilty of wrongdoing must step up and seek forgiveness, but it also implies the need for instruction, as well as reproof. I return to this important issue of church discipline in the final chapter, since I believe that in some form it can play a significant role in making good the claim about visible unity in the church.

Already sold on unity as a core principle, Warner saw with lucidity that holiness, the second work of grace, was the necessary means of producing the perfect unity that Jesus referred to in his prayer in John 17:21. Holiness, Warner believed, is the only thing that can heal divisions in the church, as well as prevent them from occurring, "for it cleanses the heart from all unrighteousness." With holiness comes the "infilling of the Holy Spirit; the return of Christ from heaven in the power of the Comforter, and bringing with him the Father, and all to abide in the church forever; thus filling his sanctified temples 'with all the fullness of God.' While the perfect cleansing feature of the sanctifying grace removes all carnality, the cause of division; the all-pervading love of God, shed abroad in the heart by the Holy Spirit that is given to us, brings all hearts into the same harmony that reigns in heaven, into perfect unity, as the Father and Son are one."[86] The indwelling of the Holy Spirit is what opens the way to the type of unity to which Jesus referred. Perfect unity is the fruit of holiness. "Both Christ and all that are wholly sanctified by him are of one, yea, of one Spirit, of one mind, of one faith, of one heart and soul, and all in 'one body,' of which he is the head, and we are members in particular."[87]

---

85. Warner and Riggle, *The Cleansing of the Sanctuary*, 272.
86. Ibid., 260.
87. Ibid., 262.

Holiness is essentially "the doctrine of Christian perfection, the state of loving God supremely and of living victorious over every form of sin."[88] It is the only principle that can unify Christians as one, in accordance with the unity prayer of Jesus. Holiness mends and serves to prevent divisions in the church. Warner came to see that important as visible unity is in the church this recognition itself was not sufficient to bring it about. Something else was needed. He found the answer in the doctrine of holiness.

The Church of God Reformation Movement under Warner was therefore founded on the twin pillars of holiness and visible unity, two interrelated principles. He took the latter emphasis on unity from the Winebrennerian churches and the former from the Holiness Alliance in Ohio. We should also see, however, that inasmuch as the Movement has not adequately addressed its embedded racism and white privilege, it has not adequately lived in accordance with the holiness principle, particularly regarding matters of racial division. It has not yet made the connection between the ethics of sanctification and social sins such as racism. In the face of racial division in church and world, what would an ethic of holiness require of those who have been sanctified by God and set apart for God in order to do God's very difficult work in the world?

D. S. Warner was absolutely adamant that the church is one. Consequently, *anything* that leads to division or separation among the members he considered to be destructive of the true church. "Where *separations of any kind* are brought in between truly converted men," Warner wrote, "the church is not in the normal state, and spiritual death must sooner or later ensue to the body thus disintegrated; and being spiritually dead it is no longer God's church."[89] No right thinking person can fail to see the far-reaching ethical implications of this, even the issue of race in the church. Few things are as divisive in the church as racism and its many tragic manifestations.

True holiness permits no place for division of any kind among Christians. Warner came to see that even many in the holiness movement only nominally took holiness as a principle. "It understood no antagonism to sectarian divisions, though it deplored them. It stood for nothing more than holiness as a subject to be taught and experienced, and satisfied itself as best it could to remain within the denominations."[90] True holiness, Warner came to believe, must be nothing short of one's entire lived-experience, affecting all that one says, believes, and does, individually and collectively. One must live holiness in one's personal and socio-political life. The true

---

88. Byers, *Birth of a Reformation*, 125.
89. Warner and Riggle, *The Cleansing of the Sanctuary*, 264 (my emphasis).
90. Byers, *Birth of A Reformation*, 271.

life of holiness is not lived only with family and close acquaintances in a church building on Sunday morning. The holy life must also be lived in the organizations and institutions with which one affiliates. From a moral standpoint holiness always has personal, social, and political implications. It must inform, indeed infuse or color, *every* facet of life, interpersonally and communally.

In *Birth of a Reformation* Andrew Byers writes that, "John Winebrenner had the correct idea of the church as comprising all the saved, and his work was on an unsectarian basis. Lacking, however, in the quality of letting the Spirit of God rule, eldership organizations were soon set up, a man rule came in, and they also became a sect. Inflexible as to doctrine, they closed the door of progress on themselves, rejected the truth of holiness, and became one of the most narrow of sects, though bearing the scriptural name, Church of God."[91]

The holiness principle implies that one who takes it serious will strive to live consistently a life of holiness; a holy life; a life pure, clean, and perfectly free of sin; a life of moral purity; a life of living consistently to be like the Holy One. In doing so the principle is applied to *all* aspects of life, not merely to the inner spiritual life of individuals. Holiness is also applied to communal or collective relations, small and large, simple and complex. The life of the individual, as well as the group or corporate entity, must be made to comply with the holiness principle. All efforts short of this must be deemed unacceptable.

D. S. Warner believed that holiness is the means to concrete visible unity. This implies that the Christian cannot be holy and comply with the expectations of the Holy One if she does not strive to achieve and maintain such unity to the fullest. To what extent may we say that Warner himself was holy in this regard? To what extent did he intentionally work to bring together in the church what he characterized as "men of the most widely conflicting idiosyncrasies, and *races* of the most opposite customs and religions"?[92] Here we see that without question, Warner was aware that the church was comprised of all races. This would have been a good place for him to intentionally link this idea and the holiness principle to the race problem in church and society. Nevertheless, how did Warner respond to the recently emancipated Afrikans? How open was he to inviting them to join the Church of God as equals among the membership?

---

91. Ibid., 23.
92. Warner, and Riggle, *The Cleansing of the Sanctuary*, 240.

WARNER AND
THE RECENTLY EMANCIPATED AFRIKANS

It is highly probable that Afrikan Americans were primarily attracted to the Church of God because of Warner's preaching and teaching on holiness and visible unity in God's church.[93] Having recently been "emancipated" from involuntary enslavement, as a result of President Lincoln's executive order (the Emancipation Proclamation), large numbers of blacks, especially in the South, would easily have found Warner's message appealing. Moreover, they very likely would have interpreted the message to be inclusive of interracial unity, even if Warner's and white pioneers' primary focus was on spiritual and denominational unity. Blacks unquestionably heard or read into Warner's message what most whites did not. They understood Christianity to be a religion of freedom, liberation and interracial unity; a religion that rejected racial prejudice, discrimination, and segregation both in and outside the church. Therefore, Warner's teaching on holiness and visible unity was good news indeed for those who had been "emancipated" less than two decades before the churches were established at Beaver Dam, Indiana, and Carson City, Michigan.

Within a few years after Warner's founding of the Church of God, Jane Williams, a black woman, was preaching and teaching on the Movement's two founding principles of holiness and visible unity, in Charleston, South Carolina and Augusta, Georgia. Williams was ordained deaconess of the Church of God in Augusta in December 1893.[94] James Earl Massey contends that Williams was preaching the core principles of holiness and visible unity before 1886. Having started a church in Charleston, she worked tirelessly to spread the holiness and visible unity message among blacks. "Based upon Black Oral Tradition, and corroborated by published reports," Massey writes, "it appears that the Church of God message in the Charleston, South Carolina, area was first carried by black believers."[95] In her letter to *The Gospel Trumpet* in 1888, sent from Augusta, Georgia, Williams requested that Warner make a trip to her area to preach, "and more fully establish the little Church of God at this place . . ."[96] There is no evidence that he did so, or that he even replied to her letter. What is known, however, is that even before Williams wrote to Warner, blacks were already joining the Movement, and establishing local churches. It is also known that Williams

---

93. See Smith, *The Quest for Holiness and Unity*, 162; Strege, *I Saw the Church*, 122; and Massey, *African Americans and the Church of God*, 90, 225–26.

94. Letter from Kilpatrick and Carter to *The Gospel Trumpet*, (column 3), 3.

95. Massey, *African Americans and the Church of God*, 26.

96. *The Gospel Trumpet* 10.10 (Aug. 1, 1888) 3 (column 4).

(and most likely other blacks joining the Movement) was concerned about the usage of the terms "colored saint" and "white saint" when referring to Movement members, as if to imply that one was the inferior and the other the superior member. Apparently having seen such references in issues of *The Gospel Trumpet*, Williams queried *The Trumpet* staff about the matter in 1893, asking: "Is it necessary for us to use the word colored, and white saint? Jesus says, 'Go ye into all the world, and preach my gospel to every creature,' without saying a word about black or white people."[97] Williams might well have been reacting (in part at least) to the question put to the editor of *The Trumpet* in the September 14, 1893 issue as to whether it was acceptable for "white preachers to preach to the colored people."[98] Williams must have known that religious groups that did not espouse the holiness and visible unity principles used these terms when they referenced white and black members of their group. Surely this should not be the case in the Church of God, she must have thought. That Williams raised the question at all suggests that some southern blacks, at least, were concerned—even before Warner's death—that there might be a color line problem in the group.

At any rate, a lengthy unsigned response to Williams's question appeared in the same issue of *The Gospel Trumpet*, most likely written by E. E. Byrum (since he frequently responded to questions submitted to *The Trumpet*). In addition, one would also think that the reply was read by Warner, who was still alive. (It is true, however, that by this time Warner was distancing himself more and more from the day to day operations of the Trumpet Company due in part to illness.) I quote at length from the response to Williams because it will give the reader a good sense of what Movement leaders were thinking about the color line even before the founder's death, and therefore *before* the turn of the century. The rejoinder is both encouraging and discouraging, but mostly the latter, since Movement people were essentially advised to adhere to custom and civil law in matters of race. After all, the responder admonishes, all are equal under God, and the Scriptures do not require that civil laws be ignored or disobeyed.

> "God has made of one blood all nations to dwell upon the earth." And of course all colors of mankind have originated from his original creation in the Garden of Eden. God himself is no respecter of persons and colors, and neither should we be. Therefore, wherein it is not necessary to do so, we should not distinguish between color. While facts clearly show a natural inequality of races, there is a Christian equality in the love of

---

97. Jane Williams, letter to *The Gospel Trumpet*, (column 4), 1.
98. See "Questions" in *The Gospel Trumpet* 13.36 (Sept. 14, 1893) (column 4), 2.

God that knows no partiality. But this impartial love to all God's creatures must be exercised within the bounds of the word of God. And that requires us to be subject to the laws of the country in which we dwell. And since the Southern States do make a distinction between the white and colored races, and demand a certain separation of the same in trains, depots, public congregations, etc., it is necessary, under the existing laws for God's children to be subject to the same. Even should it be thought that the law is unjust and contrary to the principles of righteousness to, 'resist not evil,' and 'suffer wrong rather than to do wrong,' are duties when wrong comes in the form of legislation as well as by an individual. The religion of Christ does not encourage anarchy. It teaches its sons to endure patiently under existing laws even though they be mingled with oppression and injustice ... Again, the whole tenor of Bible Christianity is against human slavery. And yet where men were in bondage, the scriptures do not encourage them to ignore existing laws and their master's right of property under the same.[99]

The responder goes on to say that those who are being unjustly treated should be consoled by the idea of being free in Christ (as if socio-political freedom is not important for those who do not possess it). They were therefore counseled to suffer and passively endure the injustice to which they were subjected, "since the word requires us to be subject to the powers that be."[100] If the responder had stopped after the fourth sentence of his long reply, his would have been a noble response; a Christ-like response. But as with the case of other responses Byrum gave regarding race matters, he seemed to speak out of both sides of his mouth.

It is most telling that the responder said that the facts reveal "a natural inequality of the races." He does not state the basis on which he made such a statement, but he was convinced that whites, presumably, are the superiors of blacks, a view that was—quite significantly—issued from the Gospel Trumpet Company itself, and most likely was read by all or most subscribers to the *Trumpet*. The responder mostly addressed what *he* considered to be of importance regarding the race question. He seemed more concerned about trying to head off the possibility of conflict and potential schism developing around the color line issue. The quite legitimate concerns of blacks like Jane Williams were apparently of little significance. One must wonder how Williams and other blacks felt about the official response given to the

---

99. Response from *The Gospel Trumpet* to the question posed by Jane Williams (Oct. 5, 1893), (column 5), 1.

100. Ibid.

question she raised. One must also wonder whether D. S. Warner saw Williams's question and the response to it, and what was his reaction. Of course, Warner could have cleared it all up—if he saw and disagreed with all or part of the response—by writing his own response in a subsequent issue of *The Gospel Trumpet*. As far as we know, he did not.

Another point of interest is that the same reasoning we see in the response to Jane Williams appears in articles to *The Gospel Trumpet* by J. C. Blaney and James E. Forrest. Each wrote an article in 1909, and Forrest wrote one in 1910.[101] The responder to Williams—intended or not—seems to have set the tone for race conversations and relations in the Movement. The Blaney and Forrest articles, written a decade and a half after the response to Williams, will be found to contain language that is very similar to what is in the response. So much for the party line that the zeal that the pioneers had for the ideal of interracial unity only began to wane *after* the turn of the twentieth century!

Many who have written on Warner believe that he had—what in those days was deemed to be—an unusual openness and friendliness toward blacks. But one wonders about the extent of this, as well as the source of such tendency in Warner. Before proceeding further, it may be helpful to say more about possible influences on Warner that may have had real significance for how he felt about the recently emancipated blacks, and for his later ministry. Or, might it be the case that the real key to blacks' attraction to the Movement was based on the way *they* interpreted and responded to those principles, and thus had little to do with how Warner and other Movement pioneers interpreted them? If this is the case—and I believe it is quite tenable—it would not matter as much whether Warner was friendly toward blacks or not. What would matter is how blacks themselves interpreted the teaching on holiness and visible unity.

It should come as no surprise that blacks understood the core principles of the Church of God to be an argument against white supremacy and the visible separation of the races. This is how blacks interpreted and understood Warner's teaching on visible unity, which explains to a large extent why they so readily joined the Movement in the early years, and perhaps why they continue to swell its membership rolls even today. Furthermore,

---

101. See Blaney, "The Unity of the Spirit," 10–11; Forrest, "National and Race Prejudices," 9–11; Forrest, "Bible Unity and the Color Line," 6–7. To Forrest's credit he noted in his February 11 article that while whites had certain advantages over blacks, these were the result of social and political causes, not natural or metaphysical ones. "Civilization, education, and refinement may excel on one side, yet this is due to the advantages to which they are fortunately heirs, and the other is rapidly advancing with the flight of time" (column 1), 10.

unless one is just a blatant racist, and I know of no evidence that Warner was in this category, the founder of a new religious group would not be too concerned about the race and socio-economic class of new members, at least not in the early stage. He would be focused on evangelizing and growing the group numerically. Sociologically, the founder at this early stage is generally interested in preaching and teaching his message or truth and drawing in converts. The hope, we have seen, is that *all* who hear will be drawn to the message. Concern about the racial-ethnic makeup of the group generally arises only after the founder falls from power or dies. This is typically when those who remain begin exhibiting concern about how or whether the group will survive. This is a second stage trait. But clearly, the Movement broke this pattern, since there were signs of concern about the color line being expressed even before the founder was no longer on the scene.

We saw previously that there is some real difficulty involved in tracing what has been frequently characterized as Warner's sense of the equality of the races. Massey speculates that Warner's brief service in the Union army might have contributed to his presumed openness to the equality of the races.[102] Warner grew up in Ohio, which after all, was an anti-slavery state. But even so, this can be tricky, for it is known that not every white person in such states believed in the equality of whites and blacks, nor did all white northerners advocate abolition.[103] Furthermore, some abolitionists did not believe in the equality of the races. And to complicate things even more, many abolitionists were colonizationists, desiring that all blacks be colonized in a country on the Afrikan continent. In addition, many, while favoring the freedom of the enslaved, desired that the process be ever so gradual.

Many abolitionists found the practice of enslavement to be repugnant for various reasons, but they were just as certain that whites were the superiors of blacks in every way that mattered. For example, many of those—including religious reformers and other church leaders who welcomed blacks into their predominantly white churches, did not consider them to be on equal footing with them. During the enslavement period, for example, many whites were critical of the practice of enslavement and of enslavers, and yet they were prejudiced against blacks and did not believe they were the equals of whites. They therefore refused to grant blacks full admission into society, including their churches. "Thus emancipation of Negroes in the North [the place that was ostensibly free of racial prejudice], though it demonstrated the strong sentiment against slavery, did not reflect a willingness to accept

---

102. Massey, *African Americans and the Church of God*, 11.

103. See the provocative study by Ratner, *Powder Keg: Northern Opposition to the Antislavery Movement 1831–1840*.

the Negro into northern society. Racism or the conviction that racism was an insurmountable barrier to racial harmony, had characterized the thinking of many northerners for a long time."[104] Consequently, we dare not uncritically assume that because Warner was in the Union army in Ohio, he was generally exposed to non-racist sentiments and an attitude of equality toward blacks. In addition, the racial and socio-economic class of Warner's army company is not known. It could well have been a lower class all-white company that lacked race sensitivity. However, the fact that he joined the Union army might well have contributed *some*thing toward his sensitivity to the race issue, for it was generally believed that the Union army was supportive of the emancipation of the enslaved blacks. Nevertheless, we have no way of knowing what the Union army experience might have contributed to Warner's stance on race. Therefore, it appears that Massey, along with Barry Callen,[105] may have made more of the Union army experience of Warner than the evidence can support.

Massey might be on more solid ground, however, when he turns to Warner's Oberlin College experience as a possible contributor to his openness toward blacks, although even in this case we cannot be certain, since indicators are that Warner did not write or speak about the effect of that experience on his racial views. However, Massey quite reasonably surmises that the residue of some of the Oberlin abolition and Underground Railroad mystique of the 1830s might have rubbed off on Warner more than thirty years later. But as stated before, we need to proceed with caution regarding this speculation as well, since Warner did not complete his college studies, and his time spent at Oberlin was relatively brief.

It appears that in terms of total time spent at Oberlin, Warner was not there much longer than a year. It is therefore difficult if not impossible to know how much of Oberlin's abolition, race, and coeducation-friendly history actually rubbed off on him.[106] We saw in the previous chapter that virtually all of Oberlin's professors and its president during that period were abolitionists. It seems reasonable to infer that Warner encountered at least some residue of this, but once again, we have no way of verifying to what extent. Furthermore, it would seem that if this aspect of the Oberlin experience were truly important to Warner, he would have left a record of it. We have seen that while still a member of the West Ohio Eldership, Warner preached on women's right to speak and pray in church. He also expressed

104. Ibid., 9–10.

105. See Callen, *It's God's Church*, 38.

106. For an excellent discussion of the Lane Seminary debate of 1834 and the connection with Oberlin College see Barnes, *The Anti-Slavery Impulse 1833–1844*, chaps. 6, 7.

his dislike for the practice of Omaha Indians treating their women as little more than servants. "How wrong and cruel such a custom," he wrote.[107] Although it is important to see that an unmistakable cultural difference existed, and despite the noteworthy fact that Warner did not try to evangelize the Indians, and also believed whites to be culturally superior to them,[108] his dislike of the custom might nonetheless be indicative of his sense of equality between women and men. However, because of the nation's treatment of Native Americans during that period, I am much less impressed by the observation that Warner's visit at the Omaha Indian village was one of the "events that sensitized him further to the injustice being done to women, an injustice about which he could not be still."[109] His visit might well have had this effect, but we cannot know for certain.

Massey considers yet a third possible source of influence on Warner's alleged openness towards blacks, namely, the ministry of John Winebrenner. We have seen that Warner was unquestionably influenced by Winebrenner's reform emphasis regarding the church, as well as a number of his doctrinal teachings, such as the relation of regeneration or conversion to church membership; foot washing; full immersion in baptism, etc.[110] At any rate, although Winebrenner had been dead for nearly seven years before the West Ohio Eldership granted Warner a license, there is strong evidence that Warner read or heard about the sage's abolitionist and anti-enslavement efforts of the 1830s; his presentation of the radical resolutions of 1845; and the moderation of his stance in the 1850s. Consequently, it is quite possible that Warner was influenced by Winebrenner's example, including the softening of his stance on slavery. For it is known that Warner was silent on such matters, perhaps desiring, like Winebrenner, to avoid conflict and division in the church. In any event, it is known that on December 12, 1872 Warner purchased two important books, one of which is critical for the current discussion. In 1848 Winebrenner edited and published *History of All the Religious Denominations in the United States*. In his journal, Warner wrote that he bought a copy of Winebrenner's "*History of all Religions* which," he said, "is the best work of the kind I know of—every church having contributed its

---

107. Warner expressed openness to women speaking and praying in church, and had no appreciation for the practice of women behaving as mere servants to men (See Byers, *Birth of a Reformation*, 71, 100).

108. Byers, *Birth of a Reformation*, 100. The Movement did not begin efforts to evangelize Native Americans until 1939. Barry Callen writes that on the same Sunday of that year two Native American worship services were held on reservations twelve hundred miles apart. See Callen, compiler/editor *Following the Light*, 329.

109. Callen, *It's God's Church*, 56.

110. Massey, *African Americans and the Church of God*, 12.

own history..."[111] Significantly, Winebrenner wrote the chapter, "History of the Church of God." Under section III of that chapter, Winebrenner listed and briefly commented on the basic beliefs and practices of the Church of God. No room was left for guessing or speculating about the church's stance on enslavement. At belief number 19 he wrote: "She [the Church of God] believes the system or institution of involuntary slavery to be impolitic or unchristian."[112] In addition, Winebrenner included the full text of the two resolutions of 1845 against enslavement.[113] Since Warner considered Winebrenner's book to be the best of its kind, and considering that he was an avid and voracious reader, it is difficult to imagine him not reading at least the chapter on the Church of God. Having done so, he would have seen with his own eyes Winebrenner's stance on the enslavement issue (although he would have seen nothing in the book about Winebrenner's later struggle and the ultimate moderation of his stance). This should remove any doubt as to whether Warner was familiar with the anti-enslavement stance of the Winebrennerian church. However, the extent to which Warner was influenced by this remains a mystery, since he himself said nothing about it.

Nevertheless, we know with certainty that the West Ohio Eldership was, by 1860, "becoming one of the strongest Elderships in the moral and intellectual strength of its teaching elders."[114] It was an Eldership that was known for its discipline and censuring of its ministers for unacceptable behavior, including the presumed ownership of blacks. An example of this was the Standing Committee's charge that J. F. Weishampel had committed a "grievous offense." He allegedly disseminated pro-slavery and sectarian principles, and circulated slanderous reports against the deceased Winebrenner.[115] The only action taken by the Eldership was the adoption of the report of the charges, although the Standing Committee made it a matter of record that the actions of Weishampel were "censurable and his guilt intolerable."[116] Although somewhat mild, it is a case of the Eldership's willingness to subject its members to censuring (or the embarrassment of the threat of censuring) if warranted by their behavior. Warner would have known that the West Ohio Eldership had one of the strongest track records regarding anti-enslavement and abolitionist efforts. Other things being true

---

111. Warner, *Journal of D. S. Warner*, 9. He bought both books from a "Brother McIntire." The other book was "Josephesus' history."

112. Winebrenner, "History of the Church of God," 179.

113. Ibid., 185.

114. Forney, *History of the Churches of God*, 557.

115. Ibid., 557–58.

116. Ibid., 558.

about Warner, it is difficult to imagine that he was not aware of and influenced to some degree by those efforts, including the anti-enslavement resolutions. Of course, this would also raise the question of why Warner made no explicit reference to these in his own preaching, teaching, and writing.

We are, nevertheless, left with questions. What specifically did Warner know about Winebrenner's abolitionist and anti-enslavement activities? Winebrenner said nothing about these in the aforementioned chapter that Warner read. Which phase or period of Winebrenner's ministry would Warner have known about and been influenced by? We have seen evidence that he likely knew about the abolitionist and anti-enslavement period from the 1830s through the late 1840s. But what, if anything, did he know of the period of the 1850s when Winebrenner moderated his earlier viewpoint because of criticisms from pastors and laity in the church, and because of his fear that the church could split over the issue of enslavement and fellowship with enslavers? It is hard to know.

What we know for certain is that Warner was licensed by an anti-enslavement Eldership that Winebrenner helped to establish. We also know that barely two years prior to licensing Warner the West Ohio Eldership "rejoiced in 'the overthrow of the Rebellion,' 'the stability of our form of Government,' 'the abandonment of the vile and damnable system of slavery,' 'the elevation of the colored race to the enjoyment of their natural and inalienable rights,' and pledged itself to 'united efforts of all true patriots to restore harmony and Christian friendship between the lately divided portions of our country.'"[117] This obviously was still fresh in the memory of the Eldership when Warner was licensed in 1867, and therefore he would have inherited this bit of history. How much of the residue rubbed off on him? We do not know. Nonetheless, it is difficult to believe that he would not have known about the Eldership's anti-enslavement witness, as well as the contributions of Winebrenner in this regard. What we do not have clarity about, and the evidence to support it, is what specifically influenced Warner's own way of thinking about church unity and about race.

Without question, D. S. Warner had contact with blacks in a ministry way, both during his active membership in the West Ohio Eldership, and after he was excised from the group in 1878. In several journal entries, beginning June 8, 1875, he wrote: "Mr. Thompson, a poor colored backslider who had been a preacher came out and went and prayed until God blessed his soul."[118] On June 21, 1875 he wrote that he baptized "Sister Stanley, a

---

117. Ibid., 560.
118. Warner, *Journal of D. S. Warner*, 118.

colored sister" in the Sandusky, Ohio River.[119] Not long after he was expelled from the West Ohio Eldership, we find him preaching the funeral of a young black woman in Dunkirk, Ohio.[120] Warner also acknowledged that a "Sister Foot (colored) from Ohio" joined their worship service at Churubusko, Indiana on November 19, 1878. Moreover, she also preached at the evening service.[121] In addition, we know that near the end of the first decade of the Movement, Warner and his team went on an evangelistic tour in the area of the Mississippi Delta where their meetings were attended by blacks. Indeed, it appears that it was largely due to this tour that Warner gained the reputation of being known to befriend blacks and to preach justice for them. We are told by standard Movement histories that as a result, Warner and those who accompanied him were mobbed and attacked at Beech Springs, Spring Hill, Meridian, Watkinsville, and other places in Mississippi. From my reading of the standard Church of God histories, as well as relevant issues of *The Gospel Trumpet*, I am left wondering about what is factual and what is fictional about the reason(s) that Warner was mobbed in Mississippi. Let's consider this for a moment.

THE 1890 EVANGELISTIC TOUR IN MISSISSIPPI

The traditional party line account of Warner's 1890–91 evangelistic tour to Beech Springs, Mississippi, in early November is that he and his company encountered persecution and attacks *because* of his strict teaching on unity and holiness "with their strong racial implications."[122] Charles E. Brown, the initial source of the party line, went so far as to say: "'It seems Warner and his company were far more rigid and stern in their stand . . . for justice to the Negro' than the 'Straight Holiness' people were."[123] Warner's "friendliness" toward blacks, he maintained, was part of the mob's charge against him.[124] Reflecting more generally on the church, Brown said that "most of the persecution which the church received in the South was due to their friendliness toward the Negro."[125] This all implies that while in Mississippi, Warner intentionally and explicitly linked the holiness and visible unity principles to interracial unity and to justice and equality for blacks.

119. Ibid., 63.
120. Byers, *Birth of a Reformation*, 171.
121. Warner, *Journal of D. S. Warner*, 380.
122. Smith, *The Quest for Holiness and Unity*, 165.
123. Brown, *When the Trumpet Sounded*, 156.
124. Ibid., 157.
125. Ibid., 360.

Following this train of thought, James Earl Massey observes that Warner sometimes reported on times "when his openness helped some persons to overcome their prejudices."[126] Like (an) earlier and subsequent generations of writers on Warner, Massey seems to assume that Warner's reference was to racial prejudice, links this to the evangelistic tour in Mississippi, and then draws the conclusion that Warner and his team were attacked *because* of his teachings on interracial unity and his openness and friendliness toward blacks. I find it interesting, however, that Noah Byrum wrote about the Mississippi tour, but at no point did he mention that blacks were in attendance at any of the meetings. In addition, he nowhere refers to race, or to Warner's attitude toward race that may have been a contributing cause of some of the attacks that Warner and his evangelistic team encountered.[127] In the next chapter we will see that neither pioneers who were with Warner in Mississippi, nor others who had contact with him and that deep South state and wrote about it, said anything at all about his relations with blacks or his preaching on justice for them.

I have struggled long and hard with Brown's, and subsequent Movement scholars' claim that Warner was attacked in Mississippi *because* he preached unity along racial lines and exhibited public friendliness toward blacks which enraged some whites to the point that they mobbed him. Massey endeavored to help clear this up for me during a telephone conversation on August 7, 2008. At that time, Massey informed me that he had the opportunity to have many conversations with Brown about blacks in the Movement, and that he later read many of the letters reporting historical facts about Movement history that were sent to Brown from all over the country and the world. A number of these letters, according to Massey, were written by blacks who had relatives and-or friends who attended the Mississippi meetings when Warner preached there. Massey specifically recalled the names of Eugene Garrett and T. H. Wingfield, Afrikan Americans, who were said to have sent letters from Mississippi. Garrett, he reported, attended one of Warner's meetings as a boy. Massey later informed me in a telephone conversation on March 25, 2015, that the land outside Beech Springs on

---

126. Massey, *African Americans and the Church of God*, 11.

127. See Stultz and Welch, compiler/editor *The Book of Noah*, 100–104. I also find it interesting and telling that nowhere in this text does Byrum even mention the presence of blacks in the Movement. There are thus no references at all to racial concerns; no reference to the Lena Shoffner sermon at the Hartselle, Alabama campground—nothing. In addition, of the numerous photos in the book of 331 pages the only picture of an Afrikan American is that of a young woman posing with about thirty other students outside the school house on the Trumpet Company grounds in Grand Junction, Michigan (159).

which one of Warner's meetings was held was actually later owned by the Garrett family.

Nevertheless, the letters to which Massey referred are among the sources that Brown apparently got information regarding blacks' attendance at Warner's meetings; how they were received by Warner; and what he reportedly said about unity along racial lines and justice for blacks that presumably stirred up mob violence against him and his evangelistic team. Warner would have done a great service to the Movement and US church history generally had he written explicitly about these matters in his journal, or in the five field reports and-or articles he submitted to *The Gospel Trumpet* (from Mississippi) so that they could be preserved for future generations.[128] Moreover, the epistolary testimony of Garrett, Wingfield, and others who either were in attendance, or knew people who were at the meetings, or were contemporaries who heard corroborating oral reports about them, would also be strong evidentiary support for Brown's and subsequent Movement scholars' claims about Warner and Movement pioneers' pre-twentieth century "zeal" about interracial unity.

During my initial conversation with Massey, he reminded me that Brown had said that support for some of the events reported on in his book came from or were corroborated by the many letters he received from people who shared memories about Warner and various aspects of early Movement history. Indeed, in the Preface to *When the Trumpet Sounded* Brown wrote: "I have also received hundreds of letters from around the world giving historical data of the early times."[129] A number of these letters reflected on Warner's evangelistic efforts in Mississippi in 1890–91. At the very least, it would have been helpful had Brown expressly stated at the appropriate places in his book that the discussion on, and reason for, Warner being mobbed was based on epistolary testimonies. For the sake of posterity, it would have been helpful had he cited the source of the letters, i.e., name of contributor, date, and location from whence the letter was sent.

---

128. In 1891 Warner sent at least five reports to *The Trumpet* during the Mississippi tour: January 1, 15; February 1, 15; and March 15. All but the February 1 report were quite detailed. In several of these reports he explained extensively how he and his company were threatened and-or attacked by mobs. In not a single instance is there reference to blacks, race, or having preached on interracial unity, or for freedom for blacks. Nor does Warner mention that blacks were present at any of the meetings or, his having been friendly toward them. We have already established that one or more blacks were very likely present at some of the meetings. So this point is not at issue. What is of concern is the claim by the party liners that Warner was attacked *because* he preached interracial unity and because of his friendliness toward blacks during the Mississippi tour.

129. Brown, *When the Trumpet Sounded*, viii.

The attention to scholarly detail in this case was lacking. This is all the more important at this writing, for I have looked in vain in the Church of God archives for the "hundreds of letters" to which Brown referred, and of which Massey has spoken. Presently, I have been able to locate less than a dozen letters from Brown's Mississippi file in the archives—all written by whites, and not a single one refers to Warner's alleged preaching on interracial unity and justice for blacks as a reason he was attacked by mobs.

As I read Warner's journal account and the five field reports on the Mississippi tour, I did not get the sense that he and his team were attacked *because* of their openness to blacks, or because Warner preached on unity along racial lines. Warner certainly did not make such claims in his journal entries or the reports from the field. Surely the presence of blacks in the meetings and Warner's alleged preaching against division along racial lines was a point worth including in his journal and the field reports to *The Trumpet*. It is strange indeed that Warner did not leave details about such matters. It should be pointed out, however, that Andrew L. Byers observed in a footnote to Warner's report written from Spring Hill, Mississippi, that "a letter had been received in the community, from Carthage, MO., written by an opposer who misrepresented the saints as believers in amalgamation with the colored people, the purpose of the letter being, of course, to stir up prejudice."[130] Indeed, in his report, Warner himself referred to "lies and slanders" being hurled at them, "such as of promiscuous kissing, free-love, etc. . . ."[131] Byers' note, and Warner's report, most certainly imply that blacks were in attendance at some of the Mississippi meetings, or were expected to be. How else can one explain the slanderous accusations against Warner and his team? Moreover, there was no need for such a letter to be sent from Carthage if it was not known that the meeting in question was to be an interracial one.

In addition, it is most interesting and telling that the letters that white Mississippians sent to editor Charles E. Brown recalling Warner's evangelistic tour made it crystal-clear that Warner was indeed attacked by mobs in Beech Springs, Spring Hill, and Meridian because he "preached the truth on holiness and unity of believers."[132] However, the letter did not expressly

---

130. Byers, *Birth of a Reformation*, 391n.

131. Quoted in ibid., 391.

132. Letter from Jones to Brown, 1. It is significant that in June 1964 James Chaney, Michael Schwerner, and Andrew Goodman (all civil rights workers) were murdered on the first day of the Freedom Summer campaign for voter education and registration, not far from Meridian, Mississippi. The three activists went out on the first day of Freedom Summer to investigate a church bombing, and disappeared. In those days, to disappear in Mississippi meant that one was dead. This was the case of the three

link "unity of believers" to interracial unity. Another letter said that Warner came "preaching clean, upright living, free from sin and sectarianism, and then the Devil sure did raise a howl."[133] On May 20, 1949, George W. Breazeale wrote that at Warner's first meeting at Watkinsville, Mississippi, the mob formed to disrupt Warner's efforts and to run he and his group out of town. The next meeting was at Beech Springs. Breazeale reports that a mob also formed there, and broke the windows at the meeting house with clubs and bricks. He said further that Warner was "cut across the face by flying glass." It was after this incident that Warner wrote the song, "Who Will Suffer with the Savior."[134] L. V. Strickland wrote that the mob at Spring Hill was heavily armed and intended to get and harm Warner, "but God made a way for his escape by being disguised in women clothes."[135] According to these letters, Warner was attacked for the reasons noted. However, *nothing* was said about him preaching explicitly on interracial unity, stressing justice for blacks, and showing more than ordinary friendliness toward them. It is most interesting that extant letters submitted by white Mississippians give not even a hint that blacks were in attendance at any of the meetings. Nor do the letters confirm or deny that Warner preached on interracial unity at any of the meetings. And yet, I am not unmindful that during the period in question blacks were essentially invisible to most whites, even if they sat right next to them in worship services. So blacks most likely attended some of those Mississippi meetings to which the white letter writers refer, but their presence was not acknowledged. In any case, what can be said of the whereabouts of those "hundreds of letters from around the world giving historical data of the early times," to which Brown refers in the Preface of his book?

It is most unfortunate that I have not been able to locate the letters written by Garrett and Wingfield to which Massey refers. By now, it may be that the letters are merely a part of Church of God lore. I say this because multiple searches at the Church of God archives at Anderson University during the summer of 2008 and on March 11, 2015 led to a dead end, despite James Earl Massey's continued insistence, subsequent to my last visit to the archives, that he himself read the letters; letters that were among the

---

freedom fighters. Warner is said to have preached against racism during his evangelistic tour in the area in 1890.

133. Letter from McDonald to Brown, 1. See also "Prologue to History of First Church of God of Meridian, Mississippi," by Sorrell and Frazier, where they write of someone having "shot a slingshot full of buckshot, which missed [Warner's] face only by inches...," but Warner "continued his sermon as if nothing had happened," 1.

134. Letter from Breazeale to Brown, 1.

135. Letter from Strickland to Brown, 4.

hundreds sent to Charles E. Brown when he was writing *When the Trumpet Sounded*. Many of the letters sent to Brown with personal stories about experience in the Church of God during the period of the pioneers ended up in the files at Warner Press. According to Massey, it was Harold L. Phillips, then editor-in-chief at Warner Press, who allowed him to read the letters,[136] among which were those written by Garrett and Wingfield.

There is absolutely no reason to doubt that Dean Massey read the letters in question. What I wonder about, however, is whether the letters were donated to the archives; whether they remain in a dusty storage room at Warner Press; or whether they were shredded. At this writing it is clear that they were not donated to the archives. In an email from Vivian Nieman (March 24, 2015), archivist of the Church of God collection at Anderson University, I learned that the aforementioned letters are not in the collection.[137] Assuming that this is in fact the case, I can only say that it is a loss beyond words for the Church of God.[138] However, it occurred to me that if nothing else, it would be immensely helpful if Dean Massey would consider drafting a letter recalling the occasion for which he read the letters written by Garrett and Wingfield, and sharing what he remembered each of them saying. Massey agreed to do so, although it turned out that the most he could remember was that he read the letters.[139] He could not recall specifics of what was said. I include Massey's letter as Appendix-A.

---

136. Massey told me about this in one of our many telephone conversations, but he also wrote about it in *African Americans and the Church of God*, 7.

137. I have a copy of this email in my personal files.

138. I initially placed this material in a footnote, but decided that it is so important that I do not want it to escape the eyes of readers. Not many people are interested or disciplined enough to read endnotes.

139. I wrote to Massey on March 28, 2015, to make this request. A copy of the letter is in my files. During a telephone conversation a few days later, he agreed to my request. On April 25, 2015, Massey phoned me to say that he had completed the letter (dated April 25) and wished to read a portion of it. He did so, and stated that he had placed the letter in the mail. When I received the hardcopy of the letter and discovered that he had not responded to the question about what he remembered reading in the Garrett and Wingfield letters, I phoned and asked if this was an intentional omission. At that time he said that he could not trust his memory about specifics in the letters. I then asked whether he thought more of the letters might still be stored away in boxes at Warner Press. We decided that I should put that question to Joe Allison, Editorial Director Discipleship Resources & Curriculum at the Press. I did so in an email on April 29th. Part of Allison's response (the same day) said: "Since 2004, our practice has been to send all historical files that we discover to the Church of God archives, so I would have thought these letters would already be in Mrs. Neiman's [sic] care. However, we have a few boxes in storage that the archive has not been able to accommodate." Allison promised to investigate to see whether any of the letters and/or other relevant research files might be in any of the boxes. On July1, 2015, I received an email from Allison saying

It is worth noting that Barry Callen contends that when Warner preached in the locations in Mississippi where he was attacked, blacks "joined the crowd each night." On one occasion "a mob of about seventy-five angry and armed white people appeared. A brick came flying through a window and Warner's face was bloodied."[140] Callen observed that Warner did not discriminate against blacks who attended his meetings.[141] There is good reason to believe that this was true. However, because of the time period and the location it stands to reason that racists who disagreed with his teachings against tobacco and alcohol usage would likely have attacked him had he said nothing at all about interracial unity. Essentially, Callen seems to follow the party line of C. E. Brown and John W. V. Smith that Warner was attacked because he preached interracial unity and was friendly toward blacks. It might well be that Callen's claim is based on information gained from letters written by relatives of attendees at those meetings in 1890—letters whose whereabouts are presently unknown, or most likely are no longer in existence. Nevertheless, Callen boldly states that "a stance [such as Warner's] insisting that racial as well as denominational barriers have no place in the church would be painful and very dangerous, but the truth is the truth."[142] I could not agree more. And yet, I am compelled to say that if Warner anywhere stated this explicitly, the definitive evidence of it should be produced to support the claim. It is absolutely true that racism has no place in the church. Without question, D. S. Warner *implies* this in his teaching on holiness and visible unity, but I have found no hard evidence that he said it as plainly and explicitly as Callen reports it. Moreover, Warner himself wrote of the attack to which Callen refers, but he said nothing about blacks being in attendance, and-or that he was attacked because of their presence

---

that having examined the aforementioned boxes and file cabinets, he and a co-worker were surprised to find "that the manuscript files ran back to the mid-1970s." He went on to say: "Unfortunately, the files contained the final manuscripts only, and none of the correspondence or research materials used in their preparation." Moreover, "there was nothing from the 1960s or the time of C. E. Brown's writing *When the Trumpet Sounded* in 1951." In any case, this certainly does not mean that the letters do not exist, but only that they are not in the storage boxes searched at Warner Press. My hope is that some Church of God scholar (perhaps historian Gary Agee) will pursue the matter of the letters to determine once and for all whether those important documents to which Massey refers still exist or not. What some of those letters may contain could be just what is needed to vastly strengthen the claim of C. E. Brown, John W. V. Smith, and others influenced by their claim that the first two decades of the Movement were characterized by a strong interracial ethic—an ethic that only began to decline in the first two decades of the twentieth century.

140. Callen, *It's God's Church*, 124.
141. Ibid., 123.
142. Ibid., 124.

or because he preached on racial justice.[143] Furthermore, white Movement people who wrote letters and books that referenced the Mississippi tour were silent as to whether race was a factor in the attacks. And yet, the party line is that Warner was attacked *because* he welcomed blacks to his revivals, and because he preached interracial unity and justice for them. Since we have yet to discover hard evidence among white sources to support this, one wonders how early black Mississippians responded to Warner's preaching and the attacks on him. I return to this important point in chapter 4.

In his report from the Oak Grove area near Meridian, Mississippi in 1891, Warner said that "there was a general blessing effected on the community in the removal of prejudice and hatred out of many hearts..."[144] We saw earlier that Massey interpreted this to mean that Warner was referring to racial prejudice. However, a close reading of what he said reveals that he was referring to religious, doctrinal, sectarian, or some other kind of prejudice. In any event, in that particular report it seemed more important to Warner to clarify for the white townspeople of Carthage, Missouri that the Church of God did not encourage "amalgamation with the colored people"; that there was no "promiscuous kissing" and "free loveism" as maliciously charged by the Fort Scott sect.[145] This seems to have been the "prejudice" that was removed from their hearts, not racial prejudice as such. Therefore, Massey's statement about the matter is misleading, and tells us nothing about Warner's actual stance on racial prejudice. As written, Warner's statement was a clarification and assurance for the whites in attendance that the Movement did not advocate racial amalgamation. His reply was acceptable to whites, but it was not evidence of the removal of racial prejudice. Furthermore, Warner makes a number of references in his journal to the removal of prejudice from one or more persons in attendance at churches where he preached. However, my reading of his journal reveals that in every instance the reference was to sectarian, doctrinal or related prejudice, e.g., prejudice against sanctification as a second act of grace. There is not a single explicit reference to the removal of *racial* prejudice in Warner's entire journal, his field reports to *The Trumpet* during the Mississippi tour, or elsewhere in his writing.

Two things, it would seem, are not open to debate. First, having examined the available evidence, one cannot question the truth of Massey's assertion that it is very difficult to trace how Warner came to believe in

---

143. See Warner, News from the Field, *The Gospel Trumpet* (Jan. 15, 1891) (column 3), 2.

144. Warner, News from the Field, in *The Gospel Trumpet*, (Feb. 15, 1891), 2.

145. Ibid.

racial equality.[146] The fact that he attended Oberlin College (an antislavery, co-educational institution) for a period of time might well be one contributing factor, but we cannot be certain to what extent.[147] Massey points to the one explicit statement (presently known to us) that Warner made that could be interpreted to mean that he unequivocally supported race equality in that instance. He observes that in the July 15, 1886 issue of *The Gospel Trumpet*, Warner wrote an article titled, "Confusion and Shaking," in which he reflected on the conflicting claims of some holiness people representing the Good Way sect in Missouri. Because individuals in this group lacked the courage and-or will to criticize those positing such contradictory opinions, Warner took them to task—among other things—for their conflicting position on the co-education of whites and blacks at one of their schools. "Some have favored the exclusion of the colored race from Pauline Holiness College," he wrote, "and others contended for the Bible equality. *Which question we are thankful to see has finally been settled, by a majority vote of the managers in favor of equal rights to the colored.*"[148] And yet, what remains unclear is whether Warner's statement about the managers' decision was polemical, or an affirmation of his own belief in racial equality. Evidence to support the latter has yet to surface which shows him arguing explicitly for racial equality within his own group, as Winebrenner at one time staunchly argued for the abolition of slavery. Furthermore, it always seems easier for many whites to take a public stand on other whites' racial position, than to clarify their own. Warner was pleased about the decision of the managers of Pauline Holiness College to include blacks, but we see no evidence in his extant writings or those of other Movement pioneers that plainly suggest a desire to both welcome blacks, and welcome them on the basis of equality. Although he acknowledged that the primitive church was a blending of people of all types and races,[149] Warner did not link this to the race question of his day. What we know with certainty from Warner's statement regarding the managers' decision about including black students is that he was, without question, aware of the color line issue in 1886. Nevertheless, one cannot help wishing that there were other, more explicit statements about racism elsewhere in Warner's writings, sermons, and speeches.

The second thing that is not open to debate is that the teaching on holiness and visible unity itself has a strong implicit interracial message.

---

146. Massey, *African Americans and the Church of God*, 11.

147. How Warner arrived at his equality of race stance warrants much deeper investigation.

148. Quoted in Massey, *African Americans and the Church of God*, 7 (my emphasis).

149. Warner and Riggle, *The Cleansing of the Sanctuary*, 240.

This is especially the case when one combines holiness and visible unity as Warner surely did. Any message that stresses the unity of all believers necessarily implies the inclusion of all people, regardless of racial and ethnic background, etc. So connected are the holiness and visible unity principles that one cannot claim true holiness and not also work to establish concrete unity along racial lines, even as she seeks spiritual and church unity as Warner and the pioneers did. We will see that for Warner it was never enough to claim that one had experienced holiness or the second work of grace. The experience of entire sanctification had to be evidenced by how one lived on a daily basis. The holiness ethic requires that what is implicit in the visible unity message not only be made explicit, but that concrete efforts are made to make it a reality.

In any case, this seems to be the logic of Warner's stance on holiness and visible unity, even if he and most of the pioneers and subsequent generations of Movement people failed to act decisively and persistently on such logic as it relates to interracial unity. At the very least, it is imperative that Movement people begin to grapple with the meaning and ethical implications of holiness and visible unity relative to interracial unity to a degree heretofore unknown. This means that Church of God educational institutions, judicatory leaders, and local churches have much educational and ethical work to do in this regard, a subject to which I return in the final chapter.

D. S. Warner saw and received the light of holiness and a new movement was born. He was unquestionably a charismatic leader to whom many were drawn because of his passionate preaching, teaching, and conviction about holiness and the visible unity of the church. As is usually the case when new religious movements form, very little attention was initially devoted to interpreting and applying the new found truths of the leader. That would come later. What is most important during the early period of a group's natural history is getting out the message, evangelizing and drawing in the people. Before too long, however, and frequently after the passing of the first generation of leaders, the need arises to explain the meaning of the founder's ideas and principles, and to determine how best to apply them. This needs to be done not only for the second and succeeding generations of converts, but for some of the old timers who may still be living. These may need to be reminded of what they once knew of the founder's ideas, while new converts often need to know the meaning of such principles as holiness and visible unity and what this should mean for how they live their entire lives—not just their lives in the church. It is therefore left to the founder's successors to clarify such matters, as well as to begin thinking about how to sustain the group and some semblance of the founding ideas and ideals.

In addition, by this time, the group begins to devote much consideration and energy to organizing in order to carry out the group's work in the most effective and efficient manner. These are marks of the second and third stage of the group's lifecycle, and the subject of the next chapter.

4

The Next Generation

Seeking to Clarify Ideas and Practices

IT IS IMPORTANT TO remember that there is frequently overlapping of the stages in the life cycle of the new religious group. For example, stage two could possibly begin even before the passing of a generation (i.e., approximately 20–25 year period of time). This is what essentially happened regarding the Church of God. Even before D. S. Warner died, he had an assistant editor, Enoch E. Byrum (1861–1942), whom he selected to succeed him. There was no process or structure in place to select leaders since the group—consistent with what frequently happens in the first stage of its development—rejected all tendencies toward organization and institutionalization. Consequently, potential succeeding leaders could be hand picked and groomed by the existing leader.

Byrum joined the Gospel Trumpet Company in 1887 during a time of intense crisis. Warner's second in command, Joseph C. Fisher, had left under a cloud of disgrace.[1] Fisher fell in love with a younger woman and divorced his wife, Allie. When Fisher would not repent, Warner would no longer fellowship with him. However, he desperately needed someone to take Fisher's place. Later we will again take up the matter of Byrum making some unfortunate statements about the relations between whites and blacks in the Movement that would tarnish its image—which remains the case

---

1. Byers, *Birth of a Reformation*, 330.

today. Nevertheless, Charles Brown contends that Byrum "has an enduring place of honor and prestige in the reformation" and that his place of importance "is second only to that of Warner."[2]

Not at all charismatic, and nowhere near the speaker that Warner was, Byrum nevertheless had an astute sense about business and management. He was pragmatic, and knew how to get things done. As Warner's health deteriorated and he removed himself further and further from daily operations at the Gospel Trumpet Company, Byrum was already making his mark and unwittingly setting the stage for the second phase of the Movement's life cycle. His focus was on sustaining the group, which of course had implications for the institutionalization of Warner's vision and teachings. In sociological terms, this opened the way for the second stage of development on the sect-church continuum.

The second phase of the new religious group is characterized by a new generation of leadership. Or, since there is sometimes overlapping, it might simply be leadership that was already developing while the founder was alive. In any case, what often happens is that the founder will have either lost favor with his followers, is no longer in the public eye, or will have died. With the founder's passing from the scene, the new leadership is confronted with the task of clarifying important matters pertaining to *core beliefs or norms, organization, doctrines* and *religious practices,* all of which are generally placed on hold during the first generation. It is now time to interpret and explain the founder's message.

By the second stage, the initial period of excitement and tension that led the first generation to its convictions will typically have diminished considerably. Moreover, seldom will the second and succeeding generations cling to those convictions with as much enthusiasm and energy as the first. H. Richard Niebuhr rightly held that, "Rarely does a second generation hold the convictions it has inherited with a fervor equal to that of its fathers, who fashioned these convictions in the heat of conflict and at the risk of martyrdom."[3] Sociologically, this is generally what happens over time, from one generation to the next.

Such change in attitude, religious fervor, and conviction is also a sign of the changing structural look of the group, as well as change in doctrine, ethics, and behavior. The group begins as one thing (in the sect stage), but over the course of a generation, it begins to exhibit characteristics of a different type of group with corresponding changes in doctrinal and ethical beliefs and practices. In sociological literature, this is the classic example

---

2. Brown, *When the Trumpet Sounded,* 128.
3. Niebuhr, *The Social Sources of Denominationalism,* 20.

of the movement from sect to denomination, or church-like organization. "By its very nature the sectarian type of organization is valid only for one generation."[4] As the transition from the first to the second phase takes place, the ethic of the earlier sect-like group begins to approach that of the denomination and the church-like organization. That is, the ethic of the sect-like group becomes watered down to accommodate people from every facet of life that are entering the group. In this respect, the group begins to take on a more universal, diverse look, but frequently at the expense of diluting its ethical ideal. The group is, at this point, being transformed into another type on the sect-church continuum.

Whereas in the first stage of its development the group was concerned only to preach and teach its truth and would allow no compromise of its doctrine and ethical ideals, with the passing of the founder the general tendency is to begin to interpret the founder's beliefs and teachings, and too often in ways that the founder would not approve. Almost always the interpretation is softer or more moderate, which generally makes it easier for others to get into the group who previously could not (or did not want to) because of the rigid requirements. Because the desire by this time is to perpetuate itself, the group's second generation of leaders interprets the founding ideas and ideals in more conservative ways that make it easier to accommodate larger numbers of people from every sector of society, including more well-to-do people. Many of these new converts have no desire to live in strict accordance with the founding core principles. Indeed, they may not even know what those principles are. The interpretations given these principles by the new leadership, then, often amount to accommodating to the ethic of society. The upside for the group is that this makes it easier for membership numbers to expand since persons are not pressured to adhere strictly to the rigorous ideals of the founder, or the perfectionist ethic of the Bible. Earlier we saw that from the sociological point of view, what we essentially have in this second stage of the group's life cycle is a movement from the stance of "Christ against culture," to that of "Christ of culture."[5]

H. Richard Niebuhr rightly held that during the first stage of a group's life cycle it "holds with tenacity to its interpretation of Christian ethics and prefers isolation to compromise."[6] During this initial stage of its natural history the group would rather be ostracized and live apart from the rest of society than to moderate or water down its ethical ideal. However, in the course of a generation, this attitude frequently changes. More and more,

---

4. Ibid., 19.
5. Niebuhr, *Christ and Culture*, chaps. 2, 3.
6. Niebuhr, *The Social Sources of Denominationalism*, 19.

the group desires to be accepted into the wider society and culture. But in truth, the group cannot avoid this in any case, since it makes the decision to receive into its body all kinds of people—regardless of social class values—*but* without also requiring strict adherence to the founding core beliefs of the group. Even more, too often the group does not even hold the feet of the new converts to the fire of the rigorous ethic of the Christian faith generally, let alone its own theological and ethical principles.

As noted before, often new converts in the second and subsequent stages of the group's life cycle do not even know what the basic core beliefs of the group are. Consequently, there is frequently a sense of not having to either give up anything from one's past or present life, or to live up to a much higher ethical standard. Therefore, the tendency to compromise is a result both of internal and external occurrences. The ethic of the gospel begins to take a back seat to that of society. At this stage, it may even be the case that the Christian ethic will be reinterpreted so that it is more palatable to broader segments of society. Niebuhr makes an instructive point in this regard when he writes: "The specifically Christian ethics is allowed to fade into the background while the ethic of the social classes takes its place, unless, indeed, it is possible to re-interpret the Christian ideal in such a way that its complete accord with social morality is demonstrated."[7] This is essentially what happened among Movement people in 1897 when Byrum—representing the leadership—opened the door for blacks and whites to divide along racial lines. Byrum's move made it possible for other whites to essentially hold that it was not necessary for racist whites to relinquish their racism before (or even after!) joining the Church of God, or to abide by a strong ethic of interracial unity in a segregated society. The gospel, it was said, has no concern for societal arrangements but only for the spiritual well being of individuals. This surely is what J. C. Blaney meant to convey in an article submitted to *The Gospel Trumpet* in 1909.

> Some have never yet learned that the gospel is not directed against the fixed customs of a country or locality where social distinctions are made. It is nowhere taught in the New Testament that a slave-master must set his slaves free or that slaves must leave their master as soon as they got saved. While such social customs are not upheld in the teachings of Christ or his apostles nowhere are they directly condemned. From this we learn that we must let the light of the gospel shine from our lives in such a way as will not disgust the world with a useless opposition against customs that do not affect our salvation. Gradually

---

7. Ibid., 22–23.

people's minds will become enlightened to the truth, and they will see less necessity for rigid caste and social customs.[8]

According to this line of reasoning, the New Testament neither confirms nor condemns social customs, regardless of how devastating they may be for a given group of people. For, if all simply live in accordance with the gospel, eventually the questionable customs will change. But until peoples' minds become gradually enlightened, the requirement is to patiently endure the inhumanity to which one or her group is subjected.

D. S. Warner advocated a church of holiness and unity, "both a spiritual and visible union."[9] Warner also declared: "Many may say we need more union of hearts, but think a visible organic union unnecessary; but remember that it was a visible organic union that Jesus prayed for, *such as the world could see and be thereby convinced and saved.*"[10] Every way I read this latter clarification of the type of unity Warner had in mind, I am left with the sense that it is inclusive of unity along racial lines, although I know of no place that Warner himself verbalized or wrote explicitly about such an expansion of the visible unity principle.

Byrum's interpretation and advice, as well as that given by Blaney and other Movement whites, was nothing short of a capitulation or narrowing of the principle of visible unity, and an accommodation to the shallow ethics of the nation that easily permitted, indeed encouraged, segregation of the races. The advice of Byrum and his supporters—and he apparently had many white supporters—made the Church of God Reformation Movement a church of racists, and essentially of sectarians, since by Warner's own definition, sectism is *anything* that is divisive in the church. Nothing is more divisive in church and world than racial prejudice, inasmuch as it alienates or segregates two or more groups of people from each other *and* from God. All of this was also an undermining of the meaning and importance of the holiness principle.

By the second stage of the group's natural life cycle then, many white Movement people were somehow unable or unwilling to see the contradiction in their teaching on holiness and visible unity on the one hand, and their encouragement and practice of racial division on the other. They essentially sacrificed the ethics of holiness and visible unity on the altar of spiritual and denominational unity. Holiness and visible unity were sacrificed for societal acceptance. Whites wanted spiritual and denominational unity, but were much less concerned about unity along racial lines, even in

---

8. Blaney, "The Unity of the Spirit," 11.
9. Byers, *Birth of a Reformation*, 236.
10. Ibid., 235 (my emphasis).

the church. Indeed, in 1909 James E. Forrest even argued in "Bible Unity and the Color Line" that racial prejudice or disunity in society is consistent with biblical unity, i.e., that the latter may tolerate the societal practice of racial discrimination. One can focus on biblical unity, and not worry about racial division supported by civil law. What was important for Forrest was spiritual, *not* visible unity along racial lines. Consequently, he argued that biblical unity is achieved, not necessarily when there is a visible gathering of believers of all races, but only when there is evidence of spiritual unity.[11] Accordingly, Forrest wrote:

> But what is unity? Is it fulfilled when we have thus literally assembled in one great body? I ask, Does this constitute Scriptural oneness? If this were true, then a union meeting of a number of sects would fulfil the Word. But not so. It is true that such a visible gathering of the saints into an assembly is beautiful and enjoyable, and is a witness in favor of unity; but if such a gathering does not necessarily constitute any part of the real unity, then the absence of this practice will not necessarily destroy or ever affect Bible unity. Here is unity: 'one mind and mouth' (Rom. 15: 5, 6); 'one faith' and practice (Eph. 4:4; Jude 3; Phil. 1:27. By the Holy Spirit we are all baptized into *one body* (1 Cor. 12:13), therefore this body is a spiritual body.[12]

The problem with denominational and spiritual unity as the sole unity emphasis is that it may be seen as being exclusive of certain races and other groups. This point did not seem to trouble Forrest, who had no problem with the practice of adjusting to prevailing social customs. "Things can be lawful and yet not be expedient," he wrote (1 Cor. 10:23). "The great apostle confesses that he made himself a servant of prevailing conditions, and adjusted himself to circumstances and to the different peoples of his day, that he might accomplish the more good."[13] Forrest then invited his readers to study 1 Cor. 9:19–23. But he was not finished yet, as he proceeded to argue that the interracial congregation might even hinder the work of the church. I personally find his illustration of the point to be chilling and disheartening at best. Said Forrest:

> A short time ago while in the South holding a meeting in a certain place, a lady several miles distant who was a stranger to us and to the truth itself, started to the place of meeting, but on her way was told by an enemy of the truth that there were

11. Forrest, "Bible Unity and the Color Line," 6.
12. Ibid.
13. Ibid., 7.

> more negroes in attendance than whites, and it so affected her that she turned aside and did not come to the meeting. It was a falsehood—only one colored person had been near, and he had humbly sat on the outside one night to listen to the Word; and the fact is, at no time had there such a scene as the persons had described to the lady. You may say that she was prejudiced and will never get to heaven that way. That may be true, but it takes salvation to deliver people from it and if conditions are such as to be uninviting to them and we never succeed in getting them to the meeting, how will they ever get saved? It is a demonstrated fact that in some places we shall utterly fail to get the truth to the white people with a mixed congregation, therefore our only alternative is to adjust ourselves to prevailing conditions, and humbly labor accordingly, that we may 'by all means save some.'[14]

Without question, interracial unity in the church was less important to Forrest than saving individual white people who were racially prejudiced, while giving no indication of desiring to extricate themselves from racism. How else does one explain the existence of such a high incidence of racism in the Movement, then and now? Furthermore, focusing primarily on the spiritual unity that Forrest called for could be seen as a convenient way of discouraging interracial unity in the church. Indeed, this most assuredly was—and continues to be—the case.

We can see that with the advent of the second stage of the group's development, the leadership becomes concerned about matters that the first generation paid little attention to—such as setting up procedures to address concerns of the group—possibly because of their zeal and excitement to just get the message out and essentially to develop a following. In the case of the Movement, this may be illustrated by considering the race question during the time of Warner, followed by the advent of the second generation of Church of God leadership. What was the response of the first and second generations to the issue of race?

EARLY CONCERN ABOUT RACE

During the first fifteen years of the Church of God Movement there was little public concern raised in the group about blacks and whites worshipping together or about existing segregation laws. For example, early Church of God literature is not replete with concerns as to whether the races should

14. Ibid.

be worshipping together. Some whites, and most blacks, seemed to assume that worshipping together was simply to be expected in a church that was founded on the principles of holiness and visible unity. They were, after all, the church of unity. However, James Earl Massey observes that as early as 1893 (two years *before* Warner's death), a concern was raised and reported in the August 3 issue of *The Gospel Trumpet* about some who wanted "to develop a separate white congregation" in Augusta, Georgia.[15] The seeds of division along racial lines were already present in the group, less than a decade after its founding. During this same period, however, there were reports from whites and blacks who wanted to worship together as one body,[16] although it was not clear that whites were advocating interracial worship that would be free of the legally required segregation. After all, it was the custom that the two groups would be physically segregated in the house of the Lord. We saw before that sometimes a rope down the center aisle was the dividing line; sometimes blacks had to sit in the back and-or in the balcony. Nevertheless, very soon after Warner's death, a growing literature began to appear about the tenability of whites and blacks worshipping together. Concerns were being raised about the need for Movement practice to be brought into line with civil law and practice in the wider society.

With the death of Warner, a new leadership came into existence. We saw in chapter 1 that in 1897, barely two years after Warner's death, the question of the races mingling together in the church became a heated issue. More and more in the field reports submitted to *The Gospel Trumpet*, there was evidence of concern over the issue of interracial worship in different localities throughout the country, especially, but not only, in the South. By 1901, for example, it was apparent that some Movement leaders were concerned about the race issue and practices of racial discrimination in and outside the church. When Robert E. Lee, "pioneer of the colored work in Florida" in 1901, inquired of local white Movement leaders whether he could attend the state camp meeting, he was told that he could, but "under certain restrictions."[17] Not long after Lee arrived, racism showed its ugly face through the innocence of a white child. "A little girl who had never seen a real black man before saw Brother Lee and she ran to her mother crying, 'Mama, don't let the devil get me! Please, mama!'"[18] Where else would a child have gotten the idea that the devil is black, and therefore a black man must be the devil, than from its parent(s), other family members, and neighbors?

15. Massey, *African Americans and the Church of God*, 28.
16. Ibid., 29.
17. Berry, *Golden Jubilee Book*, 36.
18. Lee, Letter to Berry for the *Golden Jubilee Book*, 36.

Frederick G. Smith, who followed E. E. Byrum as editor of *The Gospel Trumpet*, revealed his concern about the race question, writing: "May God hasten the time when all race prejudice may be obliterated, and every soul for whom Christ died be recognized as precious in his sight, and a worthy recipient of the redemption grace purchased in the death of our Savior."[19] Remember, however, that even during Warner's time—which was during the first stage of the group's life cycle—there were some Movement people—whites and blacks—who were not much concerned about obeying the broader society's race discrimination policy and practice, and thus worshipped together as sisters and brothers. Such a stance, although not consistently held by many whites, was a sure indicator of impending trouble.

Although there was no explicit effort on the part of Warner and others to make an issue of the race question or to even make a firm and determined public commitment against the inhumane treatment of blacks, as John Winebrenner did in the 1830s, it can at least be said that built into the teaching on holiness and visible unity was an implicit stance against racism and in favor of strong interracial relations.[20] This is about the most that one can say about the pioneer leadership's interracial stance. It is not even clear whether there was a consistent and conscious effort by white leaders during the first generation to actually evangelize blacks. John W. V. Smith reminds us that, "in the first decade no special point was made of the racial issue; the message was preached and black people responded and were accepted."[21] Merle Strege contends similarly: "The early Church of God was one of the very few groups to ignore the color line drawn through much of American Protestantism. This feature drew African Americans to the Church of God movement."[22] Elsewhere, Strege names Rufus J. Smith (1864–1925) as a southern Afrikan American who was attracted to the Movement by its teaching on unity, with its implications for racial inclusion.[23] But it is not evident from these statements that any special appeals were made to blacks to join the Movement. Moreover, in chapter two of his mostly excellent book, *I Saw the Church: The Life of the Church of God as Told Theologically* (2002), Strege focuses on Warner's theology, but fails to even suggest implications of that theology for the racism that was (and is) pervasive in the nation, as well as the churches. Furthermore, we will see that there is

---

19. Quoted Smith, *The Quest for Holiness and Unity*, 162–63. Frederick G. Smith wrote this in the preface to Schell, *Is the Negro a Beast?*, 10.

20. Ibid., 162.

21. Ibid.

22. Strege, *I Saw the Church*, 122.

23. Ibid., 81–82.

no strong extant evidence that the Movement, or any white religious group, ever entirely "ignored the color line." John W. V. Smith and Strege were more accurate in the claim that blacks heard the holiness-visible unity message of Movement pioneers, and simply joined the group. Right or wrong, blacks instinctively believed this message to be consistent with the unity message of the Bible which, in their thinking, meant that there was to be no forced separation along racial lines, in or outside the church. Black people thought (or hoped!) that the holiness-visible unity message was entirely against racial separation; that whatever else the message was about, it was about blacks and whites worshipping together as one, on the basis of equality.

Massey contends that there were a few whites who, after Warner's death, made it unequivocally clear that racism was inconsistent with the Movement's teaching on holiness and unity, and in this regard they tended to uphold blacks in the Movement. This, Massey maintains—under the influence of the Movement party line—is what William G. Schell (a white Movement minister) attempted to do in his book, *Is The Negro a Beast?* (1901). Here, Schell took issue with Charles Carroll's derogatory book, *The Negro a Beast*. Carroll's thesis was that blacks were beasts and inhuman; at best they were subhuman. Carroll also argued that the Bible was against black-white intermarriage. Schell, considered by Louisiana blacks to have shown them "much kindness," sought to prove the equality of all persons before God, as well as to call attention to Carroll's misuse of the Bible. Schell's "belief in the equality of blacks and whites," Massey writes, "was ably demonstrated both in his book and in his relations with blacks in his ministry."[24] Massey seems certain that Schell was an example of a white Movement pioneer who, according to John W. V. Smith (who Massey quotes approvingly), exhibited "very concerned effort . . . to support and uphold their black brothers."[25] Black Movement people in Louisiana, at least, believed Schell to be a white leader who was intentional about advocating unity along racial lines, as well as the principle of the equality of all races.

Church of God historian, Gary B. Agee, takes issue with claims about Schell's alleged belief in racial equality. In the 2015 Harp Lecture at the Anderson University School of Theology, "Seeing the Church of God in Black and White: The Church of God Reformation Movement and the Color Line, 1880–1920," Agee argued that in comparison to Schell's response to Charles Carroll's book, W. S. Armistead sought to discredit Carroll's claim that the Bible is against amalgamation between the races. In addition, Agee found that there is no evidence that Schell advocated full social equality for blacks

---

24. Massey, *African Americans and the Church of God*, 44.
25. Quoted in ibid., 44.

in relation to whites, as John W. V. Smith claimed.[26] Smith also failed to say that Schell uncritically espoused the party line against interracial marriage in his book, which seemed to overshadow what he said about the equality of blacks to whites under God.

Fascinated by Agee's claim that Armistead found no biblical evidence against intermarriage based on race, I felt compelled to read Armistead's book, *The Negro is a Man* (1903). Armistead did indeed succeed in proving to his own satisfaction that nowhere in the Bible is there condemnation of race intermingling on the basis of the color line. The marriage that was displeasing to God, he argued, was not that between people of different skin colors or races, but between the holy and unholy, believers and unbelievers, the righteous and the unrighteous. Nowhere in the Bible, Armistead maintained, is intermarriage drawn at the color line, but only on the basis of morals and religion.[27] Furthermore he said: "The very fact that Jesus made all nations that dwell on all the face of the earth of 'one blood' is very strong presumptive evidence that race intermingling was anticipated by God."[28] Armistead was certain that the fact that there is but one blood makes amalgamation impossible, and only an "ignoramus" would say otherwise.[29] After all, it would be intermixing of the same blood. In addition, having examined the work of scholarly scientists such as Charles Darwin, Thomas Huxley, Ernst Haeckel, Alfred Russell Wallace, Jean Baptiste Lamarck, and Carl Linnaeus he concluded that comparative anatomy demonstrates conclusively that blacks and whites were derived from a common parentage, which proves the truth of "racial unity."[30] Armistead saw no anatomical difference between blacks and whites. The structure of the brain of whites and blacks is essentially the same. In addition, he found that the reasoning powers of whites and blacks are the same; and the powers are used in the same way.[31] Blacks have a soul and moral nature, just as whites, and this makes them as much human beings, not beasts.

And yet sadly, Armistead was as much against amalgamation between blacks and whites as Carroll and Movement pioneers. He based his stance, not on race, but on geographical or continental separation. One quote from his book will have to suffice.

---

26. Smith, *The Quest for Holiness and Unity*, 163.

27. Armistead, *The Negro Is a Man*, XII. See also XX, 149, 152. Armistead's full argument and defense of this position is in chap. VI.

28. Ibid., 151.

29. Ibid., 85.

30. Ibid., 345–48.

31. Ibid., 496.

> While it is true that God interposed no *scriptural* barrier based on *physical differences*, He having 'made of *one blood* all the nations of men that dwell on the earth' (Acts 17); yet, it is equally true that God, 'in scattering the race upon the face of the whole earth,' and interposing *continental barriers*, signified, aye, expressed in no uncertain terms, His *willingness*, aye, His *imperative desire*, that *race intermingling* or *intermarriage*, *should* not *take place*. Else why separate the nations by much natural, and, withal, formidable barriers to such intermingling.[32]

God, in this view, isolated Afrika from other continents in order to prevent amalgamation, and because God presumably is against it, Armistead vowed to never advocate what God prohibits.[33] Moreover, and not unlike most white southerners of the period, he was careful to point out that he was not arguing for social and political equality between whites and blacks.[34] Indeed, although Armistead proved, against Carroll, that blacks are not beasts, and that the Bible is not against intermarriage based on race, he was infected with his own brand of racism.

The real issue, Armistead claimed, was not amalgamation between blacks and whites, but the rapes of white women by black men. "Were there no other argument against social equality of whites and blacks," Armistead proclaimed, "I would urge the brutality of such outrageous conduct as evidence of the strongest character that the blacks were not prepared for such social relations with the whites."[35] He argued, quite wrongheadedly of course, that white men never raped black women, and that any sexual relations between them, during and after slavery, was generally consensual; that "such association is sought by the white, and conceded by the colored woman or girl, of her own free will, and rarely is it ever, under any circumstances, forced."[36] The continued alleged rape of white women by black men, Armistead argued, only assures the latter's extermination.[37] Indeed, in the latter part of the nineteenth century and the first years of the twentieth, much of the white South and other parts of the country were under the illusion that black men were being lynched in such high numbers because of their rape of white women. But then, Ida B. Wells came along and waged a one person campaign against this myth. She proved conclusively that

32. Ibid., 537.
33. Ibid., 538.
34. Ibid., 536, 539.
35. Ibid., 540.
36. Ibid., 541.
37. Ibid., 541–42.

the reason given for the lynchings was nothing but a sham for keeping the recently "emancipated" blacks in a state of perpetual social, political, and economic inequality.[38]

In any event, the very thing that Schell and other Movement pioneers were so concerned about, i.e., amalgamation, was shown convincingly by Armistead not to be rejected by the Bible; that the only concern would be if the intermarriages led God's people to turn away from God.[39] But again, this would be a religious, not a color line problem. Consequently, one is forced to ask: If the Bible does not repudiate intermarriage on the basis of race or color, why did Movement pioneers do so with such frequency and passion?

To his credit, Armistead showed that according to the Bible there is both racial unity and social equality between blacks and whites, for God created blacks and whites as equals. And, he maintained, Jesus did not come to destroy that equality, or "to re-establish barriers between the whites and blacks, reds, yellows, and browns, for there never were any such barriers erected by God."[40] Nowhere in the Bible is there evidence of God inserting whites over blacks; of God making whites the superiors to blacks. However, Armistead concluded against the social equality of the two races because of his ridiculous view that black men—unlike white men in relation to black women—were indiscriminately raping white women on a massive scale.

Nevertheless, Agee is convinced that Movement pioneers were less than stellar when it came to the matter of race, and that they focused primarily on spiritual unity. They essentially ignored interracial unity, thus allowing the color line to be drawn in the church. Indeed, Agee contends that Movement pioneers failed to even see the social implications of the visible unity message relative to racial segregation in and beyond the church,[41] a point with which I wholeheartedly agree. Blacks might well have seen and made the interracial connection to the visible unity teaching even before most Movement pioneers.

And yet, there is something to be said for Schell's stance. In light of the time period, and considering that most Movement people lacked the

38. See Wells, *Crusade for Justice*, 70–71; chaps. 8, 9, and entire book.
39. Armistead, *The Negro Is a Man*, 152.
40. Ibid., 153.
41. Agee, "Seeing the Church of God in Black and White." Agee raises concerns about Movement pioneers and the color line similar to those in this book. It is hoped that as a trained historian he will be able to uncover further evidence to support my argument, as well as his own stance. I am much encouraged by this revisionist work being done by a white Movement scholar at the Anderson University School of Theology. Movement members who are aware of his work should be even more encouraged.

courage to take a public stance against racial disunity in the church and society, Schell's position was more progressive than most, and would have been even more so had he not been poisoned by the amalgamation doctrine. It is known that many whites in virtually every part of the United States—even many of those who had anti-enslavement and abolitionist sentiments—were utterly against the idea of treating blacks as the equals of whites. This was evident in—and even before—the seventeenth century. During this time, there was "a widespread and deeply planted belief in the inferiority of the Negro, whether slave or free."[42]

Many whites—south and north—who supported and even fought for abolition did not favor granting blacks full citizenship, with all the rights thereto pertaining. There are numerous examples of this, not least Samuel Sewall who, in 1700 wrote an anti-enslavement tract in Massachusetts strongly criticizing those engaged in the slavery business. But at the same time, Sewall "maintained that Negroes were inferior beings for whom there was no place in white society."[43] Many whites believed that blacks were permanently and irreversibly inferior to them.[44] This contradiction, i.e., insisting on the one hand that blacks should be emancipated, and on the other, that whites are their natural superiors, continued into and beyond the twentieth century. Indeed, it continues at this writing. There continues to be whites, in and out of the churches, who publicly criticize the most blatant forms of racism, but at the same time, find it impossible to see or think of Afrikan Americans as their equals. Many would like to think that this is less of a problem in the North. Such persons need to think again. I would suggest looking back to the period of slavery in this country, and considering why so many whites in states such as Ohio, Michigan, Illinois, and Indiana—all northern states!—fought so hard against abolition. One reason for the sympathy of many whites toward the system of slavery in these states was that they were heavily populated with southerners who migrated there, taking with them their white supremacist beliefs and practices. Therefore, a great deal of the southern mentality regarding race found its way into northern states and into the churches as well. This is a point we need to remember in any discussion on race relations in the Movement.

The problem of race, from the inception of the Movement to the present, was never just a southern problem. We will see that while there were serious issues regarding race among southern white Movement people, the same was evident in Anderson, Indiana and other places in the North. In

42. Ratner, *Powder Keg*, 5.
43. Ibid., 10.
44. Kolchin, *American Slavery 1619–1877*, 192.

fact, the state of Indiana was one of several states "carved out of the Northwest Territory—Illinois, Ohio, Wisconsin and Michigan—[that] attempted to prohibit the entrance and settlement of blacks."[45] According to state of Indiana historian, the late Emma Lou Thornbrough, the issue for the state during and beyond the nineteenth century was neither proslavery nor antislavery, but "anti-Negro." Whites hated blacks and did not want them locating to *their* state.

> There were few persons who wanted to see slavery introduced into the state, but there was widespread and intense race prejudice and fear of the competition of Negro labor—due in part to the fact that a large part of the population of Indiana came from the nonslaveholding class of southern whites. The result was a proscriptive code designed to keep the small Negro population in an inferior position and to prevent the settlement of Negroes from the slave states.[46]

The theme of "anti-Negro" or hatred of blacks is carried through in two subsequent books by Thornbrough: *The Negro in Indiana Before 1900*[47] and *Indiana Blacks in the Twentieth Century*.[48] Whites resented the idea of blacks coming to the Hoosier state. "They steadfastly believed this to be a white man's country and fought to preserve Indiana as a white man's state . . . The Indiana legislature enacted the Black Law of 1831 to discourage black settlement. The law required all blacks in the state to register with county authorities and to post a $500 bond as a guarantee of good behavior and as an added protection against their becoming public charges."[49] When all else failed, whites turned to vicious violence against blacks, committed by mobs *and* the police. "The number of lynchings in the state during the 1890s reached an all time high."[50] In *Southern Horrors* (1892) Ida B. Wells documented this tragic phenomenon in the South that saw its peak in 1892.[51]

The state of Indiana's hatred of blacks may shed some light on the confrontation between whites and blacks at the Church of God Camp Meeting in Anderson in 1912. This should not be taken to mean, however, that the anti-black sentiment existed only (or even primarily!) in white Movement people in Indiana, despite that state's reputation for lynching blacks. Indeed,

45. Clark Hine, *When the Truth Is Told*, 10.
46. Thornbrough, *Indiana in the Civil War Era 1850–1880*, 13–14.
47. Thornbrough, *The Negro in Indiana before 1900*.
48. Thornbrough, *Indiana Blacks in the Twentieth Century*.
49. Clark Hine, *When the Truth is Told*, 10.
50. Ibid., 12.
51. See Jones Royster, ed., *Southern Horrors and Other Writings*.

it is even known that in the fourteenth meeting of the Indiana Eldership of the Churches of God, October 26, 1859, the Eldership denounced slavery in the strongest possible terms, "as 'a curse upon our country; an evil detrimental to all our relations and interests, and a very evil, uncivil and unchristian system.'"[52] It is not known whether Eldership members possessed the same anti-black sentiment as most Hoosiers.

In the previous chapter, we saw that in 1890 Warner himself was the victim of vicious attacks by mobs, presumably because of his preaching on Christian unity, including interracial unity and holiness during the evangelistic tour in Beech Springs and other places in Mississippi. Warner himself reported: "Brothers Bradley and Bozeman have both been threatened in that place with violence and, we believe, even with murder, and we could expect the same animus toward us. Hence, the second night several pieces of brick and clubs came crashing through the window, all doubtless hurled in wrath at us. Nearly half of the sash was broken in and the glass flew over the house."[53] Barry Callen contends that the mobsters were enraged "because Warner showed no discrimination toward Black persons in his public meetings or his visitation of the sick."[54]

Beginning with Charles Brown's history of the Movement, *When the Trumpet Sounded*, the acceptable party line has been that, what angered white racists in Mississippi had not only to do with the *implications* for racial unity in Warner's teaching on visible unity and holiness. Rather, Brown, and a host of subsequent writers on the Movement, e.g., John W. V. Smith, Merle Strege, Barry Callen, and James Earl Massey, all claim that Warner was attacked precisely because of his strong sermonic rebukes of racism and injustice against blacks. This implies that while in Mississippi, Warner preached explicitly and uncompromisingly against racial division and injustice toward blacks.

In chapter 3, we saw that oral history in the form of reports provided in letters to Charles Brown reportedly verified this point, although at this writing all efforts to locate those letters have failed. Indeed, I have searched in vain for evidence that Warner himself named friendliness toward blacks,

52. Forney, *History of the Churches of God*, 430.

53. Byers, *Birth of a Reformation*, 390.

54. Callen, *Preparing for Service*, 65. I wish Callen had provided definitive documentation for this claim. Ironically, seventy years later (after Warner was mobbed in that part of Mississippi) J. Horace Germany, the white Movement pastor who founded Bay Ridge Christian College in Mississippi, was savagely beaten by henchmen of Governor Ross Barnett and members of the KKK and left for dead in Union, Mississippi during the civil rights movement. Bay Ridge Christian College sought to provide leadership development for blacks in what was arguably the most violently racist state in the nation.

and-or preaching for their justice as a cause for the mob attacks. This might well have been *a* cause, but the evidence has not been produced that either Warner or other white pioneers actually said so. In addition, when Warner wrote of Bradley and Bozeman being threatened in Mississippi, he did not say that it was because of their friendliness and openness to blacks. One is left with the sense that the threats occurred because of their preaching on entire sanctification as a second blessing, and possibly because of their preaching against tobacco usage and consumption of alcohol.

Moreover, I find it both interesting and telling that Andrew Byers (who joined Warner on the Mississippi tour after Sarah Smith had to drop out[55]) said nothing at all about the attacks occurring *because* of Warner's stance on race.[56] We have seen that even white Mississippians, who wrote about the tour and the persecutions Warner suffered, said nothing about blacks even being in attendance at any of the meetings, let alone about Warner's alleged preaching about justice for them.[57] One sees a similar tendency in Henry C. Wickersham, *A History of the Church* (1900). Writing about the persecution of Warner and his team during the Mississippi tour, Wickersham provides not even a hint that they were attacked because of Warner's alleged friendliness and openness toward blacks and his presumed preaching against racism in the church. Nor does he allude to blacks being in attendance at one or more of the meetings.[58] In addition, although Mother Sarah Smith was with Warner and the evangelistic company of five for a brief period during the Mississippi tour, she said nothing in the brief autobiography she submitted to Wickersham (to be included in his book) about Warner's stance on race or that he was ever attacked because of his openness to blacks. Indeed, she did not even mention the Mississippi tour.[59] William G. Schell's (along with Charles Orr's) is the longest of the autobiographical statements included in Wickersham's book (about 27 pages each). Schell made not a single reference to blacks or Warner's ministry with them, or his alleged "concerned effort" to uphold them. Not a single one of the thirteen brief biographies and autobiographies reference blacks or race in any way.

These omissions are truly puzzling, considering that the party line is that Movement pioneers had a zeal for interracial unity that only began to wane in the early years of the twentieth century. It would seem that one

---

55. Byers, *Birth of a Reformation*, 394n.

56. See Byers' discussion on the Mississippi tour in ibid., 389–96.

57. See letter to Byers from Mrs. Demaris (Smith) Vance in *Birth of a Reformation*, 466

58. See Wickersham's discussion of the persecutions during the Mississippi tour in *A History of the Church*, 297–99.

59. See Smith's brief autobiography in Wickersham, *A History of the Church*, 301–13.

would be excited to talk about such exuberance whenever the opportunity presented itself, and it surely would be the kind of news one would want to share in field reports to *The Gospel Trumpet*. If Warner and early white Movement people said nothing about him being attacked because he allegedly welcomed blacks and preached on interracial unity, one wonders whether there is evidence that black Mississippians spoke of this.

BLACK MISSISSIPPIANS AND D. S. WARNER

In the 1980s black Movement Mississippian Rosetta Rush, approaching the century age mark, told Church of God minister Rev. Glenn Hall, that as a little girl she went with her mother to hear D. S. Warner preach. Rush recalled that the most unusual thing about the experience was that, "There was a colored brother with him."[60] It is not apparent how much is to be made of this since nothing is recorded about the "colored" brother's role, or the relationship between the two men. What we do know is that if the man had been Warner's servant it would not have been unusual at all for him to have accompanied Warner, even in Post-Reconstruction racist Mississippi. Rush's statement implies that there was a much different relationship between the two men; perhaps even a relationship of mutual respect and equality. *This* most assuredly would have been unusual for that time and place. Unfortunately, Hall apparently did not press Rush for more information, and if he did, it is not recorded in his book. Moreover, even had he pressed her for more information she might not have been able to remember details about that day many decades earlier. Of course, it would have been a boon for the Movement had Hall asked (and Rush was able to respond to the question of) whether she remembered anything of substance that Warner might have said about interracial unity during his sermon; whether other blacks were in attendance; and whether Warner was attacked because of it. All we know for certain from Rush's statement is that at least two local blacks (Rush and her mother), and the black man who accompanied Warner, were in attendance at the worship service.

Hall further stimulates our curiosity when he introduces readers to Ozzie (Garrett) Wattleton (1915–2015).[61] The daughter of Eugene Garrett, Wattleton served as a Church of God minister for 75 years in the Farmhaven

---

60. Quoted in Hall, *The Mississippi Reformation Movement*, 23.

61. In a telephone conversation on April 26, 2015, James Earl Massey told me a second time that at Wattleton's earlier request he preached her funeral. He also reiterated that he had known the family for many years.

district in Mississippi.⁶² Said to have an excellent memory, even at the age of 93, Wattleton confirmed that Warner and his evangelistic team came to Mississippi knowing in advance that there were many who rejected their teaching on unity. "They set up at Union [Mississippi]," Wattleton told Hall, "inviting both whites and black" [sic].⁶³ Apparently recalling what her father told her, Wattleton reported that when Garrett was eighteen years old one of the ministers traveling with Warner's evangelistic team, Robert H. Owen,⁶⁴ returned to Mississippi in 1895 and addressed blacks in the Farmhaven district.⁶⁵ Eugene Garrett heard Owen preach and was converted under him.⁶⁶ C. E. Brown contends that not long after Owen began the vocation of ministry "he was threatened with the same kind of persecution Warner had endured."⁶⁷ If Owen preached to blacks in 1895 this would have been four years after Warner's tour, and if Wattleton was right about her father's age he would have been thirteen or fourteen years old during Warner's tour in Mississippi. This means that he might well have heard Warner preach at that time. However, Wattleton was silent as to whether her father ever heard Warner preach, or what he might have remembered others saying about Warner and the Mississippi tour.

Although what Hall reports in his book is fresh material it does not tell us whether blacks heard Warner preach on interracial unity and justice for them, and whether they believed he was attacked *because* of such preaching. Despite the fact that Hall did not obtain more relevant information during his conversations with Rush and Wattleton, he provides an important service for Church of God historians and other researchers on blacks in the Church of God. He puts these on notice that much more attention and energy must be devoted to recording the memories of elderly black Mississippians and other Deep South blacks who know first or second-handedly of blacks' experience with Warner and other Movement pioneers. Because of the age factor, however, time is of the essence to record such memories,

---

62. Hall, *The Mississippi Reformation Movement*, 24, 142.

63. Quoted in ibid., 24.

64. In a telephone conversation with Massey on May 1, 2015, he reported that Owen was the white minister to whom Wattleton referred. Charles E. Brown provides a good discussion on Owen, his relationship with Warner, and on his ministry in Louisiana and other places in the South. See *When the Trumpet Sounded*, 157–59.

65. Hall, *The Mississippi Reformation Movement*, 24.

66. This information was provided by Massey in a phone conversation on May 1, 2015.

67. Brown, *When the Trumpet Sounded*, 158.

and it might already be too late. The trained historian or other scholar will have a good sense of the types of questions that should be asked.[68]

In Appendix-A, I have included a letter from James Earl Massey which shares some of his reflections on black Mississippians and Warner. He also writes about the importance of the oral tradition in all of this. Like this writer, Massey rejects the tendency of some to uncritically privilege written literature over the oral tradition, particularly when written evidence is inadequate or even nonexistent, as regarding whether Warner was attacked in Mississippi because of friendliness toward blacks and preaching on interracial unity. See Appendix-B for a more extended discussion on the importance of oral tradition and written literature and how they may be mutually reinforcing.

When I look at the long sweep of US history and the problem of race, I am loath to say that one or two mild responses that Warner gave regarding race are *conclusive* evidence that he—unlike most whites of his day and since—fully and substantively supported the full equality of the races. I simply have not seen the evidence that Warner thought that far and deeply about matters of race. I wish there were more evidence in Warner's extant writings that he made conscious, sustained efforts to relate his teaching on visible unity to the race question. As it stands, Warner does not compare with John Winebrenner in this regard, despite the fact that Winebrenner later relinquished his earlier prophetic stance against the enslavement of blacks for a much softer, moderate position. Why was Warner so quiescent about interracial unity in the church?

Indeed, Massey himself has written that Warner was aware of the dissension that arose because of John Winebrenner's earlier, more forceful stance, that involuntary slavery was a sin and that church members would not be permitted to engage in the practice, and would be excommunicated if they did. Accordingly, Warner appears to have opted not to allow such a storm to arise in the Church of God under his leadership. "Perhaps he reasoned that, while he would honor his conscience by acting out his belief in equality of the races," Massey writes, Warner "did not need to speak out against or write about the then-current issue of how newly freed blacks in the land were being segregated and discriminated against."[69] The merit in this explanation is that it may help to explain why, in part, there is so little evidence of explicit references to race in Warner's writings and sermons.

---

68. I wrote to Hall on May 4, 2015, and inquired as to whether he could share anything else that was told him by Rush and-or Wattleton, or anybody else he might have interviewed. Sadly, Hall did not acknowledge receipt of my letter, a copy of which is in my files.

69. Massey, *African Americans and the Church of God*, 15.

However, it also lets Warner and many other whites off the moral hook. This is the downside of Massey's explanation. If Warner recognized segregation and discrimination against blacks as a sin and an injustice, as a Christian minister he should have spoken against it. Warner's approach was inconsistent with the prophetic tradition of the church. For it seems to me that if he chose to make racism a matter of individual conscience alone, he (not unlike Alexander Campbell of the Disciples of Christ[70]) sought to separate his conscience from that of the church. There should be mutual accountability and responsibility between individual Christians and the church. This is an Anabaptist stance, which I discuss at length in the final chapter. Furthermore, if Massey's line of thought is correct about the reason Warner chose not to write or speak publicly about race, it is reasonable to wonder what black Movement people would have advised had Warner sought their advice on the matter. And this is a matter on which Warner would have been well advised to have sought the counsel of black Movement people.

Massey might well be correct in claiming that because of Warner's joining of the two core principles of holiness and visible unity as fundamental needs in the church, *he* "did not discriminate against black believers."[71] However, it must also be said that Warner's individualized approach opened the door for others in the Movement to discriminate, since the church itself was apparently not held to the same standard as Warner. This meant that individuals in the church could decide the matter for themselves. However, the truth is that if racism was wrong for D. S. Warner, it most assuredly should have been wrong for the church and its members. As noted above, and will be explored more fully in chapter 7, what was needed here was a sense of mutual accountability and responsibility.

Let us remember that *during the second sociological stage of a religious group's life cycle the leadership is more likely to be influenced by the winds of prevailing secular practices,* since the leaders typically have less enthusiasm for, and are no longer preoccupied with, the principles and convictions of the founder and pioneers, to the extent they were. It is also during this stage that there arises a desire to form an organizational structure(s) in order to sustain and perpetuate the group and its ideas. This, we have seen, is a denomination and church-like trait, which means that the group begins to

---

70. Alexander Campbell was at best a gradualist abolitionist who believed the practice of forced enslavement to be a social and political, not theological or moral, issue. This religious leader made no attempt to give a theological or moral argument against the cruel practice of enslavement. By and large he considered it to be no business of the church. See McAllister, *An Alexander Campbell Reader*, 90–91. Campbell essentially advocated for a church that supported slavery.

71. Massey, *African Americans and the Church of God*, 15.

take on a much different look than during the sect stage of the charismatic leader.

In addition, as observed previously, the second generation is concerned with interpreting the meaning of the founder's core principles and beliefs, and while doing so is quite mindful of, and frequently influenced by, prevailing social and legal customs. The result, commonly, is that there will be a tendency to soften and-or compromise those principles. At best, an effort may be made to interpret the principles such that they will be acceptable to the wider society. This is something that the founder generally does not permit. Such a one tends to insist that his newfound truth is the only way. This was certainly Warner's stance regarding entire sanctification and visible unity. But with Warner gone from the scene, it was nearly impossible to escape some coloration or softening of the interpretation of these core principles during the second phase.

Because the group becomes concerned about the *forming of an enduring organization* during the second stage of its lifecycle, it starts to take on the characteristics of a denomination or church. H. Richard Niebuhr offers an instructive comment in this regard, saying: "The church as an inclusive social group is closely allied with national, economic, and cultural interests; by the very nature of its constitution it is committed to the accommodation of its ethics to the ethics of civilization; it must represent the morality of the respectable majority, not of the heroic minority."[72] The "heroic minority," in this case, represents the group in its first stage when it would not have compromised its ethic. What typically follows as the group proceeds through the second phase is a tendency to compromise its own higher principles and to accommodate more and more to the ethic of society. This is what happened in the Church of God as well. As second generation leaders sought to sustain the group through the institutionalization or routinization of its core principles and ideals, these were watered down or compromised as the group sought to be more accommodating to the wider society. In the sociology of religion the process that leads to this state of affairs is referred to as the *routinization of charisma*, which helps to solidify the group's place in the world. What does such routinization entail?

THE ROUTINIZATION OR INSTITUTIONALIZATION OF CHARISMA

Charismatic authority—prevalent in the first stage of a group's life cycle—tends to be unstable. Therefore, if the new religious group, its ideals, norms,

72. Niebuhr, *The Social Sources of Denominationalism*, 18.

and practices are to survive for more than a few years, it will be necessary for these to become institutionalized. That is, an organization needs to be formed. In the event this does not happen, it is likely that the group will not survive.

If a new religious group is to survive beyond the first stage of its life cycle, it will be during the second stage of the transformation that *charisma begins to be routinized*. That is, there is the beginning of a development of a stable set of roles, routines, and norms to guide the practices of the members. Signs begin to appear showing that what was previously charisma is now being transformed into bureaucratic or organizational forms. With the diminished fervor and excitement of the first generation, and frequently after the death of the founder, the previous charismatically-led group falls into a routine, i.e., a stabilization of ideals and practices, usually characterized by the development of some structure or organization. This inevitably causes the group's alliance with tradition, culture, and the wider society. It also puts the group on a course to become an established sect or denomination. As charismatic authority diminishes or the leader dies, there is a tendency toward the "depersonalization of charisma," either through transferability to another leader, or by becoming "a component of everyday life" through an institutional structure. Charisma, in other words, becomes transformed into an organization: "as permanent structures and traditions replace the belief in the revelation and heroism of charismatic personalities, charisma becomes part of an established social structure."[73] It has become routinized, or institutionalized. "Any group that fails to institutionalize its collective life simply will not survive."[74] If the group does not survive, it cannot continue to propagate its ideals. In order to continue promoting its core principles in any form at all, it will be necessary for the group to mobilize all of its resources in that direction.

E. E. Byrum was right in wanting to institutionalize the ideals and collective life of the Movement. However, sociologist of religion Keith Roberts rightly sees that in addition to ideal interests in a sustainable group, members also have material interests in its survival. After all, members and leaders have "invested time, energy, and financial resources in the group," and "are likely to feel that they have a vested economic interest in its survival and success. Therefore the inherent forces working for routinization are strong."[75]

---

73. Weber selection in Birnbaum and Lenzer, *Sociology and Religion*, 194.
74. Roberts, *Religion in Sociological Perspective*, 166.
75. Ibid.

The Next Generation

Even when groups, like the Church of God, initially adopt the stance of anti-institutionalism, they soon find that certain basic needs and problems of the group are best met through organized or institutionalized practices. The intention may not be to move toward institutionalization, but by pragmatically addressing certain matters the practice begins to look like movement in that direction. Although there is convincing evidence that a number of steps in the direction of organization occurred within the first couple of years of the founding of the Movement,[76] Strege is certain that within the course of a generation the movement toward institutionalization most certainly occurred. In this regard he writes:

> By 1915 the movement had grown significantly, faced serious internal disputes, was forced to deal with external requirements, and extended its mission. In the process leaders like E. E. Byrum, H. M. Riggle, and others began employing practices that were quite pragmatic in origin. Railroad clergy bureaus needed a ministers' list. Local meetings of saints wearied of waiting for the next flying messenger to land. Foreign missionaries needed financial support while the saints needed relief from incessant requests for money.[77]

Institutional structures would be needed to address these and emerging problems and concerns. Although from its inception the group had a strong disdain for, and rejected doctrine, as well as governing procedures and structures, Strege rightly contends that time and again the leadership found it necessary to develop practices to meet various needs "on the fly."[78] In the early Movement years the practices were often developed to address concerns *before* there was time or desire to focus on theory, which, in fact, did not expressly inform many early practices. That is, there was quite a pragmatic approach to problems that would arise. The intention, especially prior to 1917, was not to move toward organizing or institutionalization, but only to address problems that arose. And yet, by merely addressing some problems, unintentional moves were made in the direction of organizing. Reflection on these moves, and the production of theory, polity, doctrines, etc., would come only later. Sociologists of religion have known for a long time that in the first stage of new religious groups the leaders tend to focus little on developing theories, while in the second stage this becomes a real issue, since the next generation of leaders begin reflecting on the meaning

---

76. See Clear, *Where the Saints Have Trod*, 52, 60, 104, 115.
77. Strege, *I Saw the Church*, 89.
78. Ibid., 32, 59.

of established practices. In this regard, something similar happened in the Movement.

At this point, the concern of the leaders is to firmly establish the organization in order to insure its durability and continuation, although as happened in the Church of God in the early years, some leaders and lay members may resist this and remain uncritically devoted to charismatic governance that rejects all organizing and bureaucracy. Members of religious groups like the Church of God may never admit that they intentionally sought to develop organizations in the course of their development. They may claim, as Movement pioneers did, that all they need is the guidance of the Holy Spirit. However, the sociologist knows that in order to sustain their group it is necessary for leaders to develop organizational structures, whether they intend or want to develop them or not. The Church of God was no different, even though early in its life cycle it seemed to develop such structures willy-nilly.

SACRIFICING THE VISIBLE UNITY PRINCIPLE

Although D. S. Warner said little about interracial unity in church and society there is no question that his understanding of visible unity gleaned from the Scriptures did not stop at spiritual unity and the unity of denominational groups. It was an all-inclusive unity that included people of all races, cultures, and classes—not on a spiritual level only, but visible as well, so that all the world could see it. Warner was certain that the one God of the universe desired to save all people through the gospel of Jesus Christ, regardless of their many differences. *All* belong to God, the Parent of all, and God desires that they be united as one. Warner did not hesitate to remind his listeners and readers that the Church of God is comprised of people "*of the most widely conflicting idiosyncrasies, and races of the most opposite customs and religions.*"[79] (This is one of the few places where Warner explicitly references race.) It is through the transforming grace of God that all people—regardless of their myriad differences—are as one in the church. In John 17: 11, 20, 21 Warner finds Jesus imploring God that all who believe on him be one, even as Jesus and God are one. He believed it was not possible for one to be a Christian if she fails to take seriously Jesus's prayer for oneness.[80] Warner was convinced that this oft asserted oneness or unity in the New Testament must be a visible unity. From this, it is crystal-clear that Warner had the right pieces in place, but for reasons unknown, he did little

79. Warner and Riggle, *The Cleansing of the Sanctuary*, 240 (my emphasis).
80. Ibid., 245.

to publicly link the holiness-visible unity principle to concrete interracial unity. Had Warner and Movement pioneers made this connection with as much energy and enthusiasm as they preached and taught the doctrine of entire sanctification as a second act of grace, the group would likely not have divided along racial lines not long after the 1912 confrontation.

We saw earlier that there were rumblings by some southern white Movement people in the direction of racial division as early as 1893, two years before Warner died. Nevertheless, the infamous confrontation between blacks and whites at the 1912 Anderson Camp Meeting might not have occurred had leaders expressly linked the holiness-visible unity principle to unity along racial lines, and explicitly renounced racism in church and society.

John W. V. Smith provides an account of the 1912 confrontation.

> The zeal which the pioneers had held concerning the ideal of racial unity began to wane after the turn of the century. The pressures of society finally became so great that the worthy goal which was pursued began to crumble . . . In 1912 it was reported that there was a confrontation at the Anderson Camp Meeting at which time several white leaders suggested to the blacks that they might find it more desirable if they found some other place to worship. Their presence in such large numbers, it was felt, was hindering many white people from coming to the meetings and being saved. The blacks could well have been angered by this request, but apparently most of them were more saddened by the turn of events than angered. Many continued to enjoy the fellowship at the national camp meeting, but the open door of fellowship was partially closed and relationships were not the same. The confrontation in Anderson did not completely divide the blacks from the whites in the Church of God movement, but it did set the climate for the beginning of a separate organization among blacks in the Church of God.[81]

However, Smith is misleading in two respects. First, his book claims, as do other standard Movement histories, including the stance of Christian ethicist Cheryl Sanders[82] that the pioneers possessed a "zeal" regarding interracial unity which they intentionally sought, and that this began to diminish only *after* the beginning of the twentieth century. Based on what I have argued before, it is highly questionable that enthusiasm for interracial

---

81. Smith, *The Quest for Holiness and Unity*, 167–68.

82. Cheryl Sanders is Professor of Christian Ethics at Howard University Divinity School and Senior Pastor of the Third Street Church of God in Washington, DC. See Sanders, "Ethics of Holiness and Unity in the Church of God," 143.

unity existed among most Movement pioneers. But even if one uncritically accepts the traditional historiography on the matter, it would have to be said—based on prior discussions—that while there was much stronger evidence of the decline in "zeal" among whites after the turn of the twentieth century, there was also growing evidence of its decline during the last two years of Warner's life and immediately after his death in 1895. Secondly, the last sentence in the above quotation misleadingly implies that there was a precise correlation between the 1912 confrontation and the emergence of the National Association of the Church of God in 1917, but as we will see below, the evidence does not support this view.

In an earlier account of the confrontation, Smith wrote that "some on both sides felt that it would be better to accept the prevailing social practices and meet as separate groups. Considerable discussion arose, but the advocates of separate churches succeeded in sharpening the issue sufficiently to bring about the beginning of a Negro organization independent of the Anderson agencies. Thus the National Association of the Church of God came into being around 1917."[83] This account clearly implies—wrongly in my judgment—that there was an agreed upon mutual arrangement between blacks and whites to meet to discuss the possibility of separation, and moreover that there was a one-to-one correspondence between the 1912 confrontation and the founding of the National Association five years later. This cannot have been the case, since Ernest Wimbish (who was black) claims to have had his vision of a plot of land where all of God's people could gather for worship and fellowship around 1901, while he and his wife were still members of the Baptist church.[84] In addition, Smith's earlier account implies that whites and blacks were co-conspirators in the subsequent division along racial lines—that blacks wanted racial separation as much as whites. Here Smith may have been influenced by E. E. Byrum's claim in 1897: "I find a *prejudice on the part of each race* which should not exist . . ."[85] And then, in 1909, James E. Forrest wrote that race prejudice existed, in part, because of "the attitude [whites and blacks] held toward each other in general."[86] Byrum and Forrest implied, as did Smith, Charles E. Brown, and other early white Movement people, that blacks *wanted* to separate as much as whites, as if to imply that they were equally culpable with whites in this regard. However, this simply was not the case.

83. Smith, *Truth Marches On*, 97.
84. Massey, *African Americans and the Church of God*, 72.
85. Byrum, "The Color Line," 2 (my emphasis).
86. Forrest, "National and Race Prejudice," 10.

Strege rightly observes that black Movement people *did not* want to separate, or to even establish a separate organization within the Church of God (i.e., the National Association of the Church of God in 1917).[87] They separated because of the racism of national leaders and many other Movement whites that was communicated through *The Gospel Trumpet*, as well as actions of whites in local churches and communities. Although we cannot rule out the likelihood that *some* blacks preferred to worship only among their own, this must be put into proper context. There is no evidence that Movement blacks ever initiated and instigated separation between the races, whether in the South or the North. Rather, whites at both the local and national levels of the Movement took the lead—all over the country—in instigating division along racial lines.

Although it is true that there were pressures on the Movement from the broader society to conform to its race ethic, it is also true that many, perhaps most of the whites who joined the Movement, were already racists and segregationists and simply carried these attitudes and practices into the group and were not challenged to think and behave in accordance with the principle of entire sanctification which, according to Warner, "heals all divisions by removing the cause; for it cleanses the heart from all unrighteousness."[88] True holiness or sanctification, Warner held, radically transforms one's entire being. *This* is what makes visible unity possible. Or as John W. V. Smith contends, visible unity is "the beautiful fruit of perfected holiness."[89] There are no unholy members in the church,[90] a point apparently unknown to vast numbers of white Movement people, particularly regarding race. I know of no place where Movement scholars have acknowledged this.

The pressure to conform to the ethics of segregation and racism came both from within, as well as outside, the Movement. In any case, it was only a natural human reaction that some blacks, having been insulted and pushed away by whites, eventually decided that if whites preferred to follow the ethic of society in the matter of race they would not insist on worshipping and fellowshipping with them. Instead, some blacks decided to worship and work only among their own people. Massey reports on this in his discussion of the 1912 confrontation.

Having referred to Mother Laura Moore's recollection of the incident, Massey proceeds to share the reaction of Rev. Charles H. Hill who was also present during the confrontation. Massey writes that Hill, "a pioneer

---

87. Strege, *I Saw the Church*, 145.
88. Warner and Riggle, *The Cleansing of the Sanctuary*, 260.
89. Smith, *The Quest for Holiness and Unity*, 92.
90. Warner and Riggle, *The Cleansing of the Sanctuary*, 272.

minister from Greensboro, Alabama, gave a matching statement to that of Mother Laura Moore. Hill was present on that same occasion at Anderson in 1912. So disturbed was he by the racial rebuff they suffered, and over the evident honoring of the color bar by those brethren who presumed to speak for the Church of God, that he never returned to Anderson for another camp meeting."[91] Hill was the maternal grandfather of Massey's wife, Gwendolyn. However, it is also important to point out that even those blacks who decided they would no longer put up with such rebuffs, did not close their doors to those whites who preferred interracial worship, and thus did not mind suffering for adhering to the Movement's ethic of holiness and visible unity. Indeed, while it is certainly the case that there are segregated black churches in the Movement, these are quite different from the segregated white churches, for they are not *segregating* churches. There is a significant difference. Martin Luther King, Jr. made this point about black colleges in 1957.[92] Without question, racism is the basic reason that blacks formed separate churches. Historically, and unlike many of their white counterparts, however, black churches generally are not segregating, i.e., they do not turn whites away from their doors; are not intentional about being segregated. Whites and members of any other racial-ethnic group can join black churches as equals with all others. Historically this has not been the case with white churches.

Far too many Movement whites preferred the very thing that D. S. Warner preached against, namely sectarianism or that which divides or separates Christians from one another. Andrew Byers reminds us that in the Church of God any refusal to fellowship with others who are also Christians "would itself be sectarian, altogether unlike the true reformation, which, if it be final, must necessarily be a *restoration* and possess universal characteristics."[93] For whites to concede to separate along racial lines was, by definition, a concession to sectarianism in the Church of God Reformation Movement. And sectarianism, according to D. S. Warner and Movement pioneers, is "the essence of all sin . . . , the greatest foe to the exhibition of love which God has ever suffered Satan to beget. It hinders brotherly love among Christians . . ."[94] He characterized sectarianism as "the very mildew of hell . . ."[95] Based on Warner's view of sectarianism, then, racism itself is a

---

91. Massey, *African Americans and the Church of God*, 89.

92. Carson, et al. eds., *The Papers of Martin Luther King, Jr*, 4:281.

93. Byers, *Birth of a Reformation*, 32.

94. Warner is here quoting approvingly W. H. Starr, "a conscientious Presbyterian minister . . ." See Warner, *Bible Proofs of the Second Work of Grace*, 297.

95. Ibid., 293.

form of sectism inasmuch as it alienates and divides the people of God into factions, thereby making visible interracial unity impossible. Warner's mistake, and that of most Movement pioneers, was in failing to explicitly make the connection between sectarianism and racism; failing to say forthrightly that racism is a form of sectarianism. By failing to do this, they left it to subsequent generations of Movement people to make the connection, but these too have failed. Indeed, it is less excusable for the latter, because they have the lessons of the founders from which to learn. Presently, they have chosen not to learn.

It is to John W. V. Smith's credit that he corrected his earlier (1956) account of the 1912 confrontation after his research deepened and he discovered that the confrontation was actually instigated by whites. Later Church of God historians, e.g., Merle Strege, reveal that the chief instigator was E. E. Byrum.[96] Therefore, blacks and whites were not in mutual agreement during the confrontation. Blacks were not desirous of separating. The truth is that the confrontation was but the culmination of numerous instances of whites' concession to the societal practice of racial separation over a period of many years, dating back at least to 1893 when there were already early rumblings of instigations among whites to separate along racial lines. In addition, as reported by Massey, beginning around 1910 a pattern of separations began in interracial northern missionary homes—in New York City, Pittsburgh, St. Louis, and Detroit—that led to the establishment of several black congregations. In virtually every case the racial divisions were instigated by whites. Furthermore, the result of the 1912 confrontation as such was not the launching of the National Association of the Church of God in 1917. Rather, it would be more accurate to say that a combination of events opened the way for the appearance of the National Association, not least the clear signs of whites that they preferred to worship separate from blacks; Byrum's urging of racial separation in 1897, and supporting articles written by white pastors essentially supporting his stance; Wimbish's vision in 1901; the racial division in the northern missionary homes beginning in 1910; and the 1912 confrontation at the Anderson Camp Meeting. All of these events, taken together, contributed to the emergence of the National Association in 1917. Therefore, it is only partially true to say that there was a correspondence between the confrontation of 1912 and the founding of the National Association.[97]

---

96. See Strege, *I Saw the Church*, 147.
97. See Willowby, *Family Reunion*, 38.

RELIGION, RACIAL CONCERNS, AND THE NATIONAL ASSOCIATION

To this point in time, James Earl Massey has done more than anyone else to uncover the role played by blacks in the development of the Church of God Reformation Movement. He has also done an admirable job of discussing the causes of the emergence of two of the organizations associated primarily with Movement blacks: the National Association, and the West Middlesex Campgrounds. Massey maintains that the beginnings of these were rooted only in religious, not racial or social concerns.[98] In my judgment, this is only partially true, and must be questioned in light of the last sentence in Smith's quotation above, as well as the fact—by Massey's own admission—that many Movement whites, North and South, were instigating separation between the races as early as 1893 and possibly earlier. Also, there is the matter of Byrum's inflammatory, racially charged article, "The Color Line" (discussed in Chapter 1). In light of the core beliefs of holiness and visible unity, the advice that Byrum gave regarding race relations in the Movement was most unfortunate. His advice—intended or not—added strong support to the already growing number of incidents regarding white pastors and laity, especially in the South, who already were desirous of separating along racial lines. I suggested earlier that Byrum was less interested to announce and establish a strong platform for the Movement based on the principle of unity along racial lines, than to assure white Movement people that the leadership was against intermarriage between whites and blacks, and that it was advisable that the two groups "meet in separate meetings." He saw nothing wrong in this "where it can be done for the glory of God."[99] We can, however, be consoled by the fact that Byrum unwittingly exposed his racism, and because he did so, we should not pretend that he was not racist, for were he not, it would be very difficult to understand why he did not close the door to separation along racial lines. Byrum did those things because he himself—like most white Americans of the period—was deeply infected with racism and a sense of white supremacy. Historically, both white and black Movement people have hesitated to characterize Byrum this way. This failure, in my view, only contributes to the difficulties that the group continues to have in matters of race today, and why liberation and reconciliation continue to be elusive goals. There is too little straight talk about race in the Movement.

---

98. Massey, *African Americans and the Church of God*, 202–3.
99. Byrum, "The Color Line," 2.

All of this is to say that the founding of the National Association and the West Middlesex campgrounds may have been rooted in religious concerns, as Massey maintains, but this was not all. Cheryl Sanders is absolutely right in her claim that Afrikan Americans formed separate camp meetings and other places of worship not because they wanted to, but because "white racism essentially forced them out of fellowship with whites."[100] Racial concerns were surely a factor, and there is no way to honestly deny it. Moreover, racial concerns, as well as other divisive issues are, fundamentally, theological concerns. For anything, any practice that alienates human beings from each other and from God is a matter of utmost theological concern. That is, it is a God-concern. This makes sense for any who believes that God thoughtfully, willingly, and lovingly calls persons into being, not solely as individuals, but as individuals-in-community, united under the one God. Both the Bible and the best in the Jewish and Christian traditions teach us that the world and human beings are fundamentally relational. That is, we are always and at once, persons-in-community; persons-in-relationship with each other and with God. God creates human beings in community, to live in community, and not in isolation and alienation from each other and God. There is a fundamental interrelatedness between God, human beings, and all of creation,[101] and when actions are taken to isolate and separate people from each other and from God as racism does, it is sin. Racism is both a religious or theological concern, as well as a social concern.

Even *if* it were true that the racial concerns in the Movement arose only belatedly, after the beginning of the twentieth century, as the party liners maintain, Ernest Wimbish's vision occurred around 1901, at which time he was not yet affiliated with the Movement. However, we have seen that racism was already a glaring and disturbing factor in the Movement by 1893. It is reasonable to assume that word got around to Movement blacks throughout the country each time there was a report of whites' desire to separate along racial lines. Surely these stories found their way to West Middlesex as well. It is therefore unreasonable to argue that race (a social factor) was not an important issue that contributed to the founding of the National Association and the West Middlesex campgrounds. In short, we should reject reasoning based on the idea that there is a disjunction between religious and social factors as if the one has nothing to do with the other. If it is true that the whole world belongs to God and is loved by God, then it is reasonable to say that God is concerned about all that happens in

---

100. Sanders, "Ethics of Holiness and Unity in the Church of God," 143.

101. See the excellent treatment of this theme in Fretheim, *God and World in the Old Testament*.

the world; that God is concerned about anything that alienates or divides people from each other and from God. That God is concerned about social problems or sins, e.g., racial prejudice, means, in the deepest sense, that they are theological problems—what I like to call God-problems or concerns. The emergence of the National Association, then, was based on both social (racial) and theological factors.

James E. Forrest, who we met several times before, was a white southerner who began preaching as a Church of God minister in 1901, was persecuted for trying to live and do ministry in ways that honored the founding core principles of the Movement. Initially, at least, he tried to consistently practice racial openness to a point, although he advised black and white Movement people to adjust themselves to the prevailing societal practice of racial segregation, and that such adjustment did not preclude visible unity in the church. When preaching before blacks in Sanderville, Georgia in 1909, Forrest was arrested by the local sheriff and given a severe lecture about racial protocol in the South. Forrest reported that he was later grabbed by the collar, "shaken a little, kicked a little, and loaded onto a freight train and sent out of town at midnight."[102] Based solely on Charles E. Brown's account of the incident, one might be tempted to conclude that Forrest was deeply committed to visible unity along racial lines. However, Massey, in one of his sharpest criticisms, takes issue with such a conclusion.

Forrest, it seems, was little more than a fair weather liberal at best in matters of race. Like many well-meaning whites, he was not steady during the winds of change in the society around him. Although he started out firm in his belief that Movement principles required visible unity, not separation along racial lines,[103] he, like so many whites, Massey contends, succumbed to societal pressures and the racism that necessarily entered when more and more whites joined the group. There is simply no way to reasonably argue that many whites were not already racists when they entered the Movement (and other white religious groups), for many of these believed that blacks could never be their equals. This was the general sentiment among very many whites, North and South, and it did not automatically disappear at the point of their religious conversion. Notwithstanding this, Forrest confidently claimed that "we are delivered from prejudice toward each other only as we respectively get under the all-atoning blood of Jesus Christ."[104] This, itself, is problematic, considering that many who claimed to be converted and thus joined the Movement remained racists. The leaders had no program to work

---

102. Quoted in Smith, *The Quest for Holiness and Unity*, 166.
103. See Massey, *African Americans and the Church of God*, 35.
104. Forrest, "National and Race Prejudices," 90.

at eradicating the racist ideas and practices of new converts. Consequently, I would argue that unless those whites who experienced entire sanctification *also* literally named their own racism and sense of white superiority as sins to be eradicated, they in fact retained this attitude even after ostensibly undergoing what they considered to be complete sanctification. All of this is to say that Forrest eventually took the low road of least resistance when he later concluded that *spiritual* unity was what the Bible essentially required, and that such unity is not necessarily destroyed by the absence of visible unity along racial lines.

Massey has shown that Forrest "appealed to expediency," so prevalent was racism in virtually every sector of the nation, including religious institutions.[105] Forrest wrote: "The question with regard to the matter of Bible unity is, Is it consistent to tolerate the customs and observe them, for the present, at least, or shall we shut our eyes to everything and everybody and maintain that the only way to be Scripturally one is to ignore every ordinance, law, or custom, and let both white and colored assemble in the same house of worship and depend upon that to reach the people of the city, town, or community with the gospel?"[106] Without question, Forrest concluded as most white Movement leaders of the period that it was acceptable to tolerate and observe prevailing customs rather than to stand firm on the principles of holiness and visible unity. Forrest went on to conclude: "It has been decided by a number of reliable and worthy brethren—those who are counted sufficiently competent to look into spiritual things with sound judgment and wise discretion because of their experience and responsibility—that in some localities, in order that the cause of Christ suffer no reproach and more people be reached with the gospel, there be separate places used for public gatherings of the saints; one for white people and one for the colored people."[107]

When I read Forrest's words I could not help recalling Warner's chapter, "The Shaking Crisis Continued—Separation of the Wheat and Chaff," in which he criticized those who "think we must so temper the Gospel as

---

105. Massey, *African Americans and the Church of God*, 63.

106. Quoted in ibid.

107. Quoted in ibid., 64. In his June 13, 1913, camp meeting sermon, "The Fatherhood of God," Forrest made the claim that God receives all persons, regardless of race, ethnicity, or socio-economic class: "It does not matter with God whether a man is white or black, rich or poor. With God there is no respect of persons. I thank God tonight that he has made a way so that *whosoever will*, may freely come"; Forrest, "The Fatherhood of God," 266. One hardly knows what to make of such a claim, considering what we have learned about Forrest.

to preserve peace in the Church, notwithstanding her sin and idols."[108] For Warner, the aim was not to grow church membership as such, knowing as he did that the church that adheres to the best in the Bible and to the principles of holiness and visible unity will likely not have a large membership. In fact, he said that, "holiness beats it [the church's membership] small."[109] Large numbers of people will likely not join, because it *costs* something to do so. One has to give up cheap grace and all that it implies; give it up for entire sanctification of one's entire soul and life; give it up for an entirely radical way of thinking and living in church and world. That's what holiness does. It makes one brand new through and through.

Unquestionably, Warner was right. Strict adherence to the ethics of holiness does not lend itself to massive church growth, for the requirements of this ethic are stringent indeed. Many more people tend to avoid such an ethic than seek to comply with its expectations. This is certainly the tendency of people in the second and subsequent stages of the natural history of a religious group. Movement people who are serious about making good the claim about holiness and visible unity, would do well to read and reflect on Warner's commentary on Malachi 2:17: "Ye have wearied the Lord with your words, when ye say, Every one that doeth evil is good in the sight of the Lord, and He delighteth in them" (as quoted by Warner). Warner concluded that this verse was being fulfilled in his day, "by preachers who invite sinners into their folds, without requiring a particle of saving grace: and who even flatter them that they are already pretty good, and need but to come and join the church."[110] Warner rejected this practice, asserting instead the need for the feet of new converts to be held to the fire, and that they get good stiff doses of the Gospel truth; and that they be made to understand that the Christian standard is far more rigorous and demanding than that of society. It is most unfortunate that Forrest and other "fair weather liberal" Movement people did not heed Warner's teaching in this regard. Indeed, Warner's further assertion is most instructive: "And how many of their poor, deluded victims remain in the church for years, and never hear the Gospel lines drawn straight enough to convict them of their unregenerated hearts. The policy of these teachers has been to 'gather of all kinds,' but the next thing in order—to separate and 'cast the bad away'—has been wholly omitted."[111]

Warner would have left a very strong witness and example in matters of race had he intentionally and expressly connected this teaching to the

---

108. Warner, *Bible Proofs of the Second Work of Grace*, 289.
109. Ibid., 288.
110. Ibid.
111. Ibid.

racism and segregationist views that many whites carried into the Movement. For as it stands, most Movement people, including James E. Forrest, did not make this connection on their own. One simply cannot presume to live the life of holiness, "the one all-important, and absolutely essential attribute of the divine church,"[112] according to Warner, while day in and day out making no effort to completely dissolve his "unholy 'friendship with the world . . .'"[113]

The basic principles of holiness and visible unity are sound theological principles. Warner's and other Movement pioneers' failure was in not explicitly and consistently linking these to the issue of the color line. They also failed to *teach* this to whites who converted to the Movement. This made it easy for the pioneers and subsequent Movement people to capitulate to societal pressures, for no pressure was put on racist members to be converted from their racism. It was simply naively assumed that those washed in the blood of Jesus and who experienced complete sanctification automatically had their racism washed away.

Massey was outraged at the reasoning of Forrest. He responded by saying that, "this rule from 'reliable and worthy brethren,' *all white*, gave cover for provincialism not only in Church of God movement congregations in the South, with its one culture dominance, but also in the North and elsewhere. It was a provincialism that would negatively condition and beset the life of the Church of God movement across many decades to come."[114] Although Massey's critique has much value, I think that he was too concerned about being politically correct, since he did not call the "provincialism" among whites what it really was—racism. I think this needs to happen among Movement people—straight talk about racism, including using the term racism in verbal and written discussions. However, it is significant that in this one instance, at least, Massey was without question deeply disturbed by the concession to racism made by a prominent white Church of God pastor. One seldom sees clear-cut evidence of such agitation and disappointment exhibited in Massey's writings on the Movement. Because of his stature in the group, both whites and Afrikan Americans would be helped immeasurably to see and hear more of this from this Movement giant. This is absolutely critical for the potential opening of doors of opportunity for Afrikan Americans in educational and other agency facilities of the Movement. Massey's forthrightness about the matter of race in this instance might also be one of the keys that will unlock the cell that imprisons those

---

112. Warner and Riggle, *The Cleansing of the Sanctuary*, 268.
113. Warner, *Bible Proofs of the Second Work of Grace*, 288.
114. Massey, *African Americans and the Church of God*, 64 (my emphasis).

whites who are genuinely concerned about their own racism and unearned privilege, but have not known how to free themselves—indeed cannot free themselves without such keys.

Such vast numbers of Movement whites still hold Massey in high regard, and so thoroughly respect his counsel that if he would give himself permission to consistently speak, preach, and write forthrightly, and openly about matters of race—not hesitating to use the terms *racism* and *white privilege*, instead of using palatable, less forceful terms—like "provincialism" and "human groupings"—it might well serve to free those whites who have sought for years to find ways to give themselves permission to confess their racism and to begin the process of making good the claim about holiness and visible unity.

Should Massey find in himself or his faith the means to do this, he will likely lose some of his popularity among whites in the Movement, but it seems to me a minor loss for what is at stake, namely the authentic visible interracial unity of the Church of God Reformation Movement. I am not saying here that Massey holds the only key, and is the only one who should risk reputation and fame by being more forthright regarding the issue of race. *All Movement people, regardless of race, have responsibilities in this regard.* But make no mistake about it, for years, James Earl Massey has held *one* of the keys, and the time is long past due for him to use that key for the liberation of both blacks and whites in the Movement; to liberate them so that together they can make good the claim. I return to this important point in chapter 6.

RACIAL SEPARATION IN NORTHERN CITIES

Before looking again at the confrontation of 1912, a consideration of Massey's discussion on the pattern of division along racial lines that began to appear in northern cities in 1910 will be instructive. As noted previously, in every case, whites instigated the separations. Although D. O. Teasley, a white minister, had written to the *Gospel Trumpet* in 1909 that there was no racial division in the work in the New York City missionary home, this was soon to change. By 1910 reports of racial separation were emerging. Previously the New York City home had been an interracial mission. When the division occurred, blacks developed their own mission to continue the work. Interestingly, when Axchie F. Bolitho (1886–1974), an ordained white woman minister became the pastor of the Church of God in the Bronx (formerly the New York City Missionary home under the leadership of Teasley), the group announced several of its staunchest convictions in the church yearbook for 1932–33. The most relevant of these for our purpose is the conviction "that race, color and class prejudices are all contrary to the Christian spirit."[115] So, although there were reports of racial division in 1910, a little over two decades later the New York City congregation affirmed its commitment to racial inclusion, stating that anything short of this was a contradiction of Christian principles and the spirit of what it means to be a Christian.

Massey reports a similar occurrence of racial division in Pittsburgh, Pennsylvania, also in 1910. The city's first black Movement church grew out of a previously interracial mission that divided along racial lines. Around the same time, the races divided at the missionary home in St. Louis, Missouri. Massey tells us that J. R. Stephenson, the white pastor of the group, suggested the separation along racial lines.[116] A black congregation also developed from this division and became a strong center for the spread of the Movement's message among blacks in the state and points west.

Unlike in other instances, the missionary home in Detroit, Michigan was under the leadership of a black woman pastor, Christiana Janes. This too was an interracial home. Janes became pastor in 1910, and by 1913 the group purchased a building that ultimately had a chapel and living spaces for residential workers and visiting ministers. When an irresolvable disagreement arose between Janes and one of the white members over living arrangements, Janes was ultimately forced out, but not before the white members invited white Movement leaders to visit as reinforcements of their position. Both E. E. Byrum and W. J. Henry (a white pastor from Toledo, Ohio) supported white members' desire to have Janes removed. Henry reportedly "told the Colored saints in plain language that they wanted the place for a white church and [that] the Colored saints will have to leave."[117] Janes did what few Afrikan Americans were inclined to do at that time or since. She left and formed an independent work. Shamefully, she received neither empathy nor support from black leaders, including Daniel Oden, the man who succeeded her as pastor of what came to be the first black Church of God congregation in Detroit.

As far as we know, Janes committed no wrong that was serious enough to warrant her being forced out by the white members, supported by Byrum and Henry. Racism essentially forced her out, while black leaders in the Movement who were aware of the debacle essentially turned their heads as if what happened to Janes was of no significant consequence to them

---

115. Quoted in Strege, *Tell Me the Tale*, 38.
116. Massey, *African Americans and the Church of God*, 53.
117. See Massey's informative discussion of these separations in ibid., 48–56.

and others in the Movement—blacks and whites. Black Movement leaders allowed Janes to be slaughtered, presumably in the best interest of a fundamentally white religious group that by this time was consistently and blatantly violating its own teaching on holiness and visible unity. This was a sad commentary on white and black Movement leaders, but more so, on the latter. In any event, the blacks who remained from the earlier interracial group under Janes formed the core of what came to be The Church of God of Detroit.

Charles E. Brown has written that, it was precisely around the time the northern missionary homes ceased operation that racially separate churches began to appear. In Brown's estimation, southern Movement churches "had been *forced* by public opinion to practice segregation," and white Movement preachers and leaders paid heavy dues for their openness toward, and inclusion of blacks in the South.[118] Brown seemed not to understand that what blacks really needed was full acceptance as human beings and to be full-fledged members in Movement churches that adhered strictly to the core principles of holiness and visible unity. In addition, blacks needed to be treated, in every respect, in accordance with the principle of equality. These things done, "friendship" with them would have taken care of itself.

Two things are troubling about Brown's claims. The first is his contention that southern Movement churches were *forced* by public opinion to separate along racial lines, as if this somehow lessened their moral and religious obligation to challenge this in light of the gospel and the holiness-visible unity principle. There is no question that both the legal system and blatant white racists would have made things very difficult for Movement people and local churches that refused to adhere to the practice of segregation. Such a church would have been persecuted beyond imagination and possibly to the point that membership would have dwindled to such a degree that it was no longer possible to be a congregation. And yet, persecution is the price that Christians have been paying for their faith and commitment to the gospel since the time of the crucifixion of Jesus and the time of the early church. It is virtually impossible to *force* committed Christians who have experienced entire sanctification to behave in ways that are contrary to the teachings of Jesus Christ. One *decides* to behave in this fashion, or some other. Since one always has the choice of choosing to stand her ground, technically she cannot be forced either to stand firm, or to capitulate. In the end, *she* decides one way or the other. Freedom, the capacity to choose, is part of the very essence of what it means to be a human being.[119]

---

118. Brown, *When the Trumpet Sounded*, 360 (my emphasis).
119. Tillich, *The Protestant Era*, 115.

As morally autonomous beings, we humans are always free (within limits) to choose. Therefore, technically, even though we may feel that circumstances—social, political, economic, or otherwise—forced us to make this or that choice, the very fact that we relented *was* our choice. Even when we opt not to choose, we in fact choose. This is what it means to be a human being. To choose not to choose is itself a choice, and we need to be clear about this. The atheistic existentialist Jean-Paul Sartre put it best when he reminded human beings that we are *condemned to freedom*.[120] As human beings we cannot, not choose. Sartre maintains that, "what is not possible is not to choose. I can always choose, but I ought to know that if I do not choose, I am still choosing."[121] Because Sartre did not believe in God, he thought it necessary to place much more of the responsibility for what happens in the world on human beings themselves. He therefore argued that there are no crutches. The human being is condemned to freedom—to be free. "Condemned, because he did not create himself, yet, in other respects is free; because, once thrown into the world, he is responsible for everything he does. The existentialist . . . will never agree that a sweeping passion is a savaging torrent which fatally leads a man to certain acts and is therefore an excuse. He thinks that man is responsible for his passion."[122]

In light of this aspect of Sartre's ethic, I want to suggest that white southern Movement people and churches were not forced by outside circumstances to practice racial segregation. Without question, many of them were up against it because of the societal racial ethic of the day, but in every case, Movement people *chose* to capitulate rather than uphold the ethic of holiness and visible unity. In every case, the choice could have been made to hold on tenaciously to the Movement's holiness-visible unity ethic, even if the consequence was the disintegration of a particular local church, or even the certain deaths of some of its members. Jesus, as well as his disciples and Christians in the early church were persecuted and martyred regularly by the state for adhering to the gospel ethic that was also a critique of the State.[123] The early Christians were even falsely accused by the Emperor Nero for setting fire to Rome, for which they were subjected to "hideous tortures" by him at the close of AD 64.[124] Very many of the accusations against the

---

120. Sartre, "Existentialism," 23.

121. Ibid., 41.

122. Ibid., 23.

123. There is no more thorough treatment of the early church and the state than the massive work of Cadoux, *The Early Church and the World*. In each of the major periods of the early church's history Cadoux discusses the attitude of the state toward Christians and the nature of state sponsored persecution.

124. Lecky, *History of European Morals*, 1:429, 430.

early Christians, for which they were severely persecuted and yet stood their ground, were false.

What the historian of European morals, William E. H. Lecky, said about the false accusations that led to the persecutions and martyrs of many early Christians could well have been said about southern white Movement people had they taken the high road and stood their ground regarding the ethic of visible unity along racial lines: *"Noble lives, crowned by heroic deaths, were the best arguments of the infant Church. Their enemies themselves not unfrequently acknowledged it. The love shown by the early Christians to their suffering brethren has never been more emphatically attested than by Lucian . . ."*[125] Indeed, Justin Martyr went so far as to say that it was the brave deaths of these saints that led to his conversion. What better testimony for white Movement people to have such things said about their witness, had they been as courageous and tenacious in adhering to the basic core beliefs of holiness and visible unity as they pertained to the color line? Instead, they *chose* to capitulate. In addition, one wonders how pressure from the outside would have affected the group had there been less racism and segregationist attitudes *within* white members. And let us not forget that a few years before the first decade of the twentieth century, there was increasingly strong support among white Movement people for separation along racial lines. Therefore, Brown's claim that by 1910 the Movement "had been forced by public opinion to practice segregation" is at best a half-truth, and not an impressive one.

The second thing that is troubling about Brown's statement is his claim that white Movement preachers and leaders undoubtedly suffered more for their friendliness toward blacks in the South than leaders of any other religious group working there. There is no concrete evidence that there was ever a time when the vast majority of southern white Church of God preachers and leaders consistently and passionately preached interracial unity and oneness. If this did in fact happen, it is lost to history, since there is no extant written evidence of it. Furthermore, when it is recalled that, from its inception, the Methodist Episcopal Church built into its General Rules an anti-enslavement clause with instructions for enslavers in the group to free enslaved Afrikans or be excommunicated from the group, one would think that many of the Methodist ministers who stood firm on this matter were severely persecuted in the South and elsewhere on a scale that far exceeded that of Warner and followers of like-mind regarding race. Of course, the Methodist Episcopal Church finally split along the Mason Dixon line over

---

125. Ibid., 1:415 (my emphasis).

the slavery issue, but even after this occurrence its abolitionist ministers were persecuted for their anti-enslavement witness.

There is truth in Brown's claim that there were Church of God pastors and leaders who were persecuted because of their openness and friendliness toward blacks. However, the claim that they suffered more for their stance than any other religious group operating in the South is, for this writer, more than a stretch. In addition, indicators are that the number of Movement ministers and leaders who openly and consistently preached against division along racial lines was small indeed.

THE CONFRONTATION OF 1912: ANOTHER LOOK

The confrontation of 1912 was so outrageous, and yet so significant in Movement history that I am compelled to revisit it again, especially in light of the findings of Church of God scholars such as Merle Strege and James Earl Massey. I begin with the account of Strege. Some of what he has written about the confrontation is both fresh and instructive. In *I Saw the Church*, Strege writes:

> A strong oral tradition among African American people of the Church of God says that White camp meeting organizers encouraged Blacks to organize a separate camp meeting. Without documentation this tradition had been passed down through a series of historical essays. It may be the case that the repeated requests of the camp meeting committee in 1913 and 1914 are the origin of this tradition, in which case it would not be quite accurate to say that Whites asked Blacks to form a separate camp meeting. This much is certain: White camp meeting organizers were intent on trying to separate the races at least temporarily. It is even more certain that after 1900 White saints were willing to question the movement's practice of Christian unity insofar as race was concerned. What once had been a nearly unique practice of Christian unity that overcame racial separation began to erode.[126]

Regarding the last sentence I have argued throughout that, short of hard evidence to support it, it is a highly questionable claim. Beyond this, Strege provides a helpful interpretation regarding the oral tradition related to the confrontation. Unfortunately, he relegated the statement to an endnote rather than include it in the body of the text. Most people—including

---

126. Strege, *I Saw the Church*, 148.

many scholars—do not read endnotes, which means that many will miss his important clarification.

In the aforementioned endnote, Strege observes that the oral tradition first appeared in print form in Katie H. Davis's book on the Afrikan American camp meeting, *Zion's Hill at West Middlesex* (1953). In that book, Joseph Crosswhite, Manager of the National Association Camp Ground, wrote of having heard Mother Laura Moore tearfully tell the story of her experience at the 1912 camp meeting at Anderson.[127] Subsequently, this account was cited by a number of writers on the Movement, including John W. V. Smith, and Samuel Hines and Cheryl J. Sanders (both Afrikan Americans). Although his earlier, shorter book on Afrikan Americans in the Movement was not yet published (*An Introduction to the Negro Churches in the Church of God Reformation Movement*[128]), Massey also cited the story there, as well as in his more recent, fuller social history, *African Americans and the Church of God*. In any event, Strege contends that Moore's story was the beginning of the oral tradition regarding the 1912 confrontation that has been passed down undocumented in the black church.

Having examined the minutes of the Camp Meeting Committee of this period, Strege was able to provide supportive written documentation that the white leadership did in fact request that blacks worship at a separate, select place, but on the Anderson camp meeting grounds. "Camp meeting organizers did request blacks to hold a separate service one afternoon during the Anderson meeting," Strege writes. "The camp meeting committee micromanaged the meeting's every detail, down to the straw ordered to stuff into mattress ticks. Given this tendency, and coupled with the detailed accounts in its minutes, it seems the better part of historiographical wisdom to err on the side of caution and rely on information that can be documented."[129]

Strege appears to have a bias against the oral tradition as literature, and thus seems to assume that written documentation is necessarily more accurate or dependable than oral sources (or that written sources are the only legitimate literature and documentation). This stance is influenced by the eighteenth century Enlightenment emphasis on reason and experience. A corollary of this is the emphasis on the scientific analysis of texts of all kinds, which itself implies privileging *written* texts over others. A corresponding tendency is to minimize or downplay the value and importance of oral sources, implying that only the written text is considered to be literature.

---

127. See Davis, *Zion's Hill at West Middlesex*, 47.
128. Massey, *Introduction to the Negro Churches*.
129. Strege, *I Saw the Church*, 163–64.

Appendix-B discusses the issue that this essentially modernist stance raises, as well as the importance of the oral tradition when written sources do not exist, or have been lost or misplaced.

Based on what Strege found in the Camp Meeting Committee minutes, I see no reason to give less weight to the oral tradition that came down regarding the 1912 confrontation. The fact that blacks did not provide written documentation of the incident when it occurred, or shortly thereafter, is not evidence that it did not happen as Mother Moore and others reported it orally. If anything, the camp meeting minutes only confirm and support the oral story that blacks were asked by whites to "get a place of your own."[130] "Get a place of your own" could very well have referred to a separate place on the Anderson campgrounds, which is what Strege found in the minutes of the camp meeting committee. But it could also have meant precisely what some Afrikan Americans interpreted it to mean, namely that it would be best if they found a place to hold their own camp meetings. After all, even the minutes to which Strege refers indicate that whites were troubled by the presence of such large numbers of blacks attending the Anderson camp meetings. If this was primarily a concern expressed by southern whites, it is reasonable to assume that their preference was for blacks not only to worship separately (as in a separate tent at Anderson), but that they worship at a site away from the Anderson campgrounds.

But there is another matter that needs to be considered here as well. The confrontation between blacks and whites involved multiple representatives of each race. Strege calls attention to the story of the incident as recounted orally by Mother Moore. Inasmuch as Moore was not the only Afrikan American present at the confrontation, it must be the case that she was not the only one who gave an oral account of the incident. Daniel F. Oden, a leading black Movement minister was also present. Moreover, Massey reports that "the minutes of the 'Camp Meeting Committee' for 1913 reveal that Byrum tried to get . . . Oden to accept and endorse the suggested plan [for blacks to worship separately from the whites], but that Oden had refused to do so."[131] Byrum tried again the following year, but met with the same result. And as we have seen, Massey also reports that Rev. Charles H. Hill of Greensboro, Alabama, was also present at the confrontation, and that he too gave an oral account of the incident that apparently was little different from that given by Moore.[132] Hill reported the incident to his family and congregation, and was so disappointed, indeed was devastated, by what

---

130. Quoted in Massey, *African Americans and the Church of God*, 88.
131. See ibid., 89.
132. Ibid.

happened that he never again returned to Anderson camp meetings. It is not known how many other Afrikan Americans responded similarly after hearing the story told by Moore and Hill, but we can be sure that there were more than a few. We can only conclude that Hill's oral report corroborated that of Mother Moore, which gives added credibility to the oral historical account of the matter.

The real point about the 1912 confrontation, in any case, is that the suggestion was made (at all) by white leaders that blacks worship in a separate space, whether on the Anderson campgrounds, or in a location away from Anderson, Indiana. Imagine one group of Christians advising another group of Christians (of the same affiliation) to worship in a separate tent solely because of race. In addition, I do not buy the suggestion implied in the Camp Meeting Committee minutes that the separation suggested by white leaders was only to be temporary. Furthermore, the longevity of the separation is not the real issue at all. The real issue is that forced-separation along racial lines for any length of time was proposed by white Movement leaders in the first place.

I have been around the theological academy and churches long enough to know that minutes of meetings can be—and sometimes are—secretly altered. No, it should not happen. It simply does. Moreover, there is the matter of that troubling 1897 article written by Byrum, "The Color Line," and the advice that he gave about the separation of the races. There is no credible evidence that Byrum and other white leaders in 1912 were advising a temporary separation. In addition, let us not forget that in the early 1890s efforts were made by white Church of God pastors in the South to instigate separation along racial lines. It is therefore incorrect to say, as the party liners do, that it was *after* 1900 that white members of the Movement began to question its practice of interracial unity.

Furthermore, too many who have written on Church of God history have done so in ways that imply that although the rest of the country was embedded in racism, whites who came to the Church of God Reformation Movement were somehow completely free of racism and a sense of white superiority.[133] Or, they imply that those who were racists before joining the Church of God somehow had their racism magically washed away during the first or (most likely) second act of grace. Of course, history, experience, and the social sciences teach us that the monstrous nature of racism is such that a mere religious conversion experience alone is not sufficient to destroy this beast. The conversion experience could be an excellent step or pre-

---

133. It is true however, that John W. V. Smith seemed to be aware that racism was a problem that affected virtually every sector of American society, permitting not even the church to escape. See *The Quest for Holiness and Unity*, 166.

condition in the right direction, but it is only a beginning—a first step in a very long and difficult process. Members will have to name and intentionally work to rid themselves and their institutions of racism, something that most Movement people did not (and do not) do.

Looking at the matter sociologically and from a social systems perspective, David Moberg makes an instructive point that is quite applicable to the Movement problem of race. "Church members tend to reflect attitudes of prejudice and acts of discrimination which are institutionalized in their community, for they are members of an entire social system."[134] If the entire social system, with all its institutions, including the church, is racist, then movement from one part of the system to the next essentially means that racism is carried from one part of the system to the next, unless it has been eradicated. One can therefore join the Movement, with its emphasis on holiness and visible unity, and yet not see the evil of racial separation or segregation because racism is embedded in the entire social system such that it takes on an air of normalcy. That is, there is no need to repent of the sin of racism and white supremacy because these are thought to be the norms. Therefore, one simply undergoes the two works of grace while her racism and sense of racial superiority remain in tact and virtually unchallenged. One can then proceed to live in accordance with the Movement's emphasis on personal morality without ever feeling compelled to address one's racism and unearned privilege, or even the structural or institutional racism in the Movement itself.

The church is an integral part of the social system, and thus is mutually affected by all that happens in other parts of the system. What this means—and what too many fail to recognize—is that at some point the converted person has to acknowledge his racism as well as his desire to be completely free of it. But that cannot be all. This must then be followed by intentional, vigilant, hard work by the individual as well as church leaders and members to eradicate vestiges of racism in the new convert, as well as the church and its organizations. Merely proclaiming, "I'm saved by the blood of Jesus Christ and have experienced entire sanctification," does not in itself free one from the racism beast. If such an experience did extricate whites from their racism, no white Movement person would be a racist or would hesitate even today to fight for racial justice and equality to become a reality throughout the country. The racist who gets "saved" today is nothing more than a "saved" racist, until she acknowledges and repents of her racism, and commits herself to a program of eradicating all semblances of it. It appears to me that most white people in the Movement—past and

---

134. Moberg, *The Church as a Social Institution*, 447.

present—have not known this, or have not wanted to know it. I therefore question whether most were, and have been, liberated from their racism and unearned privilege. But I also know that if white Movement people are to be true to their founding core principles of holiness and visible unity they must be liberated from racism and unearned white privilege. I will say more about this in chapter 7. Before this, however, there is need to discuss the further expansion and diversification of the Movement into its third and most mature stages.

5

Continued Expansion and Diversification

WE HAVE SEEN THAT neither D. S. Warner nor some of the other pioneers of the Church of God exhibited much concern about social pressures outside the community of Movement believers, so focused were they on preaching and teaching their message. This is consistent with what generally occurs during the first stage of the sociological transformation of the new religious group. Leaders and pioneers are generally so attuned to their newly discovered truth and have such a burning desire to spread it among as many people as possible that they are typically oblivious to the customs and expectations of the surrounding society, including its racial ethic. They therefore preach and teach their truth as if nothing else matters for human salvation. They preach and teach it with a sense of dire urgency, as if the world is soon coming to an end, and thus there is no time to lose. We saw this very tendency in D. S. Warner, who was constantly on the go, traveling all around even in inclement weather spreading the gospel of holiness as a second act of grace and visible unity. Warner did this, regardless of his sometimes failing health; regardless of having to be away from his wife and child longer and more often than he desired. There is no evidence that Warner's excitement and enthusiasm for the holiness and visible unity message ever waned, but all the traveling and preaching he did until he was physically spent took its toll on his health and energy level such that he slowly had to remove himself from the daily operations of what was now a growing organization. This opened the door to unanticipated changes as the Movement was approaching the end of the charismatic leader stage. For it is also during the second phase that followers typically begin to exhibit less enthusiasm for the ideals and teachings of the founder. Some may not even know what those ideals were, let alone what they mean and require of them.

As the excitement and zeal began to diminish among Movement whites, and with the death of Warner, the process of routinization began picking up steam. More and more, the emphasis was placed on doing those pragmatic things that would lead to sustaining and perpetuating the still fledgling group. We have learned that this meant there was need for developing organizational structures that would effectively institutionalize the collective life, norms, and values of the group, as well as meet its growing needs. We also saw that a corollary of this is the tendency of the group to accommodate more and more to society and its ethic, as well as allow itself—wittingly or not—to be influenced by prevailing societal customs and practices.

In the case of the Church of God, the routinization of charisma also contributed to the institutionalization of the division along racial lines. This racial separation would be seen, for example, in all of the developing institutions and agencies of the Movement. Afrikan Americans would have a token presence at best in those institutions and on key boards, and where they did have such presence they typically were not in significant positions of power and authority over whites. That would have been a violation of the societal ethic to which the Movement had accommodated itself. The leaders after Warner were increasingly concerned about outside social and other pressures and sought to bring the Movement's own practices into conformity with what was occurring in society at large. Emphasis on the ideal of holiness and visible unity as pertained to race in the group was fading further and further into the background. Had attention to the Movement's basic core beliefs not diminished, instigations toward racial separation, culminating in the confrontation of 1912, might not have arisen.

In light of the foregoing discussion it can be said that in accordance with the process of the sociological transformation of religious groups there are several characteristics that distinguish the second phase of the group's natural life cycle. We were introduced to many of these in chapter 1. I list them here without comment:

- Transference of leadership due to illness or death of the leader.
- Decline in prophetic fervor and excitement over the founder's message.
- Routinization of charisma, or development of institutional forms that move the group in the direction of an established sect, denomination, or a church-like organization.

- Growing attention given to social customs and practices of society, and tendency to accommodate to them, rather than retain the group's earlier prophetic edge.
- Beginning of bureaucratization and sharper lines of authority drawn.
- Qualifications for membership made more explicit, although not as stringent.
- Religious practices and ordinances, e.g., the Lord's Supper and foot washing, develop into formally prescribed rituals.
- Struggle over leadership often occurs.
- Beliefs about God and the mission of the founder are formulated as official creeds, doctrines, and theologies.

There are other traits that distinguish the second stage, but those listed are among the most common.

As evidence of the Movement's second-generation's early efforts to develop structure and organization, the group incorporated the Gospel Trumpet Publishing Company in 1898, three years after Warner's death. The incorporation of this organization was significant because it "was for many years 'the only institution in which all the Church participated,' with its editor unanimously regarded as chief leader in the church."[1] It matters little that Movement pioneers tried to rationalize this by arguing that by placing the Company "on a thorough business basis does not make it any more worldly than if it were on an imperfect basis."[2] Sociologically, the point is that this was a move toward institutionalization, the very thing that Warner and the pioneers sought to avoid. Indeed, Val Clear has convincingly shown that within the very first year of its existence there were signs of institutionalization in the Church of God, which generally does not occur until the second stage. The signs of institutionalization in the first stage of the Movement's development included the beginning of the Gospel Trumpet Company; the naming of a trustee to hold Church of God property under Michigan law; and the appointment of A. B. Palmer to represent the church in "securing railroad passes for its ministers."[3] Such occurrences like it or not, were steps toward becoming an established-sect or a denomination. They were moves toward becoming "worldly," a primary reason that Warner left the General Eldership. One wonders how it would be possible for the church to be in the world and not be worldly to some extent. Indeed,

---

1. Massey, *African Americans and the Church of God*, 63.
2. Cole, "Is Organization Worldly?," 87.
3. Clear, *Where the Saints Have Trod*, 104; see also 52, 60, 67.

it would not be very long before the group saw the need for developing educational and related structures as well. Of course, this would also mean further movement along the sect-church continuum or life cycle of the new religious group.

THE THIRD STAGE: COMPLEX ORGANIZATIONS DEVELOP

During the third stage of the group's life cycle, institutionalization and even further diversification expands fairly rapidly as committees, boards, and the appointment of executives and paid staff, strive to meet the needs of the fast growing organization. This phase is also the period when historians and apologists begin to appear. Although the Movement had a publication arm from virtually the beginning, its use became even more important during the third phase of its life cycle, for it became even more important to publicize its activities and plans for further development and expansion. It also meant that the group began to take on an even more vivid established sect or denomination-like appearance. During this stage there is continued expansion and diversification.

In the event that a new religious group survives the second phase, the third stage is typically characterized by continued growth, and may take on a variety of complex organizational forms. By this time, the group has essentially become *established*, and also "confronts the danger of becoming the victim of its own success . . ."[4] That is, with all of its expansion, development, and increased capacity to influence society, it is frequently the case that the group's ethical ideal and-or founding principles of the leader stands to be diluted and compromised. Sociologist of religion Elizabeth Nottingham reminds us that, "In the course of its growth in members and power, the religious organization comes to include at least some elements which it has been combating."[5] The internalization of such elements may contribute to the group's failure to actualize the ideals and established goals of the pioneers. The group has taken into itself societal elements and people whose beliefs and practices are not consistent with the founding principles or goals. To be sure, such individuals in the group increases the membership and finances, but the failure to be intentional and vigilant in teaching them the true goals or core beliefs of the group leaves it vulnerable to potentially destructive ideas, attitudes, and practices both within the group and outside of it. There is always the risk of this occurring when new members join,

4. Nottingham, *Religion*, 226–27.
5. Ibid., 220.

but are not taught the group's highest ideals and expectations. This only increases the chances of the group's disintegration, especially if such internal and external challenges are not adequately addressed. Nottingham makes this point: "As the religious organization grows in responsibility and social influence, it incorporates the entire range of worldly problems: problems of policy and of government, of leadership and ambition, and of the amassing of wealth, its use, distribution, and control. Hence religion in its organizational aspects . . . is marked by the same human problems as social life in general."[6] There is no way to avoid such occurrence as long as the group continues to grow. However, the consequences may be mitigated if there is diligence in teaching members the highest principles of the group and making it clear that there will be consequences for violations.

There is no question that the Church of God, as it grew from a simple sect led by a charismatic leader, to a complex organization, inherited many problems from the outside world that it had to address. Max Weber reminds us that, "as soon as the position of authority is well established, and as soon as control over large masses of people exists, it gives way to the forces of everyday routine."[7] The critical ethical edge that characterized the group in the first stage now becomes blunted and even lost in later stages (although we have seen that in the case of the Movement the prophetic edge regarding race relations was blunted even during the first stage). This only means that there needs to be ongoing focus on the group's founding principles, their meaning, and application in succeeding generations. In the case of the Church of God there needed to be—in every stage of its development—emphasis on holiness and visible unity and their meaning and relevance for race relations in the group.

The Church of God came into existence as a protest against what was perceived as "excessive and sinful organization of the church. 'Man-rule' usurped the role of the Holy Spirit, who governed the church through the distribution of charismatic gifts."[8] To introduce organization and procedures was perceived as a movement toward institutionalization. And yet, sociologists of religion have shown that as a religious group moves beyond the first stage of its life cycle, and as its membership grows, new challenges and problems arise. In order to effectively address these issues the pragmatic leader learns rather quickly that there must be a relaxing of any ban on organization and institutionalization. This was the plight of the Church of

---

6. Ibid., 220–21.
7. See Weber selection in Etzioni and Etzioni, *Social Change*, 60.
8. Strege, *I Saw the Church*, 76.

God as well. To meet the rising needs of the growing membership it was necessary to develop organizational structures.

Growth and expansion forced Movement leaders and a few leading ministers close to the administrative operation of the church to create the Missionary Committee in 1909. According to Strege, it is not an overstatement to say that this committee "was the first bureaucratic office in the Church of God movement."[9] This was a clear shift away from the earlier stance against all organizing, but once the door was open, and as the Movement continued to grow and expand, increased organization and institutionalization followed rather quickly. There was a proliferation of organizational developments from 1916–1930,[10] what has been characterized as "a momentous decade of institutionalization . . ."[11] This growth of organizations caused much alarm among Movement members who were uncritical proponents of the old way. But once the proliferation of organizations began there was no turning back.

D. S. Warner was no longer on the scene, and his immediate successors, i.e., E. E. Byrum and Frederick G. Smith, were no longer at the helm. A new generation of leaders were emerging "that knew not the antipathy toward organization that had breathed sulfur and brimstone at denominational Babylon."[12] We have seen that the second and succeeding generations rarely exhibit the same level of enthusiasm for the ideals and practices of the pioneers. Indeed, by the third generation—the generation in which so much complex organizational development occur—members may not even know what the ideals and practices of earlier generations were. This might well have been the case with Movement leaders after the leadership of Byrum and F. G. Smith. The next generation favored the establishment of organizations as a means to addressing problems, while the passion for the founder's ideal of holiness and visible unity had diminished considerably.

It is also during this third phase that the leadership is confronted with the task of explaining why the original objectives of the founder have not yet been achieved at a time when the group is successful in expanding its membership, organizational structure, and financial base. Why, in the case of the Church of God Movement, has holiness and visible unity—especially interracial unity—not been achieved? This is an especially acute problem for groups with an apocalyptic message. Such was the case of the early followers of Jesus, who were told of his imminent and immediate second coming.

9. Ibid., 85.
10. Ibid., 134–45.
11. Ibid., 112.
12. Ibid., 137.

Continued Expansion and Diversification

When it became clear that Jesus was not coming back as soon as they imagined, however, the next generation of Christians had to contrive another interpretation of the second coming, "an interpretation which stressed His coming in the sacraments and His invisible presence in the hearts of the faithful—and necessary to transfer the hope for the establishment of God's Kingdom to a distant, other-worldly future."[13]

This is the stage at which many organizations must *rationalize* their continued existence, especially in light of their failure to reach the goals of the founder. Most simply *reinterpret the goals* or the meaning of them. We have seen that Warner's emphasis on visible unity, for example, was reinterpreted by James E. Forrest and others to mean spiritual unity. It is also common at this stage that there is *displacement of goals*, i.e., emphasis is now placed on the importance of the continued existence of the organization for its own sake rather than for the sake of realizing the ideals of the founder. "The institution has become the master of its members instead of their servant, making many demands upon them, suppressing personalities, and directing energies into serving the 'organization church.'"[14]

Further expansion and diversification during the third stage of the group's lifecycle includes, among other things, expanded evangelistic outreach, nationally and internationally. In the case of the Church of God, there was no hesitation about evangelizing immigrant groups during the first two decades of the twentieth century. This was a period of great influx of European immigrants into the United States. John W. V. Smith tells us that, "by 1920 a significant work had developed among four of these groups—the Germans, the Scandinavians, the Slovaks and the Greeks."[15] There was also a major effort to evangelize the Armenians.

Earlier we saw that Warner and other Movement pioneers initially made no effort to evangelize blacks. Blacks simply heard the unity message and responded by joining the group. But what of those we know today as Hispanics and Latinas/os? The first Hispanic Church of God congregation was established in San Antonio, Texas in 1921.[16] As early as 1900 there was evidence of evangelistic work among Hispanics and Latin Americans.[17] In a letter to *The Gospel Trumpet*, B. F. Elliott, writing from Guaymas, Sonora, Mexico, reported that he and his wife Georgia had printed and disseminated four issues of *El Evangelio* (*The Gospel Trumpet*) at 1,000 copies each

---

13. See Weber selection in Etzioni and Etzioni, *Social Change*, 61.
14. Moberg, *The Church as a Social Institution*, 121.
15. Smith, *A Brief History of the Church*, 126.
16. See Callen, compiler/ed., *Following the Light*, 238–39.
17. See Stultz and Welch, comp. and eds., *The Book of Noah*, 325.

in Mexico, the United States, Cuba, and South America. Now the largest so-called minority group in the United States, the Hispanic community is a very fertile field for continued evangelization efforts, as well as recruitment efforts for Movement schools.

This third stage of the group's life cycle teems with developments of many kinds. In addition to lively development of complex organizational structures, there also tends to be increased interest in education and training. In its early period, the Church of God had an antipathy to education and training, although from the early 1890s the Gospel Trumpet Company "served as a kind of ministers' institute, or workers' training school,"[18] and also for youth "who went to no other school."[19] On the last day of the first year of school in 1892, Warner was asked to address the students. Making clear his own sense of the importance of formal education he reportedly said: "I am a firm believer in education. In my extensive travels I have always found that the one who studies and prepares himself and prays much is the most successful in God's work."[20]

This stance should not be surprising for a couple of reasons. First, there are numerous entries in Warner's journal that reveal his own deep love for learning and studying. He read, studied, and wrote almost daily. We have seen that in addition to the Bible, he read and pondered works in theology, ethics, philosophy, history, and science.[21] Without question, Warner was a lifelong student.[22] Second, at the 1876 meeting of the West Ohio Eldership, Warner was named with G. W. Wilson and G. T. Kimmel as the committee to help determine how best to address the educational needs of the Eldership.[23] There is no evidence that Warner was ever opposed to education as such. This appears yet another way that he differed from the general sociological tendency in the transformation of religious groups. Typically the charismatic founder of a religious group does not have the love for education and learning that Warner had.

I here part company with those, e.g., Charles E. Brown, who claim that near the end of his life Warner's attitude toward ministerial education changed.[24] In Warner's case it was a matter of simply being too busy with

---

18. See Brown, *When the Trumpet Sounded*, 170.

19. Ibid., 365.

20. As quoted by Noah Byrum in *The Book of Noah*, 159.

21. See Warner, *The Journal of D. S. Warner*, 80, 83, 84, 91, 93, 94, 97, 106, 111, 166, 217.

22. Brown, *When the Trumpet Sounded*, 53.

23. Forney, *History of the Churches of God*, 566.

24. Brown, *When the Trumpet Sounded*, 170.

evangelizing to be able to take up matters of formal education. Virtually all of his energy and time was devoted to proselytizing. This fit perfectly the pattern of leaders of new religious groups. Moreover, Warner encountered indescribable ignorance in his travels. Surely one who was as well read as Warner would have known early that education for ministers and laity alike could only strengthen efforts to evangelize. Furthermore, for our purpose it is important to call attention to the fact that the founder of the Movement acknowledged the importance of education for ministers. This was during the first stage of the Movement's life cycle. The emphasis on education generally emerges during the latter part of the second or early part of the third stage of the group's natural history.

On the editorial page of the December 5, 1895 issue of *The Gospel Trumpet* Warner "outlined plans for an extensive educational project which he was never permitted to carry out."[25] According to Noah H. Byrum, the school was to begin on December 5, but Warner was ill and unable to be present.[26] E. E. Byrum, who assumed the position of editor at Warner's death, made it clear that he did not support Warner's plans for a Bible school. To establish such a school, Byrum believed, would be tantamount to "letting down the Bible standard."[27] Sociologically, this rigid stance of not wanting to do anything that might give the appearance of being worldly was an indicator that Byrum was still in the sect mode. In any event, Byrum held that what the saints needed in terms of spiritual and faith development could be provided by their regular "Bible readings and special faith meetings."[28] Two weeks after Warner died Byrum wrote in *The Gospel Trumpet*: "Some have asked if we have a theological school here. We answer 'no,' neither do we expect to have."[29] Narrowly focused and intransigent on the matter, Byrum determined that there would be no Bible school as long as he was editor.

Nevertheless, by the end of the third decade of the Movement's existence there was increased interest in training, as is indicated in a 1912 article written by H. W. Brooks and submitted to *The Gospel Trumpet*. Brooks wrote: "Men and women upon whom God lays his hand for the ministry in their youth must be public speakers, singers, readers and writers all the days of their life. Both God and men require this duty of them. They should qualify themselves to meet ably every obligation and to fulfill properly each

---

25. Stultz and Welch, compiled/ed., *The Book of Noah*, 194.
26. Brown, *When the Trumpet Sounded*, 147.
27. Quoted in Stultz et al., *Old Main*, 27.
28. Quoted in ibid.
29. Quoted in Brown, *When the Trumpet Sounded*, 171.

duty required of them in their calling."[30] Brooks' reference to "men *and* women" is significant here, as he acknowledged awareness that God may call both males and females to the ministry. In fact the entire history of the Church of God Reformation Movement reveals clearly that women were serving as pastors from the time of the pioneers. Unfortunately, the percentage of Movement women as pastors declined from a high of 32% in 1925 to a dismal 2% in 1985.[31]

By 1917, the manager of the Gospel Trumpet Home, J. T. Wilson, had pulled together a task force (one year after E. E. Byrum retired) that had the responsibility of developing a continuing program to train workers for the publishing house. Classes actually began in October of that year. By 1919 the Anderson Bible Training School had come into existence. The Training School came to be known as the Anderson Bible Seminary in 1925, and Anderson College and Theological Seminary three years later. By 1967, the official name of the school was Anderson College, now known as Anderson University and School of Theology. The school was accredited by the Indiana Department of Education in 1937. Full membership in the North Central Association of Colleges and Secondary Schools was achieved in 1946. Presently there are six other Movement schools, one of which caters primarily to blacks, Bay Ridge Christian College in Kendleton, Texas. This school was originally organized in Union, Mississippi in 1959. J. Horace Germany, its founder and first president was a white pastor who had grown up in Mississippi and received his college training at Anderson College. In 1960 Germany was beaten severely by thirty white racists in Mississippi and left for dead. Local authorities threatened to hang the black students if they remained.[32] Suffice it to say that at this writing Bay Ridge is worse off in terms of finances, staffing, faculty, administrative and Board leadership than the other Movement schools. Indeed, it has not even met the goal of regional accreditation.[33]

The Anderson school has grown by leaps and bounds. "By 1975 the campus consisted of about twenty main buildings on seventy-five acres of land. Student enrollment had reached a total of 1800, and the number of full-time faculty had increased to eighty."[34] By this time the only Afrikan American in a tenure-track faculty position was James Earl Massey. James

---

30. Quoted in Smith, *A Brief History of the Church of God*, 98.

31. See Stanley, "Church of God Women Pastors," 175.

32. See Callen's interesting and instructive discussion of the founding and development of Bay Ridge Christian College in his *Preparing for Service*, chap. 5.

33. Massey, *African Americans and the Church of God*, 233.

34. Smith, *A Brief History of the Church of God*, 100.

Marshall, and the late Thomas J. Sawyer both had teaching responsibilities, but neither was fulltime on the faculty, and neither was on tenure-track. I was a student at the College and after graduation spent one year at the School of Theology during this period. When Massey resigned in 1984 to become Dean of the Chapel at Tuskegee University there were no Afrikan Americans left on the School of Theology faculty. When he returned as dean in 1989, he was again the only Afrikan American on the faculty. When he retired for the last time in 1995, there were no blacks on the School of Theology faculty. However, James W. Lewis, an Afrikan American who, since 1992 had been Assistant Professor of Christian Ethics at Anderson University, was promoted to Professor of Ethics and Theology at the School of Theology in 2006. A tenured member of the School of Theology faculty, Lewis was appointed dean in 2014 after serving as associate dean for several years. Although his appointment as dean is a significant occurrence, it is not a gain (in faculty numbers) when we remember that for many years Massey was the only Afrikan American on the seminary faculty.

When leading ministers and Movement leaders established the General Ministerial Assembly in 1917 the creation of many church agencies followed. This made it possible for a more even distribution of power and influence in the Movement, since previously these had been centered in the editor of *The Gospel Trumpet*. By 1930, many more structural changes occurred, and this trend continued throughout and beyond the post-World War II era. From roughly 1945 to 1970 the Movement experienced unprecedented growth in membership and prosperity, unwittingly moving toward becoming the very type of religious group that early leaders sought to avoid. Sociologically, it was moving toward becoming a denomination.

In chapter 1, we saw that the denomination tends to have a complex organizational structure; tends to achieve much greater universality than the sect and established-sect; tends to be less critical of the wider society and to soften its religious and ethical ideals; thus in a related sense, it tends to be in close relationship with the power structures of society; tends to be limited by class, racial, and at times regional boundaries; tends to appeal to the middle class; tends to be receptive and open to fellowshipping with other denominations and affiliating with ecumenical organizations such as the National Council of Churches and the World Council of Churches; and tends to focus on education. Movement history, especially in the post-World War II period, exhibits all of these traits.

Although Merle Strege provides a systematic discussion of the theological implications of Church of God teachings and practices from its inception to the publication of *I Saw the Church*, and is not concerned about the sociological transformation of the group as such, his historical-theological discussion cites a number of traits that can only be characterized in the sociological sense as denominational traits. Strege uses different words, but the ideas match the traits of the denomination, as listed above. I list the characteristics as they appear in Strege's book. After each trait I place the page number in parenthesis:

- Proliferation of bureaucratic agencies and sharing of decision-making authority (217, 220)
- More accepting of other denominations and recognizing them as legitimate churches (a practice previously rejected because of adherence to the practice of *come-outism*) (218-19, 248)
- Unprecedented growth in membership in the post-World War II era (292, 297)
- Unprecedented growth in prosperity in the post-World War II era. Such prosperity is seen in the architecture of new church buildings and their locations in the nicer neighborhoods (292-93); seen also in rising pastoral salaries, and rising church property values (299)
- Increased attention to care for retiring ministers, e.g., creation of retirement funds (296)
- Change in attitude toward ecumenical groups such as the Federal Council of Churches (now the National Council of Churches) (299-300)
- Change in various practices: acceptance of medical care rather than sole dependence on divine healing (302-3); relaxing of prohibition against some forms of entertainment and consumption of coffee (305); commitment to pacifism softened (306-7); vastly increased concerns about social justice (308-9)

These traits emerged during the expansion period in the Movement from 1945-1970.[35] This was essentially a movement from the fringes and separatism to the center; toward the middle class. The movement was toward what was once referred to as "mainline" or "mainstream" American Protestantism. In the sociological sense it was a movement toward becoming a denomination.

With all of its growth in membership and its continuing prosperity, the Church of God Reformation Movement has yet to make good the claim of holiness and visible unity, especially along racial-ethnic lines. After 135 years of existence one might reasonably wonder whether Afrikan Americans

---

35. Strege, *I Saw the Church*, 297.

should remain in the group. For this writer, at least, it is a Wonder of the World that they have remained in the Movement for as long as they have, and there are no signs on the horizon of mass exiting. In any case, since for the time being blacks are intent on remaining in the group, it is reasonable to consider whether there might be things that Movement people—regardless of race and ethnicity—can, indeed must do, to finally make good the claim about holiness and visible interracial unity. This is the subject of the next two chapters. The first addresses the more general question of what whites and blacks must do in light of the centrality of the holiness-visible unity principle. There is also an extended discussion on the meaning and implications of the holiness-visible unity principle. The final chapter proposes and discusses a number of conditions for making good the claim.

6

Making Good the Claim

What Whites and Blacks Must Do

WITH ALL THE GROWTH and expansion that takes place during the third period of a religious group's life cycle there is by this time less open disagreement with outside societal forces. By now, the group has taken much more of the world (e.g., people, resources, and practices) into itself, and in this sense, has become the world. Although this tends to reduce conflict with the world, it also sets the stage for more accommodation or toleration of "the ways of the world." In this regard, David Moberg writes: "Conformity to societal folkways and mores is typical even on issues clearly in conflict with implications of the church's official dogma. Ulterior motives of 'respectability' are often involved in joining; membership standards are often relaxed as the church tries to gain all socially respectable people."[1] The group generally does a great deal of accommodating and moderating of its ethic or ideals in order to attract and retain such people. Sociologically, the religious group that exhibits these traits is either an established sect or a denomination (with signs of it approaching the church-type organization, which is even more accommodative and inclusive of the world).

A legitimate question is: Where does the group go from here, since it has nearly come full circle? That is, having broken away from a denomination or church-like organization because of irresolvable differences and

---

1. Moberg, *The Church as a Social Institution*, 121.

having existed for a period of time as a sect in the sociological sense it has, over the course of roughly two to three generations taken on the characteristics of an established sect, denomination, or church. And yet, if sociologists of religion are correct in their claim that sect-like tendencies (such as the spirit of protest) are always present in a religious group—as they surely are in the Movement—it would seem that there is a strong internal *potential* for the group to regenerate and revitalize itself and to go to yet another level of development before serious signs of disintegration begin to appear. The question is: What would be the nature of this regeneration and revitalization, and what would be its actual shape?

Such a question implies the possibility of the Movement entering a fourth stage of development. Since a most egregious weakness of the Church of God has been its failure to actualize to a significant degree the visible unity that D. S. Warner preached and taught, this could be the period in which leaders on all levels begin committing their energy, talents, and resources to making this a reality at last. Indeed, this fourth stage might well be the period in which Movement people finally begin to "make good the claim"— the claim about holiness and visible unity in the church; a unity that is not "an invisible something up in the air," declared Frederick G. Smith, but one that all the world can see; a unity "applied to the visible body of worshippers on the earth."[2] Movement people clearly did not make good the claim during the second and third stages of their natural history. Warner blew the trumpet for reform during the first stage, but it was left to his followers in subsequent generations to actualize his core principles for reform—holiness and visible unity. Perhaps *now* is the time.

Andrew Byers depicts D. S. Warner as the quintessential reformer; the trailblazer of the Church of God Reformation Movement. "There needed some one to sound the trumpet of the Lord," writes Byers, "some one to take the lead and make a positive declaration against the sin of division."[3] God had prepared Warner to be just such an instrument. Warner's was the reform stage; his "mission was strictly that of a reformer." Byers further clarified this important point, saying:

> It was his part to venture boldly with the truth God had given him, with a willingness to run the gauntlet of persecutions that were sure to greet him on the right and left. His severe denunciation of all things sectarian was consistent with his pioneer position. There first had to be an awakening, a breaking up of old conditions, particularly of the recognition (into which the

---

2. Smith, *What the Bible Teaches*, 241 (my emphasis).
3. Byers, *Birth of a Reformation*, 272.

minds of people generally had settled) of the sects as being the church of God. His work was the initial, or birth, stage of the reform.[4]

This characterization of the founder-reformer is consistent with what we saw in the first stage of the sociological transformation of the new religious group. Warner's charismatic traits aided him greatly in carrying out his reform function. But once the foundational work of reform had been done, the way had been prepared for what Byers rightly refers to as the *constructive stage*. Others, then, had to actualize the reforms and ideals of the reformer. It is during this very long, constructive stage that generations of Movement people would be expected to make sense of the basic ideals and truths that Warner preached and taught, and to determine their meaning and significance for their respective historical eras. The aim would be to concretize or actualize the core beliefs of the founder in order that all may see it. Byers said it best: "*The responsibility is to make good the claim.*"[5] Essentially this has been the task and the challenge of Movement people since Warner's death—to make good the claim about holiness and visible unity. To date this has not been accomplished to any significant degree, and thus remains a fundamental challenge for the group.

In chapter 7 I will explore some specific things that Movement people might do if they are at all serious about making good the claim about holiness and visible unity along racial lines. In preparation for this undertaking, the present chapter focuses on the need for Movement people to understand the true meaning of the holiness principle and its relation to injustice in general, and racism in particular; to understand that the visible unity principle itself is grounded in holiness, and that we cannot truly have one without the other. In the sense in which Warner understood it, there can be no holiness without visible unity, and there can be no visible unity without holiness. The two are inextricably intertwined. According to Frederick G. Smith, from the time of the early church, holiness and visible unity were inseparably linked, "for wherever perfect holiness is, there is unity of believers. In other words, there is no true and perfect unity without heart-purity, and there is no true heart-purity without Bible unity: there is no true Bible holiness without both."[6] Indeed, James Earl Massey has seen to a degree that others have not, that the integral relation between holiness and visible unity is what gave Warner and Movement pioneers their ethical edge, whether

---

4. Ibid., 31.
5. Ibid., 32 (my emphasis).
6. Smith, *What the Bible Teaches*, 227 (Smith's italics).

or not they understood the full meaning of it and consistently applied it to unity along racial lines.[7]

In this chapter, I stress the need for white and black Movement people to endeavor to be honest and forthright with each other about race; that they should strive to engage in more straight talk about racism and unearned white privilege. If they cannot, or are not willing to do this, they are doomed to being the divided church they have been virtually since the beginning. The hope is that genuine straight talk about disunity along racial lines will create openings for ways to move beyond this, and in the direction of visible interracial unity.

THE NEED TO LOOK BACK

After advancing through the continued expansion and diversification stage of its life cycle, the group is on the brink of yet another phase of development. This may be the period that requires the most imagination, creativity, courage, and newly found commitment by Movement people to its founding principles. It seems to me that this may be the point at which the members, many who may be relatively new and not well informed about Movement teachings, may begin inquiring about, and looking back to, their roots.[8] Looking back may serve two important but related functions. The obvious one for the group is that members will learn from whence they have come; who the founder was, what he sought to do and why; what were the basic core beliefs he espoused, and what was their meaning. The second function would be to assess whether the group has in fact made good the basic claims of the founder, and if not, to begin mapping out strategies *and* timetables at all levels in its organizations as to how and when it intends to do so, or *whether* it intends to do so. This could be one of the best means of renewing or revitalizing a religious group that, by now is fat and sluggish, as a result of its continued membership growth and prosperity, as well as its deepening institutional growth and complexity. The fact that the group is now *established* positions it to take the necessary steps through its institutional structures and local churches "to make good the claim."

This idea of looking back is illustrated nicely in Barry L. Callen's edited 1978 publications about the Church of God titled *A Time to Remember*, which consists of six books, each of which chronicles "a specific phase of the movement's history, teaching and future. Titles include: *Beginnings*,

---

7. Massey, *African Americans and the Church of God*, 59.

8. Cf. Callen, *A Time to Remember*. See also *Following the Light*, comp. and ed., Callen.

Testimonies, Teachings, Milestones, Evaluations, and *Projections.*"[9] For our purpose, the point in looking back to Movement roots is not to revive beliefs and practices that fostered only division and separation, e.g., the early emphasis on the absolute rejection of organization; refusal to fellowship with other denominations or to acknowledge them as legitimate religious groups; insistence on an apocalyptic ecclesiology and strict adherence to the "church-historical hermeneutic;" and rejection of medical care. Such matters were not the core beliefs on which the Movement was founded. Rather, in looking back, the point is to become acquainted with the early basic teachings that have withstood the test of time, and most particularly to become familiar with the founding core principles and what Movement members' moral responsibilities are in each generation in light of those principles. The question that remains is: Why would a group want to return to its roots to examine its beginnings and basic teachings, if not to determine the extent to which it has (or has not) made good its founding claims, and to finish the job? This cannot, indeed must not be, a purely intellectual exercise of some sort; a mere publication of books, holding forums, sponsoring lectures, workshops, etc. The intellectual engagements would be an important first step in the process, but the real revitalization will be apparent once the group begins relentlessly taking the necessary concrete, methodical steps to make good the claim about holiness and visible unity.

Throughout this book, I have added the qualifier "visible" when referring to the unity principle. The reason for doing so is that this is the aspect of Jesus' prayer to God about unity, and Warner's teaching about it, that Movement people have failed most embarrassingly and consistently to actualize, particularly in the matter of race. The tendency has been to espouse and hold up (in practice) a very narrow view of unity, e.g., spiritual or religious unity. It has always been most convenient for whites in the group to stress the spiritual and denominational aspect of unity, as if this narrow view is consistent with the visible unity espoused in the Bible and by Warner. Time and again, the Movement has sacrificed the visible unity of Christians of all races, thus making it impossible for them to worship and fellowship together on the basis of equality. Interestingly, from the time of the pioneers there was clear recognition of the differences between the members of the body of Christ. For example, in his excellent discussion on the unity of believers, Frederick G. Smith writes of members "differing in age, in sex, in intellectual attainments, in social advantages, in nationality . . ."[10] However, he fails to name race as one of those differences. It is because

---

9. Back cover of Callen, ed., *A Time to Remember*.
10. Smith, *What the Bible Teaches*, 224, 228.

of such failure and silence that this and the following chapter focus on what can be done to attain visible unity, particularly of the interracial type. There are certainly other viable issues that the Movement will need to address during this fourth stage of its life cycle, but so glaringly and consistently has it failed regarding the issue of visible unity along racial lines in virtually every area of its operations that I have chosen to focus on it here and in the remainder of the book.

NEED FOR A BROADER UNDERSTANDING OF SIN

For too long, Movement people have given only lip service to the importance of holiness or sanctification, and have too often failed to live out its meaning in race relations. It might well be that in part, the reason for this is that most have had only a narrow and superficial understanding of the holiness-visible unity doctrine and its relation to sin. Historically, members of the Movement have understood that holiness means that by the grace of God one is purged or purified of all sin and that with that same grace one is able to live free of sin. Unfortunately, there seems to be a narrow understanding of the *sin* from which holiness cleanses. The focus has generally been on purifying one of personal sins such as lying, consumption of alcohol and drugs, smoking, pre- and extra-marital sex, swearing, dancing, etc. I have yet to read where most Movement people contend that entire sanctification is a significant step toward purging one from the sin of racism; that holiness and racism are contradictory terms; or that one cannot claim holiness while simultaneously and relentlessly choosing to remain racist.

The Movement has been consistent with orthodox Christianity in its focus on sin in general and the need for its eradication. However, its understanding of sin has been too narrow. What Reinhold Niebuhr said about evangelical Christianity and sin is quite to the point of the matter. "The orthodox church still convicts people of sin, but the sins of which it makes people conscious are usually not those which are most significant in our society . . ."[11] Too often the focus is on personal sins, not social sins such as racism, and other social injustices. Niebuhr's criticism of liberal Christianity, on the other hand, was that its overly optimistic view of human nature caused many proponents to underestimate the importance of sin, such that many liberals convicted no one of sin. This was a serious error on the part of much of liberal Christianity. Although Niebuhr would have applauded the seriousness with which the Movement has historically taken sin, he would be just as emphatic in the criticism that it focused on personal sins to the ex-

---

11. Niebuhr, "The Weakness of the Modern Church," 71.

clusion of social sins such as racism. It convicts people of personal sins, but has not done enough to make them aware of, and convict them of, sins such as racism. Such sins are equally, if not more important, than personal sins, inasmuch as they devastate the lives of vast numbers of people. Although Merle Strege maintains that early Movement people considered the ethical consequences of the holiness principle, and that they "became especially concerned about the marks of sanctification in the daily lives of behavior," their emphasis was without question on personal sins, e.g., the prohibition against alcohol, drugs, caffeine, dancing, attending movies and the theater, etc.[12] They did not consider to any significant degree the ethical consequences of holiness for social issues generally, and racism most especially.

I am not here calling for Movement people to begin devaluing or de-emphasizing personal sins, but that they broaden their understanding and sense of the sins from which holiness delivers believers to include devastating social sins such as racism, sexism, heterosexism, ageism, and economic exploitation. The call is for a broader conception and understanding of holiness or sanctification, as well as the sin from which it delivers. Movement Christian ethicist and pastor Cheryl Sanders makes this point in a helpful way.

> The doctrine of sanctification proclaims that by the grace of God we can live free from sin. Our understanding of the sin from which we have been delivered, however, tends to be much too narrow, as measured by the degree of segregation and discrimination that exists within our congregations and national organizations. Since sin is manifested both in personal and social matters, so our sanctification from sin has both personal and social effects.[13]

The emphasis must be on overcoming *both* personal and social sins. I would say that in light of the Movement's dismal failure to focus on addressing and eradicating the sins of racism, sexism, heterosexism, and economic injustice there is need to be much more intentional about highlighting efforts in this direction. In a word, Movement people need to give serious and sustained attention to the socio-ethical implications of the holiness principle relative to interracial unity. Continued failure to do this can only call into question the credibility of their contention that they want to make good the claim.

Subsequently, we will see that the experience of entire sanctification does not in itself deliver one from long years of internalized racism and

---

12. Strege, *I Saw the Church*, 44.
13. Sanders, "Ethics of Holiness and Unity in the Church of God," 144.

sense of race superiority. Holiness purges such a one so that she is now positioned to work intentionally to rid herself of racism. The experience of holiness is but the first step in the process. One accepts holiness, and then chooses and strives to work diligently to eradicate her racist ideas and tendencies. Somewhere along the way the prejudiced or racist Movement person must be informed that racism is unacceptable for the individual who claims to be sanctified.

MORE FORTHRIGHTNESS REGARDING INTERRACIAL UNITY

Without question, the ideal of visible interracial unity has been implicit in the teachings on holiness and visible unity from the founding of the Movement. The focus was not solely on an inward spiritual unity or even church or denominational unity. The concern was also for that visible unity in the body of Christ that the world could see. *Every* Christian, regardless of outward features, was to be included in the unity that Warner preached and taught. That is what he took Jesus' prayer to God (for the disciples) to mean. That is what he took Galatians 3:28 to mean: that there is neither Jew or Gentile, bond or free, male or female in Christ. The Church of God is one body, notwithstanding the physical or biological traits of the members.

There are numerous places in Warner's writings where he easily could have explicitly linked his discussions on division and separation to the problem of interracial division. He writes, for example, that divisions of *any* kind between the truly converted puts the church in an abnormal state, and positions it for spiritual death and disintegration.[14] Warner was, without doubt, aware of the status of race relations in his day. What better place in his writing to have connected his criticism of divisiveness in the church to race division in the church. He could easily have named division along racial lines as an illustration of the absolutely unacceptable separation and division in the church of which he was so critical, and believed to be inconsistent with the holiness-visible unity principle in the Bible. Such specificity is always necessary in a racially divided society. One has to name it!

Warner believed strongly that ideas and actions that cause division in the church are among the worst sins cited in the Bible. And yet, he did not expressly name racism and white supremacy as divisive elements in the church. Had Warner done this, he might well have effectively silenced all guessing and speculation as to whether he was concerned only about the narrow unity of denominations, or whether his focus was on the broader,

---

14. Warner and Riggle, *The Cleansing of the Sanctuary*, 264.

more consistently biblical view that includes interracial unity. However, Warner, unfortunately, left open the door for speculation.

Reflecting on Jesus's unity prayer, Warner noted that, "the language virtually implies that if this holy unity is not seen by the world in the professed family of God, unbelief would possess their hearts, and his death on their behalf would be largely frustrated."[15] Here again, Warner failed to expressly connect visible unity to unity along racial lines. We see numerous instances of such failure throughout his writings, as well as those of subsequent and more recent Movement leaders and scholars. Indeed, even James Earl Massey has not consistently and expressly made this connection in his writings, although he does so in a mostly roundabout or indirect way in *African Americans and the Church of God*. I return to this important point below. For now, suffice it to say that Warner's tactic of not explicitly addressing the race problem, and those who have adopted this approach, has hurt more than helped the Movement to make substantive progress in race relations. Such an approach has therefore *not* been "the better part of wisdom" after all. Essentially, such a tactic leaves it to the reader or listener to figure out whether what is being said about the sin of separation has implications for race relations and what those might be. It seems to me that the better part of wisdom would be for the preacher, speaker, writer, or teacher to reveal her own stance about the matter by explicitly expressing the relation between visible unity and unity along racial lines. In other words, one should just say outright that the Movement's teaching on holiness and visible unity means that forced interracial separation is as sinful as spiritual, denominational, and other forms of division in the church.

In chapter 2, we saw that during an earlier period of his ministry, John Winebrenner focused on the visible unity principle and rejected all forms of division within the Churches of God, including racial division. However, Winebrenner later moderated his stance, seeming to prefer church unity at all cost. Unfortunately, this was done at the expense of visible interracial unity. Winebrenner feared schisms within the church and wanted to avoid it. So he sacrificed the human and civil rights of blacks on the altar of a homogeneous racial unity in the church.

We saw that D. S. Warner was excised from the West Ohio Eldership not only because he was influenced by the holiness principle, but because he was thoroughly convinced of the need for Christians to accept entire sanctification as a second act of divine grace. He therefore felt compelled to unite holiness with the unity principle, believing that holiness unites in such a way as to make the church one; that holiness is the means to visible

---

15. Ibid., 246.

unity. We have seen that while on the basis of Scripture Warner was arguing emphatically and relentlessly against divisions of all kinds in the body of Christ, white members of the Church of God were instigating separation along racial lines even before he died. Consequently, it is not helpful—if it ever was—for Church of God scholars to paint a picture of a time when the Movement exhibited no racial biases, and that somehow only at the turn of the twentieth century did Movement people begin to accommodate to the racial ethic of the wider society. This wrongly implies that there was at the turn of the century a radical shift in the Movement's race ethic.

While it is true that from the inception of the Movement blacks were welcome, we have seen that there is no hard evidence that this was based on the principle of equality and equal treatment. The evidence suggests that there were a few exceptional cases where whites who did indeed try to treat blacks as their equals but this was not the case for most white Movement pioneers. Despite the fact that early on, many blacks and a few whites fought hard to create a visible interracial unity in the church, social custom, *and much more significantly*, the failure of moral nerve and courage of many whites culminated in the unfortunate confrontation at the 1912 camp meeting at Anderson. On that day a wound was inflicted, not only on the black membership, but the entire Church of God Movement; a wound that has not yet healed, and is consequently the cause of continued division and trouble along racial lines, despite the pretense of some that significant healing and progress has been made. White and black Movement people will have to be honest about this history. They will need to see it for what it was and is, if they truly desire to make good the claim.

TALKING AND RESOLUTIONS ARE NECESSARY BUT NOT SUFFICIENT

Virtually every predominantly white religious group that has existed for at least a century in the United States can legitimately make the claim that it has made some progress in the area of race relations. In light of the amount of time that has passed in relation to the progress that has been made, however, no honest person will say that most of these groups have made significant progress toward the achievement of substantial interracial unity. To a large extent, this has not yet happened in the Church of God Reformation Movement because for far too long there has been a failure of moral nerve among both whites and blacks (especially those in leadership positions) to be vigilant about forthrightly striving to make good the claim about visible unity. I know that many, many conversations have occurred over the past fifty or so years about this matter, including the passing of a number of important resolutions on race and racial reconciliation by the General Assembly. As far back as June 1954 a resolution was adopted supporting the landmark Supreme Court decision in Brown vs. Topeka, Kansas that made the "separate but equal" ruling in Plessy vs. Ferguson (1896) unconstitutional. Ten years later, in 1964, a major statement on race was issued claiming in part: "We believe that in the Church of God there should be no racial barriers because we are all brethren in Christ." There was also affirmation of fundamental human rights and the claim that "these rights are given by God and that the church has the responsibility to defend them and work for their guarantee." The promise was also made to "work to achieve an experience of fairness and honest love toward all our brethren, free from discrimination based on race." Resolutions were also issued in June 1964 and 1965 supporting the civil rights and voting rights bill of those years, respectively. In 1964, the declaration was made that "the Church of God Reformation Movement believes that the principle of segregation based on color, race, caste, or ethnic origin is a denial of the Christian faith and ethic, which stems from the basic premise taught by our Lord that all men are the children of God." A resolution was passed in 1968 asserting that seeking racial justice was to remain a spiritual priority. In that same year, a major resolution was passed on race.[16] A Task Force on Racial Reconciliation was established in June 1998 with the understanding that it remain in existence until such time the Ministries Council determines that its work is complete. In addition, there has been acknowledgement of the failure to live up to the Movement's commitment to racial harmony.[17] Sadly, not one of the Movement's resolutions on race include the element of consequences or discipline for failure to comply. Nor were adequate timetables instituted for actually achieving the type of racial-ethnic diversity proposed in the resolutions. Therefore, presently the resolutions have no teeth.

Without question, there has been much *talk* in the Church of God about matters of race, at least since 1954. Tragically, however, when strategies have been proposed we have at times seen the "with all deliberate speed" language (of the 1954 Supreme Court decision) when the General Assembly has talked about actually following through on racial integration. For example, in 1961, the Study Commission on Race made seven recommendations on race relations to the Executive Council of the Church of God and the General Ministerial Assembly. One of these said: "Proceed

---

16. See Callen, comp. and ed., *Journeying Together*, 75, 78, 80, 85.
17. See Callen, comp. and ed., *Following the Light*, 264–65.

with all deliberate speed to integrate ratification procedures in all states immediately."[18] Historically, "with all deliberate speed" has meant little more than get to it when you can, or when you think it is most convenient. This is precisely why there are public schools in the United States that took decades before complying with the Brown decision. The language of "all deliberate speed" and "make deliberate moves . . . wherever and whenever possible" must be avoided if Movement leaders are serious about interracial unity based on terms of equality.

Notwithstanding the passing of the resolutions on race, my sense is that in their day to day relations Movement people have frequently been too timid to name the racists, the racism, and unearned white privilege that still plague the group. Many of these folks—whites as well as some Afrikan Americans—often do not even want to insert the term racism when discussing the visible unity issue. Some believe that the term is too inflammatory, and that if they are to make any progress at all toward reconciliation, it would be better to use language that is palatable to otherwise well-meaning white people, and most especially diehard racists. Indeed, Massey's apprehensiveness about using the term race in *Concerning Christian Unity* (1979), especially when discussing racial division within the Church of God, is a case in point.[19] In addition, his use of the terms "human groupings" and "provincialism" as apparently synonymous with "race," "racism," and "ethnicity" is also an example of what I am talking about.[20] This seems reminiscent of the indirect approach used by Warner, but it does not, in my judgment, contribute in any significant way toward actually resolving the Movement's ongoing race problem. Long years in the theological academy convinces me that whites who are serious about acknowledging their unearned privilege and working to eliminate their own and institutional racism, are in no way hindered from doing so because of the use of the term "racism." On the

18. Callen, comp. and ed., *Thinking and Acting Together*, 62.

19. Massey, *Concerning Christian Unity*. The following passage illustrates my point. "There are those differences that are *seen*—age, customs, culture, personal development—and there are those differences that are *known*, such as income, education, experience, and length of membership in the group" (34). He does not include race as one of those differences that is seen. Not to include this term, but to supply one that is more palatable to whites does not challenge them to address their racism and sense of privilege. However, Massey does use the terms race and racism at least three times in the book. Two of these are in connection with the World Council of Churches' initiative to address racism on a more global scale, and the other is in relation to a blatant omission on the part of the planners of the World Congress on Evangelism in Berlin, Germany in 1966. He does not explicitly use these terms when discussing unity (or the lack thereof) in the Church of God.

20. See ibid., 54, 55; and his *African Americans and the Church of God* where the term "provincialism" is used throughout.

other hand, those who are not serious about acknowledging their unearned privilege and eradicating individual and systemic racism will not do so, regardless of whether the term "racism," or a more palatable term is used.

In a word, I am saying that *there will have to be much more straight talk about matters of race and unearned white privilege* if Movement people are to do anything more than pretend that they are making significant strides toward achieving a more substantial visible unity along interracial lines; that they are in fact making good the claim, including those important offerings made in the resolutions on race during the 1960s. The time is long past due for the Movement to *show* the world (through substantive actions) that it is making good the claim. More important, the time is long past due to show the God of the Hebrew prophets and Jesus Christ that this is being done.

WHY BLACKS REMAIN IN WHITE DENOMINATIONS

A question that Afrikan Americans—whether as Movement people, Presbyterians, Disciples of Christ, United Methodists, or members of other predominantly white groups—simply *must* ask themselves is this: In light of our understanding of the holiness and visible unity principles and the fact that unity along racial lines has not been attained after more than a century, why have blacks remained in those groups? That they have done so must be enigmatic to the thinking person. Amazingly, blacks remained in the Movement after the early efforts of whites to force racial separation and to at best treat them like second-class members. Blacks stayed after E. E. Byrum's infamous article, "The Color Line" (1897); after being insulted at the 1912 Anderson camp meeting; stayed after all of that, and too much more. But why, today, after more than 100 years later, do Afrikan Americans remain in the Church of God Reformation Movement? Why do they stay and put up with the unnecessary pressures and stresses that lead to and aggravate high blood pressure, diabetes, heart disease, etc.? Why do they stay? And, at least if they must stay, why do they not exhibit more of the spirit of protest of the mid-1960s and 1970s? That is, why do they not stir and trouble the very spiritual waters of the Movement, at the local and national levels? Why do they allow the powers that be in the Movement to rest comfortably and peacefully, rather than hound them day and night until they either make good the claim, or declare for all to hear—in no uncertain terms—that they have no intention of doing so?

It is long past due for Afrikan Americans in every predominantly white religious group to ponder these questions. My personal sense is that blacks made a Himalayan mistake by remaining in predominantly white religious groups that have always treated them like unwanted stepchildren. Afrikan Americans owe it to themselves, and even more so to their posterity, to ask and seriously ponder the question: Why do we stay?

I suppose the decision of blacks to remain in the Church of God, in any case, may, among other things, be attributed to something in their character; their interpretation of the holiness-visible unity message in the Bible; the seriousness with which they apparently took Warner's teaching on holiness and visible unity (even when the pioneers did not link that teaching to interracial unity intentionally and consistently); and their sense of the deeper, more inclusive meaning of Warner's teaching on visible unity. To this, Massey offers an instructive comment.

> Early on, the unity emphasis in the message of the Church of God appealed strongly to African-Americans who were otherwise beset by restrictive segregation patterns in the land. The message of unity provided promise for needed affirmation of self-worth, on the one hand, and needed social togetherness, on the other. Unlike other church groups whose doctrinal positions accented nonrelational themes and teachings, the central theme of the Church of God movement was a relational one, the unity of believers. When social relations within this movement have been under strain, the challenge of the unity ideal has always been present as a prodding factor toward correction and reform. To be sure, the sad fact of race distancing and polarization in Church of God history can be documented as readily as that result in other church groups; but the unity ideal never has allowed that separateness to stand unchallenged. Rather, the announced ideal has stirred the most thoughtful to seek a remedy for the problem and to bridge the distances that have developed.[21]

Massey also asserts that the existence of the National Association of the Church of God is a compelling reason that blacks have chosen to remain in the Movement, even when racial tension and unrest have threatened. The National Association has in many ways provided catharsis and has at times been an open and willing advocate for racial unity. At times, it has "functioned as an active witness against racist influences at work in the church; it has been the social entity to protest when the church was not as socially responsible and active as the unity ideal seemed to demand," Massey further contends.[22]

---

21. Massey, "The National Association," 331.
22. Ibid., 332.

Without question, the ideal of visible unity still has strong appeal to those *thinking* Afrikan Americans who continue to want—more than many things—that this emphasis be inclusive of unity along racial-ethnic lines based on terms of equality, and not merely spiritual or other invisible "up in the air" unity.

Considering that blacks had been emancipated from slavery for only a few years when Warner came preaching holiness and visible unity it is very likely the case that when they heard the message they immediately interpreted its meaning much more broadly and deeply than Warner and most white Movement pioneers. For blacks, the unity message pertained not only to spiritual and denominational unity, but to concrete unity among people, regardless of race. It meant that people of all races were invited to come together to worship God as one people, equal and united under God.

Long before D. S. Warner preached his holiness-visible unity message, enslaved and nominally free blacks knew that all human beings were equal before God and were members of the one family under God, and thus that all should be treated humanely and as beings of infinite, inviolable dignity. When blacks were treated in contrary fashion in white churches some, like George Liele (Baptist) and Richard Allen (Methodist Episcopal), left and formed separate black churches in 1750[23] and 1816,[24] respectively. (Allen and a group of black parishioners walked out of St. Georges Episcopal Church in Philadelphia in 1787 for good, when they were not allowed to pray at the altar.) There is no question that Warner and other white Movement pioneers saw the implicit message of racial unity in their teaching, but the evidence suggests that their focus was on spiritual and denominational unity. This helps to explain why we see only a couple of explicit references to the race problem in Warner's teaching, preaching, and writing. Perhaps he too, like John Winebrenner, was concerned about possible schism in the church over race if too much explicit attention was given its inconsistency with the holiness-visible unity doctrine.

Black people, just a few years out of legal slavery and the post-Reconstruction era, heard Warner's message on holiness and visible unity and immediately believed that whites had finally found the truth of the Christian message and were preaching unity along racial lines in God's church (whatever else they were preaching regarding visible unity!). Blacks heard a much broader message in the teaching on unity than most whites, and thus they easily identified with it, and eagerly joined the Movement. It is no

---

23. See Lincoln and Mamiya, *The Black Church in the African American Experience*, 23–24.

24. Ibid., 49–56. See also Wesley, *Richard Allen: Apostle of Freedom*, 49–53.

wonder that blacks were devastated when, little more than a decade after the Movement was founded growing numbers of whites began questioning the wisdom of interracial worship in the group. The racial confrontation at the Anderson camp meeting in 1912 only exacerbated their sense of disappointment and frustration.

It is quite possible that blacks read more into the unity message than the pioneers themselves intended. Even if this were the case, it was nothing short of a major contribution to the Movement—this much-expanded more wholistic view of unity, as opposed to the more limited conception of spiritual and denominational unity lauded by most whites. There is no evidence that blacks rejected the latter conception of unity. Rather, they saw that the visible unity teaching of Warner was to be more broadly cast to include spiritual as well as interracial unity. In this regard, black people might well have understood the true meaning of the visible unity message better than most whites who were preaching and teaching it.

Nevertheless, if blacks just cannot bring themselves to leave the Movement, but have resigned themselves to stay—and indicators are that this is the case—what do they need to be doing (and not doing) to help insure that every conceivable effort and resource will be committed to making real the claim about visible unity along racial-ethnic lines based on the principle of equality? In addition, what are some things that whites need to do and stop doing, in order to prime the pump of visible unity and equality of treatment? Just how far are both groups willing to go in this regard? I address these matters in the next two sections, and conclude the chapter with a discussion on the centrality and meaning of the holiness-visible unity doctrine.

WHAT AFRIKAN AMERICANS SHOULD STOP DOING

If further advancement is to be made in race relations Afrikan Americans should stop allowing whites to choose their leaders and other representatives. This means that they must also stop being satisfied with *the onliest one syndrome*. Historically, too many blacks who have been firsts and the only one—even in the Movement—have been satisfied to the point that they have been so happy to just be there, to be on this or that board or faculty, or the only executive in some agency of the group, that they have done nothing substantive to open doors or create opportunities for other blacks and people of color to enter. Nor have they done much in the way of helping whites to address their racism and the institutional racism from which they benefit so much at the expense of blacks. Afrikan Americans such as these seem to fear doing anything at all that may jeopardize their own position and standing with the white leadership, or that may arouse whites' suspicions or distrust of them. Instead, too often the tendency has been to toot one's own horn—or allow it to be tooted by others—and to then pretend that he possesses admirable qualities that few others in the race possesses. This leads such a one to actually believe that he deserves all of the perks and the recognition given by whites. Such a one too often becomes comfortable with the idea that whites consider him to be the most "responsible and articulate" among Afrikan Americans in the group. Therefore, whenever whites want to know something—anything at all—since he is considered by them to be the resident expert on all things pertinent to black people and their culture, they always turn to that most "responsible and articulate" one of all Afrikan Americans. Whatever advice he gives to whites about other blacks must be true, because *he* said it! The honest person will not pretend that there is not a certain amount of psychological, emotional, and even financial satisfaction that comes from being cast into such a role by whites. But if he is truly interested in contributing to Movement efforts to make good the claim, he will admit his self-aggrandizement and uncritical individualism and commit all of his efforts and resources to making good the claim about interracial unity.

Well placed privileged Afrikan Americans in predominantly white groups who have the respect and ear of the white leadership should cease forthwith the practice of endeavoring to protect or shield white people from the contributions of other Afrikan Americans who meet every qualification to also be there except one, namely, the willingness to uncritically play by rules they did not help to develop; rules that effectively keep most blacks out, or at best in subordinate positions. The Afrikan American who is an only, and who uncritically buys into the dominant white group's easy, cheap, painless reconciliation schemes, without placing much attention on the importance of justice and liberation, is open to this criticism. Such Afrikan Americans want nothing or no person to be included that might interfere with the reconciliation schemes of otherwise good white people; schemes that have negligible input from blacks.

A certain type of Afrikan American, despite her outstanding qualifications and talents, is not supported by *the only one* because he fears that her outspokenness and "abrasive" language will only create conflict and set back efforts toward reconciliation. He does not want the waters to be troubled by the presence and voice of such a person, so he does not recommend that the white leadership find meaningful ways to include her in the organization when she applies for a vacant position. When her name is mentioned by whites as a possible applicant or resource person, the lone black among them does not lend his voice of support. His silence may be just enough to insure that the sluggish and unrealistic efforts toward reconciliation will continue as usual. Such efforts are unrealistic because the group continues to refuse to take serious the idea that the precondition to reconciliation is justice and equality of treatment. The person who might push the group in this direction does not get the chance to try, because *the only one* is more concerned about his own standing in the group, and his sense that whites must not be offended or really challenged by such a person. Like the whites who gave him so much over many years, and towards whom he has such deep respect and admiration, he believes that the only acceptable means to reconciliation is the steady but gradual movement in that direction.

Until those *firsts*—and now seconds!—in the Movement are willing to intentionally and courageously work to create openings for others who think and see differently from themselves, the possibility of visible unity along racial lines will remain a very distant and elusive ideal. Afrikan Americans who are *firsts* (and those who come after them) in the Movement, and who have managed to acquire status, prestige, place, and position have an obligation to Afrikan Americans in and outside the group. What is that obligation? In the wise words of the late legal scholar-activist Derrick Bell, "It is simply not to forget that every step we take up the ladder provides white society with another example that what they wish to believe about racism's demise is actually fact."[25] Such a one is charged to remember and to remind his white benefactors that *his* progress up the professional ladder is not synonymous with that of his race.[26] That *he* seems to be making it, is neither evidence nor proof that vast numbers of others in the race are. This way, whites cannot in good conscience pretend that most blacks are doing well socio-economically just because they know one or two in their organizations or in the broader society who are.

Racism is a reality in the United States of America and has been embedded in the very fabric of this society since the "Founding Fathers" drafted the Constitution at Philadelphia in 1787. Virtually nothing is left untouched and untainted by racism in the US.[27] Indeed, black churches and denominations came into existence precisely because of the tragic phenomenon of racism.

Racism continues to have devastating consequences for both blacks and whites, indeed for the entire country and other parts of the world. Afrikan Americans have to be willing—even against well meaning whites who prefer otherwise—to name this beast what it is—*racism*; and stop wasting

---

25. Bell, *Confronting Authority*, 157.
26. Ibid., 158.
27. See the excellent book by Feagin, *Systemic Racism*.

precious time, energy, and resources trying to produce what is deemed to be more acceptable ways of talking about it without actually naming it. I am saying that Afrikan Americans need to call racism by name, especially during interracial conversations about it, no matter how distasteful and painful it is to the ear and sensibility. If it is too awful a term to hear; if it offends the ears and sensibility of well-meaning white people and some blacks, perhaps these will work harder to address and eliminate racism if blacks persist in calling it by name, regardless. Furthermore, the presumed offensiveness of the term pales in significance in comparison to its devastating concrete effects on Afrikan Americans, and ultimately on whites as well. Offensiveness should never be the aim. Rather, the goal should be straightforwardness and honesty in discussions on racism. If we cannot or will not name the problem, how will we ever get down to the business of addressing and solving it?

I remain convinced that name-calling is counterproductive. Every effort should be made to avoid this in interracial conversations designed to work on racism and white privilege. My own experience over many years has been that we can work on this without actually pointing fingers and calling white participants racists. Indeed, more and more, I am convinced that the issue that really needs to be addressed is what white scholars have named "white privilege," often referred to in the literature as "the other side of racism."[28] This aspect of racism focuses less on how blacks feel about racism, and more on how whites—all whites, no matter how conservative or progressive—feel about their unearned privilege, how it makes them feel, what they intend to do about it, and when.[29] Every white person in the United States of America benefits from racism; benefits from it whether they are individual racists or not. Painful as it might be to some, white people need

---

28. There has been a proliferation of publications on white privilege since the decade of the 1990s. An early anthology on the subject that is an excellent introduction for college and seminary students, as well as for church study groups is Rothenberg, *White Privilege*. I recommend that whites begin with the selection by McIntosh, "White Privilege: Unpacking the Invisible Knapsack" (97–101). In addition, I have been helped much by virtually all that progressive sociologist, Joe Feagin, has written on racism. He possesses a level of sensitivity to the plight of Afrikan Americans and an insight into white supremacy and structural racism that I do not find in most whites. Throughout the Feagin corpus, and most especially in recent years, his writings are influenced by the white privilege paradigm. See Feagin, *Systemic Racism*.

29. My first encounter with the concept of white privilege occurred when I first read *The Autobiography of Malcolm X* many years ago. Commenting on Malcolm near the end of *The Autobiography*, Ossie Davis said: "Malcolm knew that every white man in America profits directly or indirectly from his position vis-à-vis Negroes, profits from racism even though he does not practice it or believe in it"; Malcolm X, *The Autobiography*, 454. The term "white privilege" was not yet in use, but Davis's statement is an excellent characterization of it.

to hear and understand this, and work relentlessly to determine the myriad ways they benefit from racism, even when they have worked so hard (as individuals) to avoid being racist, or to insure that their children will not be. Consequently, the phenomenon of white privilege must be addressed directly. In my judgment, this is done most effectively by courageous, well-meaning progressive minded and thinking white people.[30] Blacks can cheer and be supportive by encouraging such whites to step up in this regard. For these embattled whites will most assuredly pay a price in white communities.

In the matter of race, there is no question that time is of the essence. Afrikan Americans should cease the practice of trying to provide rationales for why individual whites behave as they do in race relations. Whether we name E. E. Byrum and some other Movement pioneers as racists or not, we have seen that their behavior toward Afrikan Americans was most certainly racist. Movement blacks who have the ear and respect of white leaders do not contribute in positive ways to both bridging the racial divide, and generating positive change in the racial landscape of the group, when they fail to be forthright about racism. They must name the racism of whites, as well as call attention to their refusal to acknowledge their unearned privilege at the expense of Afrikan Americans; at the expense of visible interracial unity. Forthright assertions by Afrikan Americans in this regard should create openings for sincere whites to begin acknowledging, naming, and confronting their own racism and unearned privilege. This is not likely to happen as long as Afrikan Americans speak, preach, write, and otherwise behave in ways that serve only to placate whites in the sinful state of racism. Such openings to racial inclusion will not happen if blacks do not challenge whites' refusal to acknowledge that when looked at from the long view, their privileged positions exist precisely because their ancestors stole this land from native Americans, and then ripped the Afrikans from the Afrikan continent and subjected them to what was arguably the most severe, heinous, and devastating form of involuntary enslavement ever recorded in the annals of history. In this way, whites stole the labor of the Afrikans as they forced them to develop the land to provide unearned leisure and wealth for their white captors for generations to come. It should not be difficult for whites who know the history of race relations in this country, to see how certain aspects of the country's history has provided such massive wealth and privilege for them. And yet, seeing this seems to be a most difficult task for most whites.

In 1954, Harvard social psychologist Gordon W. Allport made an excellent contribution to what will be needed to remedy the problem of the

---

30. See Wise, *Dear White America*; and Barndt, *Dismantling Racism*.

most severe form of race prejudice. Writing about this type of prejudice, Allport said that, "the basic fact is firmly established—prejudice is more than an incident in many lives; it is often *lockstitched* into the very fabric of personality. In such cases prejudice cannot be extracted with tweezers. *To change it, the whole pattern of life would have to be altered.*"[31] From within the university setting Allport was alerting people, especially other whites, to the seriousness of deep-rooted prejudice and the difficulty of eradicating the most severe types. And yet, I think that were he alive today, Allport would not disagree when I say that as important as his statement is, it does not go far enough. For just as the most severe form of individual prejudice is lockstitched into the personality structure of an individual and will require the radical altering of "the whole pattern of life," it must also be said that the severest type of prejudice, namely racism, is lockstitched into the very fabric of the society we know as the United States of America. Consequently, society too—including all of its institutions—needs radical overhauling, or a whole new structure and way of doing things, if there is to ever be a chance of Afrikan Americans and white people living in accordance with the principles of holiness, visible unity, and equality.

Afrikan Americans should cease the practice of being so willing to too easily forgive whites *before* they even acknowledge their wrongs and ask for forgiveness. This means that Afrikan Americans should be willing to forgive, but only after there has been public—not merely private—confession and asking forgiveness. The point is not to humiliate white people, but to give them the opportunity to publicly confess what has been on their part a very public wrongdoing. The suffering of Afrikan Americans has been public. Although a private apology to a lone Afrikan American might be appropriate, it is not sufficient without some public effort to express the same, especially if the offense was of a public nature.

Too often Afrikan Americans have been willing to forego requiring and hearing any public confession by whites because being human themselves they have a sense of how embarrassing and painful it is for another human being to have to do this. Notwithstanding this, Afrikan Americans have to get beyond this tendency and recognize that there will be little significant progress in the matter of race relations until they are able to allow such public confessions to take place, and until whites actually do it. When whites offend publicly in matters of race, they should seek forgiveness in a public venue, and should extend a public apology.

---

31. Allport, *The Nature of Prejudice*, 408 (my emphasis).

WHAT WHITES SHOULD DO AND NOT DO

There are also some things that well-meaning Movement whites should do, and not do. They will have to find the courage to acknowledge and address not only their own individual racism and unearned privilege, but the institutionalized racism and privilege from which they benefit in more ways than they and most Afrikan Americans can imagine and name. It is necessary that whites in the Movement "fess up" to their racism and unearned privilege, seek forgiveness from Afrikan Americans *and* God, for any practice that dehumanizes human beings is also an affront, indeed a sin, against the Creator. If it is true that every human being is a reflection of divinity, then every act of injustice of any kind is an assault on the image of God in them. Only by first acknowledging this will whites be able to begin forthwith the difficult and—what will surely be—the dreadfully painful task of eradicating their racism and taking the concrete steps to develop a welcoming and inclusive community of believers.

If true reconciliation is the desired outcome, it is reasonable to operate in accordance with the principle that at the bare minimum a public offense deserves a public, not private, apology. I referenced this in the previous section, but it is of such critical importance that it bears repeating here. If a private apology does in fact occur it should be *in addition to* the public one. This seems to me a necessary step in the direction of reconciliation. This will be very difficult to do, so prone are we humans to doing all in our power to save face. Public confession begins the healing process by sending the message that one is truly sincere about reconciliation work, which in turn will help to reduce or relieve the suspicion and distrust.

In any event, in order for there to be any chance for racial reconciliation to occur, well-meaning white people at all levels and institutions of the Church of God will have to come to the decision to which Edward Ball (author of *Slaves in the Family*, 1998) came, and then proceed with courage to get in touch with the roots of their unearned privilege and decide how they ought to respond today to past and present injustices done to Afrikan Americans; injustices that have led to and serve to shield or protect white privilege. White Movement people need to learn from the witness and moral courage of Edward Ball, who has done excellent work in terms of delving into the history of the presence of enslaved Afrikans in his family, which has helped him to see with clarity why race relations are what they are today.

Ball acknowledges feeling both shame and accountable for what happened in his own family in the South during American slavery. He noticed that whenever his family gathered for reunions and the like, there was never discussion about the role of enslaved Afrikans in the production of family wealth and the unearned privileges for whites that generally came with it. After the painful process of *first* dealing with himself, Ball could see that even when the wealth diminished over time, something very valuable indeed remained, not only for the Ball family, but for all white people. Writing in 1998, Ball declared:

> No one among the Balls talked about how slavery had helped us, but whether we acknowledged it or not, the powers of our ancestors were still in hand. Although our social franchise had shrunk, it had nevertheless survived. If we did not inherit money, or land, we received a great fund of cultural capital, including prestige, a chance at education, self-esteem, a sense of place, mobility, even (in some cases) a flair for giving orders. And it was not only 'us,' the families of former slave owners, who carried the baggage of the plantations. *By skewing things so violently in the past, we had made sure that our cultural riches would benefit all white Americans.*[32]

Ball was talking about unearned white privilege. Although he felt accountable and ashamed about what happened in his family, he rightly admits that he does not feel "responsible." From an ethical standpoint he is right about this, inasmuch as one cannot be held morally responsible either for a deed not committed by himself, or for deeds committed by family members—living or dead. The children, we could say, are not morally responsible for the wrongful deeds of their parents. And yet, I would argue that while in the moral sense Ball is neither guilty nor responsible for what happened in his family, he is absolutely responsible for how he responds to it, even today, as children who have come of age *are* responsible for how they respond to the dreadful deeds of their parents.

Do you see the difference? Since Ball himself did not commit those crimes against Afrikan American humanity during the period of American slavery, he is not morally responsible for what happened, not even for the unearned benefits that accrued to him and his family. However, he is without question morally responsible today for how he responds both to what happened and to his unearned privilege. This is what the late Rabbi Abraham J. Heschel meant when he frequently declared: "Few are guilty, but all are responsible."[33] This is a powerful claim, for it means that even those who are victimized by various oppressions and injustices are at least morally responsible for how they respond to their oppression and injustice, even though they are not guilty of causing them. Afrikan Americans are not

---

32. Ball, *Slaves in the Family*, 13–14 (my emphasis).
33. See Heschel, *The Prophets*, 16.

guilty of causing most of the conditions that have made the lives of millions in every generation little more than a living hell. And yet, while not in any way excusing or letting off the hook those who have contributed to the causes of such conditions, it must also be said that Afrikan Americans are without question responsible for how they respond to what has been (and is being) done to them. White people, likewise, even the most progressive and least racist among them, are morally responsible for how they respond to what has been and is being done to Afrikan Americans. By putting it this way, it means that no individual, no group gets off the moral hook regarding issues of race. Few are guilty of the causes and perpetuation of racism at the individual and institutional levels, but all are responsible for how they respond to it. Are they apathetic to the point that they do nothing, or do they do all within their power and means to challenge it and work vigilantly to eradicate all vestiges of the social evil?

Edward Ball decided that he would make the effort to confront his unearned privileges, that he "would make an effort, however inadequate and personal, to face the plantations, to reckon with them rather than ignore their realities or make excuses for them." When he made this decision he reported having experienced "a remarkable calm, and the rest of the path seemed clear."[34]

Ball realistically acknowledged that it would not be easy, but that openings for advancement had also been created as a result of his decision and courage to do what he could. White people in the Church of God need to have the courage to do precisely what Edward Ball did. In addition, it is sometimes the case that an Afrikan American is so positioned, has such prestige, and is respected so highly by whites that she can, *if she chooses*, play a key role in helping whites to find handles to liberate both themselves and the institutions they control. When this is done, it will be possible for Afrikan Americans and others who have been historically excluded—or included only on the basis of inequality—to now be included on the basis of equality without qualification or condition.

Earlier in this chapter I pointed to the need for Movement people to come to a greater sense of clarity about the meaning of the holiness principle, and an understanding that having experienced complete sanctification, one is responsible not only to address and fight against personal sins, but social sins such as racism. An authentic ethic of holiness has a much broader view of sin than what has historically been the case. It seems to me that a part of the problem for the Movement historically has been a failure of members to understand the theological nature of holiness and the fact

---

34. Ball, *Slaves in the Family*, 14.

that it has significant socio-ethical implications, e.g., how one who claims to have undergone the second act of grace behaves toward others, regardless of race and ethnicity. In order to position themselves to take substantive steps to make good the claim it will be necessary for Movement people to understand that holiness is *the principle of principles* in the sense that one who is its recipient should understand that it is the fundamental conditioning factor in all that they do, interpersonally and socially. By definition, holiness conditions everything that they do, including their stance on interracial unity. All that they do is informed by the holiness that is God. If this is not evident in how Movement people behave toward others, regardless of race and ethnicity, they most likely do not have such holiness in their life. What then should Movement people think about holiness? How should they think about holiness in relation to visible unity? How should they think about it in relation to sin? The final section of this chapter is a discussion on these and related questions, most particularly the meaning and implications of the holiness-visible unity principle.

THE CENTRALITY OF THE HOLINESS-VISIBLE UNITY PRINCIPLE

D. S. Warner believed that holiness suggests the infinite purity of God; that it is the very essence of God's character and who God is fundamentally. I believe that holiness is a foundational theological principle inasmuch as it has essentially to do with God. Human beings, then, are not holy in and of themselves. "Whatever holiness they possess was derived from their special relation to God."[35] This means that anything or anybody depicted as holy is holy *only* in relation to God. For God, according to Warner and a host of others, is "the Holy One." Indeed, "the Holy One" is thought to be synonymous with God; "a common and essential characteristic of Deity."[36] Paul Tillich tells us that the sphere of the divine is the sphere of holiness. Whatever is brought into the divine sphere is made holy or consecrated. "The divine is the holy,"[37] Tillich writes. The holiness experienced by we humans is therefore derivative. We are made holy and set apart by our association with the Holy One. The "Holy One" is synonymous with "God."[38]

---

35. Knudson, *Religious Teaching of the Old Testament*, 138.
36. Ibid., 143.
37. Tillich, *Systematic Theology*, 1:215.
38. Knudson, *Religious Teaching of the Old Testament*, 138.

Anthony Saldarini rightly contends that in the First Testament "God is the Holy One par excellence."[39]

Swedish theologian Gustav Aulén (who was Bishop of Strängnäs) offers some instructive comments on the meaning of holiness that may enhance the thinking and practice of Movement people. Aulén maintains that holiness is not an attribute of God, as is the case of love, justice, mercy, etc. Rather, it is much bigger than this. It is "a unique quality" or characteristic of God. Holiness, in his view, is the foundation or "background" without which one cannot even talk intelligibly about God. "Everything which belongs to God and his realm bears the imprint of holiness, and appears, therefore, in relation to everything human as separate and wholly other."[40] Here we get the sense of holiness possessing an essentially religious and ethical meaning, and has important implications for ethical behavior—indeed, for one's entire lifestyle.

The suggestion that holiness is the unique quality, foundation, or background of God, "the atmosphere of the conception of God,"[41] implies something that is quite important for Movement people. Holiness is a basic conditioning factor, which means that it thoroughly conditions the traditional attributes of God, e.g., omnipotence, omniscience, omnibenevolence, and omnipresence. Holiness suggests to us how God's power, goodness, and presence in the world are to be perceived. Holiness "gives a specific tone to each of the various elements in the idea of God and makes them parts of a fuller conception of *God*. Every statement about God, whether in reference to his love, power, righteousness, and so on, ceases to be an affirmation about God when it is not projected against the background of his holiness. Only when holiness colors the concept of love do we understand that we are dealing with divine love."[42] In addition, holiness—rightly understood—conditions and gives a certain tone to the practice or behavior of all who claim to be sanctified.

The Bible and the best in the Jewish and Christian traditions make it clear that God has from the beginning been in relationship with human beings and the world. However, it is important to understand that the concept of holiness, the idea of God as the Holy One, also suggests that even in this fundamental relatedness between God, human beings, and the world there is also a significant sense in which there is a separation between them, such that it would be inappropriate to identify the divine and the human; the

---

39. Saldarini, "Holiness," 431.
40. Aulén, *The Faith of the Christian Church*, 120.
41. Ibid., 121.
42. Ibid., 122.

divine and the world. In this sense, God is "wholly other" than creation; than human beings. Indeed, according to Aulén: "Only when the separation between the divine and the human implied in holiness is given due consideration, and the divine is allowed to appear as unconditioned majesty in relation to the human, can holiness be of fundamental significance for the Christian conception of God."[43] Holiness stands in staunch contrast to "the unclean" and "the secular,"[44] a point also made by D. S. Warner.[45]

What should it mean for Movement people when it is said that holiness should be seen as the background of every statement made about God? At the bare minimum it should say something significant about God and what God expects of human beings, especially those who claim to have experienced entire sanctification. It should also say something about human beings as absolutely dependent on God, and about whose we are. It says something about what should be our mode of behavior in church and world, as well as what we should be doing to implement God's expectations of us.

In chapter 3, I alluded to Warner's teaching that one who claims to have experienced entire sanctification must exhibit this not merely in word and confession, but in the way she lives her life. Warner made the point well in his field report that was sent to *The Gospel Trumpet* from Spring Hill, Mississippi, on February 4, 1891.

> If holiness teachers on going into a new field where people know nothing about the doctrine and experience, would faithfully tell them at once that sanctification, the second work of grace, cleanses out of man all filthiness of the flesh and spirit which includes all unholy tempers and appetites; that it can only be obtained by abandoning every sinful and unclean habit, and giving the whole man, soul, body, and spirit up to God for perfect purity of life and being, no person is prepared to contradict him, and such as conclude to seek that grace will expect to pay the full price. *And should anyone make the profession without showing the fruits of the perfect consecration, he should be at once told that he does not possess it.*[46]

The last sentence in the above quote is critical. One who makes the claim of possessing holiness but does not live it, should be told that he does

---

43. Ibid., 121.
44. Tillich, *Systematic Theology*, 1:217.
45. Warner, *Bible Proofs of a Second Work of Grace*, 19.
46. Warner, et al., News from the Field, *The Gospel Trumpet* (Feb. 15, 1891) (column 5), 2 (my emphasis).

not possess it. We have seen before that Warner was not hesitant to call out those whose behavior suggested that they were only pretending to be sanctified.[47] It is not enough to merely make the claim that one has experienced complete sanctification, important as that is in itself; one has also to *live* the claim and its deepest meanings. While one is sanctified by faith, to truly live the sanctified life means that it will be costly in terms of the type of lifestyle implied by entire sanctification. One can no longer do the things she did prior to being sanctified. Once a committed racist, racism has no place in the sanctified life. Holiness is a radical lifestyle change, and cannot exist apart from how one behaves, lives, and relates in the everyday world. John W. V. Smith offered an instructive word on the point.

> The doctrine of holiness is not just an abstract theological concept; it is a standard for everyday practical living. It is expressed in actions, attitudes, and aspirations. Paul admonished the Christians in Rome, 'Do not be conformed to this world, but be transformed by the renewal of your mind' (Rom 12:2, RSV). This nonconformity to the 'world' relates to specific aspects of the prevailing culture. It may include abstaining from or even protesting against certain practices common in our society.[48]

Smith goes on to say that early Movement people were warned "against participation in affairs of society that did not glorify God."[49] He names several of these, e.g., dressing a certain way, and eating foods that may harm the body. Unfortunately, he did not say they were warned against drawing and-or participating in the color line, and they most certainly were not warned to the extent they were warned against wearing certain clothes, eating certain foods, consuming certain beverages, and smoking tobacco. Surely participation in division along racial lines did not—and does not—glorify and please God.

This is a point that has escaped the awareness of far too many Movement whites regarding racism and the absence of interracial unity in the

---

47. In his report from the field to *The Gospel Trumpet*, sent on January 3, 1891, Warner reported on a certain minister named John McDonnal who pretended to have the truth, but whose day to day life convicted him. Warner characterized him as "crooked and disorderly in life and doctrine." He then said that he had words with him about the inconsistency, rather than allow him to think that his behavior was acceptable. "We admonished him privately, but find in him no disposition to get right with God. Therefore our duty is to thus announce him as unworthy of the confidence and fellowship of the saints. 'Them that sin rebuke before all, that others may fear'"; *The Gospel Trumpet* 11.2, (Jan. 15, 1891) (column 4), 2.

48. Smith, *I Will Build My Church*, 97.

49. Ibid., 98.

church. One obtains sanctification, Warner taught, only when she lets go of "sinful and unclean" habits and practices. For this writer, at least, I can think of nothing more sinful and unclean than racism and any other negative -ism that alienates human beings from each other and from God. If racism is deemed to be sinful, then the one who experiences sanctification must be made aware of this and helped to rid self of it. If one truly understands the meaning of holiness, she cannot continuously be sanctified and a racist at the same time. Holiness and racism are oxymoronic. The lifestyle change implied in holiness means that one has to be intentional and relentless about ridding one's life of beliefs and practices that do not glorify God. Any practice that undermines the sacredness of people because of race, gender, class, sexual orientation, age, or health falls into this category.

Holy describes both the character of God, as well as the purity of believers for God's use, i.e., to do God's work in the world. If holiness is the background or foundation without which there can be no intelligible talk about God, then one who is sanctified must also take on the quality of apartness or being set apart. In other words, such a one is made holy and set apart precisely for God, in order to do God's work in the world. Because such a one is sanctified, he is bound thusly to do the work only in ways that honor and exhibits loyalty to God alone. The work of justice, for example, must always be done in righteous ways, i.e., in ways that respect and honor the dignity of the unjustly treated. Justice must always be tempered with agape. This is the only type of justice that honors the Holy One. Inasmuch as God is holy, so must holiness of human beings reflect what they do and how they do it, both interpersonally and socially.

It is important to understand that it is not that we humans *achieve* holiness, for we cannot do that on our own. Holiness is God's gift to those who make the conscious decision to open themselves, through faith, to receive and live it. And yet, the recipient is not a mere passive vessel or onlooker in this process. Each individual must make a conscious choice to receive the gift of holiness, as well as to live in accordance with divine expectations. It is not just a matter of receiving God's gift of holiness through faith. The recipient is then expected to *live* holiness in action,[50] an idea that was also emphasized by Warner. Little passivity is involved in the decision and effort put forth by the believer. Furthermore, it should be remembered that when God confers holiness on believers it conditions all that they do. They must understand themselves to be set apart to do God's work, most especially the work of justice and liberation in the world. This is the lesson we learn from the eighth-century prophets—that because of who God is, i.e., *the Holy One*,

---

50. Hewitt, "Sanctification," 429.

Making Good the Claim 195

God demands that justice be done.[51] Likewise, the truly holy life will not rest or be satisfied as long as injustice exists. The most important mantra of the Hebrew prophets was that God expects that justice will be done in the world.

The sanctified believer is always trying to increase her knowledge of the teachings and principles of Jesus, and is always endeavoring to apply them to every aspect of her life. She models as best she can the Christ-like spirit, especially that exhibited in Matthew 25 where Jesus admonishes that what we do and fail to do to the least of the sisters and brothers, we do and fail to do to him. Such a one is also much influenced by the claim of Jesus in his inaugural address that he came to set at liberty them that are oppressed (Luke 4:18-19). In a word, she strives relentlessly to live according to God's will and applies this to all areas of life; the personal and the social; to the sins of individuals, and to those of governments and large corporations, thus holding all to the same moral standard. In this regard, she rejects "restrictionism,"[52] insisting instead that the same Christian values that apply to individuals also apply to science, politics, business, etc. Indeed, this seems to have been a real concern for the Hebrew prophets as well. How dare the powers pretend that their corrupt behavior and their undermining of justice, has nothing to do with religion. The worship of God, and the everyday world of business and politics, is not two separate, disconnected worlds. Rather, there is one world over which God reigns supreme. Consequently, all that happens in the world is of concern to God, and thus must be the concern of every sanctified believer.

All of this is to say that there is an irrevocable and inextricable relationship between holiness or sanctification and morality, on the personal as well as the social level. One is not merely to decry personal sins, but social sins as well. This latter includes racism and all forms of injustice. Therefore, the sanctified believer is set apart by God not merely to address and eradicate individual personal sins, but those of institutions, including churches and other religious institutions. Indeed, since the church is to model visible unity, social justice, etc., it is important that sanctified Christians address racial and other forms of divisiveness and injustice in churches first and

51. Snaith, *The Distinctive Ideas of the Old Testament*, 54.

52. The claim being made here is that religious values, politics and business belong to the same, not to separate realms. Thus religious values have everything to do with what goes on in these other arenas of life. Otherwise, persons in those arenas would have a kind of blank check to do whatever they want, without fear of criticism or judgment. The doctrine of "restrictionism" holds that religion and its values are separate from those of science, politics, business, etc. The idea of "restrictionism" is discussed at length in Graham, *Between Science and Values*. See "Introduction: Expansionism and Restrictionism," 1-32.

foremost, so that all of the world can see concrete evidence of visible unity and justice within their body.

Cheryl Sanders is certain that when Movement people accept and take more seriously than they do the interconnection between the ethics of holiness and the achievement of social justice, they will be better poised and positioned to dismantle structures of racism and sexism. In this regard Sanders writes:

> When more individuals and congregations within the Church of God begin to take seriously the relationship between sanctification and social change, then the barriers of sexual and racial division can be dismantled, the needed healing and reconciliation can take place, and exciting new applications of the ethics of holiness and unity to the divine task of united ministry to a divided world can emerge.[53]

In addition to more individuals and local congregations taking the holiness and social justice and social change connections seriously, the same must be done by the powers that be at all levels and in all Movement institutions and agencies. Thus, not only individuals and local churches must change, but the changes must be institutionalized such that the structures are also made to be on the side of justice and radical social transformation. Sanders rightly places emphasis on a "three-dimensional holiness ethic" where the Movement is concerned. She sees that the emphasis must be on holy living for individuals, in the church, as well as in the social order. Holy living in the world implies the necessity of doing justice. "Thus the call to holiness is not simply an admonition to stay sober and celibate" Sanders writes, "it is a vocation to bring personal lifestyle, corporate worship, and social engagement into harmony with the attributes and demands of a holy God. In the Sanctified church tradition, the possessing of Spirit is the Holy Spirit, the pursuit of social justice is a holy mandate, and the purity of the saint is a testament to God's holiness."[54]

God has but one standard, applied to both individuals and to institutions and the world, a reminder that the visible unity teaching is grounded in holiness. Persons who have experienced entire sanctification and knows what that means, also knows that there is an integral relationship between holiness, visible unity, and social change; that before healing and reconciliation can even begin, efforts must first be made to address and eradicate racial, sexual, class, and other divisions in church and world. John W. V. Smith reminds us that holiness and visible unity are inextricably bound together,

---

53. Sanders, "Ethics of Holiness and Unity in the Church of God," 145.

54. Sanders, *Saints in Exile*, 133.

"with unity being the beautiful fruit of perfected holiness."[55] When rightly understood, we can hardly speak of one of these without speaking of the other and seeing the two as interrelated.

Being spiritually one in Christ is what many have meant and mean when they talk about unity in the church. Many think that this is all that God requires. As long as they are spiritually one in Christ it is acceptable to them to remain divided along the lines of race, sex, class, etc. The holiness principle makes it impossible to be satisfied with this minimalist view of unity. This must be expanded to include a visible unity that is inclusive of *all* people on the basis of equality.

What, now, are some concrete steps that Movement people can take in order to make good the claim about holiness and visible unity, especially regarding interracial unity? Can the church and its institutions overcome this most devastating form of division? This is the subject of chapter 7, the final chapter in this book.

---

55. See Smith, *The Quest for Holiness and Unity*, 92.

7

Conditions for Making Good the Claim about Holiness and Visible Unity

John W. V. Smith was certain that in the matter of interracial unity the church has some long overdue business to which to attend. He acknowledged that there are a number of religious, theological and denominational factors that militate against visible unity in the church. Smith rightly maintains that there are other divisive factors as well, but few, he contends, are as destructive as race and nationality. These, he observes, are deeply ingrained in societies throughout the world. He acknowledges the very hard work that will be necessary to eradicate such divisive factors. "Deliberate and sometimes painful application of the Christian gospel to these societal problems is required if real unity is to be achieved. This is one area in which the church in almost every part of the world still has a great unfinished task."[1] Smith said this in his 1985 publication, *I Will Build My Church*. It is no less true today, and the Church of God is no exception.

In addition to the need for much more straight talk about race and unearned white privilege (discussed in chapter 6) there are a number of other important conditions that Movement people will have to meet if they are at all serious about making good the claim about achieving a more visible interracial unity. By doing so, they will better position themselves to more nearly approximate what D. S. Warner and early Movement leaders (should have) had in mind when they preached and taught the core principles of holiness and visible unity. My thinking about a number of these conditions is influenced by the work of my former college and seminary professor, James

---

1. Smith, *I Will Build My Church*, 129.

Conditions for Making Good the Claim about Holiness and Visible Unity 199

Earl Massey, to whom this book is co-dedicated. Although the reader has seen a number of places at which I have questioned aspects of Massey's discussion on blacks and the Church of God, I have learned much from him; both from the things with which I disagree, as well as those with which I agree. My disagreements and the reasons given are intended to create openings that will encourage all Movement people generally, to think harder and deeper about the holiness-visible unity imperative and race, and to be open to seeing through lens they are not accustomed to peering through. Indeed, my own understanding of the history of the Movement and the role of Afrikan Americans in it from the establishment of what is arguably the first black Movement congregation in South Carolina[2]—before 1886 to the present—has been immeasurably deepened by reading and pondering Massey's writings on the subject, and our many conversations about it.

In any case, in this final chapter, I introduce and discuss some conditions that may open the way for advancement toward a more visible interracial unity in the Church of God Reformation Movement. Massey introduces several of these in his trailblazing book, *African Americans and the Church of God*.[3] He lists five conditions, from which I select and expand on three. I then offer four additional conditions of my own. I first discuss the three contributions from Massey. To begin each of these three discussions, I quote verbatim what he has written, and then offer my own commentary and contribution. Each of the seven conditions is important in themselves, and in most cases they are interrelated. There is therefore some overlapping in a number of these. The seven conditions are: 1) Teach the core principles of holiness and visible unity; 2) Reconciliation must occur on all levels; 3) Need for pastors and leaders to be "called;" 4) Acknowledge God as the Parent of all persons; 5) Acknowledge the sacredness of all persons; 6) Implement the principle of equality to be applied to all persons; and 7) Call for mutual correction and accountability.

---

2. Massey observes that at least one writer contends that a black Movement church was established in Farmhaven, Mississippi in 1879, thus predating the Charleston, South Carolina church. See Massey, *African Americans and the Church of God*, 66n53. On 17 and 24 Massey refers to Michael D. Curry, "A Historical Study of the Growth of Black Congregations of the Church of God" (1983).

3. Massey, *African Americans and the Church of God*, 260.

BE VIGILANT IN TEACHING THE CORE PRINCIPLES OF HOLINESS AND VISIBLE UNITY

Massey writes: "The doctrines of Christian holiness and unity must be seriously taught again and become our core-beliefs. They must be taught again, and again, and again, until they register throughout one's being. Core-beliefs inform, shape, motivate, and determine behavior."[4] Of course, based on the foregoing discussion, I am led to wonder whether there was ever a time, during and after the Warner era, when these principles were not only taught, but were explicitly related to interracial unity in the church. My research and experience supports my sense that Warner and others did indeed teach and preach about the principles of holiness and visible unity, but that too little sustained emphasis was placed on the need to strive for concrete visible unity along racial lines. After more than a century of growth and development, and the failure to achieve such unity, we can be sure that there is need to be intentional and vigilant about teaching these core beliefs and to be explicit and unrelenting about relating them to visible interracial unity in the Movement.

One of the most significant issues that Movement pioneers—including Warner—failed to address in any significant way was the racism that most white converts, whether in the South or the North, carried with them into the Movement. There seemed to be a false and devastating assumption among whites that by being converted and then "perfected" through a second work of grace, the new converts were automatically cleansed entirely of racist attitudes and assumptions. Moreover, it is quite possible that most whites gave no thought at all to their racism upon entering the Movement. To make things worse, Warner himself took an individualistic stance on matters of race that was similar to Alexander Campbell's stance on slavery. Campbell, a leader of the Christian Church (Disciples of Christ), believed that as an individual Christian one has to decide the rightness or wrongness of such matters for herself. According to Campbell, the race question was a matter for political, not religious leaders. The slavery question, in other words, was a political problem to be addressed by politicians. It was not a theological or moral issue to be addressed by the church, although each individual Christian could decide where they should stand on the matter. This was all too convenient, since it meant that some could decide—as many did—that slavery and racism was not a violation of the Christian ethic, and thus they could continue to enslave their black sisters and brothers and comfortably remain members of the church.

4. Ibid.

Warner's stance on race relations was similar to Campbell's since as an individual he was against injustice toward blacks, but, according to Massey, he apparently "thought it the better part of wisdom" to avoid explicitly preaching or teaching about the predicament of blacks after Emancipation and Reconstruction.[5] I would argue that an even "better part of wisdom" tells us today that Warner's decision was a monumental mistake. Here Warner could have taken a lesson from the vigilant stance and witness against enslavement in the West Ohio Eldership of which he was a member for a decade. Because Warner decided as he did, there was a lack of clarity as to the meaning of visible unity relative to race, not only for individual Movement people, but for local churches throughout the country. Explicit sermons and articles by Warner linking visible and interracial unity in the church would have sent a clear message of a different kind to the fast growing Movement. Members and churches would have known, without question or guessing, that they were not to accommodate to the racial ethic of the larger society, but instead were to see clearly the implications for unity along interracial lines in such teachings as: "All the saved of God in any place constitute his church in that place";[6] and God "forbids all divisions. The community of God is not only one body, but *all* divisions of that one body are condemned in the strongest terms."[7] Warner's mistake, as that of most Movement leaders then and since, was that he only allowed himself to talk in a roundabout way about the race question, rather than to address it forthrightly, and to insist on the responsibility of both individuals and the church to eradicate racism, most particularly and immediately in the church and its institutions. Movement people can be helped much by a more direct approach to addressing division along racial lines. Although he apparently did not often address the race question in a forthright and systematic manner, John W. V. Smith periodically named racism as an impediment to unity, and also noted the difficulty in overcoming it, as well as the need to make sustained efforts to do so.

Much, much more of this kind of straight talk about race and the holiness-visible unity connection are needed among white leaders in the Movement.

In his examination of scriptural teachings on visible unity, Warner only implied what he should have made explicit. For example, we saw earlier that he wrote that the language of the Bible points specifically to a unity that can be seen by the world, and that failure in this regard opens the church

---

5. Ibid., 15.
6. Warner, *The Church of God*, 16.
7. Warner and Riggle, *The Cleansing of the Sanctuary*, 244 (my emphasis).

to spiritual death and disintegration. The reasonable person who desires understanding cannot read Warner's words, be aware of racial segregation and discrimination in the church and the wider society, and not see the implications of those words for *visible* interracial unity in the church, and beyond. Furthermore, in one of the few places where Warner even used the word *race* he made it clear that the church is an amalgam of "the most widely conflicting idiosyncrasies, and races of the most opposite customs and religions," and that God does not permit them to be separated from each other because of such differences.[8] Warner certainly understood this as not merely an invisible spiritual unity, but a unity that was to be visible to the world, and inclusive of all races of people. Indeed, some later problems regarding race might have been avoided had Warner preached and taught expressly about visible unity and its meaning regarding interracial unity. As noted in the previous chapter, he might well have been concerned about schisms occurring in the church had he not taken the cautious means to addressing race, rather than a more direct and prophetic approach. But even so, such an approach says a great deal about those who would essentially sacrifice an entire race of people who are already victimized by racism and racial discrimination on a massive scale. I simply cannot imagine the God of the entire human family being pleased with such a sacrifice, even for the sake of building the church. After all, according to the Christian faith, human beings are sacred beyond all measure, and are God's special creation, imbued with God's image.[9] All people have absolute dignity, sacredness, and preciousness to God by virtue of God's love and infinite care and compassion for them.

D. S. Warner was convinced absolutely that any belief or practice in the church that leads to separation and division was sinful. Nothing, in his view, was more sinful than causing division in the church. "There is then a solemn and awful weight of importance connected with this divine unity. For this cause there is perhaps no one thing more frequently enjoined in the New Testament than the oneness of all believers; no evil more peremptorily forbidden than that of schisms; and no sin more strongly denounced than that of 'causing division.'"[10] Racism is a sin because it divides and alienates human beings from each other and from God. As far as I can tell, this is a point that E. E. Byrum did not fully grasp. He cannot have understood Warner's teaching in this regard, given his advice to separate or divide along racial lines in his infamous 1897 article, "The Color Line." Nor would By-

---

8. Ibid., 239, 240.
9. See Tournier, *A Doctor's Casebook*, 122–23.
10. Warner and Riggle, *The Cleansing of the Sanctuary*, 246.

rum have given the same advice at the 1912 confrontation at the Anderson camp meeting, had he understood fully Warner's teaching on the sin of division in the church. Moreover, Byrum might not have been so quick to help push out Christiana Janes as pastor of the interracial mission home in Detroit (chapter 4). What Warner and other Movement pioneers failed to make explicit regarding the interrelationship between the holiness-visible unity principle and interracial unity must be taken up by Movement people today with an urgency and sense of duty heretofore unknown. Members of the Church of God are not responsible for the moral failure of the pioneers, but they most assuredly are responsible for how they respond to it.

By Warner's definition the advice that Byrum gave to separate along racial lines amounted to sin. This may be hard for many white Movement people to swallow, but I cannot see how Byrum's advice can be called anything other than heresy, divisiveness, or sin. According to Warner, sectism is the most hateful sin to God because it divides the church. It did not seem to matter to Warner what was going on in the wider society at the time. What mattered was holiness and visible unity in the church. Since Warner considered anybody, regardless of gender, race, or class who had experienced salvation to be a member of God's church, this must mean that every Afrikan American who was converted to the Christian faith was a member of the church, pure and simple. Therefore, anything that anybody said or did that led to Afrikan Americans being asked to separate from the body of Christ because of what civil and other societal authorities required, was guilty of the sin of sectism in the church.

From the foregoing discussion it should be easy to see why it is so important at this juncture in Movement history for there to be a return to remembering, teaching, and understanding the founding core beliefs of holiness and visible unity. What did Warner mean by these, and what was the general drift of his thinking about their implications for the church and its ministries? These two principles—holiness and visible unity—need to become more than abstract concepts to be discussed and analyzed among Movement people. Even more so, today, they need to become a way of living and relating in church and world, and allowed to be infused in everything that Movement people do, individually, interpersonally, and collectively, both in the church and all of its institutions and agencies. Massey is right in suggesting that a good way to get at this is to teach—unrelentingly—the basic core beliefs of the Movement, and to do so relentlessly until they become the very culture of the Church of God.

Movement leaders at the local, state, and national levels need to pull out all stops in order to insure that these principles are taught and modeled for every member. I see this as essentially a teaching-learning issue for the church. Consequently, the place to begin such systematic teaching of this kind is in the Movement's theological school, since this is where it will be most evident that individuals sense a call to ministry and the need for theological education. Such teaching needs to be carried forth in the local churches as well, but I will say more about this subsequently.

Historically, a high percentage of students enrolled in the Movement seminary are affiliated with the Church of God Reformation Movement. These students should be *required* to take a course that focuses on the core beliefs of holiness and visible unity and how these are manifested in each of the theological disciplines, at the local church level, and in Movement agencies. This could conceivably be a one semester intensive course in which a faculty member representative of each of the theological disciplines has the responsibility of teaching a 2–3 week segment with an emphasis on how these core principles are manifested in her or his discipline and how they may be concretely applied in ministry. Such a course would be enriched immeasurably if a pastor and-or agency executive is invited to share in such teaching. In the case of the pastor and agency executive, there should be intention about insuring that a person of a different gender and race is selected for this function each time the course is taught. Furthermore, if the seminary has no Afrikan Americans and other people of color on its faculty the academic dean should secure such person from outside the institution. Such ones could be retired Movement persons who are well versed in a particular theological discipline. It could even be an "outsider," i.e., a non-Movement person, who seriously engages and examines Movement ideas and practices.

In such a course, students should be challenged to see and understand that both Jesus Christ and D. S. Warner were concerned not merely about spiritual and denominational unity, but a visible unity that the world can see. In every case, instructors should not only show how the principles of holiness and visible unity are manifested in her or his theological discipline, at the local church level, or in Movement agencies, but should also make a special effort to relate those ideals to race relations, and any other practices in the group, e.g., sexism, classism, and heterosexism that cause division. This is absolutely critical. In order for the teaching of these core beliefs to have the hoped for effect on would-be pastors and other church leaders, those who do the teaching must themselves be witnesses to how the principles are related to race relations in the church and all of its agencies. Teaching these Movement core principles in the seminary will insure that would-be pastors and church professionals are grounded in the biblical, historical, theological, ethical, educational, and practical aspects of holiness and visible unity.

Conditions for Making Good the Claim about Holiness and Visible Unity 205

Robert L. Berry reported that as a result of D. S. Warner's preaching in Wichita, Kansas in 1890, several ministries developed, and that when whites failed to keep the work going, Cornelia Bateman, a black woman, saw the truth of Warner's teaching and provided leadership until whites took it up again.[11] Often the only black person photographed with ministerial groups of early Movement years, Bateman was one of Warner's Bible students in the early1890s. Massey has written: "Cornelius Bateman knew Daniel S. Warner and, according to a reference to her that appeared in the January 28, 1896, issue of the *Gospel Trumpet*, she worked hand-in-hand with the Gospel Trumpet Family while one of the students Warner was teaching the Bible at Grand Junction."[12] Notwithstanding Rev. Bateman's contributions to the Movement, she was frequently the token black, even during her student days under Warner. Perhaps at some point a Church of God historian will uncover how she came to be part of the Gospel Trumpet Family, and whether concrete steps were taken by leaders to attract other blacks as well. To be sure, such persons, if asked and prodded, may not have wanted to come, but it is most important to know that genuine efforts were made to insure that the group looked more like God's heterogeneous creation. The Gospel Trumpet Family would have been the perfect place to model visible interracial unity during Warner's time. What a message that would have sent! In any event, Movement seminarians today must be taught that tokenism is only a first step in the process toward establishing visible interracial unity.

Of course, it goes without saying that the makeup of the university and seminary faculty and administration should be a concrete model of interracial unity. Since the end of the Civil Rights Movement tokenism as an end in itself, has been unacceptable to the intelligent mind. The church and its institutions ought to lead society in going beyond the practice of tokenism in their staffs and faculties. As a church related institution, universities and seminaries should never be satisfied with the societal standard that ten percent of the work force should be comprised of people of color and other historically excluded groups. Indeed, these institutions should uphold and model a far superior standard by seeking to include a "critical mass" of such people, thus providing leadership for society, rather than being led by it.

If the Anderson School of Theology (and the University) does its work well in this regard, the next phase of teaching and witnessing to the basic core beliefs of the Movement will still be challenging, but should not be as difficult. Obviously the theological seminary and university is not the only

---

11. Berry, *Golden Jubilee Book*, 37.
12. Massey, *African Americans and the Church of God*, 48.

place where teaching should occur. Just as the would-be pastor's theological education should not end when she graduates from seminary, education in the local church and in church agencies should be ongoing as well. In conjunction with the lay leadership in the local congregation the pastor should structure the ministry such that, everything done will have an educational component to it. The Sunday sermon, as well as Sunday school and mid-week services can be used creatively to include periodic, planned and structured sessions that focus on the meaning and ethical implications of the basic core beliefs. If this is done several times each year it can be reasonably assured that all diligent members will know what these are, what they mean, and how they ought to be lived out in their day to day lives, as well as in the church. Every local church will do this differently, since the people and the context will be different. However, in every case there will have to be strong leadership by the pastor and lay leaders. It will be important for these to let the congregation know how important it is for members to understand the Movement's founding core principles and what these mean in the most concrete sense, especially as they relate to unity along racial lines. In addition, this unity should be reflected in the local congregation, particularly if the community where the church building is located is a multi-racial, multicultural community.

RECONCILIATION MUST OCCUR AT ALL LEVELS OF THE CHURCH

Regarding this condition, Massey writes: "Reconciliation must be effected between the congregations in every town, city, and state where the 'color line' brought division."[13] Of course, this literally means every city in the United States of America where a Movement church has grown up, for there is no place in the country—from the first days of the Movement to the present—that does not evidence division along the color line to some degree. It is not difficult to see how efforts towards reconciliation—the resolving of differences and establishing a relationship based on equality—can be aided by the creative educational endeavors of the seminary, local churches, and Movement agencies. In order for there to be even a possibility for reconciliation to occur there must first be awareness that there is a problem, followed by efforts to resolve it in ways that are equally beneficial to all concerned parties. This necessarily implies give-and-take. Educating members on the core principles of the Movement can contribute significantly toward reconciliation.

13. Ibid., 260.

What Massey proposes in this emphasis on reconciliation is true as far as it goes, but it does not go far enough. Reconciliation that means anything at all, will not be possible until white people repent, acknowledge their racism and unearned privilege, decide what they intend to do about it, and when. Although such acknowledgement will be very difficult for most whites, it is absolutely necessary as a precondition for reconciliation to occur. For essentially what whites do in such acknowledgement and repentance, is to begin the process of liberating themselves from their racism. This enables them to begin the movement toward racial inclusiveness and equality.

More and more, my sense is that white Movement people will not even be able to hear the truth of what is said about anti-racism and pro-reconciliation efforts if they do not first acknowledge their racism and unearned privilege. In addition, and equally important in the pre-reconciliation stage, one will first have to be reconciled to self and to one's group if there is even to be a chance of reconciliation with blacks. Reconciliation between whites and blacks presupposes each group's having first resolved issues of race with itself. William Stringfellow, a white Episcopal layman and lawyer who lived and served in East Harlem from the late 1950s to 1964 reflected on this precise point after it was made clear to him by a black resident that it was important that as a white person he simply be himself; that he not renounce any part of his heritage and past, but that he simply present himself as authentic to blacks and Puerto Ricans in Harlem. Nor was it necessary or appropriate for him to try to imitate blacks and Puerto Ricans and their culture, or for them to imitate his. Stringfellow had only to be himself, as was the case of life-long residents in Harlem.[14] By acknowledging and appreciating his own culture and customs, Stringfellow was able to be reconciled to himself, and this opened to him the possibility of being reconciled to others—both within and outside his group. From this, he drew the conclusion that for blacks and whites to be reconciled, they had first to experience intra-group reconciliation.[15]

Although an important point for both groups seeking inter-group reconciliation, it is most important for Afrikan Americans to seek intra-group reconciliation, in part, to present themselves as a united front when working toward reconciliation with whites. More than ever before, this is a crucial point for Movement blacks. Had there been more evidence of this intra-group reconciliation, Movement black leaders would not have pretended that what happened to Christiana Janes in Detroit had nothing to do with

14. Stringfellow, *My People Is the Enemy*, 25.
15. Ibid., 148.

the status of blacks in the Movement. Nor would they likely have made the mistake of not standing by her. Although Janes chose to sever ties with the Movement, she was more faithful to the holiness and visible unity principles than most whites and some blacks during that time. In any case, the point to be made here is that when a person and-or group is reconciled to self or its group, this does much in terms of clearing the way for reconciliation with another. This pre-reconciliation step is really the only means to preparing the way for healing, and ultimate reconciliation.

There is one Creator who is the source of all life. Every person is imbued with the image of God and possesses inestimable worth because created and loved by God. Over the years, some of my white students expressed hatred for themselves and their race because of the history and practice of racism in the United States. I have always been quick to remind them that they belong to the one God of the universe, and therefore are required to maintain a healthy sense of love for self and their group. One can be angry about racism, its perpetrators, and the devastation it causes, without hating self and other white people. Besides, self-hatred does not move us closer to solving the race problem and moving toward reconciliation.

Reconciliation will not be easily attained, nor should whites and Afrikan Americans expect to achieve it cheaply. Whites will have to go through the confessing, repenting, asking for forgiveness process, while deciding what to do about their unearned privilege. In this regard, reconciliation will be costly. Rabbi Heschel was very clear about this at the Conference on Race in Chicago in 1963 where he was the co-keynote speaker with Martin Luther King, Jr. He said: "It is time for the white man to repent. We have failed to use the avenues open to us to educate the hearts and minds of men, to identify ourselves with those who are underprivileged. But repentance is more than contrition and remorse for sins, for harms done. Repentance means a new insight, a new spirit. It also means a course of action."[16] It's not enough just to confess, repent, and ask forgiveness in matters of race. One's life and practice must then be brought into conformity with the change that occurs in one's soul and spirit.

In any event, it must be seen that Afrikan Americans who desire reconciliation will also be heavily taxed in terms of cost. Having already been the long time victims of individual and institutional racism, they are now being asked to participate in reconciling activities with those who continue to benefit from racism in numerous ways. Afrikan Americans are being asked to suffer doubly. Already the victims of hundreds of years of white supremacy and institutional racism, they are now asked—even as their

---

16. Heschel, "Religion and Race," 96.

suffering continues—to join with whites and to willingly suffer with them through processes intended to achieve some semblance of reconciliation and anti-racism. For we can be sure that although whites can do a great deal on their own toward addressing this issue, the nature of the problem is such that they cannot solve it alone—without the willing participation of Afrikan Americans. The most sensitive and committed whites will also be troubled by blacks having to suffer doubly. They too will sense the injustice and inhumanity of it, but finally will know that this is one of the cruel consequences of racism in this country—that both the perpetrators and the victims hold a key to its solution, and that without one or the other the problem cannot be resolved to the extent that reconciliation between the two can become a reality.

There is no question that racism is a monster problem for Afrikan Americans as well as whites, which makes it so difficult and painful for the two groups—in any setting, religious or non-religious—to discuss and work at it in ways that will lead to its eradication, and opening the way to reconciliation. Louise Derman-Sparks and Carol Brunson Phillips have made a helpful statement in this regard as they remind us of the impossibility of even studying the problem of racism dispassionately, let alone the difficulty of discussing it across racial lines. "Victims of racism harbor anger, frustration, impatience, and so forth," they write. "Perpetrators and beneficiaries of racist systems exhibit various forms of denial and other defenses."[17] However, on their worst days whites do not experience the pain and frustration from racism that Afrikan Americans experience every waking moment of every single day. To require, or even expect that Afrikan Americans will, when racially offended, always respond in ways that are palatable to white offenders is asking too much, and at best borders on blaming the victim. Such an approach means that the pursuit of anti-racism and reconciliation is being done solely at the expense of Afrikan Americans. Anti-racism and pro-reconciliation efforts ought always to be based on the principle of *shared-suffering* between the races, and all participants should be helped to understand this.

I know that there are those who will immediately think of Martin Luther King, Jr. in this instance. They will remind us of one of King's favorite statements: "Unearned suffering is redemptive." While it is true that King frequently made this statement in sermons, speeches, books, and articles, it is also true that most people have misunderstood his meaning. They have done so because they have not read far enough or deep enough into the King literary corpus. It was never King's intention to convey the idea

---

17. Derman-Sparks and Brunson Phillips, *Teaching/Learning Anti-Racism*, xi.

that the mere subjection of a person or people to suffering that they do not deserve guarantees their redemption or that there is anything necessarily redemptive about suffering. And yet, we can be sure that this is precisely what many oppressors want oppressed people to think, namely that there is a kind of nobility or virtuousness in suffering as such. This, however, is the furthest thing from what King had in mind.

King knew that much of the suffering of his people and other oppressed people is unearned and undeserved. When he declared that such suffering is redemptive, he did not mean that suffering as such is redemptive or good in itself, or even that Afrikan Americans, by virtue of their suffering, possessed a kind of moral superiority over others. Rather, he meant that *undeserved suffering can be made to be redemptive by the sufferers.* In other words, they have to be willing, not to merely endure the suffering, but to do everything in their power to nonviolently defeat and eliminate the suffering and its causes, and to intentionally begin moving in the direction of establishing the beloved community. The struggle against the suffering and its root causes is what opens the way to redemption. In this sense, and this sense only, did King believe unearned suffering to be redemptive. Since God did not create human beings to suffer unnecessarily, it is always their responsibility to fight to eradicate undeserved suffering of all kinds.

Movement people should be much, much more deliberate in doing all that is humanly possible to clear the way to reconciliation between the races, for only in this way can they show not only their Christ, but the world, that they have finally come to the point of making good the claim about visible unity in the Church of God. Clearing the way to reconciliation means working vigilantly to remove all vestiges of racism, in its individual and institutional forms. It should not be expected that Afrikan Americans will passively endure racial insults or to always respond in ways that are most acceptable to the one(s) doing the offending. While it is reasonable to expect that Movement blacks will do all in their power to respond to racial offenses as lovingly as they can, it is just as reasonable to expect that whites will work harder than ever before to actually think before they open their mouth and let slip a foul racial comment. Whites should not be given a license or a kind of permission by school administrators, church executives, and others to say whatever they want to say to Afrikan Americans (or about Afrikan Americans to other whites!). In fact, not trying to protect such whites from possibly getting criticized by offended Afrikan Americans may actually be educational for them, since it will force them to take the extra time and make the extra effort to *think* about what they might say and how it may be received. I am not speaking here about situations involving a long time close friendship between an Afrikan American and a white person.

Such persons relate on a much different, mutually trustworthy level. Their relationship may be such that each has permission to say to the other what they would not say to others outside their racial-ethnic group. My concern, rather, is with the more casual relations that exist between whites and Afrikan Americans in employment situations, for example, and the tendency of whites to speak without first thinking about how it might be received by blacks in the room.

Reconciliation can only occur between equals, and only *after* each group has been reconciled to itself. This means that something else that can be quite painful is also necessary. Afrikan Americans must be honest with white Movement people about how they really feel about their racism and unacknowledged unearned privilege; how they feel about whites' racism and their efforts both to divide along racial lines and to do all in their power to sustain the division in the church and its agencies.

In other words, there needs to be much more honest straight talk about racism in the Movement by both blacks and whites. Anna Arnold Hedgeman, a black educator and civil rights worker, made this point in a different context. In a conversation with William Stringfellow she said quite poignantly: "Very few Negroes and white people are in real communication with each other. Those of us who can and do speak honestly, as you and I do, must keep in touch and help others to learn the quality of communication necessary if the races are to be reconciled. This will be very hard and will become more difficult as the crisis deepens, but that just makes it all the more important that we keep in touch."[18] And no person was more forthright about the need for such direct straight talk about race than Malcolm X. Not one for sugar coating what he believed to be the truth, Malcolm said: "You *never* have to worry about me biting my tongue if something I know as truth is on my mind. Raw, naked truth exchanged between the black man and the white man is what a whole lot more of is needed in this country—to clear the air of the racial mirages, clichés, and lies that this country's very atmosphere has been filled with for four hundred years."[19] Based on my experience growing up in the Movement, graduating from one of its colleges, attending the Anderson School of Theology for one year, and observing the behavior of whites and blacks in the group, I am left with the awareness that not nearly enough of this kind of straightforward talk about race has taken place. An effort was made in the 1960s, but that was a long time ago. If reconciliation is to be anything but an abstraction, straight talk

---

18. Quoted in Stringfellow, *My People Is the Enemy*, 125.
19. Malcolm X, *The Autobiography*, 276.

about race must become part of Movement culture, and thus be expected to occur on all levels.

As we can see, both whites and Afrikan Americans will likely pay a heavy price for reconciliation, but it is important to acknowledge and understand the differences involved in each case as well as the possible consequences for each group as they work toward this end. Moreover, if Movement people today are truly serious about the core principles of holiness and visible unity, it will be necessary for reconciliation to be effected not only in every local church, but in every institution affiliated in any way with the Church of God Reformation Movement.

As for me, I do not see how the Movement's schools and other agencies can honestly claim to be serious about their basic core beliefs as long as there is not a critical mass of people of color, especially Afrikan Americans, in tenure track faculty positions, and in upper level administrative and managerial positions. At some point, somebody in a significant leadership position will have to step up and say: "This is what we need to do, and this is how we can do it. Furthermore, we need to do it right now," a point, we will see, that black Movement leaders—portraying the sect or ethical prophetic element in the church—made in the late 1960s. I have lived long enough and have seen enough to know that without this type of leadership initiative, the Movement will remain in the "all deliberate speed" or gradualism mode relative to the issue of race. As long as this is the prevailing approach, there is no sense expending valuable time and energy discussing the need for reconciliation. However, inasmuch as there are some signs here and there of a desire to make good the claim, the hope must be that a cadre of white and black people will soon emerge who will be so determined and committed to make real the claim about visible unity along interracial lines that their actions in this direction will ignite and incite a revival throughout the Movement.

I do not believe that God has ever needed massive numbers of people to do the work of establishing the community of love, i.e., to do *kin-dom* work.[20] The small remnant of committed, courageous Christians has generally been the spark for igniting such work and regeneration. God just needs a few genuinely committed people. The question for Movement people is: Who will be among these few, and when will they take the stage?

---

20. Following the late Mujerista theologian, Ada María Isasi-Díaz (who was influenced in her use of this term by Georgene Wilson, O.S.F.), I substitute "kin-dom" for the more traditional "kingdom" since this latter has sexist and elitist connotations. Kin-dom represents more of the sense of "family of God" that is similar to the historic emphasis on family in Latina and Afrikan American women's culture. See Isasi-Díaz, *Mujerista Theology*, 83n14.

One last point should be stressed before proceeding to a discussion of the third condition. Those in leadership positions in Movement institutions who claim to be serious about making good the claim will need to be willing to put their money and other resources where their mouth is. Every conceivable effort should be made to avoid the serious mistake of failing to appropriate sufficient monetary funds and other resources to support the stated goal of reconciliation. Hopefully, this was one of the lessons that Movement leaders learned during and after the May 28, 1968 meeting of the 50th Annual Business Session of the General Assembly in Anderson, Indiana. For the first time, Movement leaders publicly faced up to, and acknowledged, the seriousness of the race problem, internally and externally. Charles Weber, Executive Secretary of the Executive Council boldly told the attendees: "The racial crisis is the most pressing matter confronting the church today."[21] This was a first in Church of God history, and is, in my estimation, the quintessential model for straight talk about race. It was apparently a highly charged meeting in which white and black Movement leaders engaged in long over-due straight talk about racism in the church, its agencies, schools, and other institutions. The late Rev. Thomas J. Sawyer, one of those black leaders present, who once said that he frequently "sat and dreamed of what real unity would be like in the Church of God . . . ,"[22] reflected: "Angry young black leaders, for the first time voiced their bitterness toward a 'racist' Church of God . . . Time after time the issue of racism was joined in heated, but healthy dialogue . . . At the end of the meeting it was evident to many that the era of equivocation had passed. The Church must act—now!"[23] And, there was a strong sense that proposed changes must begin within the church's own fellowship.

Before presenting a new resolution on race relations from the Executive Council at the 50th General Assembly of the Church of God, June 18–20, 1968, Weber forthrightly and honestly proclaimed: "While gains are encouraging, they have not kept up with the changes in society; the progress is much too slow and the urgency is increasing . . ."[24] At the end of that Assembly a final resolution—hard to swallow by some and not swallowed at all by some others—was offered up, debated, and finally passed in its original form. The resolution was presented by Rev. Edward L. Foggs, a black member of the Business Committee: "Resolved that this Assembly call

21. Quoted in Sawyer, "A Survey Analysis of Christian Unity within the Church of God Community," 94.

22. Sawyer, "Racial Separation and Christian Unity," 112.

23. Sawyer, "A Survey Analysis of Christian Unity within the Church of God Community," 93.

24. Quoted in ibid., 94.

upon the Church to repent for the deficiencies and failures as a people on the point of race relations, turning to God for renewal and grace during this International Convention."[25] Tempers flared on both occasions that year, and feelings and egos were likely rubbed raw. However, attendees learned of changes and progress being made throughout Church of God institutions, many with significant financial implications, e.g., the hiring of a token number of blacks in staff and administrative positions, and also faculty positions.

Liberation and reconciliation work is, and will continue to be costly, financially and otherwise; costly also because those who for years have been recipients of unearned privilege and advantages must be willing to acknowledge this, declare what they intend to do about it, and when. None of this will be easy. All of it will be painful. Indeed, this too is putting the money where the talk is regarding interracial unity in the Movement.

For those who are quick to say that we are living in economically challenging times I say only that, having taught in the theological academy for over thirty years at this writing, I know from experience that even in economically tough times administrators and boards of trustees find—indeed *make*—ways to do what *they* really want to do. I have seen the same tendency among pastors who spearhead campaigns to raise money to build expensive church buildings during economically depressed times and put everything into the effort. However, when approached about making a sizable donation or raising money for a community center or social programming to address serious needs in the immediate vicinity of the church, they exhibit a failure of will. In 1892 Borden P. Bowne, the father of American personalism (the philosophy that God is personal and loving, and that human beings are sacred because loved by God and endowed with God's image), declared that, "The greatest need in ethics is the impartial and unselfish will to do right. With this will, most questions would settle themselves . . . One bent on doing wrong never lacks an excuse; and one seeking to do right can commonly find the way."[26] My own experience corroborates this view. If one has the will to do the right thing, she can generally find a way(s) to do it.

---

25. Quoted in ibid., 95. Edward L. Foggs is now General Secretary Emeritus, Church of God Ministries, and Distinguished Minister at Large, National Association of the Church of God.

26. Bowne, *The Principles of Ethics*, 305.

PASTORS AND OTHER LEADERS SHOULD BE "CALLED" BY GOD

Regarding this condition, Massey writes: "Those who lead congregations must be persons 'called' by God to that work, and must be conditioned by gifts, knowledge, and experience for that leadership."[27] In my view, few terms receive as little attention and discussion as the concept of *the call* to ministry. Very seldom indeed do we hear—in seminaries and local churches—discussions on its meaning and how one discerns whether she has been (or is being called) to ministry. Generally, what I experience in seminary communities is that students have decided on their own at some point that they want to "try out ministry." When asked about their interest in ministry, they usually do not put it in terms of a call, but even when they do, I am often left feeling that they are really not experiencing a call at all. Rather, in far too many cases they say: "I have tried everything else and failed, so I thought I would give ministry a chance." WOW! They treat ministry not like a vocation, but like a profession, i.e., that which one chooses to do as her life's work in order to earn a living. Of course, what I always want to hear—but seldom do—in student's comments about their experience of a call is that something of a deeply spiritual nature seems to be tugging at them every which way they can imagine and just won't seem to let them have peace. What I then hope to hear—but again seldom do—is something like: "So I went to my pastor, elders, and-or spiritual advisor to discuss what I had been experiencing and asked for advice on how best to discern whether I am being called to ministry."

To be called to ministry is about much more than making a conscious choice about one's life profession, although it does involve conscious choice. A divine call is more about God's business with one's life, than what one might otherwise wish to do with his life. To experience a divine call is to simultaneously experience a sense of the overwhelming ethical or moral significance of what one is being called to do. The focus has to be on "divine" because a higher than human power is doing the calling. It is God who calls and sets the life-task or agenda for the called.[28] Therefore, the divine call to ministry is first, foremost, and last about God and God's agenda, while the one being called is a conduit or vessel through which God will participate in doing the work associated with the call.

To be called is to be drawn into the *vocation* of ministry. Many have adhered to the false notion that the only real ministry is ordained parish

---

27. Massey, *African Americans and the Church of God*, 260.
28. See Weber, *The Protestant Ethic and the Spirit of Capitalism*, 79.

ministry. But we know that this is not true, and that one may be called by God to any one of a number of different types of ministry. My calling, for example, is to teaching ministry. For more than thirty years I have lived out my vocation as a theological educator.

It is not true that there is only one way to be called into ministry. There are more ways of being called into ministry than many of us can imagine. Some people have a clear, immediate, and dramatic call experience that comes with clarity about the nature of what they are being called to do, such as the call experience of Saul[29] or Martin Luther.[30] Others experience a lengthy, drawn out call process, as was the case with Martin Luther King, Jr.[31]

The concept of "call" is from the Latin word *vocatio* (vocation), which means God's summoning of a person to a particular work of service in ministry. That God does the calling implies that God also does the choosing of the person, calling her by name. Who can forget God's words to the prophet Jeremiah: "Before I formed you in the womb I knew you, and before you were born I consecrated you. . ." (Jeremiah 1:5)? This means that the call is a very personal encounter between God and the one called. One writer contends that this call by name "can have the effect of bringing to pass what the caller intends; especially, to call someone by name is frequently to invest them with the qualities which the name connotes."[32] In addition to selecting the person, God also chooses the service to be done.

This is quite different from the way seminary students often talk about the call. They frequently imply that the choosing was all theirs, and that God played a relatively minor role. It is what they themselves decided to do. Such a view is precisely why pastors and other leaders in the church should not only be called, but should know precisely what it means to be called to ministry. If pastors and would-be pastors and other leaders in the church knew the meaning of the call, they would know that ministry is much more than a profession or job that they must be committed to do only forty hours a week. Rather, they would know that as a vocation, ministry is one's life, which means that by and large one is always on call. They would also know that ministry is not that which one simply tries out because he has tried everything else and has failed. Nor is ministry that which one does for a few months or years and then decides that it's not working out, and thus he will leave in order to do something else.

---

29. See Acts 26:12–18.
30. See McGiffert, *Martin Luther*, 16–17.
31. See King, Jr., *The Autobiography*, 14–16.
32. Davies, "Calling," in *The Westminster Dictionary of Christian Theology*, 79.

Conditions for Making Good the Claim about Holiness and Visible Unity 217

I believe that part of the reason the Movement has to this point blundered in its efforts to make good the claim about visible unity is related to the matter of substantial numbers of pastors and leaders not knowing what it means to be called, and correlatively, that they should be devoted to ministry as long as they have reasonably good health and are in control of their faculties. If they had the type of understanding and commitment about ministry that is implied in the call, they would know to whom must be their first and last loyalty, and why God does not call them to be successful in ministry. Rather, God calls them to be faithful to God's expectation, namely that they do justice, love mercy, and walk humbly with God (Micah 6:8). Faithfulness to God and what they are called to do is the test, not success in increasing the membership roll, the budget, or the size and expensiveness of the church building.

Progress toward making good the claim is dependent in a substantial way on whether ministers and other Movement leaders understand the true meaning of what it means to be called by God, and that when she is called she is in it for the long haul. An excellent illustration of this is the witness that my late teacher, Dean Walter G. Muelder (of Boston University), made to his retired clergy colleagues of the New England Conference of The United Methodist Church in June, 2004. At 97 years of age, Dean Muelder challenged his colleagues to keep calling the church back to its foundations. He threw down the gauntlet, declaring that their ministry must continue throughout their lives, "even in retirement." They were no longer actively engaged in pastoral ministry, but with all of their experience, connections, and other resources at their disposal they could still make a positive impact on church and world. Even in their retirement they are still part of the ongoing dialogue with the church and its work.[33] When one is called to ministry, she must be helped to understand that she is in it for the remainder of her life, for, as Dean Muelder admonished in an interview in his 91st year, "it is not my show."[34] It is God's show, or there is no show worth the admission.

No one has spoken more forcefully and passionately about the meaning and cost of being called to ministry than Martin Luther King, Jr. Two years before he was assassinated, King preached a sermon at Ebenezer Baptist Church in Atlanta, where he was co-pastor with his father, in which he was compelled to clarify the source of his call to ministry and what was required of him in light of that call. King was reacting to the concern of a fellow clergy person who, like himself, talked much about civil rights in his

---

33. See *The United Methodist Newscope*, 8.
34. Moorehead, "It's Not Our Show," interview with Walter G. Muelder, *Bostonia*, 33.

sermons. Some members of the church pastored by the man were critical of his linking the fight for civil rights to ministry. King advised the pastor as follows:

> I said, 'Don't pay any attention to them. Because number one, the members didn't anoint you to preach. And any preacher who allows members to tell him what to preach isn't much of a preacher.' For the guidelines made it very clear that God anointed. No member of Ebenezer Baptist Church called me to the ministry. You called me to Ebenezer, and you may turn me out of here, but you can't turn me out of the ministry, because I got my guidelines and my anointment from God Almighty.[35]

From this we see that God, not the local congregation, is the chief Subject and sole Authority in the calling process. This is not to minimize the importance and role of the one being called and-or the congregation. But it is a reminder that God alone calls persons to ministry and selects the ministry to be done, and it is to God that the one called owes ultimate loyalty, allegiance, faith, and obedience. A local congregation participates in the formal selection of a ministerial candidate and in this sense "calls" her to that church. The difference is that God alone calls her to ministry, commissions her, and gives her authority to do what she is called to do.

When pastors and other leaders in the church understand that God calls them to ministry, they also understand that they are in ministry for the long haul; that while they will need to be mindful to do those things that contribute to their physical, emotional, and psychological health each day, the nature of the call is such that ministry becomes for them a way of life, not until they get tired of the hassles and frustrations of ministry, but until they are separated from it by mental or other incapacitation, or death.

Pastors and leaders in local congregations should be called to their work in ministry and should know in the uttermost depths of their being what this means and requires of them. They should be able to articulate what it means to be called and the work they do in ministry should reflect it. Like the first two conditions above, this third one implies the need and importance of education and knowledge. Theological education is an important component of the process of discerning one's call to ministry. This, in turn, means that seminarians must take their seminary course work much more seriously than many do. They should be as serious and dedicated to their studies as we expect of one who is studying to be a cardiologist. This is not to say that the focus should be on getting top grades in order to graduate

---

35. King, "Guidelines for a Constructive Church," 110–11.

with honors. If the student focuses on the most important thing, namely, learning, in most cases the grades will take care of themselves.

Furthermore, the attitude that students have toward ministry and theological education is important. Vast numbers of people in the United States tend to look upon ministry and theological education as secondary in importance to other vocations and fields of study. Frequently this happens because the mentality in this country is such that when most people think about graduate level academic and professional study, they also have in mind the possibility of getting a well paying job at the end of the degree program. It is known that many ministers who have invested in theological education are barely able to eek out an existence, a problem that is exacerbated when a family is involved. And yet, I maintain that those who are called, and who understand what that means, will be able to find ways to both survive with dignity and to do the work to which God summons them. When God calls one to ministry it is also with the assurance that God will provide what they need to do the work to which they are called. What we need more of in the church is a sense that ministry is the greatest vocation in the world, far transcending in importance all of the professions. The remaining four conditions that will contribute to better positioning Movement people to make real the claim about holiness and visible unity are my own offerings.

ACKNOWLEDGE THAT GOD IS THE PARENT OF ALL PEOPLE

This condition and the two that follow, are fundamentally theological, and should have been expressly built in to the theological and ethical foundation of the Church of God Reformation Movement in the days of Warner and beyond. It is obviously too late to go back more than 130 years to insert them. However, they can—indeed must be—inserted from where we are today. Moreover, I would say that failure to act on this and the following two conditions forthwith can only mean that racism and unacknowledged white privilege will continue to be alive and well in the Church of God, making it virtually impossible to make good the claim about holiness and interracial visible unity. This can only mean that too many whites will continue to feel comfortable living with their unchallenged racism and unearned privilege.

In the Christian tradition it is believed that God, as Creator, is the Parent of all people—regardless. This includes even people such as Adolph Hitler who have engaged in genocidal practices. It includes those—poisoned by the doctrine of "manifest destiny"—who forcibly took this country from native people and massacred thousands. It includes those who forced Afrikan people into dehumanizing slavery. No matter what human beings do to violate the worth of each other, the environment, and the animal kingdom, we are all children of the one God of the universe—without exception—and at the appointed hour every one of us will answer to God for how we treated God's creation and all that is in it. Of course, this must also mean that what we humans do in the world not only affects each other, but God as well.

Reflecting on the subject of religion and race in the early 1960s, Heschel reminded us that the world belongs neither to whites, Afrikan Americans, or any other race. It is, rather, God's world. "No man has a place in this world who tries to keep another man in his place,"[36] Heschel proclaims. It is God's world, and not that of any particular individual or group.

That God lovingly and willingly calls each person into existence and imbues in each the image of God means that there is a fundamental inextricable interrelationship between human beings as such, and God. This means that whatever happens to human beings anywhere in the world affects—directly or indirectly—all other human beings. But this is only part of the truth. The other part—the part that we humans so conveniently forget or ignore—is that what we do to each other also affects God. Because God is both personal and is love, and is the Mother-Father of all, whenever we humans disregard and mistreat each other we do the same to God. Think about that! "When I hurt a human being, I injure God,"[37] said Heschel. To harm any human being in any way, for whatever reason—even if it is state-inflicted death (or capital punishment) for a heinous, murderous crime—is to also harm the creator and sustainer of us all. This is because God has constructed reality as social, and has created humans as relational beings. You cannot insult me without also insulting yourself, other human beings, and the God of the Hebrew prophets and Jesus Christ.

No reasonable person would argue that when a child veers from the path of righteousness his behavior does not affect other human beings and his parents as well. Theologically, this means that what affects one affects all, including God. What we do to each other affects all of humanity, as well as the God of us all. This must be the case since members of the Jewish and Christian communities live by the faith that God is Personal, and as such cares about and responds to all that happens to us. By viewing God as Creator it is reasonable to say with Heschel that, "God is every man's pedigree. He is either the Father of all men or of no man. The image of God is either in every man or in no man."[38] In this regard, God is as hurt and troubled

---

36. Heschel, "Religion and Race," 96.
37. See Stern, "Interview with Dr. Heschel," 399.
38. Heschel, "Religion and Race," 95.

over the lethal injection given the convicted mass murderer, as God was hurt and troubled over each of the murders he committed. And yet, as the God of justice, God does not allow such heinous crimes to go unpunished in a moral universe.

By acknowledging that the God of the Hebrew prophets and Jesus Christ is the God of every person or no person, Movement people should be able to support the idea that every person, regardless of race, ethnicity, gender, class, sexual orientation, age, ability, or health belongs equally to the one God of the universe, and that whenever any one of these is treated unjustly or in other cruel and inhumane ways, these same things are done to God, who we claim to love and serve. We are, ultimately, one people under God, infused equally with God's image. Moreover, when we honor each other, rather than do mean and vicious things to demean the other, we also honor God and the image of God in each other. Such acknowledgement contributes greatly to any effort to make good the claim.

ACKNOWLEDGE THE SACREDNESS OF PERSONS AS SUCH

This condition is not intended to advocate a crude anthropocentricism that implies the absence of intrinsic dignity in non-human life forms, e.g., plants and animals. Human beings have supreme worth, but they are not the only life forms that possess intrinsic value, and in the Biblical view are "not the most highly evolved of the animals . . ."[39] Nevertheless, God created all life and declared it to be "very good" (Gen. 1:31). By virtue of this, both human and non-human life forms have intrinsic worth. Notwithstanding this, the aim of this fifth condition is to focus on the inviolable worth and sacredness of human beings who are—each and every one—dear to the heart of God.

With all of the convenient talk about pluralism, multi-culturalism and inter-culturalism, this country still fundamentally thinks of itself as white. One need only discipline oneself to see and hear what actually comes over televised and other media on a daily basis. We have been conditioned to see as true only the things we have always "known." Many of us were taught that all people are created equal; that we are, all of us, Americans—black, white, brown, red, and gold people. And yet, virtually everything that we see and hear in the media implies another reality. We cannot see this reality, i.e., cannot seem to know what we really see, because we have been conditioned to see only what we have been taught; we see only what we know, or more accurately, what we think we know.

39. Tournier, *A Doctor's Casebook . . .* , 122–23.

Let me illustrate what I mean. A twenty-four hour period seldom passes that one is not inundated with commercial adds and news stories about white Americans. In fact, when reporters use the term "American" and include pictures of these "Americans," pay attention to the race of these people. It is not uncommon for the station to flash pictures only of whites. More often, the vast majority of the scenes are of large numbers of whites with one or two very light complexioned Afrikan Americans. Some times we see one or two East Asians or one or two Hispanics among the throng of whites. In any case, this is what is meant by the term "Americans." It is no wonder that for many people of color—including this writer—whenever most whites use the term "American" they mean *white* American. Similarly, when most white women talk about women's rights, they mean "white" women's rights. Those who were alert witnessed many instances of this during Senator Hillary Clinton's race for the democratic nomination for President in 2007.

Recently I saw a clip on the evening news about Americans returning to college. Several college campuses were featured in the story. I did not see a single student of color moving into dorms or walking across those campuses. So I said out loud: "I guess Afrikan Americans, Indians, Hispanics and Latinas/os don't go to college." I saw another clip about single moms and their struggle to manage a job, a home, and childcare. Not one of the women featured in the story was a woman of color, but the byline was about the challenges of single moms, not single *white* moms. For anybody who is alert and actually thinking when they watch anything at all on television, the clear message is that this nation is fundamentally white, for the references to "Americans" in special news stories are too frequently accompanied by pictures of white Americans only, or primarily. These types of examples can be produced *ad infinitum*, and we are in the twenty-first century! "The principle to be kept in mind," writes Heschel, "is to know what we see rather than to see what we know."[40] What does it really say about Afrikan Americans and other people of color when we see such frequent instances of their being completely left out, as if they don't even exist? They are clearly thought to be invisible, or at best what Latin American liberation theologians used to refer to as "non-persons."

I began this section on the sacredness of persons as I did because the practice and behavior of far too many people in this country, including churches and other religious institutions suggests, intended or not, that only white people are fully human, and thus are the only ones who matter. And of course, if this is the case it must also be true that only the fully human

---

40. Heschel, *The Prophets*, xv.

person is sacred, which would mean that some human beings are sacred and some not. I think this has been a problem for Movement people at least since the second phase of its development, roughly after the death of D. S. Warner in 1895. That is, many Movement white people, like much of white America, still treat Afrikan Americans like they are less human than they. The Frenchman, Alexis de Tocqueville, traveling in the Untied States in the early 1830s, drew this same conclusion in his classic book, *Democracy in America*, as he tried to show how the condition of equality manifested itself in political institutions of the nation, as well as in the customs, manners, and intellectual habits of the people. For example, Tocqueville wrote words that I wish had no relevance today, but they do. In describing how white Americans thought of the enslaved Afrikans he wrote that "we scarcely acknowledge the common features of humanity in this stranger whom slavery has brought among us. His physiognomy is to our eyes hideous, his understanding weak, his tastes low; and *we are almost inclined to look upon him as a being intermediate between man and the brutes.*"[41] Tocqueville also wrote that there was no evidence that whites and blacks would ever co-exist on the basis of equality and equal freedom in the United States.[42] To this point in US history we can only say that he was prophetic (in the predictive sense).

Lest we think that this was only the view of some whites in the 1830s, let us not forget Andrew Hacker's more recent provocative book, *Two Nations: Black and White, Separate, Hostile, Unequal* (1992). Hacker, a white political science professor, was teaching at Queens College in New York City when his book was published. He is convinced that whites are still generally racist, but are more careful as to how they speak and act publicly regarding matters of race.[43] In this regard, most adhere to political correctness, thus hiding behind a façade of racism. Much of present-day white society believes that Afrikan Americans' lives are less valuable than theirs, and there is a presumption among whites that blacks represent an inferior strain. "In this view, Africans—and Americans who trace their origin to that continent—are seen as languishing at a lower evolutionary level than members of other races." Although this is not often said in public venues, "the fact remains," writes Hacker, "that most white people believe that, compared with other races, persons with African ancestries are more likely to carry primitive traits in their genes."[44] Suffice it to say that what too many whites

---

41. Tocqueville, *Democracy in America*, 415 (my emphasis).
42. Ibid., 432–33.
43. Hacker, *Two Nations*, 52.
44. Ibid., 23, 24.

thought about Afrikan Americans during Tocqueville's day is not much different today.

It is important to understand this reality if Movement people are to make significant strides in race relations. Even more so, Movement people need to see this as their own reality, and not solely the reality of "those other white people" or of other segments of American society. Movement people are also American society. The problem is that since the second stage of their development as a religious group, too many have uncritically behaved in ways consistent with the American practice regarding race relations.

If members of the Church of God concede that there is but one God of the universe who is the Parent of all people or of no people, they must also admit that persons as such, i.e., every human being called into existence by God, has a sacredness and preciousness all their own, because they are willed and loved into existence by God. In other words, *every* person has infinite, inviolable sacredness because each is a child of God. If God is truly the Parent of all, and if God loves all persons equally as the Bible teaches, and if God implants equally in all persons the image of God, then it must be the case that there are no *more* or *lesser* human beings in the eyes of God. All are equal before God. Whites are not more human than Afrikan Americans or other groups; nor are these more human than whites. The one God of the universe has created autonomous human beings, all who have equal value before God. Martin Luther King, Jr. said it best: "Every man from a treble white to a bass black is significant on God's keyboard, precisely because every man is made in the image of God."[45] Nevertheless, as morally autonomous beings, it is quite possible that individuals may choose to behave in ways that give them a tarnished image. But this applies only to the individuals who so choose, and not to entire races of people.

God implants the divine image in every person, regardless of race, ethnicity, gender, class, and sexual orientation. My regard for a human being must be based, not upon his merit, or my sense of my own merit, but on my sense that the image of God inheres in him, as in me—for neither of us has done anything, nor can we do anything, to merit God's grace, for example. In addition, only God bestows inherent worth in human beings.

Whenever and wherever any two persons meet in the world they owe the other respect and acknowledgement of mutual dignity, and for no other reason than they are persons—called into existence and sustained by God. Similarly, no person should ever be used as fuel to warm society.[46] Along this same line, Heschel declares: "No person may be sacrificed to

---

45. King, "The American Dream," 88.
46. Bowne, *The Principles of Ethics*, 106, 199.

save others. If an enemy said to a group of women, 'Give us one from among you that we may defile her, and if not we will defile you all,' let the enemy defile them all, but let them not betray to them one single soul."[47] *This is how important and precious is even one individual human being to God.* It should be no different for us. But whites in the Movement will miss the full significance of this principle if they fail to first come home to the idea that Afrikan Americans and other people of color are as human as they, and are as important and valuable to God, who is no respecter of persons (Acts 10:34). That every person is sacred means that every one is owed respect and has a right to be treated like a child of God. Such an attitude and stance will make it easier for Movement people to make good the claim about holiness and visible unity regarding race.

IMPLEMENT THE PRINCIPLE OF EQUALITY AS APPLICABLE TO ALL PERSONS

The principle of equality or equal treatment of all individuals and groups should be basic and prominent in every religious group, especially in the democratic society. It is difficult to come to this sense if one does not believe that all individuals or groups are as fully human as others. Nor does it help if one believes that there is less of the image of God in Afrikan Americans and other people of color than in his own group. At some point it will have to occur to such persons that how they think of themselves, of others, and of the mutual relationship among all human beings has a great deal to say about how they think about God, and how they understand the nature of God and God's relationship with human beings and the world.

For now, it is important to understand that without a built-in principle of equality we can be assured that racial and other types of injustice will continue, whether in the Movement or in other places in the US and the world. There is no question that John Winebrenner, and later D. S. Warner, was right in their teaching on visible unity in the church. To the extent that both men failed to incorporate the principle of equality, however, they also failed in their teaching on visible unity as it pertained to racial relations. By not incorporating the principle of equality, the door in the group led by each man was left wide open for the unequal treatment of blacks. Since the equality principle did not apply to Afrikan Americans (as was also the case in the wider society) it was permissible for them to be treated like second-class citizens in (as well as outside) the church.

---

47. Heschel, "Sacred Image of Man," 155.

During this period of remembering and looking back, Movement people need to see the importance of incorporating the principle of equality in every phase of the church's operation, assuming that the group is really interested in making good the claim of being one body of people—inclusive of all races—under God. An enforced principle of equality would mean that all persons are to be treated equally in hiring and employment practices, as well as in worship and related contexts. There will not likely be any significant progress in the direction of reconciliation between white and black Movement people if there is no concrete evidence of a real push to systematically treat all persons on the basis of the principle of equality. The work that lies ahead will be both difficult and costly to achieve, and yet, it is work that must be done by all who are genuinely concerned about making good the claim.

CALL FOR MUTUAL CORRECTION AND ACCOUNTABILITY

Movement people who say they are serious about making good the claim about uniting holiness and visible unity should have little difficulty understanding the need for a disciplinary component that will keep all members honest about, and open to, the issue of accountability. The individual members as well as the ecclesial community need to be accountable to each other regarding the basic core beliefs of the group. Notwithstanding critics' claim that the Churches of God (General Eldership) was a sect that engaged in its own lawmaking,[48] a form of the principle of mutual correction (or discipline) and accountability existed during John Winebrenner's leadership where individual members *and* the churches were held accountable regarding the enslavement issue. According to the anti-slavery resolutions of 1845, those who enslaved Afrikans were required to free them if they wanted to join the church or to retain membership. In any case, they could be censured or even excommunicated if they refused to discontinue the practice of enslavement. This mutual accountability was a disciplinary mechanism for the group. Individuals were accountable to the church as the church was on the slavery question.

---

48. Warner might well have had groups like the Churches of God (General Eldership) in mind when he wrote: "Had the founder of the church of God left her without a creed, or system of cooperation, it might have been taken for granted that men were left at liberty to draft such rules as they thought best; and so have an excuse for different creeds, and divisions that would arise therefrom. But Jesus has forever excluded all who would be lawmakers in the kingdom of heaven"; Warner and Riggle, *The Cleansing of the Sanctuary*, 258.

Indeed, we recall that Warner himself was censured when he was brought up on charges by W. H. Oliver in 1877 for presumably bringing in bands of holiness groups into the Churches of God, and for his constant preaching and teaching entire sanctification as a second act of grace. He was given a warning, and a restriction was placed on his license by the West Ohio Eldership. In addition, he was admonished to not bring holiness workers or other outside elements to hold meetings in the Churches of God without the consent of the Eldership.[49] When Warner was not able and willing to stop preaching and teaching sanctification as a "second blessing," he was excised from the group.

It will also be recalled that Warner himself implied the need for mutual correction and accountability when he discussed the matter of persons who behave in ways that unfit them for membership in God's church. We saw in chapter 4 that Warner imposed discipline on Joseph Fisher in 1887, then co-owner of the *Gospel Trumpet*. Fisher fell in love with a younger woman, divorced his wife, and married his lover. Warner interpreted the Bible to say that the divorced person was to remain celibate and single until the other died. When Fisher refused to repent, Warner insisted that he leave *The Trumpet*. Able to convince E. E. Byrum to buy Fisher's share of *The Trumpet*, Warner was essentially able to get rid of Fisher, and ceased to fellowship with him. In this way, he was able to enforce church discipline.

Moreover, in 1899, Byrum sought to impose discipline on a group who began teaching Zinzendorfism, the view that one is justified and sanctified at the point of conversion, as opposed to the Movement teaching that one first experiences justification and then, through faith, experiences a second act of God's grace. As Merle Strege tells the story, Byrum imposed discipline on what was a substantial group, thus "risking the possibility of major defections."[50] Byrum refused fellowship with the group (deemed by him to be heretics). What I find most interesting is that Byrum was willing to risk the defection of a substantial number of Movement leaders over this issue, but nowhere is there evidence of discipline being imposed on racists in the group during that period. Perhaps a reason for this is that racism was endemic to the group—from its inception—as it was to the nation. Therefore, to impose discipline would virtually deplete the white membership if the vast majority refuses to repent of the sin of racism. In any event, Movement people need to be accountable to each other on the issue of visible unity along racial lines—especially at this advanced stage of the group's life cycle. Even if such accountability was not required during the earliest stages of

---

49. Warner, *D. S. Warner's Journal*, 248.
50. Strege, *I Saw the Church*, 43.

the Movement's natural history, it is most certainly applicable in its most mature stage today.

I have believed for a long time (and it has been confirmed by my own experience and the experiences of many other people) that most individuals who join Christian communities do not have much awareness of what will be required of them and the theology behind it. They have little sense of what it means to be Christian, let alone what it means to live the Christian life. They have no idea that having converted to the Christian faith means that they must no longer conform to the ways of society and the world; that there is a much higher ethical standard that they must now live by—the imperative of agape love, that unconditional and overflowing love that flows directly from God and requires that we humans love one another without condition or qualification, just as God loves us. In a word, new converts—indeed many long time Christians—have little awareness that being a faithful member of the Christian community requires a level of maturity and dedication that escapes most. The regenerated life in Jesus Christ requires the willingness to discipline one's self to live in accordance with his teachings and example. What this means, of course, is that too little attention is devoted to teaching converts the faith and what is required of them in their daily living. My sense is that this type of training and the discipline that comes from it is not a short-term affair, but one that must continue throughout each member's life of faith. It is a life-long process.

We saw in chapter 3 that the Anabaptists have some instructive things to say and teach about the importance of mutual correction and accountability among Christians. Such teachings, I believe, are quite relevant and applicable to Movement people as well, most particularly for those who want to make good the claim. But it is not just the Anabaptist tradition that has instructive offerings in this regard. We saw above that both Warner and Byrum invoked the practice of church discipline, although one wishes that they had applied it explicitly to white racist behavior, and the unequal, and unjust treatment of Afrikan Americans. We also find that Charles E. Brown, appointed fourth editor of the *Gospel Trumpet* in 1930, gave considerable attention to the matter of church discipline, mutual accountability, and the responsibility and expectation of members essentially to prove that they are true Christians and dedicated workers in the faith. I return to Brown's contribution in a moment.

Being a Christian, unlike what far too many proponents believe, is not based on cheap grace. Dietrich Bonhoeffer taught that being a Christian is based on costly grace. It is costly because it calls one to drop everything, deny everybody and everything, and follow Jesus Christ. "It is costly because it costs a man his life," Bonhoeffer said, "and it is grace because it gives a man the only true life."[51] Those who come to the Christian faith but continue to believe that it is acceptable to persist in living their old ways are recipients of cheap grace. Bonhoeffer characterized the receiver of such grace saying:

> The Christian life comes to mean nothing more than living in the world and as the world, in being no different from the world for the sake of grace. The upshot of it all is that my only duty as a Christian is to leave the world for an hour or so on a Sunday morning and go to church to be assured that my sins are all forgiven. I need no longer try to follow Christ, for cheap grace, the bitterest foe of discipleship, which true discipleship must loathe and detest, has freed me from that.[52]

The short of it is that it *costs* something to be a Christian—to be a true Movement person. Every member—especially new members—must be taught (even as long time members should be relentlessly reminded) to understand that by being converted to the Christian faith and joining the church she is saying No to sin of all kinds, and Yes to unequivocal faithfulness to God and God's expectation that justice be done in the world. Having forsaken the old life, the new member lives only for God and the church. This will require vigilance, dedication, and discipline on the part of members. What Franklin Littell has said of the Anabaptists is applicable here: "The new member must be deeply aware that he has foresworn the world, sin, and the devil, and in whole heart and soul and body set out to live for God and His church."[53] Indeed, none was more emphatic about this than D. S. Warner. We get a sense of this from his reflections (in 1886) on men in the Good Way group in Missouri. Concerned that many of them were unwilling to take a firm stance against those whose views and practices deviated from the expectations of holiness, or whose views vacillated to and fro, because they did not want to be thought ill of, Warner reflected: "These men talk of contending earnestly for holiness, but want to avoid disturbing men's conflicting opinions, imbibed in sect education. This is silly child's play. There is no consistency in calling men out of the sects, and letting them still retain the errors of sect education. The Good Way is really a Babylon sheet. Though it teaches against sects, it is inconsistent in itself."[54] The way they have chosen is not an easy way, and before they can be critical of those outside the group, they must first rid the contradictions and inconsistencies within the group.

51. Bonhoeffer, *The Cost of Discipleship*, 37.
52. Ibid., 42.
53. Littell, *The Origins of Sectarian Protestantism*, 84.
54. Warner, "Confusion and Shaking," (column 2).

The members must be clear about what holiness requires and hold firm to it. Members must be willing to renounce old habits and practices for ones that are thoroughly Christ-like. But not many in the Movement seem to really understand that this also applies to the requirement of interracial unity; that racism is not a Christ-like idea and practice, and therefore members must not be fearful or hesitant (to the point of incapacitation) to take sides against those who are friendly toward it. There must be no fence-straddling, or unwillingness to take a stand.

There is no question in my mind that the idea that to be a Christian is costly, is a novel idea for far too many proponents of the Christian faith today, and has been so in the Movement for too, too long. Too many people who come to the Christian faith believe that they do not have to give up anything in order to be a Christian. If they were chronic liars before, they think they can continue to lie. If they were heavy drinkers and smokers before, they think it acceptable to continue. If they stole from the poor and needy before, they think it is permissible to continue to steal from them. If they were sexists before, they think it is acceptable to continue being sexist, and the same applies to racism. They think they can continue being the racists they were before experiencing conversion and sanctification. The even greater tragedy is that the religious group with which they affiliate does not teach them any differently; does not watch what really comes through the door to membership. If more attention were given this latter, there might be the heightened possibility that "a strong and true church could be maintained."[55] As far as the Movement is concerned, precisely this will have to happen if there is to be any hope of making good the claim.

Writing on the Anabaptist tradition of discipline among members and the church and the importance of mutual accountability, homiletician and Christian ethicist Mary Alice Mulligan, writes that the Anabaptists understood the Christian life to be a total commitment and response to Jesus Christ. This in itself implies that the new convert is expected to be committed to an entirely different lifestyle than in the pre-conversion period. It also implies that such a one must commit to expending the time and energy to be taught as well as to work hard and diligently to learn what is expected of them. This is part of the cost for membership in the group. Mulligan writes: "Those who believe in him commit their lives to God and pledge to live in a way worthy of Jesus, which means following his way. To become a Christian is to belong to (to become the possession of) Jesus Christ."[56] Anyone desiring conversion to the Christian faith must be made aware that she is

---

55. Littell, *The Origins of Sectarian Protestantism*, 85.
56. Mulligan, "Remodeling Word and Table in the Believers Church," 131.

expected to lead a radically transformed life, and to be a radical transformer of the world; a life based on the teachings and witness of Jesus Christ. Mulligan contends that the sign that such a lifestyle is being lived is indicated by one's effort to live out of "a commitment to 'holiness,' that characteristic of striving toward a more perfect pattern of the Christian life. Believers are to live lives not conformed to the world but transformed by the power of God at work within them. . . They are convinced their lives can be exemplary, not by their own willfulness alone, but because of God's holy power at work within them."[57] Although the power of the Holy Spirit is at work in this process, it is also understood that each member, and the ecclesial community, will help and support each other in the effort to achieve this more perfect state. Sometimes this may mean carrying out one's role and responsibility in helping the community to reach a consensus as to whether to ban or shun a member who has strayed from the requirements of the faith and refuses to acknowledge and correct the wrong done.[58]

It is important that Christians, most especially Movement people, understand that membership in the church exacts a price. The issue here is not what it takes to be a member of the Church of God. Warner saw that that puzzle was solved in the Holy Scriptures. One need only be converted or regenerated to gain membership. The issue here concerns what is expected of one in order for her to retain and remain in good standing. The question is, what happens, or what must one be willing to do, should her life prove not to be in harmony with holiness or perfection? What happens when one begins saying and doing things that are not consistent with the life of holiness?

Warner was certain that "no person can remain in the church when ceasing to be holy."[59] He was critical of those sects (including the Winebrennerian Churches of God) that had a prescribed course of discipline that could lead to the expulsion of a person from the group. Warner believed there was no need for rules that could lead to revoking one's membership in the church, since "men becoming unfit for membership in the body of Christ, are already without the same. God's church is self-adjusting."[60]

There need be no rules that lead to excommunication, according to Warner, because the fact of one's sin alone cancels his membership in the Church of God. That one is a Christian does not mean that she is no longer capable of sinning, for as long as she is an autonomous human being with freedom to make choices, she is capable of sinning. As a human being, she

---

57. Ibid., 132.
58. Littell, *The Origins of Sectarian Protestantism*, 94.
59. Warner and Riggle, *The Cleansing of the Sanctuary*, 270.
60. Ibid.

will always be susceptible to making errors in judgment or simply making mistakes, but these are not always what one should view as sin. In fact, just because one commits a sin does not mean that she is no longer a member of the church. If she repents, seeks forgiveness, and receives the counsel of other members and the church, she is restored. This must happen if one is to remain a member of the church. Warner taught that, "There never was, nor ever can be a sinner or unholy person in the church, which is the body of Christ."[61] One cannot remain in the church if she ceases to be holy, and fails to do those necessary things to restore herself to the church. This has real implications for Movement people who are racists. Such ones must be willing to work unrelentingly to overcome their racism and their unwillingness to acknowledge their unearned privilege in order to restore themselves fully to the church.

According to Warner, to have rules of discipline that might lead to excommunicating a person whose behavior suggests he is unfit to remain in the group is a sectarian practice and thus unacceptable. The church belongs to God, he reasoned, and therefore human beings have no church from which to expel or excommunicate anyone. Nevertheless, Warner understood the need for Christians to live holy lives, since God does not dwell among the unholy. Persons should be allowed to seek restoration, Warner believed. But this is not unlike what we find in sects that have rules of discipline. Enslavers in the Churches of God (General Eldership), for example, were given the opportunity to liberate those they enslaved. They had to make a choice. Failure to liberate the enslaved meant excommunication of the enslaver. Warner found this procedure to be problematic, and yet he himself, following the teachings of the Bible, implied the need for some type of discipline or ongoing effort on the part of individual Christians to remain saved. One enters church membership through salvation, but by committing sin and failing to overcome it, Warner maintained, "his name is blotted out of the book of life. 'And the Lord said unto Moses, Whosoever hath sinned against me, him will I blot out of my book.' Ex. 32:33. But, 'He that overcometh, the same shall be clothed in white raiment; and I will not blot out his name out of the book of life' (Rev. 3:5)."[62]

It is the member's responsibility to clear her name, i.e., to overcome the sin committed. Unfortunately, what we do not see here is any required involvement on the part of other members and the church community to assist in the restoration process. Warner did not point to the biblical foundation for such a process, despite the fact that such exists. Indeed, the prospect for

---

61. Ibid., 271.
62. Ibid., 272.

such a process seems to be implicit in the Exodus and Revelation scriptures cited above. Furthermore, it will be recalled that, although Warner rejected the idea of a formal procedure for discipline, this did not preclude him from subjecting Joseph Fisher to discipline when he divorced his wife and married another woman. Nor did he see as problematic the dis-fellowshipping of Elder S. Ensminger in 1872, for "immoral conduct."[63] (Warner was still a member of the General Eldership at the time.)

How else does one overcome, if he does not will to do so and put forth effort in that direction; if he does not have the aid and assistance of other members and the broader church community? This implies the need for a process. But to the question: Can the local church receive or expel members, Warner's response was no. What it can do, however, is to recognize (or not) members based on how they live, which puts much of the onus on an individual member. He must prove his *worthiness to be recognized as a member of the church* by the way he lives his life. This, Warner believed, is different from the General Eldership's rule about excommunication. He seemed to think that the refusal to recognize one's membership is qualitatively different from such a one being excommunicated from God's church.

While growing up in the Church of God, I used to frequently hear the following statement recited to new members: "We will accept you on your testimony, until your life proves otherwise." As I got older I understood that the new member was essentially being told that we recognize your membership in the church until your life proves that we should no longer so recognize your standing. The pastor and laity did not say that we receive you, or we will expel you; only that we recognize your membership based on your testimony, and the way you live your life henceforth. This is different from official excommunication, since it is not a matter of putting one out of God's church, but rather of refusing to recognize her membership if she fails to work toward an acceptable testimony. It is refusing to fellowship with such a one, much as Warner did in the cases of Elder S. Ensminger and Joseph Fisher.

CONTRIBUTIONS OF CHARLES E. BROWN

As implied above, Charles E. Brown went much further in his treatment of mutual correction and accountability than Warner did. As human beings, we will make mistakes, and we will periodically sin. But rather than wallow in self-pity, we are charged by the Scriptures to work to overcome the sin in order to clear our name and be restored. The onus is strictly on the

---

63. Warner, *Journal of D. S. Warner*, 5.

individual concerned, although Brown, unlike Warner, and apparently in agreement with the Anabaptists, seemed to acknowledge the importance of possible contributions and the participation of other members and the church community. In this regard, Brown writes:

> We have attempted to prove that the burden of a member's recognition rests primarily upon the member himself. It is his duty to produce satisfactory evidence that he is a member. Undoubtedly the same thing is true with regard to excommunication. If a member's conduct or attitude becomes such as to threaten the withdrawal of recognition, it is clearly the duty of this accused member to make every reasonable effort to clear his reputation.
>
> Here it is not possible to follow completely the analogy of the civil court. In the criminal courts a man cannot be tried nor condemned unless he is physically present to hear the charges and to make such reply as he is able. But a criminal court has the power to compel a man's presence, whereas the councils of the church do not have this power. Consequently, the best the church can do is to honor completely the spirit of this principle of justice, giving the accused person every reasonable opportunity to appear and to answer for himself. Should the accused person neglect or despise this opportunity, here the church would seem justified in taking an analogy from the civil courts of law wherein judgment by default is taken against the man who refuses to appear and to plead at the time and place appointed by the court.[64]

In the case of the church, the judgment by default would mean that one is no longer to be recognized as a member of the church. Brown was aware that church discipline (even in his day) received virtually no attention, and he gave a number of plausible reasons why this was the case. He acknowledged that there are scriptural foundations for church trials that might lead to excommunication. As examples, Brown cited Acts 5:1–11, 8:18–24, and 1 Corinthians 5:1–5. He also included the famous passage in Matthew 18:15–20 (which, as we will see presently, has been of critical importance in the Anabaptist tradition). Brown concludes—and I believe rightly—that "the only good which can be accomplished through excommunication is *to deliver the church from the shame and scandal of giving her indorsement and consolation to persons of known evil lives and reputations.*"[65]

The very subject of excommunication is serious business and should not be easily invoked. However, Brown, as well as the Second Testament,

64. Brown, *The Church Beyond Division*, 132.
65. Ibid., 135 (my emphasis).

contends that excommunication has its potential value for the church. In this regard, it "must be of a nature to carry with it the assent and approval not only of the church members themselves, but of the sober-minded better element of the public as well." He goes on to say that, "the proper excommunication is not essentially a judgment of the heart of the man or woman excommunicated [for this is virtually impossible for we humans to judge]; it is the judgment of his life, and that judgment must be sufficiently clear, sound, and unprejudiced to carry the moral conviction of the large part of the good people concerned, both in the church and in the general public."[66] Persons should not be called up on frivolous charges or charges that reasonably mature and intelligent people in and out of the church do not see as being real problems. Of course, we have to be able to see that a problem of a different sort could emerge if a large segment of the church and the society carries a bias. What happens, for example, should a person be called out because of his consistent practice of racial prejudice, but the vast majority of the local church and community are filled with people who are similarly racially biased?

In any event, Brown saw that any group that appealed to the Scriptural foundation of the subject of excommunication should do so in a loving and respectful spirit, and on the basis of fairness and justice and "performed according to the Scriptures and in the Spirit of Christ." When an excommunication is done in this accord, "it constitutes one of the gravest sentences that could ever be pronounced upon a human being prior to that solemn day when he stands at the judgment seat of Christ."[67]

Brown argues that even the foundational text, Matthew 18:15–20 was not meant by Jesus to be a formal judicial proceeding in the church, but merely a way for Christians to settle deviations from accepted teachings, and in a particular spirit. Brown saw the text as placing more emphasis on the spirit in which conflicts should be resolved between members, than on the need for a legal procedure. He was just as adamant, however, that the truly saved should be willing to talk things over with each other, and to be open to both giving and receiving advice that will help to restore one whole. The sister or brother who is unwilling to do this, he maintained, is no sister or brother and such a one's membership should no longer be recognized. The point of such proceedings, according to Brown, is never to destroy, "but to restore, the offender."[68] This, he maintains, is in the spirit of Jesus Christ.

---

66. Ibid.
67. Ibid., 139.
68. Ibid., 138.

Brown's stance actually comes close to the Anabaptist view as espoused in the work of James Waltner, who writes: "It became the conviction of the Anabaptists that the locus of the living Word was the congregation. Each believer had something to gain from, and contribute to the shared life of the congregation."[69] Brown seemed to see that it is not only a matter of the role of individuals, but of the ecclesial community as well. Both have responsibilities to assist in correcting those who stray from the core teachings. Although it is the individual who makes the decision to undergo regeneration, it is not an individualistic decision when the church community itself also plays a significant part, from beginning to end. This is where the principles of *mutual correction* and *mutual responsibility* come in. Reflecting on the Anabaptist tradition, Mulligan views these as proper functions of the church community. "People in the fellowship were bound together in their relationship to God and to each other . . . In their life together then, members of the group were expected to give and receive counsel from each other concerning matters of faith."[70] Mulligan also maintains (not unlike Brown) that because believers are united on the basis of certain principles and beliefs, "certain expectations of lifestyle and behavior resulted naturally from the understanding of the faith, the commitment to follow the teachings of Jesus Christ."[71] To be a Christian meant that one would think and behave differently than she did in her pre-Christian life. To receive Christian teachings and the example of Jesus Christ meant giving up the old ways for the new. It also meant that this was to be reflected in the things one said and did.

One will not be perfect after the initial conversion experience. However, one's attitude should certainly change dramatically, even if it may take time, hard work, and vigilance in order for one's thinking and behavior to catch up. One might be a diehard racist, sexist, or heterosexist at the time of conversion. We know from experience and the sound work of social scientists and clinical psychologists that these are not completely eradicated at the point of religious conversion, and will not be if there is not ongoing concerted effort, methods, and therapies to help it to happen. At the point of conversion, however, there should at least be an attitudinal change regarding racism, etc.; a sense, sparked by solid teaching and counsel by longstanding church members (who both know and live the way), that such things are considered sins because they alienate and divide people and also dehumanize both the victim and the perpetrator. All of these things are contradictions to the spirit of the gospel and the love that is Jesus Christ. With

---

69. Quoted in Mulligan, 132.
70. Mulligan, 132–33.
71. Ibid., 133.

this attitudinal change, the new convert willingly submits self to the wise counsel of the church, the Bible, and the best in the Jewish and Christian traditions.

Although I find the Anabaptist tradition to be strong regarding matters of discipline and mutual correction and am much helped by it, we have seen that something like this exists in the history of the Church of God Reformation Movement. Movement people, therefore, do not have to look far for instruction on such matters. We see inklings of it in Warner's writings, but we have seen that the more full-blown treatment appears in the writings of Charles E. Brown. In every religious group there needs to be a means by which disagreements are settled, and by which persons—and the church!—are held accountable for deviations from the teachings and witness of Jesus Christ, as well as the core beliefs of the group.

Unfortunately, even though in some form such an instrument has been present in the Movement since the time of Warner, it has not frequently been invoked in matters pertaining to the failure to make good the claim about visible unity and oneness, and most especially interracial unity. Individuals and clusters of white Movement people should have literally been called out over the years—and even today—for their adherence to racism. Too few have been willing to see their own complicity in racism, and have only been able to see the blatant racism of other whites in the Movement, or in other groups. *Every* white person benefits from racism, whether this or that one is an individual racist or not; and there is no question that there are some whites—even in the Movement—who work hard and relentlessly against racism in all forms. But even these benefit from racism by virtue of their white skin. Until Movement people—blacks and whites alike—understand this, the pattern of not calling people to account for their racism will continue, which means that reconciliation is little more than a hopeless, impossible ideal.

The text of Matthew 18:15–20 is just as relevant to this matter as to any other that a person or group in the church may be called up for correction. Perhaps it will be helpful to cite the text.

> If another member of the church sins against you, go and point out the fault when the two of you are alone. If the member listens to you, you have regained that one. But if you are not listened to, take one or two others along with you, so that every word may be confirmed by the evidence of two or three witnesses. If the member refuses to listen to them, tell it to the church; and if the offender refuses to listen even to the church, let such a one be to you as a Gentile and a tax collector. Truly I tell you, whatever you bind on earth will be bound in heaven, and whatever you

loose on earth will be loosed in heaven. Again, truly I tell you, if two of you agree on earth about anything you ask, it will be done for you by my Father in heaven. For where two or three are gathered in my name, I am there among them.

This is the Christ-like means for discipline and correction in the church. Since the church is a voluntary institution, it is true that no member need allow self to be subjected to such mutual correction, and many do not. Often they simply leave a given local church altogether, or join another one. But what is important is that when such a one refuses to receive the decision or judgment of the ecclesial community concerning his behavior, his membership is no longer acknowledged by the group.

Brown and Mulligan remind us that the point of such mutual correction is not to demean or destroy the person, but to restore such one to the community of believers, as well as deliver the church from the appearance of supporting shameful, scandalous, and sinful behavior.[72] *Retaining fellowship* with the wrongdoer is the aim of mutual correction in the church. But when it becomes evident that such a one rejects correction and persists in wrongful behavior, the church needs to have enough of the Christ-like spirit, as well as common sense, to let that person exit the group—regardless of how wealthy such a one may be, or what may be his race.

At no level of the church should the membership be comprised of people who absolutely refuse to work hard and unrelentingly to eradicate either their own, and-or the racism of the church or any of its agencies. D. S. Warner sought to reform the church from within such that it would be purged of all sectarian or alienating elements. There is no question that racism in the church continues to be among its most divisive and shameful elements. This is particularly important for the Movement at a time when many seem to have an interest in remembering and looking back to its roots, and thinking about what they need to be doing in order to make good the claim about holiness and visible unity along interracial lines.

Finally, from the inception of the early church over 2,000 years ago, Christians have known that theirs would be a life of persecution, not unlike that of the One they served who was beaten, nailed to, and crucified on an old rugged cross. Over the years, it was increasingly the case that proponents of Christianity believed and behaved like they expected the world to treat them respectfully, and not subject them to cruel and unusual punishment. Christians forgot almost entirely that the church was from the very beginning a counter-cultural community, and as such, it will generally always find itself on the wrong side of what is expected by the wealthy,

---

72. See Brown, *The Church Beyond Division*, 135, 138; and Mulligan, 134.

and the powers and principalities. What these expect, generally contradicts what the Christian ethic requires of believers and the church.

This all means that members of the church who take their faith seriously will be persecuted both by forces within and outside the church. Persons should learn this basic fact as soon as they join the church, or soon thereafter. Furthermore, it is a point to which Movement people need to come to terms. The attempt to walk the straight and narrow way will be costly. There is no other conclusion to be drawn. This has always been the case, and there is no evidence that it will ever be different. Those who truly believe in the core ideas of holiness and visible unity in the Church of God Reformation Movement should understand that adherence to such principles means that they will be persecuted in some form or fashion, particularly when everything they stand for as a church is against the ethic of society, but is consistent with the radical ethical imperative of Jesus Christ. This is the price of the crown that Christians seek to wear. No less is it the price of making good the claim about holiness and visible interracial unity in the Church of God Reformation Movement.

Afterword

MAPPING THE PAST

THE CHURCH OF GOD Reformation Movement was birthed in October, 1881.[1] Incidentally, this was the same year that the Tennessee legislature passed the first Jim Crow Law. Even as the message of holiness and unity was being spread by recognized Movement founder, Daniel Sidney Warner (1842–1895), and other early Church of God pioneers, one state after another followed Tennessee's lead, passing legislation to racially segregate schools, trains, hospitals and other institutions. To combat this polarizing force in society, the Church of God might have seemed well-positioned declaring as they did a message of visible unity in the Body of Christ.

Indeed, church leaders were genuinely committed to the teaching of holiness and unity. They brooked no compromise as they decried the evils of a church divided by denominationalism. These early "saints" were willing to divide family and communities for the cause, a unity without which one could not live the holy life. It is clear from the historical record that these early "come-outers," so labeled because they urged their hearers to come out of sects and denominations, were often more than a little disruptive in passionate pursuit of church oneness.

What becomes disturbingly clear, however, is that this radicality was not directed toward the eradication of the color line, which, at the time, was being divisively drawn across society. In other words, the same commitment to suffer for the cause of oneness was, as a general rule, not risked in any initiative to bring blacks and whites together in a demonstrable, visible unity. Justification for this accommodation took many forms including the fear that holding interracial meetings would damage efforts to win souls for Christ.

1. Smith, *The Quest for Holiness and Unity*, 2nd ed., 35.

In the historiography of the Church of God the record of race relations in the Movement is one that begins well. Examples of interracial meetings were highlighted, and early Church of God pioneers were portrayed as being largely untainted by the stain of racial prejudice. Though there were certainly instances of interracial gatherings in these early decades, Rufus Burrow, Jr.'s critical work effectively challenges more institutionally friendly accounts of relations between whites and African Americans. As Burrow's study demonstrates, few sources show unequivocally that Movement leaders, with any real intentionality, made an effort to welcome African Americans into the Church of God fold. This remains true even in the earliest years of the life of the Movement when blacks and whites worshipped together in many communities.

Sometimes Warner's June, 1890, *Gospel Trumpet* article condemning a decision by administrators at Pauline College to bar African Americans from the campus is cited as evidence of the founder's progressive views on the subject of interracial worship and unity. In the article, Warner does indeed make a strong stand against the Good Way Holiness group's decision to close the school to blacks. He even referred to the decision to dispel them as "sin." He also pointed out the fact that God had "made of one flesh all men to dwell upon the earth."[2] Warner's condemnation of this group's actions is for me the strongest indication of Warner's position on racial matters. Still yet, Burrow is right to contend that Warner says little to indicate his convictions about interracial fellowship as an aspect of visible unity. Moreover, the founder's personal convictions don't seem to become instantiated in the doctrinal platform of the emerging Movement.

In my own research on racism in the Church of God tradition which began in 2003 as a doctoral student, I found little evidence that white Movement leaders gave much thought to addressing the color line. In March of 2014, I had the opportunity to return to the subject of race and the Church of God tradition when asked to give the Harp Lecture for Anderson University's School of Theology in Indiana. In putting together this project, I planned to bore down into three areas of the Movement's tradition in order to look for clues as to the nature of race relations throughout the first couple of decades of the Movement's history. I imagined the project to be analogous to what climatologists do when seeking to examine climatic and atmospheric conditions from a previous era.

First I examined the hymnody of the Church of God. Next, I read early issues of *The Gospel Trumpet*, specifically those having to do with race. Finally, I chose to examine William G. Schell's book, *Is the Negro a Beast?*,

---

2. A loose quotation from Acts 17:26. Warner, "Good Wayism," (column 1), 4.

a defense of the humanity of African Americans, published by the Gospel Trumpet Company in 1902.

SONGS AND HYMNS OF THE CHURCH OF GOD

Music has always played a central role in the life of the Church of God Movement. In short, members sang what they believed.[3] Even Warner himself wrote songs and hymns. Both what is addressed and not addressed in these musical compilations is telling. Absent from *Songs of Victory* published in 1885 by the Gospel Trumpet Company is any real celebration of the distinctives of the Movement's teaching, particularly holiness and unity. On the other hand, a theme conspicuous in the tradition is the need for every individual to be saved. But this theme, no doubt, was a common one in the songsters of other evangelical traditions competing for souls during this era. Moreover, publishing songs with a theme common to many church traditions would have aided in the sale of songsters. As a result, one is left to wonder whether or not market considerations were a motivating factor in what musical compilations were eventually included in the Movement's first song book.[4]

A further examination of the musical tradition of the Church of God reveals that Charles Wesley Naylor was instrumental in highlighting the charism of unity within the Church of God's musical tradition. For example, Naylor had a hand in writing the song "Let Us Be United," published in 1907, as well as in the production of "The Church has One Foundation" published the same year. In this latter composition, the lyricist wrote, "Back to the one foundation, From sects and creeds made free, Come saints of every nation To blessed unity. Once more the ancient glory Shines as in the days of old, And tells the wondrous story—One God, one faith, one fold."[5] Naylor's circumscribed views on unity, poetically expressed as they were, did not, however, appear to give him pause when called upon to articulate the Church of God's position on racial unity. In a *Gospel Trumpet* article he remarked:

---

3. See Adams, "The Hymnody of the Church of God (1885–1890) As a Reflection of That Church's Theological and Cultural Changes," 1.

4. Fischer, *Songs of Victory*.

5. Naylor, *"The Church has One Foundation"* (No. 163), in *Select Hymns for Christian Worship*. Naylor added two verses to this song penned by Samuel J. Stone, verses three and five. The lyrics here quoted make up verse five. See Timeless Truths Free Online Library, accessed November 24, 2015, http://www.Library.timelesstruths.org/music/The_Church_Has_One_Foundation/.

> We teach that we should give no offense neither to the Jew nor the Greek, neither to the church of God, as the Bible declares; or, in other words, we teach people to be subject to the social customs of the community wherein they reside. Most certainly we do not advocate the marriage of a white and a colored person, and I would not perform the marriage ceremony under such conditions even if the law did not forbid it. In all things we believe in both races keeping their proper places and relations.[6]

THE GOSPEL TRUMPET AND RACE

In preparation for the Harp Lecture, a second sampling conducted in this 2014 study was drawn from early issues of *The Gospel Trumpet*. With regard to race relations, the *Trumpet* seems to have blown with an uncertain sound. In other words, some contributions written for the newspaper condemned racial prejudice. At other times, however, Movement leaders gave a rationalization for the accommodation of the Jim Crow system.

It is also true that articles from *The Gospel Trumpet* give credence to Burrow's contention that white pioneers displayed no real sustained commitment to evangelize African Americans. Moreover, at times contributors to the *Trumpet* were eager to refute any notion that their friendliness to African Americans went beyond the bounds of either God's law or human law. In one instance J.F. Lundy, a contributor to *The Gospel Trumpet* writing from Anderson, South Carolina, gave a glimpse of the Movement's treatment of its black worshipers. Further, he appears to play down any substantive differences between the manner in which blacks were treated in Church of God meetings and in the way they were treated in meetings of rival groups. In speaking of a disturbance in one such Church of God gathering the contributor wrote,

> The great opposition came up nominally over two colored saints, one from Charleston, S.C. and the other from Augusta, Ga. These saints with a few colored people from this neighborhood occupied seats in the rear of the room. All they did was sit peaceably in the room and testify to salvation when opportunity afforded. The general custom of the country is to extend to the colored people the privilege of seats in the back part of all meeting houses. The only difference between God's way of doing business and sect machinery was that in the saints meetings

---

6. Naylor, *The Gospel Trumpet*, (Column 3), 9.

they testified when the Spirit moved, but in Babylon, after all the whites had spoken.[7]

IS THE NEGRO A BEAST? BY WILLIAM G. SCHELL

Lastly, in this 2014 study I examined the text, *Is the Negro a Beast?*, by Church of God leader William G. Schell. The reason for my interest in this text had to do with the role it has played in the historiography of the Church of God. More specifically, historian John W.V. Smith cites this source as evidence that Schell supported the "full equality" of blacks and whites.[8] A close reading of this volume, however, might lead one to think otherwise. Schell's condemnation of "amalgamation," for example, reveals a lack of commitment to the fullest expression of social equality, a complete eradication of the color line in all relationships.

Burrow staunchly contends in this book that little evidence can be mustered to support a claim that most white Movement pioneers were committed to addressing the color line in either society or in the church. From the earliest days of the Movement's history, Church of God leaders seem to have concerned themselves primarily with a circumscribed, spiritual unity rather than a more robust understanding of unity which might have taken into account social realities in the late nineteenth and early twentieth centuries.

This is not to say that African Americans were blind to the social implications of a message of holiness and unity. Indeed, blacks did enter the Movement. But right away they began showing evidence that they were not reading the tradition nor hearing the rhetoric of unity and holiness in the same way as their white counterparts. For example, one of the first African American ministers to fellowship with the Church of God, Jane Williams, contributed a question which was subsequently published in *The Gospel Trumpet*.[9] She asked, "Is it necessary for us to use the word colored, and white saint?"[10] In response to this query the following rationale was given for the continued use of this apparently offensive identifier. The writer stated that "God has made of one blood all nations to dwell upon the earth.' And of course all colors of mankind have originated from his original creation in the garden [sic] of Eden." This same writer went on, however, to claim

---

7. Lundy, *The Gospel Trumpet*, (Column 2,), 3.
8. Smith, *The Quest for Holiness and Unity* 2nd edition, 156–57.
9. Massey, *African Americans and the Church of God*, 25.
10. Williams, "Question," *The Gospel Trumpet*, (Column 3–4), 1.

that there was a "natural inequality of the races," and that the laws requiring separation of the races in the South had to be observed.[11]

LOOKING FORWARD

Burrow's contribution to the Church of God Movement moves beyond simply mapping its racial history. He offers instead some helpful suggestions as to how to move forward in an effort to live into the best of the theological heritage of the church. Doing so would result in a practice of visible unity that would in the end address divisions between blacks and whites within the Movement. Recognized in this approach, however, is the conviction that a commitment to visible unity would have a transformative effect on relationships between whites and all other diverse constituencies whether divided by race, class, gender or sexual orientation.

In demonstrating a streak of optimism the author contends that he believes that the Movement could be entering a fourth stage of development, one in which its past convictions regarding a holiness expressed in a visible unity would become a reality. Make no mistake, however, for Burrow's recommendations for "Making Good the Claim" are not for the faint of heart. Truth-telling, straight talk and church discipline are all elements of what might be necessary to take on this seemingly intractable social issue. Moreover, the author acknowledges just how ensconced are the ugly habits of heart and mind which have brought the Movement to its current position. Still yet he offers hope.

A step toward healing, Burrow contends, will require that white members first acknowledge their racial prejudice and their enjoyment of white unearned privilege. Having lived in the white community all of my life, I fear Burrow's prescription will be a hard sell for many. He also states that in order to address racism a broader definition of sin must be employed. My years of ministry in the church, however, leave me with the impression that structural evil is not a concept well-understood by the average church goer in our Movement. Nor do individuals in the dominant racial group, as a rule, believe that they have been negatively impacted by the kind of racist ideology widely disseminated to justify human slavery and, more recently, Jim Crow segregation. Consequently, racial prejudice finds its home in the subconscious, hiding out until some trigger forces it out of the underbrush and into the full view of everyone, including its host. Only after such a traumatic event might one seek to address what had been a previously unrecognized racial bias.

11. Ibid.

Burrow contends, nevertheless, that the Movement may be getting back to the best of its theological heritage. For the author it will be necessary for the church's institutions of higher learning including his alma mater, Anderson University in Indiana, as well as the Movement's only seminary, Anderson University School of Theology, to work together toward a real, lasting commitment to visible unity.

ENCOURAGING DEVELOPMENTS AND A PROPHET OF RECONCILIATION

Over the past few years there have been some hopeful signs that such a commitment could be on the horizon. For example, some states and regional governing bodies in the Church of God have voted to merge their black and white assemblies. Though these mergers are a good start, much trust building and cooperative work still needs to be done to effect a genuine coming together.

At the seminary then Dean, David Sebastian, led the faculty and staff in a process which resulted in the reworking of the seminary's mission statement. The final product seems to pick up on relational aspects of the holiness and unity message not always emphasized by early church of God pioneers. "The mission of the Anderson University School of Theology is to form women and men for the ministry of biblical reconciliation."

The above commitment recognizes that human relations are broken by sin. Such an undertaking further necessitates that individuals become reconciled to God, to themselves, to the cosmos, and to each other. A genuine embrace of biblical reconciliation, therefore, requires that we eschew any tendency to view people of another race, class, gender or sexual orientation as somehow less than.

Though not well versed in efforts to promote the cause of unity and racial reconciliation by other Church of God institutions, I am in a position to speak to exciting developments at Anderson University. In 2013 Aleza Beverly was promoted to serve in a newly created position, Dean of Intercultural Engagement. The creation of this deanship demonstrates a commitment on the part of the university to promote intercultural competency among administrators, faculty, staff, and students. In this role, Beverly has led a number of initiatives and training events which are yielding positive results.

Recently, the university's Mosaic team proposed an institutional hiring process subsequently affirmed by university president, John Pistole. The goal of this initiative is to redouble efforts to hire diverse candidates to fill open faculty and staff positions. Results over the past five years show that the number of diverse faculty as a percentage of the entire faculty has increased from 2.9% in the 2009–10 school year, to 8.9% in the 2014–15 school year. More modest gains were made in the retention of diverse staff at the university. In the 2009–10 school year diverse staff made up 5.9% of the entire staff. In the 2014–15 school year that number increased to 6.9%. Despite the successes, the work continues.

Burrow's book offers a way forward, a divine challenge that the Movement should take up. There are, however, complicating factors at work. For example, something of an identity crisis seems to have exercised the Church of God for the past couple of decades. It was this dilemma that the late Gilbert Stafford considered in a series of books before his death in 2008.[12] The need for Movement leaders to address this lingering existential issue is imperative. It is exacerbated by the fact that denominational centers in North America no longer seem to retain the necessary magnetism to hold their respective churches in orbit.

It remains to be seen what impact a new focus for ministry in the Church of God initiated by its visionary General Director, Jim Lyon, might mean with regard to recovering a ministry of visible unity. Trumpeting a "Jesus is the Subject" message might fire a new desire to live out the prayer of Jesus offered in John 17—a prayer for oneness. It is, after all, a petition that if it is to be realized will require human and divine cooperation. The Movement's call for a ministry of "reclamation" might also inspire among its constituents an interest in retrieving from its past a commitment to bible unity, a unity characterized by a people whose aim it has been to "reach their hands in fellowship."[13] Moreover, the kind of work prescribed by Burrow will require a steadiness of purpose and a collective "boldness" heretofore unknown among the saints. Burrow's work assumes such a continued loyalty to the message of holiness and unity. Inherent in the author's argument as well is the suggestion that many in the Movement have failed to grasp the transformational potential of a commitment to a more robust expression of unity lived in holiness—"visible unity." Indeed, such an aspirational goal might begin by addressing racial divisions within the Body of Christ, but will necessarily inspire work to build bridges of holy love to all diverse demographics represented in our churches and communities.

On the other hand, the Church of God Ministries' new organizing focus might, for some, displace a commitment to visible unity lived in

---

12. Stafford, *Signals at the Crossroads*. This volume is a compilation of three earlier works.

13. Naylor, "The Church's Jubilee" (No. 312) in *Worship the Lord*.

holiness, especially if the holiness and unity message is viewed as having more or less exhausted its relevance in a post-denominational church era. What might replace these traditional theological foci then could be a more mainstream, evangelical gospel message minus the Church of God distinctives forged in earlier decades. Proponents of such a pivot away from earlier theological emphases might first carefully consider the opportunities opened up by trumpeting a unity message in the United States, a country whose demographics are rapidly showing signs of increasing diversity. Such exigencies may be the reason that the largest church group in the U.S., the Catholic Church, has foregrounded the promotion of genuine church unity in its push to reach an increasingly diverse world with the message of the gospel.

The Church of God Reformation Movement came into existence in difficult days. Walls between people groups were real, and portended much pain and destruction, divisions between North and South, rich and poor, capital and labor, native and immigrant, black and white, liberal and conservative. It was in this season that the Lord raised up a people who sincerely sought to live the life of the holy, manifested in a visible unity among the saints of God. Though they missed the mark at times, still yet they pressed forward. May we do the same. And let us hear again a prophet of reconciliation from our own tribe, the late Samuel G. Hines, whose commitment to holiness and visible unity inspires and challenges us yet.

God has a new world order. It is not racial; it is not national; it is not Jewish; it is not Gentile; it is not east or west. The Church of God is either going to demonstrate, dramatize or display this solidarity, or become a contemporary scandal, bringing blame and shame to the Gospel by virtue of blatant contradiction between what we preach and what we practice.[14]

Gary B. Agee
Associate Professor of Church History
Anderson University School of Theology

---

14. "God's Agenda Our Mandate," A sermon delivered at the International Camp Meeting held in Anderson, Indiana, on June 16, 1991. Hines was not originally scheduled to speak in this service. He was asked to fill in for the ailing Benjamin F. Reid.

Appendix A

Letter from James Earl Massey

When Charles E. Brown wrote that Daniel Sydney Warner and his evangelistic team of five were mobbed in Mississippi in 1890–91 *because* of their friendliness toward blacks and because Warner preached interracial unity and justice for blacks, I immediately thought that this was a truly uncommon occurrence in a nation not known for such treatment toward blacks. But just as quickly, I had to pause, because I was unable to find written sources to support Brown's claim (even in his book!). Brown's assertion would be repeated uncritically in future histories on the Church of God Reformation Movement, thus producing the party line stance that Church of God pioneers possessed a "zeal" for interracial unity as no other denomination did; a zeal, we are told, that only began to diminish at the turn of the 20th century.

When Brown was researching and writing *When the Trumpet Sounded* (1951) he sent out a request for letters from those who had experiences with Warner and other Movement pioneers. The relevant information from these hundreds of letters Brown said he received from around the country and the world would be weaved into the story of the Movement. In the Preface of his book Brown mentioned receiving these letters. When I read those places in the book where he tells the reader that Warner was mobbed and beaten because he welcomed blacks to the services and preached justice for them, I tried to verify the source of his information. From which letter(s) did such information come? One would expect a historian—any scholar—to name the source(s). It would have been immensely helpful had Brown expressly stated at the appropriate places that the information about Warner and blacks in Mississippi was supplied in letters from Eugene Garrett, T. H. Wingfield, and other Movement blacks, or even from certain whites. At the very least, it would have been helpful to have included the names and locations of the most important letter writers in an appendix. At any rate, upon visiting the Church of God archives, I found about a dozen letters that were sent from white Mississippians who encountered Warner during his tour. All indicated that Warner had been mobbed and attacked a number of times, but not a single one mentioned the presence of blacks at the meetings, or that the attacks occurred because of Warner's friendliness toward blacks, or because he preached on interracial unity.

It was only in conversations with James Earl Massey that I learned that letters had been sent by Garrett and Wingfield. Massey had the good fortune to read these and other letters during his research on blacks in the Church of God. The letters were brought to his attention and shared with him by Harold Phillips, then editor-in-chief at Warner Press. To my dismay, I was not able to locate those letters in the Church of God archives. The archivist checked in a number of places, but to no avail. Indicators are that the letters no longer exist.[1] In any event, I have seen no reference to these letters in the historical work of Strege and Barry Callen, which leads me to think that they, unlike Massey, did not see or read them. It is quite possible that Massey is the only living connection to those important letters that told about black pioneers' experience with Warner during the Mississippi tour.

Because the letters might well be lost to posterity, I asked Dean Massey if he would write what he remembers reading in them. Unfortunately, he could not remember details of what he read, but agreed to send reflections on oral and written sources regarding blacks in the Movement, especially in the South. What follows is the verbatim account of his letter.

---

1. In an email dated April 29, 2015, Joe Allison, Editorial Director Discipleship Resources & Curriculum at Warner Press, Inc., told me that these few boxes remain in storage at Warner Press because the Church of God archives have not the room for them. Allison promised to go through the boxes within several weeks, and did so, but without finding anything at all relevant to my search. I have a copy of Allison's email in my files.

Letter from James Earl Massey

April 25, 2015

Dear Dr. Burrow:

By now, you have probably received the book I mailed to you. The author of the book is Rev. Glenn Hall, pastor of the Eighth Street Church of God in Meridian, Mississippi, a congregation that was founded in 1903, and its history is connected with blacks who came to faith through the preaching of Church of God pioneers who ministered openly and purposely in that area during the Post-Reconstruction Era.

You will have noticed the pages on which Hall reported about Eugene Garrett, among others, and, also about what Garrett's daughter, Ozzie Garrett Wattleton, reported about his life and ministry as one of the early black converts in Mississippi. Given our trenchant as blacks for "talking our history" rather than writing it down, we must give due honor to that tradition as a main primary source whenever no written records are available for our research.

As for written resources: I had access to, and read, many letters from black leaders who were in ministry in Church of God congregations during the early Twentieth Century. Most of those letters were shared with me in 1978–79, when I was at work amassing data for what was published in 2005 as *African Americans and the Church of God: Aspects of a Social History* (Anderson University Press). Dr. Phillips had retired in 1977 from his post as editor-in-chief at Warner Press and was at work preparing a history of Warner Press, Incorporated (=Gospel Trumpet Company, publisher of the Church of God's denominational journal *The Gospel Trumpet*), and he voluntarily passed on to my scrutiny many letters in which he saw details in which he knew I would have interest. All of those letters were from the Gospel Trumpet Company files, letters sent to earlier editors through the years. Some were letters submitted to editor Charles E. Brown (whom Phillips followed) when Brown was writing his *When the Trumpet Sounded: A History of the Church of God Reformation Movement* (1951), and some were letters sent earlier, in the late 1920s, when the Gospel Trumpet Company was preparing to celebrate its fiftieth year of service for the Movement. Those earlier letters contained historical information about progress among the churches, and that progress was reported in a Golden Jubliee Book, published in 1931, with R. L. Berry, editor.

I have detailed all of this to indicate some of what I had available as documentation when I was preparing my book on our group history. I not only had access to letters from the Gospel Trumpet Company archives, I also interviewed many black elders who succeeded the black pioneers in the churches those leaders had founded—and I had initiated amassing those interviews as early as 1948, one year after my call to ministry, acutely aware that I was heir to a history and heritage to be both honored and documented. I must also report that being elected to membership on the Publication Board of the Church of God in 1961, and serving as an active board member until 1978 (and as one of the directors, and vice-chairman from 1974–1977) also placed me in a prime position to research and report on our Movement's life and direction. Mindful of all this, Dr. John W. V. Smith, official historian for the General Assembly, and professor of church history at the School of Theology, had me lecture to his classes about my findings, which allowed an early "public airing" of what was later published in my book.

If you wish to re-check any published reports, gain access to the files which contain the materials for *The Golden Jubilee Book* (1931); supporting documents for Charles E. Brown's *When the Trumpet Sounded: A History of the Church of God Reformation Movement* (1951); supporting documents for Harold L. Phillips's *Miracle of Survival* (1979), and diary entries from Daniel Sidney Warner as reported by A. L. Byers in *Birth of a Reformation, or the Life and Labors of D. S. Warner* (1907).

Take advantage, as well, of the thousands of "Reports From the Field" which were published regularly in issues of *The Gospel Trumpet*, from its earliest years, especially the period from 1884 down to the 1930s. Many early volumes are presently available on-line through the Nicholson Library at Anderson University.

Happy Hunting!!!!

James Earl Massey

Appendix B

Validity of Oral and Written History

I HAVE A STRONG appreciation for the significance of the oral tradition among Afrikan Americans and others in the Afrikan diaspora. In addition, I am aware that there is a bourgeoning school of thought for which orality is viewed as literature, even if it still needs other sources to support it. Of course, even written history sometimes needs the support of other sources, including oral ones.

Many scholars still seem to be more influenced by the traditional Eurocentric and modernist stance that history, in order to be valid, must be written down. In fact, Europeans, most glaringly the philosopher Hegel, argued quite emphatically that Afrika, and its essentially oral culture, had no history at all prior to the arrival of the Europeans on the continent. Presumably, the history of Afrika began at the precise moment that Europeans began *writing* about it. Everything Afrikan was subsumed under everything European. Indeed, the sense that one comes to when reading Hegel is that the Afrikans benefited a great deal from the Europeans who essentially gave them civilization, morality, and a history. Such a stance gave no credence at all to the art of Afrikan *griots* who gave extensive detailed oral narratives of hundreds of years of their culture and history. Hegel wrote in 1830 that Afrika "is no historical fact of the World; it has no movement or development to exhibit."[1] He claimed that any evidence of historical movements even in the northern parts of Afrika actually "belong to the Asiatic or European

---

1. Hegel, *The Philosophy of History*, 99.

world."² Hegel viewed Afrika as being, at best, "on the threshold of the World's History," but it had no real history as such.³

Clearly exhibiting a postmodernist stance, Steven J. Salm has made an instructive point about orality and European nations that set out to conquer and colonize Afrikan nations from the fifteenth century onward.

> When the colonial powers set out to assert their dominance over the African societies they encountered, they denied the historical existence of African civilization. It suited their hegemonic aims to view Africans as culturally inferior, or 'without culture' and 'without history.' They wanted to believe that Africa's past was devoid of any significant events, and that its society must be in its infancy and thus ripe for the 'civilizing mission' of colonialism. *History, it was assumed, must be recorded in a written form to be valid.* This notion was later dismissed, largely through the acceptance of oral literature as an historical source to reconstruct the African past.⁴

Because the Afrikans had no written history, the earliest European invaders commenced almost immediately to construct fictitious histories of Afrikan nations. These histories were primarily about *European culture in Afrika*, not about Afrikan histories and cultures as such. They conveniently ignored the contributions of the great ancient Afrikan civilizations, and presented the Afrikans as a savage people, all the while pretending to forget about their own savage treatment of the Afrikans. Few white scholars have written more cogently and convincingly about the European construction of early relations with Afrika than the British historian, Basil Davidson, who clarifies the matter of just who was more savage and vicious—the Europeans or the Afrikans.

> All this [the slaughter of Afrikans] was as easy for the Portuguese, and for much the same reasons, as it was in India whenever they met with resistance to their greed and theft. They were better armed. They were trained to ruthlessness. They wanted more than a simple monopoly of trade, ruinous though that would be for the coastal cities; they wanted loot as well. African warfare, like Indian warfare, was designed to minimize casualties, not maximize them. These invaders had no such care.⁵

2. Ibid.
3. Ibid.
4. Salm, "Written and Oral Literature," 286 (my emphasis).
5. Davidson, *The Lost Cities of Africa*, 200.

In time, as the Portuguese and other European nations grew wealthier through their pillaging and exploitation of Afrikan nations, they would conveniently forget how they came by their wealth, believing instead, that "they had always enjoyed a higher civilization than Indians or Africans. They forgot the past, which told another story."[6] Their all too convenient loss of memory caused them to believe that, but for the civilizing hand of the Portuguese (and other European nations) the Afrikans would have remained the murderous savages they were thought to be.[7] Even the great Thomas Jefferson wrote that any "improvement of the blacks in body and mind" was due solely to their contact with whites.[8] Jefferson, like many whites of his day, believed that the enslaved Afrikans should be freed, but because they were thought to be naturally inferior to whites and could not function well alongside whites, it was argued that they should be colonized in an Afrikan country.[9]

Many still see little credibility or value in the idea of the oral tradition as an acceptable historical source. It has in fact been an acceptable historical source for more than fifty years in expanding sectors of the academy. Samuel Imbo is instructive in reminding us that: "Equation of literature with writing is symptomatic of the bias of European thought systems. The bias accomplishes two feats simultaneously: The mode of expression that many Africans find meaningful for communication is denigrated, and the elitism of an outlook that divides the world into competing camps goes unchallenged."[10] In addition, it has been found that many oral histories on Afrika throws "light into many obscure places," and have "become a wide-ranging and fruitful addition to historical and sociological knowledge in Africa."[11]

Like their Afrikan ancestors—both on the continent and during the period of American slavery—Afrikan Americans are an oral people whose appreciation for written literature is as deep and intense as any people. Therefore, many Afrikan Americans argue for the validity of *both* orality and the written word, believing that each potentially enriches the other. Afrikans and Afrikan Americans reject the practice of subsuming orality

---

6. Ibid., 199.

7. Ibid., 200.

8. Jefferson, *Notes on the State of Virginia*, 141.

9. Ratner, *Powder Keg*, 12–13.

10. Imbo, *Oral Traditions as Philosophy*, 60. See also the excellent chapter by Salm, "Written and Oral Literature," chap. 16; and p'Bitek, *Africa's Cultural Revolution*.

11. Davidson, "Africanisms and Its Meanings," 91.

under the written text rather than highlighting it. In addition, they challenge the tendency to attribute "special status" to the written word.

What seems to elude most whites is that orality was (and continues to be) an art form for Afrikans on the continent and in diaspora, and therefore is taken much more seriously by them. That is, one entrusted with important information or historical facts, for example, was expected to work hard and incessantly to remember and report as accurately as possible. It has also long been understood that the bearer of such information may engage in a bit of embellishing, depending on the context in which the reporting is done. In every case, however, the basic facts of the matter were to be told accurately.

This is the sense in which we should understand the case of the oral telling and re-telling of the story of the Lena Shoffner sermon against the dividing rope in 1897; the story of the 1912 confrontation at the Anderson camp meeting as told by Mother Laura Moore, Rev. Charles H. Hill, and others; as well as the stories that blacks reportedly told Charles E. Brown in letters about D. S. Warner's friendliness toward blacks during the Mississippi tour in 1890–91, and how he was mobbed, in part, *because* he preached justice for blacks. Careful archival research and questioning Movement leaders has not, at this writing, provided the location of those letters, or whether they still exist. All that remains is the memory of a few Movement people, like James Earl Massey, who assured this writer that he read many of the letters, and verified orally that what Brown wrote about Warner's relationship to blacks during the Mississippi tour is consistent with what he read in those letters. Without the developing oral tradition regarding such important incidents in Movement history, it might be necessary to discredit, or at the very least, to lower significantly the credibility of the party line stance that the primary reason that Warner was mobbed and attacked in Mississippi was because of his welcoming stance toward blacks, and his preaching justice for them. Charles Brown was the first scholar to report this in his history of the Movement. In the passages where he discusses the matter,[12] he does not tell readers the source of his information. However, because he writes in the book's Preface that hundreds of letters from around the nation and the world supports the discussions in his book, it is reasonable to assume that what he writes about Warner and race during the Mississippi tour is based on information revealed in some of the letters from that state, most likely from black Mississippians, such as Eugene G. Garrett and T. H. Wingfield.

Sadly, Brown did not name the authors and letters from which he extracted the information about the mob attacks in Mississippi. Had he explicitly named the letters from Garrett and Wingfield, for example, the questions

---

12. Brown, *When the Trumpet Sounded*, 156, 157, 360.

about whether Warner was mobbed *because* of his liberal interracial stance would less likely have arisen. Since the letters are no longer available, it will be necessary to depend on the most credible oral sources available, e.g., James Earl Massey, who read the letters before they disappeared.

When I think about the importance of the oral tradition my mind goes immediately to those phenomenal story and history tellers in Afrika called *griots*. Their memories are amazingly accurate and long. They had to be, since there was a time when so much of the history was not written down and preserved on paper for all to read. It was preserved in *well-trained, well-disciplined minds*. Because enslaved Afrikans in the United States were denied the right to learn to read, they kept alive the art of developing powerful memories in order to convey the stories and history orally to future generations.

It is true that orality is limited by the fact that embellishing may occur, and the mind may forget important facts. Without question, one must look critically at *any* source of history, including written sources. "As with any historical source, oral tradition must be understood to represent only a limited reality. It must be carefully analyzed, always within the wider cultural context of the society producing it, to decode the messages it contains."[13] But we also know that written literature may be limited by the cultural, racial, class, and gender biases that the writer brings to the task. Such biases even affect one's choices of written sources to use in one's work, or even the choice to prefer written sources over oral ones (or vice versa).

I do not see privileging one of these sources over the other as necessarily problematic. It seems to me that the problem arises when one fails to use every possible available source as she tries to get at the truth, or if she pretends that one or the other is necessarily more objective. There are frequently both written and oral sources that have important bearing on an issue. Each may inform and-or enrich the other, or may corroborate some aspect of what the other proposes, as in the case of the 1912 confrontation.

There may even be times when only the written can support or document the written text, or when only the oral can support the oral text. For example, who can forget Alex Haley's amazing discovery, what he called a "peak experience," in the village of Juffure in the back-country of West Afrika? Determined to corroborate the oral stories he had heard all his life from family members about his Afrikan ancestors of the Kinte clan, Haley was told about an elderly *griot* who could orally corroborate or verify the life-long oral stories he had been told by his family members regarding their distant relatives in Afrika. These *griots*, "still to be found in the older

---

13. Lamphear and Falola, "Aspects of Early African History," 74.

back-country villages, men who were in effect living, walking archives of oral history,"[14] wrote nothing down. (It is only in recent years that attention has been given women *griots* or *griottes*. Alex Haley only sought out *griots*, since he had not heard of *griottes*, and thus simply assumed there were none.[15]) Because there were few written sources in Afrika before colonialism, oral history was essential if one wanted a glimpse of ancient Afrika.

In order to qualify as a senior *griot* one must apprentice under a senior *griot* for forty or fifty years, during which time she learns a particular line of narrative, etc. (It is important to understand that during this training and education, women tend to learn from the women, and men from the men. It is also known, however, that fathers sometimes contribute to educating their daughters in this process.[16]) Qualifying as a senior griot(tes) is a serious matter that requires intensive and long-term training and discipline. The apprentice is trained from childhood for the purpose of narrating the story. Such a one would, on special occasions, tell "the centuries-old histories of villages, clans, families, or great heroes. Throughout the whole of black Africa such oral chronicles had been handed down since the time of the ancient forefathers . . . , and there were certain legendary *griots* who could narrate facets of African history literally for as long as three days without ever repeating themselves."[17] In every case, these were persons with extensively trained memories, who were selected and "entrusted with the memorization, recitation, and passing on of oral history from one generation to the next."[18] These were the *griots*, walking libraries of key information about their homelands and who were highly admired for their memory, knowledge, and creativity in narration.[19] But in addition to serving as historian, the *griot* has been known as adviser, spokesperson, diplomat, interpreter and translator, musician, composer, teacher, exhorter, warrior, witness, and praise-singer. In addition, they have been known to participate in a host of ceremonies, e.g., namings, initiations, courtships, etc.[20]

It was one of these *griots* who narrated for nearly two hours according to Alex Haley, before coming to the point in the history of the Kinte clan when Haley's relative, Kunta, was mentioned. After what seemed an eternity, the *griot* said:

14. Haley, *Roots*, 674.
15. See the instructive book by Hale, *Griots and Griottes*, chap. 7.
16. Ibid., 224. See also chap. 5.
17. Haley, *Roots*, 674.
18. Lamphear and Falola, "Aspects of Early African History," 74.
19. Salm, "Music," 271.
20. See Hale, *Griots and Griottes*, chap. 1.

'About the time the King's soldiers came'—another of the griot's time-fixing references—'the eldest of these four sons, Kunta, went away from his village to chop wood . . . and he was never seen again. . . .' And the griot went on with his narrative.[21]

But Haley had heard what he had hoped to hear about his ancestor. He was transfixed, unable to move or say anything. He wrote:

I sat as if I were carved of stone. My blood seemed to have congealed. This man whose lifetime had been in this back-country African village had no way in the world to know that he had just echoed what I have heard all through my boyhood years on my grandma's front porch in Henning, Tennessee . . . of an African who always had insisted that his name was 'Kin-tay'; who had called a guitar a 'Ko,' and a river within the state of Virginia, 'Kansby Bolongo'; and who had been kidnapped into slavery while not far from his village, chopping wood, to make himself a drum.[22]

Haley had always known this story through oral narratives in Tennessee. He now had the word of mouth story corroborated by the oral narration of an old Afrikan *griot*. Haley needed nothing that might have been written in order to confirm the *griot's* narration, other than the oral stories heard on his grandmother's doorstep.

This is a long account of Haley's experience, but it makes my point about the validity of oral tradition and how, at times, the best source to support the oral is the oral, and similarly regarding the written literature. It also further supports my contention that as a source, the oral may enhance or enrich the written and vice versa, or the oral may serve to corroborate and enrich the oral, as we saw in Alex Haley's case. Therefore, we dare not uncritically disparage the potential contribution of oral narrative in history, any more than the written.

My sense is that oral sources can benefit and enrich traditional written histories on the Church of God, including what is written in the camp meeting committee minutes of 1912 and 1913 (chapter 4). The primary source of the infamous confrontation of 1912 is the oral account of Mother Laura Moore and Reverend Charles H. Hill. What Merle Strege uncovered in the Anderson camp meeting committee minutes, and wrote about, is not superior to the oral narrative of Moore and Hill, but rather is an important supportive or corroborative source. It in no way undermines or destroys the

21. Quoted in Haley, *Roots*, 679.
22. Haley, *Roots*, 679.

credibility of the oral account given of the confrontation. The two compliment, and enhance each other. Taken together, the end product is a much enriched, fuller account, of a tragedy in the Movement's history that should not have occurred, and for which the consequences are still forthcoming.

Acknowledgments

I WOULD NOT HAVE been inspired to write this book were it not the case that for more than thirty years I was befriended and taught by two giants in the Church of God Reformation Movement: Rev. Theodore Baker, Sr. who was my close friend, confidant, and surrogate father; and Dr. James Earl Massey, who was my teacher at Anderson University and during the one year I was a student at the Anderson School of Theology. In addition to my own personal experience growing up in the Movement, I learned much about other aspects of it from these two giants, through extended conversations over many years, observing their behavior and treatment of others, and through reading and reflecting on books written by Massey.

I met both of these men in the fall of 1969 when all three of us arrived at Anderson University for various responsibilities. I was an entering freshman. Massey was called to be Campus Minister and a member of the faculty. Baker was called to perform significant staff responsibilities in the business office. During my student days, he was the university bursar, and I spent many hours in his office at Decker Hall discussing my financial woes, and how or whether I would be able to survive and graduate. No matter what I at times said to the contrary, Ted Baker always believed that I would not only survive, but thrive, and he did everything that he could to help make it so.

In those days, James Earl Massey seemed to me to be untouchable and even unreachable. Initially he was a bit too formal for my taste. However, his mannerisms in the classroom were such that I knew, even in my freshman year, that I would want to emulate some of his moves in whatever I would ultimately do professionally or vocationally. Any student of Massey's who sees me at work in the classroom will immediately recognize the Massey influence. Not only was James Earl Massey dead serious about his classroom preparation (of lectures, assignments, etc.) and what he expected of students, he was also the sharpest dresser of any professor I had known at the time, or since. I always appreciated the fact that he dressed the part for the classroom, a practice I took as my own when I became a seminary professor fifteen years later. One scene is indelibly emblazoned in my mind. One day, Massey entered the large, filled-to-capacity lecture room in Hartung Hall, casually removed a clean white handkerchief from his suit coat pocket, never once glanced at the class, and commenced dusting the chair before sitting at the lectern. Afterward there was a long silence on his part. And then, without any explanation whatever, he began the lecture for the day. I remember thinking: "The Professor's got style!"

During my student days at Anderson, no professor was more prepared for the day to day work in the classroom than James Earl Massey. Moreover, I have read and pondered the work of several men said to be (or have been) theologians in the Church of God Reformation Movement. Although these were primarily white males, my judgment is that Massey is *the* Church of God theologian to be reckoned with, considering the breadth and depth of his understanding of the theological landscape in and beyond the Movement. Add to this his consistent efforts to make good the claim regarding holiness and visible interracial unity, and I do not see how one can fail to conclude that as theologian in the Movement he is truly a man among men.

After graduating from AU, I spent one year at the School of Theology. During this time, I did a guided research on Social Christianity under Massey's supervision. I was required to read and write on a number of books for him that semester. Four are etched into my memory: Richard Quebedeaux, *The Young Evangelicals* (1974); Carl F. H. Henry, *Aspects of Christian Social Ethics* (1964); David Moberg, *Inasmuch: Christian Social Responsibility in 20th Century America* (1965), and also by Moberg, *The Great Reversal: Evangelism Versus Social Concern* (1972). I later learned that Moberg not only did excellent work in evangelical Christian social ethics, but in the sociology of American churches as well, especially his excellent book, *The Church as a Social Institution* (1963, 1984). His scholarship in both fields influenced my own work at various points in my scholarly development. Although not in the conservative evangelical camp myself, I am much appreciative to have had the opportunity to read, write, reflect on, and discuss with Massey the work of a number of top notch evangelical thinkers. I have, for many years, thought of myself as one of the theological sons of James Earl Massey, although I have also been quick to say, that I am very likely the son who fell the furthest from the tree, so to speak. Because Massey has written a seminal book on blacks in the Church of God Movement, has served in a number of major leadership capacities in the group, and has distinguished himself as an outstanding preacher, academician, scholar, and author, I address a number of his ideas in this book. I challenge a number of ideas in Massey's otherwise excellent text, all in the interest of pushing Movement people to be much more intentional than ever before about actualizing in its own body what is required by the founding core principles of holiness and visible unity.

Although the quintessential professional, Theodore Baker, Sr. (Ted) was easygoing, earthy, and street-wise enough to really have at it with students from inner cities around the nation—many who thought they were the hippest of the hip and the slickest of the slick. As university bursar, Ted was not one over whose eyes students could easily pull the proverbial wool. It was always humorous to me when he would best them at their own game.

Once, during my sophomore year at AU (before Ted and I became good friends), I was returning to school from my home in Pontiac, Michigan. I ran out of gas at a rest area about thirty miles from Anderson and had less than two dollars in my pocket. Embarrassed beyond words, I called the AU switchboard and asked for Ted's home number. It was a Sunday afternoon. When Ted answered the phone I told him what happened. Sensing my embarrassment and not wanting to exacerbate it, he said quickly and unhesitatingly: "We'll be there within the hour." Sure enough, after about forty-five minutes he drove up in his dark blue Chrysler with his entire family (at the time) in the car—Mary, Teddy, Beckie [now a tenured professor at AU], and Steve. Daughters Mary and Leah came along a few years later. Ted retrieved the gasoline can from the trunk, emptied it into my tank, waited for me to start the car, inconspicuously slipped some money into my hands, and said: "Let me know when you get back to Anderson." I knew at that moment that Ted was that "ram in the bush" my Mother said God would always provide, just when I needed it most. Ted was truly that ram in the bush for me more times than I can remember.

Significantly, Ted Baker was in many ways a surrogate father to me. He followed closely my journey from college, to graduate school, to seminary professor, and author of more than a dozen books. Across the years, Ted always made two things absolutely clear: his love for Mary Baker (his wife, best friend, and soulmate), and his children. He could, and often did, talk much about Mary, her goodness and her many virtues. She was, without question, his heart. In addition, Ted expressed a strong desire to be supportive of my efforts to get through college and to find my own path thereafter. He more than succeeded, and when I completed doctoral studies at Boston University in 1983 he lavished me with congratulatory words that nearly brought me to tears.

Not long before he died, Ted told me something that touched me deeply, and also encouraged me as I was nearing the completion of an early manuscript draft of this book. He said that he had gotten "saved" in 1961, and that he came to the Movement in late 1962. He went on to say that he remembered that every place he went in Church of God circles in Michigan and other places he heard the constant refrain: "We don't have all of the truth; but we are *committed* to the whole truth." He said that his lifelong desire, from that point, was to get and witness more and more of that truth, although it was frequently more elusive than he would have liked. This was especially the case regarding the truth about holiness and interracial unity in the Movement. *This* truth, more than any other, Ted Baker wanted to witness first hand and to see it actualized and lived on a grander scale in the Church of God. He always believed the Church of God could be better than it was in the matter of interracial unity, and he was devoted to doing all he could to make it a reality.

Long after I graduated from AU, Ted and I continued to talk regularly by telephone, and periodically enjoyed a meal and *more* hearty conversation on the AU campus, at a local restaurant (where he *always* insisted on paying for my meal), at his house, and occasionally on my turf in Indianapolis. Not unlike many black southerners, Ted loved good well-seasoned foods, warm friendly conversation, and lots of hefty laughter. For as long as I knew him, Ted believed in me and stood with me in some of my toughest hours. (Lord knows I yearned for his presence and voice when I and several distinguished colleagues suffered a devastating professional setback a few years after his death.) As I said in the Acknowledgements of my first book, *James H. Cone and Black Liberation Theology* (1994), and believe it bears repeating here: Through all the years I have known him, Ted Baker, Sr. "has been a constant source of inspiration. . . . He has truly been like the wind beneath my wings. No man has been more of a fan and big brother to me than he." I miss him. I miss the many long conversations we used to have about making good the claim, and what was needed in order for that to happen. I miss his regular, often unexpected, much desired telephone calls to my office or home. When I was a student at AU Ted once said to me laughingly as I was about to leave his office: "You know, you think funny with those way-out ideas of yours. I'm gonna keep my eye on you." True to form, more than thirty years later, Ted Baker, Sr. was still keeping his eye on me, and I have good reason to believe that he is still doing so today.

Both Massey and Ted eagerly and graciously read an earlier manuscript draft of this book during the fall of 2008. Massey sent written comments and suggestions from Alabama. Thereafter, we talked many times on the telephone and also exchanged a number of letters regarding my line of discussion in the book. He also read and commented on revised drafts of chapters 1, 3, 4, and 7. Unlike many scholars, Massey was generous beyond words in his suggestions and recommendations about additional resources that might be helpful. He never hesitated to say that he believed my book was an important contribution to the Movement, and urged me (during an unexpected and difficult lull in my career) to get it completed. To my delight, my Teacher never failed to treat me to good dosages of that well known Massey humor, reminding me all along of the need and importance of just going on anyhow, and to not allow would-be obstacles to thwart the work I am called to do as theological educator.

Ted and I spent an afternoon at his home discussing his comments, and suggestions for improvement of the manuscript. He talked and I took notes. Afterward, we talked about the manuscript a number of times on the telephone. He believed the manuscript was accessible to the college level student, but he challenged me over and over again to make the language more accessible to others as well. He wanted the book to be comprehensible to the common every day lay person in the Movement; wanted it to be a book that would spark excitement and energetic conversation among Movement people of all races and classes. I promised him that I would work hard at this, and I truly did. I just do not know at the moment the extent to which I succeeded (if at all!). At any rate, this book is intended to provide another chapter on the way to the truth that Ted so much wanted to witness and experience in the Church of God Reformation Movement.

I am deeply indebted to both of these larger than life men of the Church of God Reformation Movement—James Earl Massey and Ted Baker, Sr.—and hope that this meager contribution toward making good the claim is a worthy companion to what they themselves contributed on the way to truth.

I want also to acknowledge the painstaking efforts of Vivian Hampton Nieman, archivist of the Church of God collection housed at Anderson University. Mrs. Nieman exhibited a keen sense of curiosity and wonder about the Movement, which aided immensely her outstanding investigative skills in the archives. She was always forthcoming in offering helpful suggestions that sometimes sent me to places I had not expected to go, but was generally well rewarded when I went.

I am most grateful for the kind and generous assistance of Anne Roberts, former administrative assistant to the academic dean at Christian Theological Seminary in Indianapolis (and grandmother of Ava!). Under the most trying circumstances, her high level of commitment, generosity and professionalism never wavered in the area of faculty support. She was a paragon among those professionals without whom academic deans could not function well. What a person she is!

Last, but certainly not least, I want to thank Barry L. Callen and Gary B. Agee, authors of the Foreword and Afterword, respectively. Both men are among the world's top authorities on Church of God history today, and each is passionate in his view that the God of the Hebrew prophets and Jesus Christ expects that the Church of God will make good—sooner than later—on its claim about holiness and visible unity along racial lines. It is not lost on this writer that Callen and Agee are white men, proof positive that in the matter of interracial unity the Church of God can be better than it has been in its local churches, schools, and agencies if it wills to be, and if it dares to speak and witness in God's name.

Bibliography

Adams, Robert A. "The Hymnody of the Church of God (1885–1890) as a Reflection of that Church's Theological and Cultural Changes." D.Div. diss., Southwestern Baptist Theological Seminary, 1980.
Agee, Gary B. "Seeing the Church of God in Black and White: The Church of God Reformation Movement and the Color Line, 1880–1920." The Harp Lecture at Anderson University School of Theology, 2015. http://drive.google.com/a/anderson.edu/file/d/0B56sbqn97cS10ME9PeXNzT1kview.
Ahlstrom, Sidney E. *A Religious History of the American People*. New Haven: Yale University Press, 1972.
Allport, Gordon W. *The Nature of Prejudice*. 1954. 25th Anniversary ed. Reading, MA: Addison-Wesley, 1979.
ARDA (Association of Religious Data Archives). http://www.thearda.com/Denoms/D_1349.asp.
Armistead, W. W. *The Negro Is a Man: A Reply to Professor Charles Carroll's Book, The Negro is a Beast*. Tifton, GA: Armistead & Vickers, 1903.
Aulén, Gustav. *The Faith of the Christian Church*. Translated by Eric H. Wahlstrom and G. Everett Arden. 1948. Reprinted, Eugene, OR: Wipf & Stock, 2002.
Ball, Edward. *Slaves in the Family*. New York: Farrar, Straus & Giroux, 1998.
Barndt, Joseph. *Dismantling Racism: The Continuing Challenge to White America*. Minneapolis: Augsburg, 1991.
Barnes, Gilbert Hobbs. *The Anti-Slavery Impulse 1833–1844*. New York: Harcourt, Brace & World, 1964.
Bell, Derrick. *Confronting Authority: Reflections of an Ardent Protester*. Boston: Beacon, 1994.
Berry, Robert L., ed. *Golden Jubilee Book*. Anderson, IN: Gospel Trumpet, 1931.
Birnbaum, Norman, and Gertrud Lenzer, eds. *Sociology and Religion: A Book of Readings*, 184–96. Englewood Cliffs, NJ: Prentice-Hall, 1969.
Blaney, J. C. "The Unity of the Spirit." *The Gospel Trumpet* (February 4, 1909) (column 2), 11.
Bonhoeffer, Dietrich. *The Cost of Discipleship*. Rev. ed. New York: Macmillan, 1959.
Bowne, Borden P. *The Principles of Ethics*. New York: American Book Company, 1892.
Breazeale, George W. Letter to Charles E. Brown. May 20, 1949. Church of God Archives, Mississippi file of Charles E. Brown, 1.
Brown, Charles E. *The Church Beyond Division*. Anderson, IN: Gospel Trumpet, 1939.

———. *When the Trumpet Sounded: A History of the Church of God Reformation Movement*. Anderson, IN: Gospel Trumpet, 1951.
Byers, Andrew L. *Birth of a Reformation: Life and Labors of D. S. Warner*. Anderson, IN: Gospel Trumpet, 1921.
———. "Warner: Life in Brief." In *A Time to Remember: Testimonies*, edited by Barry L. Callen, 9–12. Anderson, IN: Warner, 1978.
Byrum, E. E. "The Color Line." *The Gospel Trumpet* 17.25 (Sept. 2, 1897) (column 5), 2.
Cadoux, Cecil John. *The Early Church and the World: A History of the Christian Attitude to Pagan Society and the State Down to the Time of Constantine*. Edinburgh: T. & T. Clark, 1925.
Callen, Barry L., ed. *Following the Light: Teachings, Testimonies, Trials and Triumphs of the Church of God Movement, Anderson*. Anderson, IN: Warner, 2000.
———. *It's God's Church: The Life & Legacy of Daniel Sidney Warner*. Anderson, IN: Warner, 1995.
———. *Journeying Together: A Documentary History of the Corporate Life of the Church of God Movement (Anderson)*. Anderson, IN: Warner, 1996.
———. *Preparing for Service: A History of Higher Education in the Church of God*. Anderson, IN: Warner, 1988.
———. *Thinking and Acting Together*. Compiled ed. Anderson, IN: Executive Council of the Church of God and Warner, 1992.
———, ed. *A Time to Remember: Evaluations*. Anderson, IN: Warner, 1978.
———, ed. *A Time to Remember: Teachings*. Anderson, IN: Warner, 1978.
Carson, Clayborne et al., eds. *The Papers of Martin Luther King Jr.: Symbol of the Movement*, 4:281. Berkeley: University of California Press, 2000.
Carver, Cecil C. *Church of God Doctrines*. 1948. Reprinted, Guthrie, OK: Faith Publishing House, 1979.
Clear, Valorus B. "The Church of God: A Study in Social Adaptation." *Review of Religious Research* 2. 1–4 (Winter 1961) 130–32.
———. *Where the Saints Have Trod: A Social History of the Church of God Movement*. 1977. Reprinted, Jackson, KY: Reformation, 1998.
Cole, George, L. "Is Organization Worldly?" In *A Time to Remember: Evaluations*, edited by Barry L. Callen, 87. Anderson, IN: Warner, 1978.
Corbin, Don. "Slavery and the Civil War as Viewed by the Churches of God." *The Church Advocate* 135 (Sept. 1970) 7.
Davidson, Basil. "Africanisms and Its Meanings." In his *The Search for Africa: History, Culture, Politics*, 79–93. New York: Random, 1994.
———. *The Lost Cities of Africa*. Rev. ed. Boston: Little, Brown, 1987.
Davies, Rupert. "Calling." In *The Westminster Dictionary of Christian Theology*, edited by Alan Richardson and John Bowden, 79. Philadelphia: Westminster, 1983.
Davis, Katie H. *Zion's Hill at West Middlesex*. 1951. Prestonsburg, KY: Reformation, 2007.
Dorchester, Daniel. *Christianity in the United States*. New York: Hunt & Eaton, 1889.
Douglass, Frederick. "The Church and Prejudice." In *Narrative of the Life of Frederick Douglass & Other Writings*, 143–45. Ann Arbor, MI: Ann Arbor Media Group, 2004.
Durnbaugh, Donald F. *The Believers' Church: The History and Character of Radical Protestantism*. New York: Macmillan, 1968.

Epstein, Daniel Mark. *Sister Aimee: The Life of Aimee Semple McPherson.* New York: Harcourt Brace Jovanovich, 1993.
Feagin, Joe R. *Systemic Racism: A Theory of Oppression.* New York: Routledge, 2006.
Filler, Louis. *The Crusade Against Slavery 1830–1860.* New York: Harper & Row, 1960.
Fischer, Joseph C. *Songs of Victory.* Williamston, MI: 1885.
Forney, Christian Henry. *History of the Churches of God in the United States of North America.* Harrisburg, PA: Board of Directors of the Publishing House and Book Room of the Churches of God, 1914.
Forrest, Aubrey Leland. "A Study of the Development of the Basic Doctrines and Institutional Patterns in the Church of God (Anderson, Indiana)." PhD diss., University of Southern California, 1948.
Forrest, James E. "Bible Unity and the Color Line." *The Gospel Trumpet* 30.7 (Feb. 7, 1910) (column 3), 6.
———. "National and Race Prejudice." *The Gospel Trumpet* 29.6 (Feb. 11, 1909) (column 1), 10.
———. "The Fatherhood of God." In *Camp-Meeting Sermons: 1913*, edited by Gospel Trumpet, 266–73. Anderson, IN: Gospel Trumpet, 1913.
Frazier, Mae McDonald, and Essie Lee McDonald Sorrell. "Prologue to History of First Church of God of Meridian, Mississippi." Church of God Archives, 1.
Fretheim, Terence E. *God and World in the Old Testament: A Relational Theology of Creation.* Nashville: Abingdon, 2005.
Fudge, Thomas, A. *Daniel Warner and the Paradox of Religious Democracy in Nineteenth-Century America.* Studies in American Religion 68. Lewiston, NY: Mellen, 1998.
Gerth, Hans H., and C. Wright Mills. eds. *From Max Weber: Essays in Sociology,* 51–54; 245–52; 267–301. New York: Oxford University Press, 1946.
Gossard, J. Harvey. "John Winebrenner: Founder, Reformer, and Businessman." In *Pennsylvania Religious Leaders*, edited by John M. Coleman et al., 93. University Park: Pennsylvania Historical Association, 1986.
Graham, Loren. "Introduction: Expansionism and Restrictionism." In *Between Science and Values*, 1–32. New York: Columbia University Press, 1981.
Hacker, Andrew. *Two Nations: Black and White, Separate, Hostile, Unequal.* New York: Ballantine, 1992.
Hale, Thomas A. *Griots and Griottes: Masters of Works and Music.* Bloomington: Indiana University Press, 1998.
Haley, Alex. *Roots.* Garden City, NY: Doubleday, 1976.
Hall, Glenn E. *The Mississippi Reformation Movement: An Overview of the History of the Farmhaven District.* Xulon Press, self-published, 2014.
Hartman, Marvin J. "Reasons for our Growth." In *A Time to Remember: Evaluations*, edited by Barry L. Callen, 79–83. Anderson, IN: Warner, 1978.
Hegel, Georg W. *The Philosophy of History.* Translated by J. Sibree. New York: Dover, 1956.
Heschel, Abraham J. *The Prophets.* New York: Harper & Row, 1962.
———. "Religion and Race." In *The Insecurity of Freedom*, 85–100. Philadelphia: Jewish Publication Society, 1966.
———. "Sacred Image of Man." In *The Insecurity of Freedom*, 150–67. Philadelphia: Jewish Publication Society, 1966.
Hewitt, Glenn. "Sanctification. In *A New Handbook of Christian Theology*, edited by Donald W. Musser and Joseph L. Price, 429. Nashville: Abingdon, 1992.

Hine, Darlene Clark, and Kathleen Thompson. *A Shining Thread of Hope: The History of Black Women in America.* New York: Broadway, 1998.

Hine, Darlene Clark. *When the Truth is Told: A History of Black Women's Culture and Community in Indiana, 1875–1950.* Indianapolis, IN: The National Council of Negro Women, 1981.

Hume, John F. *The Abolitionists: Together with Personal Memories of the Struggle for Human Rights 1830–1864.* New York: Putnam, 1905.

Imbo, Samuel. *Oral Traditions as Philosophy: Okot p'Bitek's Legacy for African Philosophy.* Lanham, MD: Rowman & Littlefield, 2002.

Isasi-Díaz, Ada María. *Mujerista Theology: A Theology for the Twenty-First Century.* Maryknoll, NY: Orbis, 1996.

Jefferson, Thomas. *Notes on the State of Virginia.* Edited by William Peden. Chapel Hill: University of North Carolina Press, 1982.

Johnstone, Ronald L. *Religion in Society: A Sociology of Religion.* 8th ed. Upper Saddle River, NJ: Pearson Prentice Hall, 2007.

Jones, T. A. Letter to Charles E. Brown. Church of God Archives. Archives C526 1994. Congregational and Regional History, Box 22, Minnesota, Mississippi, 1.

Kern, Richard, ed. *A History of the Ohio Conference of the Churches of God, General Conference 1936–1986.* Nappanee, IN: Evangel, 1986.

———. *John Winebrenner: Nineteenth Century Reformer.* Harrisburg, PA: Central Publishing, 1974.

King, Martin Luther, Jr. *The Autobiography of Martin Luther King Jr.* Edited by Clayborne Carson. New York: Warner, 1998.

———. "The American Dream." In *A Knock at Midnight,* edited by Clayborne Carson and Peter Holloran, 85–100. New York: Warner, 1998.

———. "Guidelines for a Constructive Church." In *A Knock at Midnight,* edited by Clayborne Carson and Peter Holloran, 101–15. New York: Warner, 1998.

Knudson, Albert C. *Religious Teaching of the Old Testament.* New York: Abingdon, 1918.

Kolchin, Peter. *American Slavery 1619–1877.* New York: Hill & Wang, 1993.

Lamphear, John, and Toyin Falola. "Aspects of Early African History." In *Africa.* 3rd edition edited by Phyllis M. Martin and Patrick O'Meara, 73–96. Bloomington: Indiana University Press, 1995.

Lecky, William E. H. *History of European Morals: From Augustus to Charlemagne.* 3rd edition, Revised. Volume 1. New York: Appleton, 1879.

Lincoln, C. Eric, and Lawrence Mamiya. *The Black Church in the African American Experience.* Durham: Duke University Press, 1990.

Littell, Franklin Hamlin. *The Origins of Sectarian Protestantism: A Study of the Anabaptist View of the Church.* New York: Macmillan, 1964.

Lorman, Ratner. *Powder Keg: Northern Opposition to the Antislavery Movement, 1831–1840.* New York: Basic, 1968.

Lundy, J. F. "Anderson, S.C., August 15, 1895." *The Gospel Trumpet* 15.33 (Aug. 22, 1895) (column 2), 3.

Macy, Jesse. *The Anti-Slavery Crusade: A Chronicle of the Gathering Storm.* New York: United States Publishers Association, 1970.

Massey, James E. *African Americans and the Church of God: Aspects of a Social History.* Anderson, IN: Anderson University Press, 2005.

———. *Concerning Christian Unity.* Anderson, IN: Warner, 1979.

Bibliography

———. *Introduction to the Negro Churches in the Church of God Reformation Movement*. New York: Shining Light Survey, 1957.

———. "The National Association: A Positive Force." In *Following the Light: Teachings, Testimonies, Trials and Triumphs of the Church of God, Anderson*, compiled and edited by Barry L. Callen, 330–33. Anderson, IN: Warner, 2000.

Mathesen, Lena L. "Miscellaneous" section in *The Gospel Trumpet* 29.8 (Feb. 25, 1909) (column 1), 10.

McAllister, Lester G., ed. *An Alexander Campbell Reader*, 88–92 St. Louis: CBP Press, 1988.

McDonald, W. A. Letter to Charles E. Brown. Church of God Archives. Archives C 526. 1994 Congregational and Regional History, Box 22, Minnesota, Mississippi, 1.

McGiffert, Arthur Cushman. *Martin Luther: The Man and His Work*. New York: Century, 1919.

McIntosh, Peggy. "White Privilege: Unpacking the Invisible Knapsack." In *White Privilege: Essential Readings on the Other Side of Racism*, edited by Paula Rothenberg, 97–101. New York: Worth, 2002.

Moberg, David O. *The Church as a Social Institution: The Sociology of American Religion*. Englewood Cliffs, NJ: Prentice-Hall, 1962.

Moorehead, Kent. "It's Not Our Show." Interview with Walter G. Muelder. *Bostonia*. (Summer 1997) 31–33.

Mulligan, Mary Alice. "Remodeling Word and Table in the Believers Church." PhD diss., Vanderbilt University, 2001.

Naylor, C. W. "The Church Has One Foundation" (No. 163). In *Select Hymns for Christian Worship and General Gospel Service*. Anderson, IN: Gospel Trumpet, 1911.

———. "The Church's Jubilee" (No. 312). In *Worship the Lord: Hymnal of the Church of God*. Anderson, IN: Warner, 1989.

Niebuhr, H. Richard. *Christ and Culture*. New York: Harper & Row, 1951.

———. *The Social Sources of Denominationalism*. New York: Holt, 1929.

Niebuhr, Reinhold. *An Interpretation of Christian Ethics*. New York: Meridian, 1958 [1935].

———. *The Nature and Destiny of Man: A Christian Interpretation*. Complete in 1 vol. New York: Scribner, 1941, 1943, 1949.

———. "The Weakness of the Modern Church." In *Essays in Applied Christianity*, edited by D. B. Robertson, 69–77. New York: Living Age, 1965.

Norwood, Frederick A. *The Story of American Methodism: A History of the United Methodists and their Relations*. Nashville: Abingdon, 1974.

Nottingham, Elizabeth. *Religion: A Sociological View*. New York: Random House, 1971.

p'Bitek. *Africa's Cultural Revolution*. Nairobi: Macmillan, 1973.

Phillips, Carol Brunson, and Louise Derman-Sparks. *Teaching/Learning Anti-Racism: A Developmental Approach*. New York: Teachers College, 1997.

Plato. *Gorgias*. Translated by Walter Hamilton. New York: Penguin, 1982.

Quarles, Benjamin. *Black Abolitionists*. New York: Da Capo, 1969.

Ratner, Lorman. *Powder Keg: Northern Opposition to the Antislavery Movement 1831–1840*. New York: Basic, 1968.

Roberts, Keith A. *Religion in Sociological Perspective*. 3rd ed. Belmont, CA: Wadsworth, 1995.

Ross, George. "Biography of Elder John Winebrenner" (1880). http://www.mun.ca/rels/restmov/texts/believers/ross/BEJW.HTM,2.

Rothenberg, Paula S., ed. *White Privilege: Essential Readings on the Other Side of Racism*, 97–101. New York: Worth, 2002.

Rowe, A. T. "What We Believe." In *A Time to Remember: Teachings*, edited by Barry L. Callen, 70–74. Anderson, IN: Warner, 1978.

Royster, Jacqueline Jones. ed. *Southern Horrors and Others Writings: The Anti-Lynching Campaign of Ida B. Wells, 1892–1900*. Boston: Bedford, 1997.

Russell, Bertrand. *A History of Western Philosophy*. New York: Simon & Schuster, 1945.

Saldarini, Anthony J. "Holiness." In *The HarperCollins Bible Dictionary*, edited by Paul J. Achtemier, 431. New York: HarperCollins, 1996.

Salm, Steven J. "Music." In *Africa: African Cultures and Societies before 1885*. Edited by Toyin Falola, 2:265–84. Durham: Carolina Academic, 2000.

———. "Written and Oral Literature." In *Africa: African Cultures and Societies before 1885*, edited by Toyin Falola, 2:285–301. Durham: Carolina Academic, 2000.

Sanders, Cheryl J. "Ethics of Holiness and Unity in the Church of God." In *Called to Minister . . . Empowered to Serve*, edited by Juanita Evans Leonard, 131–46. Anderson, IN: Warner, 1989.

———. *Saints in Exile: The Holiness-Pentecostal Experience in African American Religion and Culture*. New York: Oxford University Press, 1996.

Sartre, Jean-Paul. "Existentialism." In his *Existentialism and Human Emotions*, 9–51. New York: Philosophical Library, 1957.

Sawyer, Thomas J. "Racial Separation and Christian Unity." In *A Time to Remember: Evaluations*, edited by Barry L. Callen, 110–12. Anderson, IN: Warner, 1978.

———. "A Survey Analysis of Christian Unity within the Church of God Community—1950–1970: Focus Upon Black-White Relationship." In *The Church of God in Black Perspective*, 70–97. Shining Light Survey, 1970.

Sherwin, Oscar. *Prophet of Liberty: The Life and Times of Wendell Phillips*. New York: Bookman Associates, 1958.

Singleton, George A. *The Romance of African Methodism: A Study of the African Methodist Episcopal Church*. 1985. Reprinted, Nashville: AME, 2001.

Smith, Frederick G. *What the Bible Teaches*. Anderson, IN: Gospel Trumpet, 1914.

Smith, John W. V. *A Brief History of the Church of God Reformation Movement*. Rev. ed. Anderson, IN: Warner, 1976. [*Truth Marches On*. Anderson, IN: Gospel Trumpet, 1956.]

———. *I Will Build My Church: Biblical Insights on Distinguishing Doctrines of the Church of God*. Rev. ed. Anderson, IN: Warner, 1999 [1985].

———. *Truth Marches On: A Brief Study of the History of the Church of God Reformation Movement*. Anderson, IN: Gospel Trumpet, 1956.

———. *Quest for Holiness and Unity*. Anderson, IN: Warner, 1980. [2nd ed. edited by Merle Strege. Anderson, IN: Warner, 2009.]

Smoot, J. D. "Our Mission in the World." In *Camp-Meeting Sermons: 1913*, edited by Gospel Trumpet, 253–64. Anderson, IN: Gospel Trumpet, 1913.

Snaith, Norman. *The Distinctive Ideas of the Old Testament*. London: Epworth, 1944.

Stafford. Gilbert W. *Signals at the Crossroads*. Anderson, IN: Warner, 2011.

Stanley, Susie. "Church of God Women Pastors: A Look at the Statistics." In *Called to Ministry . . . Empowered to Serve: Women in the Church of God Reformation Movement*, editd by Juanita Evans Leonard, 175–79. Anderson, IN: Warner, 1989.

Stern, Carl. "Interview with Dr. Heschel." In *Moral Grandeur and Spiritual Audacity: Essays Abraham Joshua Heschel*, edited by Susannah Heschel, 395–412. New York: Farrar, Straus & Giroux, 1996.
Strege, Merle D. *I Saw the Church: The Life of the Church of God Told Theologically*. Anderson, IN: Warner, 2002.
———. *Tell Me the Tale: Historical Reflections on the Church of God*. Anderson, IN: Warner, 1991.
Stringfellow, William. *My People Is the Enemy: An Autobiographical Polemic*. 1964. Reprinted, Eugene, OR: Wipf & Stock, 2005.
Strickland, L. V. Letter to Charles E. Brown, February 18, 1949. Church of God Archives. Mississippi file of Charles E. Brown, 4.
Stultz, Dale E., and Douglas E. Welch, comp. and eds. *The Book of Noah: Memoirs from Our Past*. Anderson, IN: Historical Society of the Church of God, 2007.
Stultz, Dale E. et al. *Old Main*. Anderson, IN: Historical Society of the Church of God/ Anderson University, 2008.
Thornbrough, Emma Lou. *Indiana Blacks in the Twentieth Century*. Edited by Lana Ruegamer. Bloomington: Indiana University Press, 2000.
———. *Indiana in the Civil War Era 1850–1880*. Indianapolis: Indiana Historical Bureau & Indiana Historical Society, 1965.
———. *The Negro in Indiana before 1900: A Study of a Minority*. Bloomington: Indiana University Press, 1993 [1985].
Thrash, Catherine (Hyacinth). *The Onliest One Alive: Surviving Jonestown, Guyana*. As told to Marian K. Towne. Indianapolis, IN, 1995.
Tillich, Paul. *The Protestant Era*. Translated by James Luther Adams. Chicago: University of Chicago Press, 1948.
———. *Systematic Theology*. 3 vols. in 1. Chicago: University of Chicago Press, 1967.
Tocqueville, Alexis de. *Democracy in America*. Complete and unabridged, Vols. 1 and 2. 1835. Reprinted, New York: Bantam, 2004.
Tournier, Paul. *A Doctor's Casebook in the Light of the Bible*. New Yor: Harper & Row, 1960.
Troeltsch, Ernst. *The Social Teaching of the Christian Churches*. Translated by Olive Wyon, 2:993–99. London: George Allen & Unwin, 1931.
United Methodist Newscope. 32.30 (July 16, 2004) 8.
Upchurch, Matthew. "No Holiness without Unity, No Unity without Holiness: Becoming the Church of God in the Image(s) of God." MTS thesis, Christian Theological Seminary, 2009.
Warner, Daniel S. *Bible Proofs of the Second Work of Grace*. 1880. Reprinted, Prestonsburg, KY: Reformation, 2007.
———. *The Church of God or What Is the Church and What Is Not*. Anderson, IN: Warner, n.d.
———. "Confusion and Shaking." *The Gospel Trumpet* (July 15, 1886) (column 2).
———. *D. S. Warner's Journal 1872–1880*. Transcribed by Fred Shively and Verne Tedder. Unpublished.
———. "The Experience of Oneness." In *A Time to Remember: Teachings*, edited by Barry Callen, 15–17. Anderson, IN: Warner, 1978.
———. "Good Wayism." *The Gospel Trumpet* 10.12 (June 15, 1890) (column 1), 4.
———. "News from the Field." *The Gospel Trumpet* 11.2 (Jan. 15, 1891) (column 3), 2.
———. "News from the Field." *The Gospel Trumpet* 11.4 (Feb. 15, 1891) (column 4), 2.

Warner, D. S., and Herbert M. Riggle. *The Cleansing of the Sanctuary*. 1903. Reprinted, Guthrie, OK: Faith Publishing House, 1967.

Warner, D. S. et al. "News from the Field." *The Gospel Trumpet* (February 15, 1891) (column 5), 2.

Weber, Max. *The Protestant Ethic and the Spirit of Capitalism*. Translated by Talcott Parsons. New York: Scribner, 1958.

———. "The Routinization of Charisma." In *Social Change: Sources, Patterns, and Consequences*, edited by Amitai Etzioni and Eva Etzioni, 53–63. New York: Basic, 1964.

———. *The Theory of Social and Economic Organization*. Translated by A. M. Henderson and Talcott Parsons. Edited by Talcott Parsons, 358–92. New York: Free Press, 1947.

Wells, Ida B. *Crusade for Justice*. Edited by Alfreda M. Duster. Chicago: University of Chicago Press, 1970.

Wesley, Charles H. *Richard Allen: Apostle of Freedom*. Washington, DC: Associated Publishers, 1935.

Wickersham, Henry C. *A History of the Church*. 1900. Reprinted, Prestonsburg, KY: Reformation, 2007.

Williams, Carl C. "Are We a Sect?" In *A Time to Remember: Evaluations*, edited by Barry L. Callen, 21–23. Anderson: IN, Warner, 1978.

Williams, Jane. Letter to *The Gospel Trumpet* 13.39 (Oct. 5, 1893) (column 4), 1.

Willowby, Richard. *Family Reunion: A Century of Camp Meetings*. Anderson, IN: Warner, 1986.

Winebrenner, John. "History of the Church of God." In *History of All the Religious Denominations in the United States*, 170–87. 2nd ed. Harrisburg, PA: Winebrenner, 1848.

Wise, Tim. *Dear White America: Letter to a New Minority*. San Francisco: City Lights, 2013.

X, Malcolm. *The Autobiography of Malcolm X*. As told to Alex Haley. New York: Grove, 1964.

Yahn, S. G. *History of the Churches of God in North America*. Harrisburg, PA: Central, 1926.

Yinger, J. Milton. *Religion in the Struggle for Power*. Durhan: Duke University Press, 1946.

———. *Religion, Society and the Individual: An Introduction to the Sociology of Religion*. New York: Macmillan, 1957.

———. *The Scientific Study of Religion*. New York: Macmillan, 1970.

Index

African American Alumni Luncheon, 6n8
African Americans and the Church of God, xiii, xviii, xxvii, 174, 199, 253
Agee, Gary B., 101n139, 115, 116, 118, 118n41, 267–68
A History of the Church, 122
Alabama Camp Meeting, 21
"all deliberate speed," 176–77
Allen, Richard, 180
Allison, Joe, 100n139
Allport, Gordon W., 185–86
Ambrose, 29
American Anti-Slavery Society, 45, 52
Anabaptists, 228, 230, 234
Anderson Bible Seminary, 162
Anderson Bible Training School, 162
Anderson Camp Meeting, 79, 131, 147, 149, 178
Anderson College and Theological Seminary, 162
Anderson School of Theology, 115, 163, 205–206, 211, 254
Anderson University, 6n8, 115, 205, 247, 265
Anderson University School of Theology, 162, 242, 247
An Introduction to the Negro Churches in the Church of God . . . , 148
anti-racism, 209
ARDA, 7n10
Arkansas Eldership ("colored"), 43, 44
Armistead, W. S., 115, 116, 117, 118
"As Others Knew Him," 66–67

Aspects of Christian Social Ethics, 264
A Time to Remember, xivn2,
Augusta, Georgia, 86
Augustine, 29
Aulén, Gustav, 191, 192

Baker, Beckie, 265
Baker, Leah, 265
Baker, Mary, 265
Baker, Steve, 265
Baker, Teddie, 265
Baker, Theodore, xi, xiii, xxvii, 263, 265–66, 267
Ball, Edward, 187–88, 189
Bateman, Cornelia, 205
Bay Ridge Christian College, 121n54, 162
Beaver Dam, Indiana, 5, 15, 86
Beech Springs, Mississippi, 95, 96, 98, 99, 121
Believers Church, 50, 231
Bell, Derrick, 183
Berry, Robert L., 67, 205, 253
Bessemer, Alabama, 22
Beverly, Aleza, 247
Bewley, Anthony, 44
"Bible Unity and the Color Line," 111
Birth of a Reformation, 85, 254
Bishop Sybert, 44
black oral tradition, 86, 255–62
Blaney, J. C., 89, 109–110
Bolds, Otto, 21
Bolitho, Axchie, 142
Bonhoeffer, Dietrich, 228–29
Boston University, xvi, 265

Bowne, Borden P., 214
Breazeale, George W., 99
Brooks, H. W., 161–62
"Brother" Bozeman, 121, 122
"Brother" Bradley, 121, 122
Brown, Antoinette, 64
Brown, Charles E., 21, 22, 23, 25, 31, 64, 82, 95, 96, 98, 100, 101, 107, 121, 124, 132, 138, 144, 146, 147, 160, 228, 233–39, 251, 253, 254, 258
Brown vs Topeka, Kansas, 176
Burrow, Fannie B., xviii
Business Committee, 213
Byers, Andrew L., xxi, 66, 85, 98, 167, 168, 254
Byers, J. W., 67
Byrum, Enoch E., 24, 25, 26, 27, 28, 29, 30, 69, 73, 77, 87–88, 106, 107, 110, 128, 129, 132, 135, 136, 143, 149, 158, 161, 178, 185, 202–203, 227
Byrum, Noah, 25, 69, 96

Cadoux, C. J., 145n123
call, 215–19
Callen, Barry L., 17, 63, 66, 91, 101, 121
Campbell, Alexander, 33, 126, 126n70, 200, 201
Campbell, George, 79
Camp Meeting Committee, 148, 149, 150
Canterbury Church, 47
Canterbury, Connecticut, 47
Carroll, Charles, 115, 116
Carson City, Michigan, 5, 15, 86
Carter, Thomas, 23
Carthage, Missouri, 98, 102
Carver, Cecil, 8, 17
charisma (of Warner), 66–75
charismatic, xix
charismatic authority, 127–28
Charleston, South Carolina, 86, 199n2, 244
"cheap grace," 140, 228
"Christ against culture," 18, 58, 108
Christian Catholics, 58

Christian Church, 37, 200
Christian masons, 58
Christian Odd fellows, 58
Christian Pedo-Baptists, 58
Christian Science, 11
Christian soldiers, 58
"Christ of culture," 58, 108
Church Advocate, 48, 49, 52, 57
Church of God archives, 100n139, 267
Church of God Doctrines, 8
Church of God of Detroit, 22
Churches of God (General Eldership), xviii, xixn5, xxiii, xxiv, 12, Ch. 2, 60, 69
church type 2–6, 166
Civil Rights Movement, 205
Clear, Valorus, xi, xiv, xivn2, xv, xxii, 15, 73, 155
Clinton, Hilary, 222
Cogswell schoolhouse, 66
Colder, James, 57
"come-outers," 241
commitment mechanisms, 7
Committee on Slavery, 42
Concerning Christian Unity, 177
"condemned to freedom," 145
Conference on Race (Chicago, 1963), 208
Confrontation of 1912, 131, 133–34, 135, 147–52, 154, 175, 178, 261
"Confusion and Shaking," 103
Constitution and "Declaration of Sentiments," 45, 46
constructive stage, 168
Corunna, Indiana, 63
"costly grace," 228–29
counter-cultural community, 238
Crandall, Prudence, 47, 48
critical mass, xxi
Crosswhite, Joseph, 148
Curry, Michael D., 199n2

Darwin, Charles, 116
Davidson, Basil, 256
Davie, Grace, 3
Davis, Katie H., 148
Declaration of Sentiments, 45, 46, 52

Index

Democracy in America, 223
denomination, 3, 9–11, 60, 163, 164
depersonalization of charisma, 128
Derman-Sparks, Louise, 209
Detroit, Michigan, 22, 143
Disciples of Christ, 7, 33, 37, 126, 178, 200
Displacement of goals, 159
Dunbar, C. R., 14
Dupree, Eliza B., 43

East Pennsylvania Eldership, 40, 41, 44, 49, 55
Eastside Church of God (Pontiac, Michigan), xviii
Ebenezer Baptist Church, 217–18
Eighth Street Church of God (Meredian, Mississippi), 253
El Evangelio (The Gospel Trumpet), 159
Elliott, B. F., 159
Elliott, Georgia, 159
Emancipation Proclamation, 30, 33, 59, 60, 86
Emperor Nero, 145
Enlightenment, 148
Ensiminger, S. (Elder), 233
entire sanctification, 74, 75–85
Episcopalian, 37
established sect, xxii, 10, 60, 156, 163
Evangelical Association, 44
"Evening Light" church, 18
excommunication, 146, 233
Executive Council, 176
"extraordinary enthusiasm," 74

Farmhaven district, 123–24, 199n2
Feagin, Joe, 184n28
Federal Council of Churches, 164
Fertility rates, 7
Filler, Louis, 64
Finney, Charles G., 64, 65
Fisher, Allie, 106
Fisher, Joseph C., 106, 227, 233
Foggs, Edward L., 213
Forney, Christian Henry, 12, 13, 35, 36, 43, 56
Forrest, Aubrey Leland, xiv, xv, 138

Forrest, James E., 89, 111, 112, 132, 139, 140, 141, 159
Fort Scott sect, 102
"Founding Fathers," 183
Free Will Baptist Church, 49
Fudge, Thomas, 55

Gandhi, Mohandas K., 72
Garrett, Eugene, 96–97, 99, 100, 123, 124, 252, 253, 258
Garrison, William Lloyd, 45
General Assembly, 176, 213
General Eldership, 12, 13, 40, 41–43, 44, 55n70, 56, 57, 58, 69, 226
General Ministerial Assembly, 163, 176
General Rules, 146
"generation," xxii
German Reformed Church, 35, 37
Germany, Horace J., 121n54, 162
"gift of grace," 71
Goings, Henry, 44
Golden Jubilee Book, 253, 254
Good Way sect, 103, 229, 242
Gorgias, 36
Gospel Trumpet Home, 162
Gossard, J. Harvey, 51
Grand Junction, Michigan, 205
Green County, Pennsylvania, 56
Greensboro, Alabama, 134, 149
Grimké, Angelina, 45
Grimké, Sarah, 45
Griots, 255, 260, 261
Griottes, 260
Guyana, South America, 72

Hacker, Andrew, 223
Haeckel, Ernst, 116
hairesis (heresy), 14
Haley, Alex, 259, 260, 261
Hall, Glenn, 123, 125n68, 253
Hamer, Fannie Lou, 72
Hayesville, Ohio, 63
Hargrove, Barbara, xixn6, 3
Harn, George U., 42, 55
Harp Lecture, 115, 242, 244
Harris, Sarah, 47

Harrisburg Anti-Slavery Society, 45, 46, 52
Harrisburg, Pennsylvania, 35
Hartselle, Alabama, 21
Hartung Hall, 264
Hedgeman, Anna Arnold, 211
Hegel, G. W. F., 255–56
Henry, Carl F. H., 264
Henry, W. J., 143
Heschel, Abraham J., 188, 208, 220, 224–25
Hill, Charles H., 133–34, 149–50, 258, 261
Hines, Samuel, 148, 249
Hispanics (Latinas/os), 159–60
History of All the Religious Denominations in the United States, 18n64, 92
"History of the Church of God," 18n64, 40, 93
Hitler, Adolph, 72
holiness, 172–73, 190–97
Holiness Alliance Band, 12, 84
"human groupings," 142, 177
Huxley, Thomas, 116

ideal type, 71n39
Inasmuch, 264
Indiana Blacks in the Twentieth Century, 120
Indiana Department of Education, 162
Indiana Eldership, 5, 40, 121
International Church of the Foursquare Gospel, 67
International Youth Convention, xviii
Isasi-Díaz, Ada María, 212n20
I Saw the Church, xiii, 114, 163
Is the Negro a Beast?, 115, 242, 245–46
I Will Build My Church, 198

James H. Cone and Black Liberation Theology, 266
Janes, Christiana, 22, 143, 144, 203, 207
Jefferson, Thomas, 257
Jerome, 29
"Jesus is the Subject," 248

Jim Crow Law, 241
Johnstone, Ronald, 3, 10
Jones, Jim, 72
Juffure, 259

Keller, Sarah, 14
Kendleton, Texas, 162
Kern, Richard, 39, 40, 45, 49, 51
Kilpatrick, A. J., 23
Kimmel, G. T., 160
kin-dom, 212, 212n20
King, Martin Luther, 72, 134, 208, 209–10, 216, 217–18, 224
Kinte clan, 260, 261

Lamarck, Jean Baptiste, 116
Lane Seminary, 64
"leader principle," 31
Lecky, William E. H., 146
Lee, Robert E., 113
"Letter on Slavery," 41, 58
"Let Us Be United," 243
Lewis, James W., 163
Liele, George, 180
Linnaeus, Carl, 116
Lincoln, Abraham, 33, 86
Lincoln, C. Eric, 3, 7
Littell, Franklin, 229
Lovejoy, Elijah, 44
Lucian, 146
Lundy, Joseph F., 23, 244
Lutheran Church, 11
Luther, Martin, 216
Lyon, Jim, 248

Mahan, Asa, 64
Mamiya, Lawrence, 7
"man-rule," 34
Marple, E., 57
Marshall, James, 162–63
Martyr, Justin, 146
Mason Dixon line, 146
Massey, Gwendolyn, 134
Massey, James Earl, xi, xiii, xviii, xix, xxv, xxvii, 8, 22, 26, 27, 28, 29, 86, 90, 91, 96, 98, 99, 100, 100n139, 102, 113, 115, 121, 124n64, 125, 126, 133–34, 137,

138, 141, 142, 143, 147, 149, 162, 163, 168–69, 174, 177, 179, 199, 200, 205, 206, 215, 253–54 (letter), 258, 259, 263–65, 266–67
McDonnal, John, 193n47
McGuire, Meredith, 3
McIntosh, Peggy, 184n28
McPherson, Aimee Semple, 67, 72
Mennonite, 69
Meredian, Mississippi, 95, 98, 102
Methodist Episcopal Church, 8, 33, 47, 53, 146
Mexican American War, 55n70
Michigan Eldership, 44
Ministries Council, 176
Miracle of Survival, 254
Missionary Committee, 158
Mississippi tour, xxv
Moberg, David, xixn5, xxvi, 2–3, 151, 166, 264
Moore, Laura, 133–34, 148, 149, 150, 258, 261
"movement," 9
Muelder, Walter G., xvi, 217
Mulligan, Mary Alice, 230, 231, 236, 238
mutual correction and accountability, 51, 226–39

National Association for the Promotion of Holiness, 14
National Association of the Church of God, 22, 132, 133, 135, 136–42, 148, 179
National Camp Meeting, xviii
National Council of Churches, 163, 164
Native American, ix
Naylor, Charles Wesley, 243–44
New England Conference of the United Methodist Church, 217
"new measures," 65
New York City missionary home, 142
Niebuhr, H. Richard, xiv, xixn6, 2, 18, 107, 108, 109, 127
Niebuhr, Reinhold, 171
Nieman, Vivian, 100n139, 267

North American Convention of the Church of God, 6n8, 22
North Central Association of Colleges and Secondary Schools, 162
Northern Indiana Eldership, 5, 15
Northern Michigan Eldership, 5, 15
Nottingham, Elisabeth, xixn6, 3, 69, 156, 157

Oak Grove, Mississippi, 102
Ober, Benjamin, 57
Oberlin College, xxiv, 14, 33, 63, 64–66, 91, 103
Oden, Daniel F., 22, 23, 143, 149
official charisma, 73
Oklahoma Assembly, 30
Oliver, W. H., 12
Omaha Indian, 92
oral history, xxvi, 22, 86, 121, 147, 255–62
Orr, Charles, 122
"Our Position on Slavery Re-defined," 56
Owen, Robert H., 124

Palmer, A. B., 155
Pauline Holiness College, 103, 242
Peoples Temple, 72
perfectionist sect, 13
personal charisma, 73–75
personalism, 214
Personalist, xvi
persons-in-community, 137
Phillips, Carol Brunson, 209
Phillips, Harold L., 100, 252, 253
Pistole, John, 247
Plessy vs Ferguson, 176
Pope, Liston, xiv
Pontiac, Michigan, xviii, 265
post-Reconstruction, xv
pre-reconciliation, 207, 208
Presbyterian USA, 7
principle of equality, 225–26
principle of mutual correction, 50
"principle of principles," 190
pro-reconciliation, 209
"provincialism," 142, 177
Publication Board, 254

282　Index

Quarles, Benjamin, 64
Quebedeaux, Richard, 264
Queens College (New York City), 223

Racism, 142, 152, 177, 183–84, 185, 186, 237
Reconciliation, 182–83, 187, 206–14, 247
Reconstruction, xvi, 30, 60
redemptive suffering, 209, 210
Reid, Benjamin, 249n14
religious training in home, 7
"Reports from the Field," 254
Resolutions of 1845, 40, 41–42, 52–53, 57, 58
"restrictionism," 195, 195n52
Riggle, H. M., 129
Roberts, Anne, 267
Roberts, Keith A., xixn6, 3, 7, 128
Robinson, Henry, 22, 23
Roman Catholic Church, 8
Rothenberg, Paula, 184n28
routinization of charisma, 127–30, 154
"Rules of Cooperation," 12
Rush, Rosetta, 123
Russell, Bertrand, 29–30

sacredness of persons, 221–25
Saldarini, Anthony, 191
Salem Reformed Church, 35
Salm, Steven J., 256
sanctification, 13, 14, 171, 194
sanctified church tradition, 196
Sanders, Cheryl J., 131, 137, 148, 172, 196
Sanderville, Georgia, 138
Sapp, Beatrice, 22
Sartre, Jean-Paul, 145
Sawyer, Thomas J., 163
Schell, William G., 115, 118, 122, 242, 245–46
Scott, Matthew Moses, xvii
Sebastian, David, 247
second phase, 107–108, 110, 112, 154–55
second work of grace, 12, 13, 200
sect, 1, 2–6, 16, 18, 60, 163

sect type, 16, 108, 167
Sewell, Samuel, 119
shared suffering, 209
Shoffner, Lena (later Matthesen), 21, 22, 23, 24, 30, 258
Sin, 171–73
"Sister" Foot, 95
"Sister" Stanley, 94
slavery, 38–61
Slaves in the Family, 187
Smith, Frederick G., 114, 158, 167, 168, 170
Smith, John W. V., 101, 114, 115, 116, 121, 131, 132, 133, 135, 148, 159, 193, 196–97, 198, 201, 245, 254
Smith, Rufus J., 114
Smith, Sarah, 67, 122
Smoot, J. D., 79
sociological transformation, Ch. 1, 61
sociology of religion, 1, 5
Socrates, 36
Sohm, Rudolph, 71
Songs of Victory, 243
Southern Horrors, 120
spiritual democracy, 31
Spring Hill, Mississippi, 95, 98, 99
Stafford, Gilbert, 248
Stanton, P., 44
state camp meeting, xviii
Stephenson, J. R., 143
St. Georges Episcopal Church, 180
Straight Holiness people, 95
Strege, Merle, 19, 25, 114, 121, 147, 148, 149, 163, 164, 172, 227, 252
Strickland, L. V., 99
Stringfellow, William, 207, 211
Study Commission on Race, 176
Sunday School Advocate, 47

Task Force on Racial Reconciliation, 176
Teasley, D. O., 142
Texas Eldership, 57, 58
The Black Church in the African American Experience, 7
The Church as a Social Institution, 264
"The Church has One Foundation," 243

"The Color Line," 25, 136, 150, 178, 202
The Gospel Publisher, 36, 39, 44, 45, 46
The Gospel Trumpet, xiv, 87, 89, 97, 98, 103, 109, 113, 114, 123, 133, 142, 161, 192, 227, 244, 245, 253
The Gospel Trumpet Company, 22, 30, 77, 88, 106, 107, 155, 160, 205, 243, 253
The Great Reversal, 264
"the Holy One," 190-91, 194
The Negro a Beast, 115
The Negro in Indiana before 1900, 120
The Negro is a Man, 116
The Onliest One Alive, 72
The Quest for Holiness and Unity, xiii
"The Shaking Crisis Continued…," 139
The Social Sources of Denominationalism, 2
The Social Teaching of the Christian Churches, xivn3
The Young Evangelicals, 264
third phase, xx-xxi, 105, 156-65
Thomas, George, 42
Thornbrough, Emma Lou, 120
Thrash, Hyacinth, 72
"three-dimensional holiness ethic," 196
Tillich, Paul, 190
"time servers," 46
Tocqueville, Alexis de, 223
Tournier, Paul, 221n39
Towne, Marian K., 72
Troeltsch, Ernst, xiv, xixn5, xixn6, 4, 16
Tuskegee University, 163
Two Nations: Black and White, Separate, Hostile, Unequal, 223

"ultraism," 49
Underground Railroad, 64-65, 91
undeserved suffering, 209, 210
unearned privilege, 152, 177, 178
Union, Mississippi, 121n54, 124, 162
Union Town, Maryland, 44
United Brethren, 69
United Churches of Christ, 11
United Methodist Church, 7, 178
Upchurch, Matthew, 22n74

Vermillion College, 63
visible organic union, 17
vocatio (vocation), 215, 216
von Zinzendorf, Graf Nicholas, 77

Wallace, Alfred Russell, 116
Waltner, James, 236
Warner, Daniel S., xvii, xviii, xxii, xxiv, xxv, 5, 12-20, 24, 29, 33, 34, 37, 38, 43, 50, 51, 54, 59, Ch. 3, 110, 113, 123, 130-31, 134, 140, 141, 160, 173, 174, 190, 192, 200, 201, 202, 227, 231, 233, 238, 251
Warner, Joseph, 63
Warner Press, 253
Watkinsville, Mississippi, 95, 99
Wattleton, Ozzie (Garrett), 123-24, 253
Weber, Charles, 213
Weber, Max, xixn6, 3, 16, 67, 68, 71, 72, 157
Weishampel, J. F., 93
Welch, Douglas, 22
Wells, Ida B., 117-18, 120
West Middlesex Campgrounds, 136, 137
West Ohio Eldership, 12, 13, 34, 40, 43, 44, 59, 60, 66, 81, 91, 92, 93, 94, 160, 201, 227
West Pennsylvania Eldership, 40
what is, xvi, xvii
what ought, to be xvi, xvii
When the Trumpet Sounded, xiii, 97, 121, 251, 253, 254
Where the Saints Have Trod, xiv
white privilege, 142, 177, 178, 184, 184n28, 185
Wichita, Kansas, 205
Wickersham, Henry C., 122
Williams, A. D., 49, 50, 52, 53
Williams, Carl, 9
Williams County Ohio, 62, 66
Williams, Jane, 86, 87, 88-89, 245
Wilson, Bryan, xixn6
Wilson, G. A., 12

Wilson, Georgene, O.S.F., 212n20
Wilson, G. W., 160
Wilson, J. T., 162
Wimbish, Ernest, 132
Winebrenner, Eve C., 35
Winebrenner, John, xviii, xix, xixn5, xxiv, 12, 15, 15n46, 18n64, Ch.2, 71, 76, 92, 93, 94, 114, 174, 180, 226
Winebrenner, Philip, 35
Wingfield, T. H., 96, 97, 99, 100, 252, 258
Wise, Daniel, 47, 48

"with all deliberate speed," 177
women as pastors, 162
World Council of Churches, 163

X, Malcolm, 72, 184n29, 211

Yahn, S. G., 55n70
Yinger, J. Milton, xixn6, 3, 4, 5, 70, 74

Zeaney's Chapel, 43
Zinzendorfism, 13, 26, 76, 77, 227
Zion's Hill at West Middlesex, 148